THE BRITISH ISLES

Green **Line**
3

von
Marion Horner
Stephanie Ashford
Jennifer Baer-Engel
Elizabeth Daymond
Paul Dennis
Axel Plitsch

herausgegeben von
Harald Weisshaar

Ernst Klett Verlag
Stuttgart • Leipzig

Green Line 3 für Klasse 7 an Gymnasien
und für den Bildungsstandard Klasse 8 in Baden-Württemberg

Herausgeber: Harald Weisshaar, Bisingen
unter besonderer Mitwirkung von Frank Haß, Kirchberg.

Autoren: Marion Horner M.A., Cambridge; Stephanie Ashford M.A., Brigachtal;
Jennifer Baer-Engel, Göppingen; Elizabeth Daymond M.A., Kiel; Peter Lampater, Ehingen
sowie Paul Dennis M.A., Lahnstein; Axel Plitsch, Wülfrath
unter Mitwirkung von Hamida Aziz, Tübingen; Dr. Gregory Fuller, Stuttgart;
Michael Mattison, Stuttgart; Susanne Steiert, Wendlingen

Berater: Paul Dennis M.A., Lahnstein; Hartmut Klose, Seevetal; Antje Körber, Merseburg;
Axel Plitsch, Wülfrath; Elisabeth Renner, Freiburg.

1. Auflage 1 5 4 3 2 | 2012 11 10 09 08

Alle Drucke dieser Auflage sind unverändert und können im Unterricht nebeneinander
verwendet werden. Die letzte Zahl bezeichnet das Jahr des Druckes.

Internetadresse: www.klett.de

Redaktion: Andrew Hutchins M.A., Anette Dangelmaier M.A.

Gestaltung: Anita Bauch
Illustrationen: David Norman, Meerbusch; Dorothee Wolters, Köln; Uwe Häntsch,
Berlin *(Zusatzgeschichten)*; Lars Benecke, Hannover
sowie Naomi Fearn, Berlin *(Kelsey, British History Comic und Grammar)*
Umschlaggestaltung: Koma Amok, Stuttgart
Umschlagfoto: Ariel Skelley/Corbis
Reproduktion: Meyle + Müller, Medien-Management, Pforzheim
Satz: Satzkiste – Böhler | Frerichs | Warkus GbR, Stuttgart; Wiebke Hengst, Ostfildern
Druck: Stürtz GmbH, Würzburg

Printed in Germany
ISBN 978-3-12-547140-5 (fester Einband)
ISBN 978-3-12-547141-2 (flexibler Einband)

Hallo und herzlich willkommen bei Green Line 3!

Units und Buchaufbau von **Green Line** sind dir gut vertraut. Die **Units** mit ihrem klaren Aufbau, die **Revisions**, **Free section**, **Mediation** und der gesamte Anhang mit **Grammar**, **Vocabulary**, **Dictionary**, **Classroom phrases** und **Irregular verbs** sind auch in Band 3 zu finden. Aber in diesem Band gibt es natürlich viel Neues.

Ich fange mal mit den kleinen Änderungen an:

- In den meisten Units gibt es nur **zwei** und nicht mehr drei oder vier ***Language***-Teile.
- In jeder Unit findest du eine ***Did you know?***-Box mit erstaunlichen Fakten, die nicht mal deine Oma glauben würde!
- In jeder Unit hilft dir eine Übung zu ***Writing texts*** beim Schreiben. Du lernst, wie du eigene Texte verfassen und interessant gestalten kannst.
- In der ***Grammar*** findest du nach jedem Pensum eine englische Zusammenfassung ***(English summary)*** – du kannst also Grammatik auch auf Englisch lernen.

Nun zu den **großen** Änderungen, *so listen to this:*

- Zwischen den beiden *Language*-Teilen steht die neue Seite **Talkwise**. Hier geht's nur um das Sprechen, in jeder Unit mit einem anderen Schwerpunkt.
- Nach den beiden *Language*-Teilen (in Unit 1 nach dem *Text*) gibt's in jeder Unit eine neue **Skills**-Seite. Das ist die erweiterte *Skills*-Box, die du aus Band 1 und 2 kennst. Die ***Skills***-Seite bietet dir viele nützliche Lernhilfen zum Lesen, Hören, Schreiben usw. an.
- Nach jeder zweiten Unit findet sich ein spannender **Text** (Units 2, 4 und 6).
- Nach den Units 1, 3 und 5 machst du, wenn du willst, die Doppelseite **Project** mit deiner Klasse, vielleicht mit einem anderen Fach zusammen: Biologie, Erdkunde und Informatik. So kannst du diese Schulfächer auch auf Englisch erleben.

Alles klar? Dann los und viel Spaß!

- Diese Texte und Übungen sind nur auf den Lehrer-CDs zum Schülerbuch enthalten.
- Diese Texte und Übungen sind auf der Schüler-CD im Workbook *und* auf den Lehrer-CDs.
- Partnerarbeit
- Gruppenarbeit
- Schreibübungen
- Übungen/Übungsteile für den *English folder*
- ⟨ ⟩ Wahlfreie (fakultative) Übungen/Übungsteile oder Kapitel
- Besonders knifflige oder anspruchsvolle Übungen/Übungsteile

Unit 1 The world of sport

A

B

C

1
started in 1823 at famous school in England • kick or carry oval ball • grass pitch • referee controls game

2
fast sport from Canada • 2 teams of 6 players on ice • game in 3 parts of 20 minutes • use sticks to score goals

3
very popular in America • 4 bases on field • hit ball with bat and run from one base to another

4
first club in England 250 years ago • sport for men or women • bat in front of legs • matches can go on for 5 days!

baseball

cricket

athletics

1 Work with the photos

a) *Match the photos and the names with the correct notes for the sports. Guess the meaning of the new words in blue.*

WB p. 4/1; 3

TIP

Different people need different words. What words do **you** need when you write or talk about your favourite things? Collect useful new words and keep this 'personal vocabulary' in your folder.

b) *Do you know more about these sports? Tell the class.*

c) *Make a sports quiz.*

1. Make your own notes about sports: where people play, what equipment they need, how many players there are in a team etc. (For new words, use a dictionary or ask other people).
2. Write 5–6 questions about the information in your notes.
3. Test your partner with your quiz!

5
one of oldest sports in the world • run, jump or throw • track 400 metres • Olympic Games every four years

6
started because American kids wanted to surf on land! • jump and do tricks in air • helmet to keep head safe

7
sport of European kings 400 years ago • use racket to hit ball • umpire can see whole court from tall chair

rugby | skateboarding | tennis | ice hockey

2 Listening: Sports news

a) *Listen and say what sports are on the radio. What sounds or words help you?*

b) *What sports are or aren't easy to enjoy on the radio? Try to explain why.* WB p. 4/2

DID YOU KNOW?

- Bikes in track races don't have brakes.
- Sisters Venus and Serena Williams have both been Wimbledon tennis champion.

You will learn more fun sports facts on page 13!

3 Your turn: You and sports

a) *What sports are popular or not so popular in Germany? Why? Talk in groups.*

b) *What sports do **you** do? Tell the others in your group.*

A new trick

Laura is practising at Epic Skatepark in Birmingham for a big event next weekend.

Harry: Wow, Laura! I've never seen that trick before! It's brilliant! Who taught you?

Laura: Nobody. It's my own special trick. I'm going to do it in the competition next weekend.

Harry: With a great new trick like that I'm sure you'll win. Will you teach me, please? Then I'll have a better chance in the boys' competition.

Laura: Oh, I – I haven't got time now. My dad's picking me up soon.

Harry: Well, let's meet again here tomorrow. I'll pay for your ticket, no problem.

Laura: Hm. I'm watching the big football match on TV tomorrow.

Harry: Me, too. But the match doesn't go on the whole day, does it?

Laura: No, but – er – I'm – I mean, I've got other arrangements tomorrow.

Harry: I thought we were mates! Why do I have the feeling that you don't want to teach me?

Laura: Sorry, Harry. But the boys' competition starts at 10 o'clock next Saturday, right?

Harry: Yes. What has that got to do with it?

Laura: Well, the girls don't start until the boys finish. And if you do the trick first, everybody will think it's yours, not mine. I'll show you how to do it next Sunday, OK?

1 Put the right parts together

1. Harry is sure Laura	will teach Harry her trick	the whole day tomorrow.
2. Laura's dad	starts	next weekend.
3. The football match	is picking her up	next Sunday.
4. The boys' competition	will win the competition	soon.
5. Laura	doesn't go on	at 10'clock next Saturday.

2 What do you think?

Is Laura fair when she offers to teach Harry her trick ***after*** *the competition? Why or why not?*

3 Your turn: What, where and when?

a) *What sports or other events are there in your town in the next few weeks? Find out about them and make notes like this:*
volleyball match – sports centre – next Sat. – 2 pm

b) *Tell your partner about your events. Example:*

There's a volleyball match at the sports centre **next Saturday.** It **starts at 2 pm.**

WB p. 5/4

GRAMMAR

For 'timetable' information about events in the future (dates, times etc.), use the simple present:
The train **leaves at 4 pm** this afternoon.

(→ G2)

4 What is happening next week?

a) *Danny Way, a famous American skateboard champion, is visiting the UK next week. Laura has seen his website diary for the trip. What does she tell Harry? (Find out why she is excited!)*

On Monday he's arriving in the UK.
On Tuesday morning **he's** …
In the afternoon he … *Go on, please.*

Mon	arrive in the UK
Tues	**(am)** do an interview with 'Sidewalk' magazine **(pm)** talk on the radio
Wed	make a skateboard video at Playstation Skatepark in London
Thurs	**(am)** open a sports shop in Swansea **(pm)** meet fans at Swansea Skatepark
Fri	teach tricks to kids in Leicester
Sat	give prizes at a skateboard competition in Birmingham

⟨b)⟩ *Ask what your partner is doing next week.*

Example:

"What **are you doing** after school on Monday?" – "**I'm training** at the judo club."

WB p. 5/5; 6

GRAMMAR

When you talk about arrangements for the future, use the present progressive:
We'**re watching** the big match at Phil's house **next Saturday**.

(→ G 3)

5 Events and arrangements

Complete the information with the correct tense: simple present or present progressive.

1. There **is** a big basketball game tomorrow. I **am playing** in it.
2. My father ___ (take) me to a rugby match next Saturday. It ___ (start) at half past two.
3. Our German partner school ___ (send) a girls' football team to England next week. Their plane ___ (arrive) at Heathrow at 10.30 on Monday.
4. The easy fitness course ___ (finish) on October 1st. After that we ___ (start) a harder course.
5. The tennis fans ___ (go) to Wimbledon by bus on Friday. Their bus ___ (leave) at 9 am.
6. The new sports centre ___ (open) on September 15th. Kelly Holmes ___ (open) it.

WB p. 6/7

6 Asking for help and giving help

a) *Find the rule: Look at the pictures. In what situations can you use the will future?*

b) *What can you say?*

I'll … / **Will you** …, please?

get | be | lend | play | tell | explain | help | put

(→ G 4)

1. You need a partner for tennis.
2. Your friend hits a golf ball into some trees.
3. You don't know the rules for baseball.
4. You can't mend your skateboard alone.
5. A boy doesn't know the way to the skatepark.
6. There are two football teams, but no referee.
7. You haven't got your own cricket bat.
8. Somebody must put the sports equipment away.

WB p. 6/8; 9

TALKWISE

Is it important to win?

It's not always easy to talk about a new subject. But it can help if you practise and learn some good phrases. Use these new **Talkwise** pages to improve your conversation skills! You'll find one in every unit.

1 A cartoon

What can you say about the wheelchair basketball player in the cartoon?

2 Listening: A sports discussion

a) *Before you listen: Why do people think it* ***is*** *or* ***is not*** *important to win? Make notes in two lists.*

b) *Now listen once and collect more ideas for your lists.*

c) *Check the Useful phrases on the right. Then listen again. Which phrases do you* ***not*** *hear?* WB p. 7/10; 11

USEFUL PHRASES

You want to say: Yes!	You want to say: No!
I agree.	I don't agree.
You're right.	Sorry, but you're wrong.
Exactly!	Don't be silly!
That's what I think, too.	Rubbish!
	I don't think that's true.

3 Short answers

a) *When you don't agree, you can use short answers. Read the examples and make a rule.*

1. It isn't important to win. – Yes, it is.
2. When you lose, people laugh. – No, they don't.

b) *The second speakers don't agree. Show this with short answers.*

1. "The best players don't always win." – "..."
2. "It's more important to win than to play fairly." – "..."
3. "There are more important things than sport." – "..."
4. "When you lose, you can't smile." – "..."
5. "In sport you always need luck, too." – "..." WB p. 7/12

4 Your turn: Is it important to win?

Explain what you think and why. Say if you agree or not with the others in your group.

Did you know?

The Superbowl is a big event which millions of American football fans watch on TV. But when the second half of the 1967 Superbowl started, there was a problem. The TV channel that was showing the game was still in a commercial break. So the game stopped and the players waited until the commercial break ended. It's not only the referee who controls the game. It's also money!

Cool Runnings is a film which tells the true story of an unusual bobsleigh team. The men in the team trained in the country that they came from – hot Jamaica. The first snow they saw was when they arrived in Canada for the 1988 Winter Olympic Games!

Tanni Grey-Thompson from Wales is a disabled athlete whose success in wheelchair races made her famous everywhere. Between 1988 and 2001 she won fourteen gold medals, broke over twenty world records and won the London Marathon five times!

Winners in sport are often people whose bodies are different in some way. Olympic rowing champion Matthew Pinsent has much bigger lungs than other people. Swimming champion Michael Phelps has very large feet. Sports scientists help to find young people who will be the champions of the future. They can match them with the sports they will be good at.

Tennis players that have love aren't happy. Why? Because in tennis 'love' means zero! It comes from the French word *l'oeuf* because zero looks like an egg.

In 2005 Danny Way did one of the craziest things anyone has ever done on a skateboard: He jumped almost nineteen metres over the Great Wall of China!

1 Play a game with the texts

a) *Choose a sentence from every text. Write the sentence again, but change it so the information is wrong (or funny!).*

b) *Can your partner correct the mistakes in your sentences without the book?*

2 Find the rule

a) *Look at the texts again. Collect all the nouns in front of the relative pronouns* ***who, which, that*** *and* ***whose****.*

b) *Check if the nouns are people or things. Then make a rule about when you can use the relative pronouns.*

noun	who	which	that	whose
event		✓		
channel			✓	
referee				
…				

3 What relative pronouns can you use?

a) "I've got a book **that / which** has all kinds of facts about different sports. It explains the rules and the equipment 1 players use. And it tells you about the stars 2 have had the greatest success. You can read about records 3 people have broken, too. I found out about a football player 4 twenty-two goals helped her team to win a match! There are also stories about funny things 5 have happened. I like the story about the tennis player 6 got lost on the Tube on the way to Wimbledon! The book is great for someone 7 hobby is sports quizzes. It has all the answers 8 you'll ever need!"

WB p. 8/13

(b) *What sports can you see on the book on the right?*

4 A game: Sports words

Give definitions with relative clauses. Your partner must guess the words.

Examples:

It's someone **who** controls a game.
It's a thing **which** you use in tennis.

a person someone a thing a sport …	+	**who** **which** **that** **whose**	+	controls a game job is to help athletes is popular in the US / … you use in tennis / … …

WB p. 8/14

5 What can sports fans buy on the Internet?

Example: a bag – Tiger Woods kept golf balls in it
→ There's **a bag that Tiger Woods kept golf balls in**.

1. a pair of shoes – Kelly Holmes won a gold medal in them 2. a cricket bat – the English team wrote their names on it 3. a tennis racket – Roger Federer played at Wimbledon with it 4. a bottle – Lance Armstrong drank water from it 5. a skateboard – Danny Way broke a record on it 6. a ball – David Beckham scored a goal with it 7. … *(any more ideas?)*

WB p. 8/15

6 Contact clauses

a) *Look at the relative pronouns in sentences 1 and 2. Are they the subject or the object of the clause?*

1. It is a film **which** tells a true story.
2. It is an event **which** fans always watch.

If the relative pronoun is the object, you do not need it:

It is an event (which) fans always watch. → It is an event fans always watch.

TIP
If the word after the relative pronoun is a verb, the relative pronoun must be the subject: S-V-O!

(→ G 5)

b) *Check these sentences. Do you need the relative pronoun or not? Make contact clauses.*

1. Sports scientists are people who use science in sport. 2. They test athletes that trainers send to them. 3. The information which they collect is useful. 4. They can find the athletes who have the best chance. 5. They know about the food that athletes should eat. 6. They also help athletes with the computer technology which they use.

7 Make one sentence from two

Example: The Marathon is a sports event. I really love it.
→ The Marathon is a sports event I really love.

1. Last year I went to London with a friend. I know her from school.
2. We waited in a good place. We found it near the Cutty Sark.
3. Then we saw the car. The athletes were running behind it.
4. This was the big moment. Everyone was waiting for it.
5. It was so exciting to be near famous athletes. You usually only see them on TV.
6. Lots of people were also running for charities. They wanted to make money for them.
7. A man shouted 'thank you' for the money. We threw it in his box.

WB p. 9/16

8 Listening: A cricket bat

a) *Before you listen: Tim has just started cricket at school and wants his own bat. So his father takes him to a sports shop. What problems can there be?*

b) *Now listen to the dialogue. Explain in no more than three sentences what the problem is. How do you think the story ends?*

WB p. 9/17

9 How to: Explain words you don't know

Sometimes you don't know the exact word you need. So you must explain it.

Examples: Schwimmbrille They're things swimmers put over their eyes.
or: If you wear them under water, your eyes won't get wet.

sich beschlagen When this happens to glass you can't see through it.
or: Warm air on cold glass does this.

Explain these new words. There is always more than one way to do it, so compare your ideas in class. (You will find out the correct English words later in the unit!)

Kleinbus • Brille • winken • rutschen • Skier • Zahnweh • Adler

WB p. 9/18

USEFUL PHRASES

It's a kind of … It's got … It can …
They're things that help you to …
You get this feeling when …
If this happens, you …
This happens when … / You do this when …

10 Revision: Simple present or present progressive?

a) *What does the athletics star tell the reporter? Make sentences with the correct tenses.*

1. for the Olympic Games • I • at the moment • train 2. to this track • I • come • every day 3. usually • meet • at 2 o'clock • my group 4. our trainer • us • always • lots of help • give 5. today • check • he • our fitness over 400 metres 6. I • to feel • start • really strong • now 7. wait • right now • for me • the others 8. never • champions • stop and talk

b) *Imagine you are the reporter. What questions would you like to ask?*

Eddie the Eagle

1 Before you read

Think of sports stars you know. What are they like? What words do you know that describe them best? Collect ideas.

It was late in the evening when an unusual hero got off the plane and walked into the airport in Calgary, Canada. A short man with glasses, he didn't look like a sports star.

Eddie Edwards from Britain was in Calgary for the ski jump competitions at the 1988 Winter Olympics. He didn't expect to win. He was just glad to be there.

Accidents always happened to Eddie. While he was walking through customs his clothes fell out of his bag. He got a big surprise when he saw that a lot of people were waiting for him. His fans were holding up a message for him: "Welcome to Eddie the Eagle Edwards".

Wow, that's brilliant, he thought. He didn't know he had a fan club in Canada. He was still looking at the fans when he walked into a door.

It was now very late in the evening but he didn't know how to get to the Olympic village. At last he found someone from the British Olympic ski team who could tell him. It was 2 am when he finally arrived at the village.

The next morning Eddie Edwards couldn't practise because he was sorting out problems with his equipment. He was even an hour late for his press conference.

"You can't come in here," said a man on the door. "There's a press conference for Eddie Edwards."

"But I *am* Eddie Edwards."

"You? No, never. You're not an athlete." When Eddie was finally in the room there were questions from 130 reporters.

"Do you wear your glasses when you jump, Eddie?"

"Yes. They mist up when I put my goggles over them. I just hope they'll be clear again before I get to the bottom."

The reporters liked Eddie's friendly face and the stories of his adventures. He told them how he became a ski jumper although it was a very unusual sport in Britain. He told them how hard it was to start in the sport. He slept in his van in very cold weather when he travelled to other countries for competitions. That helped to save money. He also told them about his accidents.

The reporters weren't sure what to think about Eddie. His eyes were bad, he had no money, and one accident after another happened to him. What was he doing at the Winter Olympics? He had no chance

of success. Was he somebody they should laugh at? Somebody who shouldn't be there? Or was he somebody in the true Olympic tradition who showed that it was more important to be there than to win?

The reporters and people everywhere in the world wanted to see Eddie in the ski jump competitions. Some of the other ski jumpers weren't so sure. Some were at the Olympics after twenty years in the sport. Now everyone was interested in someone with no chance.

The day of the first competition came.

There are two ski jump events at the Winter Olympics. The 70 metres was the first, a few days before the 90 metres.

While Eddie Edwards was going to the top of the mountain for his first jump in the 70 metres, he heard the names of the others and how far their jumps were.

"Lotric of Yugoslavia … 85 metres."

"Collins of Canada … 83.5 metres."

Eddie was the twenty-fourth ski jumper that day. From the top of the mountain he looked down. There were 40,000 people, and TV cameras were everywhere. There was a good chance he might look very silly. But he was there, at the Olympics.

Eddie Edwards was ready. He started to slide over the snow. Fast, then faster. His goggles misted up, but he tried to keep his skis straight. He could feel the cold wind on his face. He was ready to take off.

Some people say that Eddie the Eagle didn't jump, that he fell out of the sky. But it was still a long time before he came down. Alone in the air, he flapped his arms and tried to go as far as he could.

"Edwards of Great Britain … 55 metres."

It was good enough for last place.

Matti Nykanen of Finland jumped 89.5 metres, so some people laughed at Eddie. But he was enjoying the competition. Before his second jump he waved to all the people and the cameras. Then he took off again.

"Edwards of Great Britain … 55 metres."

He couldn't improve.

A week later in the 90 metres ski jump competition, on a clear day with no wind, Eddie Edwards jumped a new British record of 71 metres in front of 80,000 people. He was very happy, even if Nykanen won the gold medal with 118.5 metres.

The day after the 90 metres competition, Eddie Edwards was more popular than the winner of the gold medal. He got invitations to talk on TV, to open events and to sing on records in England and Finland. Why was he so popular? Maybe it was because he was just a normal person. He lost but he celebrated. He also showed he could do something most people never do – he could get to the Olympics.

(adapted from: *True Sport Stories* by Tim Lardner)

2 Talk about Eddie Edwards

a) *Look at the text again. Compare your ideas from exercise 1 with Eddie.*

b) *Explain why you think these phrases are or aren't good ways to describe Eddie.*

a great athlete • very clever • an idiot • a crazy character • a normal person • a special person

c) *Find your own words to describe Eddie and explain why you chose them.*

3 ⟨Feelings in sport⟩

a) *Look at the photos of Eddie on page 16 and 17. What do you think his feelings are right now?*

b) *Look in magazines etc. for photos that show feelings in sport. Bring your photos to school. Say how the people feel and why.*

4 Role play: Eddie's press conference

Work with the photo of Eddie's press conference on page 17. Think what the reporters are asking and what Eddie's answers are. Write six questions and answers. (Lines 26 to 68 in the text can help to give you ideas.) Act the interview with your partner. WB p. 10/19

5 Writing texts: Write your own *Did you know?* sports text

a) *Work alone or with a partner. First choose a sport or a famous or unusual athlete. Then use books or the Internet to find some interesting or funny information. Write a short text of ~~6–8~~ 10–12 sentences for your folder.*

⟨b)⟩ *Copy your texts from a) and make a* Did you know? *poster for your classroom. Use photos or draw pictures that go with your texts.* WB p. 10/20

6 ⟨A song: You'll never walk alone⟩

Listen to the song that fans of Liverpool Football Club always sing at matches. Do you think it is a good football song? Why/why not?

When you walk through a storm,
Hold your head up high,
And don't be afraid of the dark.
At the end of a storm,
There's a golden sky,
And the sweet silver song of a lark.
Walk on through the wind,
Walk on through the rain,
Though your dreams be tossed and blown.

Walk on, walk on, with hope in your heart,
And you'll never walk alone.
You'll never walk alone.

©Text: Richard Rodgers / Oscar Hammerstein

VOCABULARY SKILLS

Using a German-English dictionary

You can look up English words you don't know in a **German-English dictionary**. But watch out, because there are often different English words or phrases for one German word. So look for information about the context.

You've already learnt lots of skills in *Green Line* 1 and 2. Now you'll find a whole page of Skills in every Unit – for vocabulary, reading, listening, writing and speaking.

1 What's 'null' in English?

Check the words for 'null' on the right.
How do you say '0' in these pictures?

null ❶ zero ❷ *(bei Telefonnummern)* O [əʊ] (GB), zero ❸ *(im Sport)* nil; *(beim Tennis)* love [lʌv]

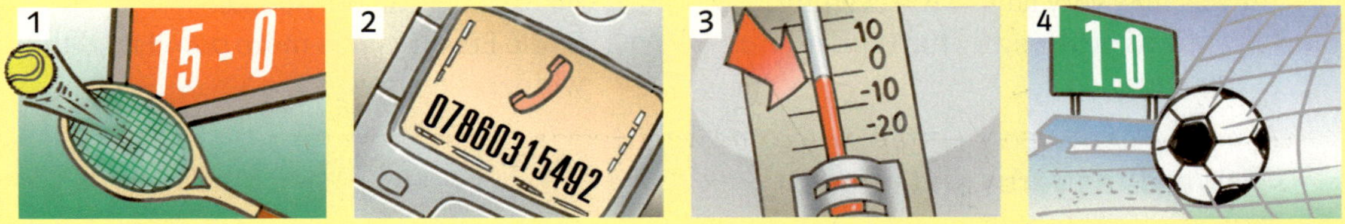

WB p. 11/21

2 Not word for word

You often can't put German into English word for word.
Check the phrases with 'Glück' on the right.
What can you say to these people?

1. someone who wins a ticket for a big game
2. someone who has got a match tomorrow
3. someone whose helmet broke (not his head!)
4. someone who fell in a 100 metres race

Glück ❶ luck; **viel Glück!** good luck; **was für ein Glück!** what a stroke of luck! ❷ **Glück haben** be lucky; **kein Glück haben** be out of luck, be unlucky!; **Glück gehabt!** that was lucky!; **da hast du aber Glück gehabt!** you were lucky there

3 Put it into English

A German girl is writing to an English friend about a football match she played in. Put these ideas into English. Use a German-English dictionary for words you don't know.

1. My first goal didn't *(zählen)*. 2. I was standing *(abseits)*. 3. Our team was the better team in the first *(Halbzeit)*. 4. I took a *(Elfmeter)*. 5. The other team played better after *(Halbzeit)*. 6. The game ended *(unentschieden)*.

WB p. 11/22

TIP
Don't forget to look at the context when you look up a word in the dictionary.

4 ⟨A joke⟩

Jokes are often funny because a word has two meanings.
Use a dictionary to find out another meaning of 'racket'!

What sport is bad for your ears?
– Tennis. Because you can't play it without a racket.

1 Make a grid for sports words

Find as many words for your grid as you can.

sport	place	equipment etc.
cricket	pitch	ball, bat, helmet
baseball		
...		

WB p. 12/24; 25

2 Put in the correct prepositions

When you have finished, you can check your own answers in the text Eddie the Eagle.

1. He didn't look ___ a sports star.
2. Accidents always happened ___ Eddie.
3. A lot of people were waiting ___ him.
4. It was now very late ___ the evening.
5. What was he doing ___ the Winter Olympics?
6. The day ___ the first competition came.
7. He could feel the cold wind ___ his face.
8. Some people laughed ___ Eddie.
9. He waved ___ all the people.
10. Eddie Edwards was more popular ___ the winner.

WB p. 12/26

3 Words as verbs and nouns

Some words can be verbs ***and*** *nouns. So if you already know one form of the word, you can understand the other form.*

a) *Write these sentences with verbs, not nouns. (You already know the verbs.)*

Example: He gave a *wave* to the TV camera. → He **waved** to the TV camera.

1. There was a *shout* from a fan in the crowd.
2. His *jump* was over 100 metres.
3. He gave the ball a *kick*.
4. Two bikes in the race had a *crash*.
5. Athletes should get a lot of *sleep*.

b) *Write these sentences with nouns, not verbs. (You already know the nouns.)*

Example: I know the boy who *is batting*. → I know the boy with the **bat**.

1. It *surprised* everyone when I won.
2. I think it will *snow* before the game ends.
3. She *dreams* about the Olympics.
4. A reporter *interviewed* the winner.
5. Look, we must *queue* for tickets.

4 Sounds: Words that you link

a) *Listen and repeat these sentences from* Eddie the Eagle.

An‿unusual hero got‿off the plane. – His clothes fell‿out‿of his bag. –
He had‿a fan club‿in Canada. – You're not‿an‿athlete. –
He also told them‿about‿his‿accidents. – It was good‿enough‿for last place.

b) *Find more examples in the text of words that you link.*
Choose three sentences and read them to the class.

NOW YOU CAN

- ✓ Give information about sports.
- ✓ Talk about 'timetable' events in the future with the simple present.
- ✓ Talk about arrangements for the future with the present progressive.
- ✓ Ask for help or give help.
- ✓ Say if you agree or not.
- ✓ Use relative (and contact) clauses.
- ✓ Explain words you don't know.
- ✓ Use a German-English dictionary.

1 A game

Choose a sport you are interested in and make notes about it. Look up new words you need in a German-English dictionary. Make a word web for your sport.

Then play a game in groups of four or five. Use your notes and talk about your sport. Who can talk longest without any long pauses?

2 What are they doing at the weekend? (→ G3)

Example: Bill: Let's watch a rugby match on Saturday. – Jon: Good idea!
→ John and Bill are watching a rugby match on Saturday.

1. Anne: Can I play tennis with you on Sunday? – Fiona: Sure. → Anne is … with … on …
2. Phil: Let's meet at the sports centre on Saturday. – Ben: OK. → Phil and Ben …
3. Rob: I'll teach you to row on Sunday morning. – Jill: Oh, thanks! → Rob …
4. Tina: I must train at the weekend. – Justin: Let's train together. → Tina and Justin …
5. Father: I can drive you to the skatepark tomorrow. – Laura: Thanks! → Laura's father …

WB p. 13/28

3 Make sentences with relative clauses (→ G5)

a) *Put the right parts together with a relative pronoun.*

1. An umpire must be someone	+	they follow.
2. Fans often wear the colours of the team		you play with an oval ball.
3. Everyone wants to work with a trainer	who	are very tall.
4. Rowing champions are often people	that	athletes win a lot of races.
5. Wheelchair athletes use wheels	which	you are playing against.
6. Basketball is easier for players	whose	knows the rules of the game.
7. Rugby is a sport	+	don't weigh much.
8. You should always be polite to the person		lungs are very big.

b) *In which of the sentences you made in a) do you not need the relative pronoun?*

WB p. 13/29

4 Your turn: Do you agree?

Give an answer to these people. The Useful phrases in Talkwise on page 12 can help you.

1. "Skateboarding isn't a sport for girls."
2. "I think there's too much sport on TV."
3. "Golf is a boring game."
4. "People with no chance shouldn't be at the Olympics."

WB p. 13/30

⟨Project⟩ English and Computing[1]

English is not only for English lessons. You can also speak English in other subjects. On these **Project** pages you talk about Computing, Biology and Geography. The **Skills** boxes will help you with your project work.

DID YOU KNOW?

- … that 1946 was the date of the first all-electronic[2] computer?
- … that the Internet started in the year 1969?
- … that in 2004 60 % of all households[3] in Germany were on the Internet?
- … that more than 80 % of the homepages on the World Wide Web are in English?

STEP 1: Look at the keyboard[4]

Work with a partner. Can you find these keys[5] from an English keyboard on ***your*** *keyboard? Find the German words and write them in your exercise book. Which team is the fastest?*

1 @ (= 'at')
2 ↵ return / enter
3 space bar
4 ⇧ shift
5 ctrl control

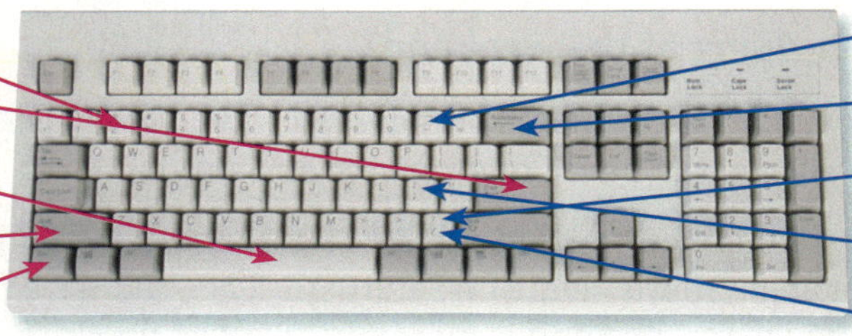

6 - hyphen
7 ← delete
8 : colon
9 ? question mark
10 / slash

STEP 2: Work with a word processor[6]

Follow these instructions[7].

1. Start a new text file[8] 🗋.
2. Type[9] the text *Who is the mystery[10] man?*
3. Save your text 💾.
4. Now put the sentences in the right order:

   ☞ With the help of your mouse, highlight[11] the sentence you want to move.
   ☞ Click on the **cut**[12] ✂ button.
   ☞ Move the cursor ↖ to the new position[13] of the sentence and click.
   ☞ Click on the **paste**[14] 📋 button.

5. Use ↖ and 📋 to put the other sentences in the right position. Then fill in the man's name.

Who is the mystery man?

- He played for hours when he was a kid.
- His name is ______ ______.
- He went to play football for Manchester United's Jr.[15] Team.
- In 1997/98 he became an English international[16] football player.
- So he was never that good at school.
- Two years later he played his first Premiership match.
- 1 He was born on May 2nd, 1975.
- In 2003, he went to Real Madrid.
- He left school when he was 16.

[1] **Computing** [kəm'pju:tiŋ] = Informatik • [2] **all-electronic** [ɔ:l‿elek'trɒnɪk] = vollelektronisch • [3] **household** ['haʊsəʊld] = Haushalt • [4] **keyboard** ['ki:bɔ:d] = Tastatur • [5] **key** [ki:] = Taste • [6] **word processor** ['wɜ:d ˌprəʊsesə] = Textverarbeitungssystem • [7] **instruction** [ɪn'strʌkʃn] = Anweisung • [8] **file** [faɪl] = Datei • [9] **(to) type** [taɪp] = tippen • [10] **mystery** ['mɪstri] = Geheimnis, Rätsel • [11] **(to) highlight** ['haɪlaɪt] = hervorheben • [12] **(to) cut** [kʌt] = ausschneiden • [13] **position** [pə'zɪʃn] = Stelle, Position • [14] **(to) paste** [peɪst] = einfügen • [15] **Jr.** ['dʒu:nɪə] = (Abkürzung für) Junior • [16] **international** [ˌɪntə'næʃnl] = international

STEP 3: Collect words for the Web

Can you match and explain the Internet words? (Check the spelling in the Dictionary.)

down, log ✓, web, user, search, on, web, e-mail, home, pass

engine, word, address, name, page, on ✓, line, load, site, browser

STEP 4: Find information on the Internet

PROJECT SKILLS

If you want to find information for a project you can use the Internet. These project skills can help you.

a) Start a new text file. Type in your name, the date and the numbers one to six.

b) Read the tasks[17] on the right. Write down keywords[18] you need to look for the answers on the Internet.

c) Go to an Internet search engine[19] (Google™, Yahoo®, etc.). You have 20 minutes to find useful information. Only use the facts you need.

d) Write the answers in your text file. Type your answers or use the commands[20] copy and paste.

e) Read your text again and look for mistakes. Then save it and print it out[21].

Tasks:

1. Find three British football clubs.
2. Find two important Welsh sports.
3. Find two Scottish football clubs.
4. What are the Highland Games?
5. What is the 'Man versus[22] Horse Marathon'?
6. What is 'Gaelic[23] football'?

STEP 5: Do a project: Sports in the USA

In Step 4 you learnt how to look for information on the Internet. Now it's time to use these skills in a project about sports in the USA.

1. *Work in groups of four or five. Find information about a popular American sport, a sports star or a famous team.*
2. *Look at interesting websites and think about what people should know about the sport.*
3. *Make a poster for your class. Use the texts and photos you have found.*
4. *Give a presentation and show your poster to your classmates. They may want to ask you some questions, so be prepared!*

[17] **task** [tɑːsk] = (Arbeits)aufgabe • [18] **keyword** ['kiːwɜːd] = Stichwort • [19] **search engine** ['sɜːtʃ ˌendʒɪn] = Suchmaschine • [20] **command** [kə'mɑːnd] = Befehl • [21] **(to) print out** [prɪnt 'aʊt] = ausdrucken • [22] **versus** ['vɜːsəs] = gegen • [23] **Gaelic** ['geɪlɪk] = gälisch

Unit 2 Once upon a time . . .

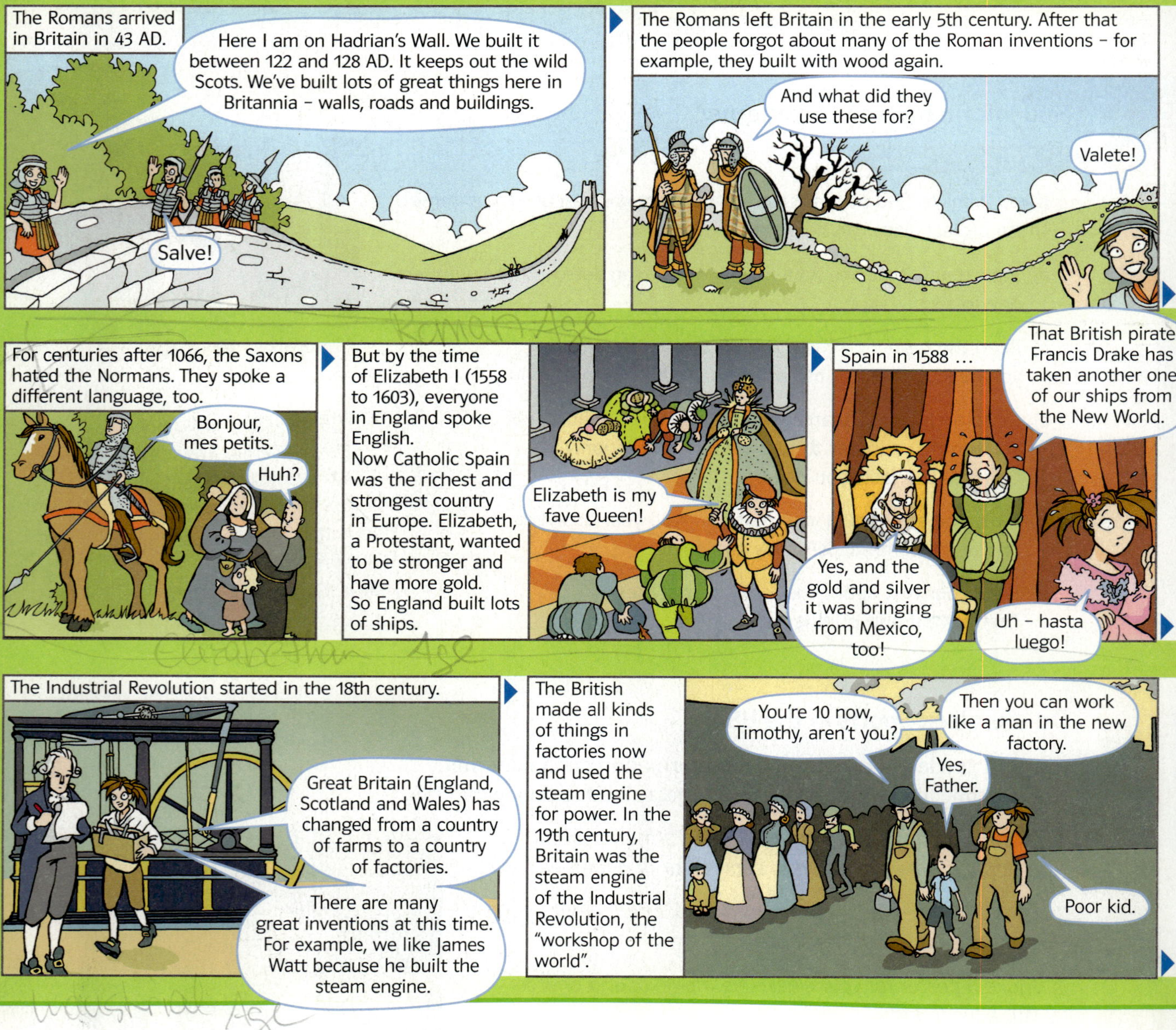

1 What happened in history?

a)
1. What was "Roman Britain"?
2. What did the Battle of Hastings mean for Britain?
3. Why was the Elizabethan Age important for Britain, and for the world?
4. What was the Industrial Revolution?

b) *Find the events on this page on the time line of British history at the back of the book.*

WB p. 15/1

DID YOU KNOW?

- The Romans also used elephants when they attacked Britain.
- Factories in Birmingham first made steel pens in the 1830s.
- At *Shakespeare's Globe Theatre* in London, the plays and the building are just like they were in the 16th century.

2 Listening: When is it?

Listen to the people. They all lived in one age. Which age is it, and what information tells you this?

WB p. 15/2

3 Your turn: Comics

a) *Talk to your partner: Do you read comics? If so, which ones? Why do you like them?*

b) *Compare this comic to other books about history. What is different?*

Visit the *World Stage*

Tracy: Hey, Mark! Look at this dress! Were they really able to make things like that in those days?

Mark: How should I know? Do we have to look at all these dead people, Tracy?

Tracy: Will you just be quiet? Oh, here's a guide. I must ask him about the dress. Excuse me, can I ask you a question about this person? I can't believe this dress is real!

Guide: I've had to answer that question many times, but it's real. This is Queen Elizabeth I: She really wore dresses like this.

Mark: Come on, Tracy, I want to see some other people – what about pirates?

Guide: Pirates? Oh, you needn't look far. You could call Sir Francis Drake over here a pirate: the Queen's pirate. Thanks to him, England – and Elizabeth, of course – got very rich in the 17th century. Spanish ships brought home gold from colonies in the New World, and Drake attacked the ships and took the gold.

Tracy: No way! Was he allowed to do that?

Guide: Well, he didn't have to worry about Elizabeth. She knew that if a country wanted to be strong, it had to be rich. You mustn't forget that Elizabeth was in many ways a modern woman. She was the first queen of England who wasn't married. She had a very strong will, and she thought, "People see a weak woman in me. If I want to make England strong, I will have to be as strong as a man." And she was. Have you seen any of Shakespeare's plays?

Tracy: Oh, I've read *Romeo and Juliet*.

Mark: Oh no! More dresses!

Guide: Simple people liked the plays because they had a lot of action. But they weren't able to see that some plays also tried to show how important England – and Elizabeth – was in the world. Shakespeare was a 17th century pop star. If you look, you'll be able to find him in this room, too. Ask your teacher, and maybe you'll be allowed to go to Shakespeare's Globe Theatre while you're in London. Hundreds of kids have already been able to do some great workshops there.

Tracy: Oh yes! Then we won't just have to imagine what a 17th century theatre looked like. The Globe is open-air, isn't it?

Mark: Well, I'm glad some *modern* pop stars are here, too. But I can't see Robbie Williams. Can you?

1 Read the text, and then say ...

1. ... what you like or don't like about Elizabeth I. What makes her special?
2. ... what you know about William Shakespeare.
3. ... whether you think a wax museum like Madame Tussaud's is good if you want to learn about history. Why or why not?
4. ... who you would like to see at Madame Tussaud's.

2 Revision: Modals

1. Here's a museum guide. If you want, you
2. The faces are wax. They
3. This dress is very beautiful. It
4. Today, captains of British ships
5. If our teacher says yes, we
6. Is Robbie Williams here? I
7. I've got a map of the 'World Stage', so you

- can do a workshop at the Globe Theatre.
- mustn't steal gold from other ships.
- needn't ask a guide.
- can't see him anywhere.
- can ask him a question.
- must be very expensive!
- mustn't get too hot.

WB p. 16/3

3 Find the rule

a) *Try to explain the two different meanings of **can** in these two sentences:*

Can I ask you a question? *(lines 8–9)* – I **can't** see Robbie Williams. *(lines 60–61)*

b) *Look at the dialogue again and find examples of the new forms **able to** and **allowed to**. We use these forms as past, present perfect and future tense of **can**.*

c) *Copy the grid into your exercise book and fill in the correct forms for the four tenses.*

WB p. 16/4

		Present	Past	Present perfect	Future
können	+ –	can can't			
dürfen	+ –				
...					

TIP

The verb **to be** is important when you use *able to* and *allowed to*.

4 Complete Mark's text about the Queen's pirate

Example: At 18, Drake (be able to) get his first job on a ship. → At 18, Drake **was able to** get …

Francis Drake was born in 1540. At 20 he **1** (be able to) cross the Atlantic for the first time. And at only 24 he **2** (be allowed to) become captain of a ship. From 1572 to 1587 his ships **3** (be allowed to) attack Spanish towns and ships and steal their treasure. In 1580, Drake **4** (be able to) finish a trip all round the world and he became *Sir* Francis Drake. The Spanish attacked England in 1588, but they **5** (not able to) defeat Drake's smaller but faster ships. Drake died at sea near Panama in 1596. People **6** (not yet allowed to) look for the box they put his body in; it is at the bottom of the sea.

5 At the Globe

*What **will** Tracy and Mark **be able to** do at the Globe? What **won't** they **be allowed to** do?*

go to | use | meet | wear | try on

WB p. 16/5

6 Your turn: What can you do?

a) *What were you not able or not allowed to do in the past? Tell your partner about three things.*

Example: Last year I **wasn't able to** swim under water. Now I can.

b) *What new things will you be able or allowed to do in the future? Tell your partner about three things.*

Example: I'**ll be allowed to** drive a car when I'm 18. I can't yet.

swim under water • drive a car • go to bed after 12 pm • go to a disco alone • ride a bike • speak English • watch TV in my room • …

WB p. 17/6

7 *Have to*

a) *Find the rule: Look at the dialogue on page 26 again and find the past tense, present perfect and future forms for **must** and **needn't**. Put them in your grid, too.*

b) *The Globe Theatre website answers everybody's questions. Complete the text with forms of **have to**. Be careful: present tense, past tense, present perfect or will future?*

WB p. 17/7; p. 18/8; 9

TIP

You can see that **to have** is also an important verb. Remember: You make the negative and questions with forms of *do*, in the past tense with *did*. You make the present perfect with forms of *have*.

1. ***I've heard that only men and boys acted in Shakespeare's time.***
   That's right. The boys **had to** play women's roles.
2. ***Did Shakespeare become famous quickly?***
   Yes. He / not wait long for success.
3. ***we / wear warm clothes when we come to watch a play?***
   Yes. Because the Globe is an open-air theatre, it might get cold.
4. ***Can we sit down in front of the stage?***
   No, you / stand, sorry.
5. ***Is there a hotel near the theatre?***
   Yes, but it's very popular. If you want a room, you / call early.
6. ***Did people ever think the plays were boring in those days?***
   Yes, and the actors / be careful, because people threw food at them then!
7. ***modern actors / watch out for food yet?***
   No, not yet!
8. ***Can children come to see a play?***
   Of course, and you / not / worry if they walk around: You're allowed to, like in Shakespeare's time!

8 How to: Visit a museum

You (A) are in a museum. Act the following scenes with a partner (B). The Useful phrases can help you.

1. A: You want to buy tickets for your family.
   B: You work at the ticket office.
2. A: You want to get a map of the museum.
   B: You work at the museum shop.
3. A: You can't find the rooms about the 17th century.
   B: You are a museum guide.
4. *(Your ideas.)*

WB p. 19/10

TIP

Remember:
You can use **may** to ask for things:
May I ask a question? – Yes, you **may**.

USEFUL PHRASES

How much are the tickets?
Are there special prices for families / … ?
Where can I get souvenirs / a brochure / … ?
Can you tell me the way to …, please?
May I take a photo of … ?
Are we allowed to use mobiles / eat in … ?

TALKWISE

Planning a special event

1 Before you listen

a) *Look at the photo on the right. Collect ideas about:*

- who the people are;
- where they are and what they are doing.

b) *Listen once. Were your ideas for a) right?*

2 Collect ideas for a trip

a) *When you are planning a special trip, you have to think of lots of things. Collect ideas and make a list.*

transport
price
lunch
...

b) *Now listen to the conversation again and take notes about the ideas the pupils have about their trip. Put any new ones into your list from exercise 2 a).*

3 Where shall we go?

a) *What can you say? Match the suggestions with one or more of the answers.*

1. I've got an idea. → Yes, what is it?
2. I think we should check the weather first.
3. Why don't you ask at the tourist office?
4. Shall I buy the tickets?
5. How about lunch at a nice restaurant?

Oh, that's a good idea. I'll do that.
Yes, OK. Thanks very much.
I'm not so sure. Won't that be expensive?
Yes, what is it?
You're right. It might rain.

(b)) *You and a friend want to go out one afternoon. What can you do? Make a short dialogue. Use the Useful phrases.*

WB p. 20/11

USEFUL PHRASES

How about a trip to ...?/We could go and see ...
I suggest we go by bus/train/...
Shall I get the timetable/map/...?
Why don't you check the Internet?
I think we ought to phone the tourist office/the station/...
Shouldn't we take sandwiches/water/...?

4 Your turn: Plan your event

a) *In groups of 3 or 4, choose one of these situations for a class event. You want to:*

1. ... have a school open day.
2. ... go on a trip to a museum.
3. ... collect money for a children's hospital.
4. ... have your own idea.

b) *Now work alone. Prepare what you want to suggest. Use the Useful phrases and make notes. Think of reasons for your suggestion.*

c) *Now talk about your ideas with the others in your group. Choose one suggestion and then make a plan: Who is going to do what, and when?*

WB p. 20/12

Get the facts: Victorian Britain

What was "hot" in Victorian England? *TV People* wanted to find out and "talked" to two very different Victorians.

Queen Victoria
(1819–1901)

What should people remember most about you?

My long reign. When I died in 1901, I had spent more than 63 years on the throne.

What about the Empire?

Oh, that old thing. Don't you call it the Commonwealth now? Well, the Empire made Britain very rich because we had chosen colonies which were able to give us cheap raw materials and food. When I became Empress of India in 1877, we had taken Australia, Canada, Egypt, India … and lots of little islands all round the world. But we had already lost the Thirteen Colonies in North America. Of course I can see now why many people in the colonies were not happy. But after they had become independent, lots of countries which had been colonies wanted to join the Commonwealth.

"The Empire made Britain very rich"

Stephen Hoskins
(1810–1847)

You were a farmer's son?

Yes, that's right. Factory workers were often people from the country who had worked on farms or in small workshops before they went to the towns. There they lived in tiny, dirty slums because they didn't have money for better houses.

Tell us about your work.

My first day at the factory was in March, 1820. Work started at 5.30 am. I was hungry because there had not been any bread at home for breakfast. In the factory, it was my job to keep the machines clean. I hadn't done any training, so I could only do this simple job. In the evening, after I had sat on the floor all day, my back hurt.

"Work started at 5.30 am"

Didn't you have to go to school?

The government had not opened any free schools yet when I was a boy – this didn't happen until 1870 – and my family needed the money I got in the factory.

■ *Watch* **Get the facts** *at 9 pm on Monday on* **BBC1.**

1 Look at the text

a) *Correct these sentences about Victorian Britain.*

1. Victoria was Queen for nineteen years. → No, she was on the throne from … until …
2. Britain wanted to improve the lives of people in her colonies. → No, Britain wanted …
3. Only people from the towns worked in the factories.
4. All of Britain's colonies had to join the Commonwealth when they became independent.
5. Children who worked in factories got breakfast from the factory owner.

b) *Look at the photos of Victoria and Stephen. What questions would **you** like to ask them?*

2 The past perfect

a) *You use the past perfect to show that one event happened before another one in the past. Find more examples of the past perfect in the text and say which action or event happened first.*

b) *You will also often find the past perfect in sentences which say* ***why*** *things happened. Complete these sentences with ideas from the text.*

GRAMMAR

When I died in 1901, **I had spent** more than 63 years on the throne. — **This** event happened after **this** one.

(→ G10)

TIP

I was hungry **because** there **had not been** any bread …

I **hadn't done** any training, **so** I could only do this simple job.

(→ G10)

1. Many factory workers were people who …, **so** they did not know what towns were like.
2. The Empire made Britain rich **because** the British …
3. On his first day in the factory Stephen Hoskins …, **so** his back hurt in the evening.
4. Stephen did not go to school after work **because** the government …

WB p. 21/13

3 From fortress to museum: Simple past or past perfect?

fortress

royal palace

prison

museum

London Zoo opened in Regent's Park in 1847. From the 13th to the 19th century people **had kept** wild animals in the Tower of London, but these animals 1 (go) to the new zoo in 1831. William the Conqueror 2 (build) the Tower as a fortress in 1078, twelve years after he 3 (become) king. But when William 4 (die), they 5 (not finish) it yet. When they 6 (finish) it, people called it the Great Tower, and later kings 7 (use) it as a royal palace. After they 8 (build) a lot of new towers and buildings, the Tower 9 (become) a castle and a prison. Visitors first 10 (come) to the Tower in the 16th century, and today it is a museum.

WB p. 21/14

4 Listening: The news at ten

Some TV People *readers have made a funny radio show about Queen Victoria. Listen, and put these events in the right order.*

a) walk the dog
b) go shopping
c) shout at cook
d) get up
e) sleep badly
f) have lunch
g) be tired

5 Your turn: One thing after another

Tell your partner about funny or interesting things that happened to you in the past. Say why they happened. What had happened before, or what happened next? Example:

Last Wednesday I arrived at the station **after** the train **had left**. I was lucky because there was another train an hour later.

READING SKILLS

A historical story

There are different ways to read a story. Here is one way. Before you read, it's important to **get ready**. When you start, read for **gist** first, then for **detail**.

Pre-reading

1 Getting ready to read

How can you get "into" a story even before you start to read? You must find out as much as you can about the text first.

a) *Look at the title and the pictures on p. 33–35. Can you guess what the story is about?*

b) *What stories or films do you know that are about the past? Tell the class about them.*

First reading

2 Reading for gist

The first reading – or reading for gist – gives you more information: Now you find out what the story is about and what characters are in the story. But you do not try to understand every word yet.

a) *Read the whole story quickly. Don't stop if you find words that you don't know.*

b) *Now you know better what the story is about. Did you guess right in exercise 1a)?*

Second reading

3 Reading for detail

Now you have got the most important ideas, but many things are not clear yet. So you read for detail.

a) *Read the story slowly – first one part, then the next.*

b) *If you find words which you don't understand, think before you look them up: Can I understand enough without them? If the answer is "yes", don't look them up.*

c) *There are really two stories in this text. Draw two action lines and put in the parts of the text and the most important events. How are the two stories connected? Draw connecting lines between the two action lines.*

TIP

Write down interesting words for your 'personal vocabulary' and put them in your folder.

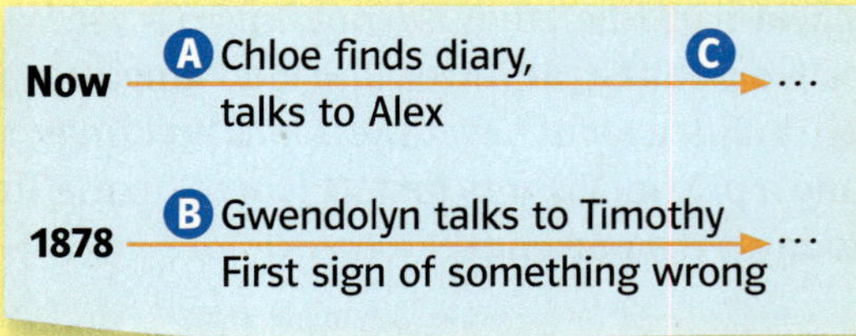

A closer look

4 Thinking about the story

Do a) ***or*** *b).*

a) *Look at the text again and make a list: How was life in 1878 different from now? What other things do you know about the 19th century? Put them in your list, too. Compare Gwendolyn's life to Chloe's, and Timothy's to Alex's.*

b) *Look for adjectives or phrases in the text that describe the characters well. Make a list and use it to write a few sentences about the four most important characters.*

WB p. 22/15

The diary

A "So where did you find it?" Alex asked his girlfriend, Chloe, while they were on the phone.

"In an old box. I was looking for some jewellery in my mum's wardrobe," she explained. "And then I found this Victorian diary. Someone in our family wrote it."

"It must be funny to read."

"Yes, the first few pages are so … *different* from today! I mean, 1878 wasn't that long ago, but everything is so old. They've all got these funny, old-fashioned names – Gwendolyn, Reginald, Henrietta, Timothy, and then Lord this and Lady that."

"Hey, I've got an old-fashioned name, too, so be careful what you say!" Alex said and laughed.

"Oh please, 'Alex' isn't old."

"But 'Clarence' is. That's my first name – terrible, isn't it?" Alex smiled. "I never use my first name, I hate it. Alexander is my middle name."

"You're joking! My mum has never liked the name Clarence – don't ask me why. Anyway, I've only read the first few pages, but I guess our family was very poor in the 19th century. Gwendolyn's parents have sent her to work as a servant girl for some rich people in a big house near Regent's Park. Listen to this: *'I can't let dear Mother know how much I miss her. It might break her heart. But she and Father are right: I must help to feed my dear little brothers and sisters, it is my duty. I love them so. I'm very lonely, but Lady Cumberland is good to me.'*"

"Hm, that's a bit sad," replied Alex. He looked out at the sun which was shining on the cars in the street outside.

"Well, that was the second page; she had only been with this Cumberland family a few days. On the fourth page she's already got a friend in the house. His name is Timothy."

B "Oh, what a long day it's been. It's nice to be up here in the servants' rooms again," Gwendolyn said tiredly. She put a candle on the table.

"Yes, life downstairs with Lord and Lady Cumberland is just too perfect. And boring!" Timothy laughed.

"Well, Timothy, *you* aren't boring – it's so nice to talk to someone of my own age. Everyone else in the house is so much older."

"Yes, but Gwendolyn, it may not be good for you if the others see that you and I talk a lot."

C "Chloe, please. I think I've heard enough about these Victorian people," Alex said into the phone the next day. "Let's talk about something less boring – like our flight to Spain this summer! Hey, I think that language school in Majorca sounds better than the one in Malaga. What do you think?"

D "I don't understand," Gwendolyn said. "You're so kind and gentle. There's nothing wrong with you."

"I'm afraid there is. Do you really want to know?" Timothy asked. He wasn't smiling.

"Yes, yes, what is it?" Gwendolyn asked.

"Well, I – I can see things."

"And so can I, Timothy."

"No, Gwendolyn, you don't understand. I can see things that haven't happened yet."

"What things?" Gwendolyn was curious now.

"Oh, usually it's just silly things, really. Like last week. I was cleaning the fountain in the garden when suddenly, in my head, I saw Mrs Lacy – she had fallen into the fountain. The next day I walked into the garden: There was Mrs Lacy in the water and she was shouting. The two young Cumberland children had just pushed her in!"

"That *is* funny!" Gwendolyn laughed. "She really isn't a very nice tutor, you know. But Timothy – why is your face suddenly so sad?"

E "I'll have to ask Mum," Chloe said. "Every time I talk about our flight to Spain she looks funny and doesn't say a word."

"How strange," Alex said. Suddenly, he had an odd feeling in his stomach, a feeling he had never had before. But he didn't say a thing. He looked up as the room became dark; a cloud had moved in front of the sun.

F "Well," Timothy went on, "I don't always see funny things like tutors in fountains. The things I see are sometimes terrible."

"Terrible?"

"I once had a vision about Her Ladyship's son, who was in India at the time. I saw him on a ship. It was sinking. I could see his white face in the water. Three days later, a telegram arrived with the news: He had drowned. That's when I started to become scared."

"Oh no!" Gwendolyn gasped. "I'm so sorry you have to see such things. You've – you've got what they call the sixth sense."

"Yes, that's it. But there's more. Are you sure you want to hear it?" he asked.

"Yes – yes, I am. Go on."

"Now that you are here at Cumberland Hall," Timothy continued, "I have the same scary vision every day."

Now Gwendolyn was scared, too.

G Alex couldn't get Chloe on his mobile any more. She had not been at school that day. He walked to her house through the rain, but nobody was there – the house was empty. A neighbour called to him, "Looking for the Robinsons? They're on holiday, I think – away from this rainy weather!" At that moment, Alex got that strange feeling in his stomach again. He was scared now. Where was Chloe?

H "Did you get it again today?" Gwendolyn asked Timothy the next evening. He nodded.

"The same people? The same situation?"

"It's always the same," he answered.

"But who are they?" wondered Gwendolyn. "And why did this vision start when I came to work here?"

"I don't know. I've never met them. They look like you and me, but they're different. I don't know – they must be from a different time and place. Sometimes I can see their names, but then the vision ends and I forget them. But it doesn't matter: We can't help them anyway. There's nothing we can do for them," Timothy said sadly. He put his face in his hands. Gwendolyn just looked at her friend, and then at the candle. She felt terrible.

I "What's wrong, Mum?" Alex wanted to know when he got home. His mother looked as white as a ghost.

"Chloe's mother phoned while you were at school. They're staying with her aunt in Manchester. Alex … I don't think Chloe is coming back to London. You aren't going to believe what I have to tell you."

J "Our names are *where*?!" Alex couldn't believe what he was hearing.

"In Chloe's great-great-grandmother's diary. Listen: *'Poor Chloe and Clarence, whoever they are, wherever they are. If they stay together, that accident will happen: The metal flying machine will fall from the air. Clarence will live. Chloe won't. Can't Timothy and I do anything to help? But maybe it's already too late …'*"

"And Chloe's mum believes what someone says he could 'see' back in 1878?" Alex shouted. He was angry.

"Yes, Alex. She believes it. A lot of the things that Timothy saw actually happened. Chloe's mum found some information about it in the town library years ago. That's why she's scared for her daughter. When she found out that your real name was Clarence, she got a big shock. She really feels that something bad will happen to Chloe if you two stay together. And your trip to Spain this summer – *'the metal flying machine will fall from the air'* – don't you see? Chloe's mum feels terrible. But she says Chloe mustn't see you any longer."

K "Are you sure, Chloe? Really?" Alex asked that night. Chloe had phoned him, but hadn't told her mum.

"Do you see any other way?" Chloe replied. "Maybe we can still be friends. Later. But I don't know. I've read the whole diary now and I really believe that something bad could happen. Maybe I'm just silly, and I'm sure you don't understand. But please, try."

"What else can I do?" Alex said. Before he could say more, there was a 'click', and the line was dead.

Quietly, slowly, Alex put the phone down. He was shocked. He watched the rain against the window and thought about Chloe. When might he see her next? In a month? A year? Never again? He had no idea.

1 Believe it or not?

a) *What do you think about the story: Can you believe it? Why or why not?*

b) *What do you know about the "sixth sense"? Do you know any examples? Tell the class.*

WB p. 23/16

2 Writing texts: Write an ending to the story

1. ***First think and then make notes:*** *What happens to the characters? You might need two paragraphs – one for Gwendolyn and Timothy, one for Alex and Chloe.*
2. *Don't forget the four 'W'-questions:* ***Who … ? • What … ? • When … ? • Where … ?***
3. *To* ***improve your style****, use adjectives and adverbs, and connecting words like "because", … Look at exercise 3 on page 36, too.*
4. ***Use the new words from the story****, for example "vision", "sixth sense", "strange", etc.*

WB p. 23/17

1 French words in English

a) *The Normans brought their language, a kind of French, to England. Lots of French words became part of the English language. Look at these modern French words and say what they are in English.*

b) *Say the English words out loud. If you know French, compare the way you say them in French and English.*

acteur · arriver · changer · cousin · grands-parents · départ · dialogue · histoire · danser · excuser · famille · différent · problème · répéter · visiteur · musique · théâtre · station

2 Sounds: Sentence stress

Long sentences can be a problem when you speak or read out loud. It can help to stress important ('meaning') words.

a) *Listen to these sentences:*

1. King **Philip** of **Spain** wanted to **attack England** with his **famous Armada**.
2. If I **want** to make **England strong**, I will **have** to be as **strong** as a **man**.

Can you find rules for the words that you don't stress?

b) *Now find the important words in these sentences and say the sentences out loud. Then you can compare your ideas with the CD.*

1. Maybe you'll be allowed to go to the Globe Theatre while you're in London.
2. I think we ought to phone the tourist office before we go.
3. The government had not opened any free schools yet when I was a boy.
4. Gwendolyn's parents have sent her to work as a servant girl for some rich people.

WB p. 24/19

3 Improve your style

When you write a story or a dialogue, it is boring always to repeat 'said'. Find other verbs in The diary.

1. "I was looking for some jewellery," Chloe **said** to Alex.
2. "That *is* funny," Gwendolyn **said**.
3. "It's always the same," Timothy **said**.
4. "The Spanish are leaving!" the men **said**.
5. "Romeo, Romeo, wherefore art thou Romeo?" Juliet **said**.
6. "You can work in the factory," the man **said** to his son.

4 ⟨A song: Greensleeves⟩

Alas, my love, you do me wrong,
To cast me off discourteously.
For I have loved you well and long,
Delighting in your company.

Chorus:
Greensleeves was all my joy,
Greensleeves was my delight,
Greensleeves was my heart of gold,
And who but my lady Greensleeves?

NOW YOU CAN

- ✓ Talk about British history.
- ✓ Use *able to, allowed to*, and *have to* correctly.
- ✓ Visit a museum.
- ✓ Talk about suggestions and ideas for activities.
- ✓ Use the past perfect.
- ✓ Read a text carefully.

1 Complete Gwendolyn's diary (→ G 9)

*Use **have to, able to** or **allowed to** in the correct tense. Watch out for signal words.*

It has been a hard week in Lord and Lady Cumberland's house. On Monday I 1 clean all the bedrooms, so I (not) 2 sit down until the evening. On Wednesday Lord Cumberland's brother visited. He plays the bagpipes, and we servants 3 listen to him when he played for the family. Friday was very rainy – it was so wet that I (not) 4 walk in the park. Cook is ill, and so far this week, I 5 prepare breakfast, lunch and the evening meal for the whole family every day – that's nine people! If Cook is better tomorrow, I 6 have a free afternoon: My brother is coming to London! I hope that I 7 find him at the busy train station! Timothy's visions have stopped: If I live to be 100, I (not) 8 forget the things he told me about!

WB p. 25/21

2 Plan a class trip

Make suggestions for a class trip with these ideas. Use the Useful phrases on page 29.

Example: **I suggest** we collect …

1. collect ideas • in class • at home …
2. visit • London Zoo • Tower of London • …
3. look for tips • on the Internet • …
4. go • by train • …
5. check • times • prices • …
6. phone • information centre • …
7. where • lunch • sandwiches • …
8. make report • give presentation • …

WB p. 25/22

3 Retell Chloe and Alex's story (→ G 10)

Start like this: 1. After Chloe **had found** …, she **went** … 2. After she …, she …

WB p. 25/23

4 Your turn: Plan a visit to the museum

a) *Suggest a museum you want to visit in or near your town.*

b) *Talk about five things you want to find out, or questions you want to ask there. Write them down.*

⟨The ruby[1] in the smoke⟩

The year is 1872. Sally Lockhart, 16 years old, is in the middle of a mystery[2]. Her mother died in India when Sally was only a baby. Her father died three months ago when his ship sank in the South China Sea. And somebody has just sent her a strange letter from Singapore:

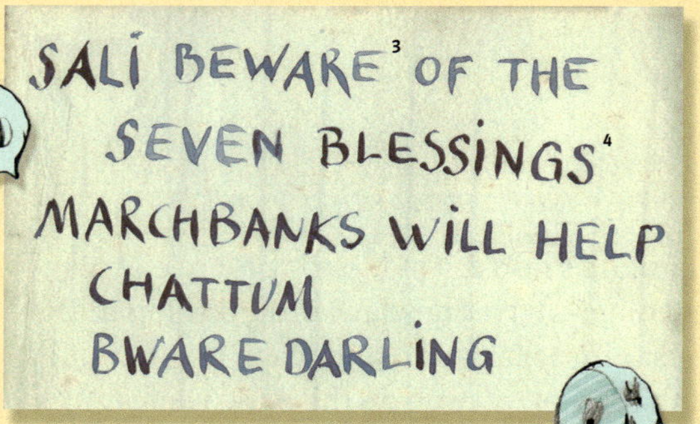
SALI BEWARE[3] OF THE SEVEN BLESSINGS[4]
MARCHBANKS WILL HELP
CHATTUM
BWARE DARLING

She goes to her father's old office to ask someone about this strange message and talks to Mr Higgs. But when he hears the phrase 'The Seven Blessings', he falls over dead. Major[5] Marchbanks reads about this in the newspaper and sends a letter to Sally right away. He tells Sally that she is in great danger[6] and that she should come to his house in Kent as soon as she can; he must give her some very important information …

She watched the grey city turn into the grey country, and looked at the sea to her left. There were always five or six ships going up or down the Thames.

The town of Swaleness was not very large. She decided not to take a cab[7] from the station, but to save her money and walk.

"Foreland House is not far away, maybe a mile," a man told her. "Take the river path."

She went at once. The town was sad and cold, the river was brown, and the country around her was empty.

The path followed the bank[8] of the river, and finally she came to some trees. There was the house – the paint was old; the garden, too, was untidy[9]. It was a very unhappy place.

She went up to the door and was ready to ring the bell when the door opened and a man came out. He put his finger to his lips[10] and closed the door. He was careful not to make a sound.

"Please," he whispered[11]. "Not a word. Follow me, quickly …"

Sally followed and he took her quickly around the side of the house and into a little verandah. He closed the door behind her, listened, and then held out[12] his hand.

"Miss Lockhart, I am Major Marchbanks." She shook his hand. He was about 60, she guessed. His face was thin and his clothes were a little too big for him. His eyes were dark and fine. His voice was familiar[13] in some strange way. There was something in his face that scared her, until she realized that he was scared, too: much more than she was.

"Your letter came this morning," she said. "Did my father write and ask you to see me?"

"No …" He sounded surprised.

"Then – have you ever heard the phrase 'The Seven Blessings'?" Sally asked.

[1] **ruby** ['ru:bi] = Rubin • [2] **mystery** ['mɪstri] = Geheimnis • [3] **(to) beware of** [bɪ'weə‿əv] = sich in Acht nehmen vor • [4] **blessing** ['blesɪŋ] = Segen • [5] **major** ['meɪdʒə] = Major • [6] **danger** ['deɪndʒə] = Gefahr • [7] **cab** [kæb] = Droschke • [8] **bank** [bæŋk] = Ufer • [9] **untidy** [ʌn'taɪdi] = unordentlich • [10] **lip** [lɪp] = Lippe • [11] **(to) whisper** ['wɪspə] = flüstern • [12] **(to) hold out** [həʊld‿'aʊt] = reichen • [13] **familiar** [fə'mɪlɪə] = vertraut

Major Marchbanks' face didn't change[14]. "I'm sorry," he said. "Did you come here to ask me that? I'm so sorry. Did your father –" Major Marchbanks suddenly looked sad and lost. "I have an enemy[15], Miss Lockhart," he whispered, "and that enemy is now yours, too. She – it is a woman – is wholly evil[16]. She is in this house now, which is why we must hide out here, and why you must leave very soon. Your father –"

"But why? What have I done to her? Who is she?"

"Please – I can't explain now. I shall, believe me. I know nothing of 'The Seven Blessings', nothing of the South China Sea, nothing of ships. Your father could not know … I can't help you. I can do nothing."

She saw terrible unhappiness in his face. She saw that he had no hope and it scared her. She could only think of the letter from the East. "Did you once live in Chatham?" she asked.

"Yes – a long time ago. But please – there's no time. Take this – "

He took out a brown paper package[17] that was about six inches long.

"This will tell you everything. Maybe, because he said nothing to you about it, I shouldn't either[18] … You will have a shock when you read this. Please be ready for it. But your life is in danger if you know it or not, and at least[19] you'll know why."

She took the package. Her hands were shaking badly; he saw it, and for one strange moment took them in both of his and put his head on them.

Then a door opened.

He jumped away, grey in the face; a woman looked around the door.

"Major – she's in the garden, sir," she said.

She looked as unhappy as he did. Major Marchbanks looked at Sally.

"Through the door," he said. "Quickly now …"

The major took her through the house; she felt empty rooms, cold floors and sadness.

"Please," she said as they arrived at the door, "who is this enemy? I don't know anything! You must tell me her name, at least."

"She's called Mrs Holland," he whispered and opened the door a little. He looked through. "Please – leave now. You walked? You're young, strong, quick – don't wait. Go straight to town. Oh, I'm so sorry …"

He almost cried.

And she was outside, and he closed the door. Ten minutes after her arrival, she was leaving again. She looked up at the wall of the house and thought: was this enemy watching?

Halfway along[20] the river bank, she stopped and looked back. Why she looked she did not know, but she saw a small figure[21] by the trees – a woman in black. An old woman. She was hurrying after Sally.

Sally finds out that Mrs Holland is looking for a beautiful ruby from India that is missing and which she says is hers. She also finds out that not everything she has heard about her parents is really true …

adapted from: *The ruby in the smoke* by Philip Pullmann

[14] **(to) change** [tʃeɪndʒ] = (sich) verändern • [15] **enemy** ['enəmi] = Feind • [16] **evil** ['i:vl] = böse • [17] **package** ['pækɪdʒ] = Paket • [18] **not either** [nɒt 'aɪðə] = auch nicht • [19] **at least** [ət 'li:st] = wenigstens • [20] **along** [ə'lɒŋ] = entlang • [21] **figure** ['fɪgə] = Gestalt

⟨Revision for tests⟩ Unit 1–2

These Revision pages will help you to prepare for tests. You will practise reading, writing, listening and speaking on them.

1 Mixed bag: Mixed tenses

*Put in the verbs in the right tenses. ('•' means: Use **have to, able to** or **allowed to.**) Sometimes there is more than one right answer.*

It is Saturday morning, and Debbie 1 (surf) on the Internet. Next week she 2 (do) a project on the history of sport. At the moment she 3 (download) early photos of tennis players. She 4 (be) happy because she 5 (• show) these photos in her presentation on Friday. She 6 (already start) to write her text: "A hundred years ago tennis players 7 (• wear) terrible clothes. I'm glad girls 8 (not • wear) long skirts today! In 1900 many girls 9 (not • play) tennis because their parents 10 (be) against it."

Debbie 11 (look) quickly at her watch: 12 o'clock. Her tennis team 12 (play) a match against Redwood College this afternoon. She is sure her team 13 (not • win): The Redwood girls 14 (be) too good! Last year Redwood 15 (not • try) very hard, they 16 (win) easily! The match 17 (start) at 2 o'clock, so Debbie 18 (• leave) the house at 12.30. Suddenly she 19 (remember) something. "Oh no! Grandma 20 (come) for lunch today! Mum 21 (be) angry if I 22 (not be) here. What shall I do?"

2 A reader's letter: Do you agree?

A reader wrote this letter to a magazine which had done an article about people like Timothy (in Unit 2). Do you agree with Laura? Make notes. Then write your own letter to the magazine to say what you think. The Useful phrases on page 12 can help.

Dear *Look!* Magazine,
Your article about the 'sixth sense' was silly. Nobody can see into the future. I only believe what I can see – and I don't see ghosts or have visions! Today we can use science to explain strange events. Scary things are great for films – I love all those technology tricks. But there's no 'sixth sense' in real life!

Yours, Laura

3 Plan a trip to a sports event

You want to go to Berlin and watch the Berlin Marathon. Suggest this to your partner, then talk about your plans together. Use the Useful phrases on page 29.

Example:

You: How about a trip to Berlin to watch the Marathon?
Your partner: Good idea! We could go …

4 Make a word web: Sport

tennis • race • pool • Winter Olympics • Wimbledon • field • referee • athletics • goal • with a ball • track • ski jump • court • athlete • football • umpire • snow • without a ball • swimming • marathon • water • kick • goggles • racket • 400 metres

a) *Find two words or phrases you can use as headings. Then write all the other words under one or both of these two headings.*

b) *Make smaller groups with the words in your word web. You can put some words in more than one group.*

5 London, 1666

a) ***Pre-reading:*** *Look at the title and the picture. Say what you think the story is about.*

b) ***Reading for gist:*** *Read the story once quickly and answer these questions:*
- **Who** is it about?
- **What** happens?
- **When** does it happen?
- **Where** does it happen?

Sam was 13, and he was learning to become a shoemaker. He worked for Mr Fenton, and he lived and worked in the Fentons' house. Mr Fenton taught Sam how to make new shoes and mend old ones. Sam's own family lived in another part of London. He visited them when he had a holiday, but that was not very often, and he missed them.

On 2nd September 1666 Mr Fenton woke Sam up very early. "Quick!" he shouted. "Get up!" People were shouting, and there was a terrible smell. Something was burning. The buildings in the next street were on fire. The houses were of wood, so they burnt easily. The strong wind was bringing the fire nearer. Everybody ran through the smoke down to the River Thames. Mrs Fenton, her children and Sam got into a boat, then Mr Fenton went back and helped to fight the fire.

Sam stayed with Mr Fenton's family for five days. He found out later that the fire had started in a baker's house in Pudding Lane. Only six people died in the fire, but it burnt down more than 13,000 houses.

On 7th September Sam went back to where Mr Fenton's house and workshop had been. The buildings were not there any longer, but Mr Fenton was – he was busy with plans for a new house. "Your family is OK," Sam said, "but I have no news of mine. Please let me go and look for them!"

Mr Fenton was a kind man, and Sam was allowed to go. His parents' house had burnt down, and he could not find his family anywhere. Some neighbours said, "They've gone to the country to stay with a man called Will. He's a farmer somewhere." Sam had an uncle whose name was Will.

Sam went back sadly to Mr Fenton. "I want to go and look for my family," he said. Mr Fenton was angry. "I made an arrangement with your parents," he said. "I teach, and you help. And I really need your help now. You can look for your family later."

Sam knew Mr Fenton was right: He wasn't allowed to break the arrangement. That could mean prison! But he was so worried about his family. Should he walk to his Uncle Will's farm anyway? Should he risk his job and his future?

c) ***Reading for detail:*** *Which people are important for Sam? Why? What makes Sam's problem at the end of the story so hard?*

d) *Sam must choose between Mr Fenton and his family. In what way is Mr Fenton right? In what way is Sam's family more important? Put your ideas in two lists.*

e) ***Writing texts:*** *What do you think Sam does next? Write an ending to the story.*

Unit 3 Living together

1 Listening: Favourite TV shows

a) *Look at the scenes from famous TV shows. What do you think each show is about?*

b) *Listen to the conversations and check your ideas. Were you right?*

⟨c)⟩ *Do you know any other TV shows about family life or friends? Talk about the characters and their problems.*

DID YOU KNOW?

- In the 1950s, mothers spent 13 hours every week in the kitchen. Today it is six hours.
- One in four British children live with just one parent.
- British children between four and 15 years old watch 17 hours of TV a week. Only five hours of the 17 hours are children's TV.

Meet the Pattersons

Here is another family, the Pattersons from England.

Grandpa Patterson's wise words

- Brush your teeth three times a day or they'll all fall out.
- Don't eat apple pips or a tree will grow in your stomach.
- Eat up your crusts so that your hair will go curly.
- Don't sing at the table or you'll marry a crazy person.
- It's bad luck to put a hat on a bed.
- Don't tell a lie or your nose will grow.

1

Mum, please don't put meat in my sandwiches any more. I've become a vegetarian – remember?
Amy

2

Sorry Jake, I want to split up. We'll never get on. You're already 16 but you behave like a 6-year-old. Miriam.

3

I have to share a room with my twin sister and it's driving me crazy. She's selfish and she never tidies up, and she 'borrows' my make-up.
Mel, Essex

4

No, Mel, U can't go to Katie's party. It's 2 L8 and UR only 13! I don't care what your friends say.
Mum

5

microwave chips
frozen Brussels sprouts
crisps
pizzas

6

Have gone to DIY shop to get wood for shelves. Back soon. Dad.

7

2 The Pattersons

What do you find out about the Patterson family – their problems and what they are interested in? How do they talk to each other?

WB p. 28/1; 2

3 Your turn: Family life

Compare life in the Patterson family with your own life at home. Talk to your partner.

WB p. 28/3

4 Listening: A telephone message

a) *Grandpa Patterson lives alone. Listen to a message that his cleaning lady has left on the Pattersons' answerphone. Write down the important information.*

b) *What should the Pattersons do now?*

WB p. 28/4

Sunday lunch

Dad: Well, this is nice. When was the last time we had Sunday lunch together?

Mum: I can't remember. Oh – is Jake still in bed? He came home very late last night.

Amy: I know, but he didn't enjoy himself at all. He and Miriam have just split up.

Mum: Oh no, really? And I liked Miriam. Oh dear. Well, I'll call Jake on my mobile. Jake? Are you OK? What? … You feel tired? … Well, lunch is ready.

Dad: I'll put the meat on the plates, and everyone can help themselves to vegetables.

Amy: No meat for me, please. I've decided to become a vegetarian, remember?

Dad: Then help yourself to extra sprouts.

Amy: I can't stand Brussels sprouts! I'll make myself a sandwich and take it to my room.

Mum: No, you won't! We're having a meal together as a family. We never see each other these days.

Mel: I see too much of Amy. And what do you mean *your* room, Amy? It's mine, too.

Mum: Behave yourselves, you two! Why can't you be nice to each other?

Dad: Oh, and here's Jake. You're half asleep, boy!

Mum: And you haven't even got dressed, Jake! Sit down first. Your dad cooked lunch himself!

Jake: Did you really, Dad? So who taught you how to cook?

Dad: Nobody taught me. I taught myself! – Ouch! I've just hurt myself with this knife! – Come on, have some lunch before it gets cold.

Jake: Could you put it in the microwave for me, please? I'm meeting my friends in ten minutes.

Mum: Do it yourself, Jake! This isn't a hotel, you know. Next weekend you kids will have to cook for yourselves. We're visiting Grandpa because he can't look after himself now.

Jake: So are you going to put him into an old people's home?

Mum: We don't know yet. But you'll be OK on your own while we're away, won't you?

Mel: Relax, Mum. Why do you always imagine the worst? We can look after ourselves.

1 Funny or not?

a) *Do you know this kind of family situation? Talk about any examples you know.*

b) *What do you think of the Pattersons?*

2 What do the Pattersons say?

Example: Mrs Patterson thinks the twins are very polite at the table. – That's wrong. She says: "Behave **yourselves**, you two!"

1. Mr Patterson gives everyone vegetables. – That's wrong. He says: "Everyone …"
2. Mr Patterson says that Amy should take some bacon. – That's wrong. He says: "…"
3. Amy wants to get some chips. – That's …
4. Mr Patterson hurt Mrs Patterson with a knife.
5. Mrs Patterson will put Jake's lunch in the microwave.

3 *Myself* or *me*?

a) *Find the rule for reflexive pronouns:*

Nobody **taught me** how to cook.
I **taught myself** how to cook.

Grandpa's cleaning lady can't **look after him**.
Grandpa Patterson can't **look after himself**.

b) *Mel is describing herself and her family. Put in* ***me / you / us*** *etc. or* ***a reflexive form****.*

Example: "Amy and I fight over clothes, but at parties we enjoy **ourselves**."

1. "I'm a bit shy. **I** don't like it when people look at …"
2. "Amy can be a bit selfish. **She** only thinks about …"
3. "Amy often makes … a sandwich and takes it to our room."
4. "**Jake** often falls off his skateboard and hurts …"
5. "When Mum is alone, **she** often talks to …"
6. "**I** know lots of card tricks because my dad taught …"

WB p. 29/5

GRAMMAR
Reflexive pronouns

I've hurt **myself**.
You'll enjoy **yourself**.
He taught **himself** to swim.
She has hurt **herself**.
It (the computer) turns **itself** off.
We can look after **ourselves**.
You can all help **yourselves**.
They behaved **themselves**.

(→ G11)

4 Reflexive in German, not in English

a) *Look at the dialogue on page 44 and answer the questions. Choose from these verbs.*

1. What happened to Jake and Miriam last night?
2. Why doesn't Amy want any meat?
3. What hasn't Jake done yet?
4. What should Jake do first at lunch?
5. Why is Jake in a hurry to finish his lunch?

relax | feel | meet | remember | sit down | split up | decide | get lost | hurry up | get dressed | imagine

⟨b)⟩ *Make sentences with the verbs you did not use in a).* WB p. 29/6

5 *Themselves* or *each other?*

Use ***each other*** *or* ***themselves****.*

TIP
The twins are looking at **themselves**. … sich …
The twins are looking at **each other**. … einander …

Start like this: The twins are taking a photo of …

(→ G11, 12)

WB p. 29/7

6 Stress the subject in a sentence

If you want to stress the subject of a sentence, you can sometimes use a reflexive pronoun:

1. Mel, could you get me a drink of water? – No, Amy, get it **yourself**!
2. Amy, I'm going to call Charlie. – Wait, Mel. I'll call him …
3. Who told you about Miriam's new boyfriend? – Miriam …
4. Maybe Dad can build a wall in our bedroom! – No, let's … ! WB p. 30/8

TALKWISE

Meet halfway

1 Before you listen

Some conversations become fights while others stay friendly.

a) *Sort these tips into two lists:* 'Right way' *and* 'Wrong way'.

Get angry. • Ask what the other person thinks. • Shout. • Show you understand what the other person feels. • Always agree with the other person. • Cry – then the other person will feel sorry for you. • Explain your feelings or ideas. • Stay cool. • Show you are listening. • Be polite. • Say "You always …" or "You never …" a lot. • Be positive before you say what you really think. • Walk away if someone gets aggressive.

b) *Compare your lists with a partner. Talk about any differences.*

2 Listening: Right way / wrong way

a) *You are going to hear two conversations. The first is between Kim and her parents, the second is between Jill and her parents. For each conversation, write down:*

- what the girls want to do;
- how their parents feel about the idea;
- why the girls think their parents should say 'yes';
- what the parents decide in the end.

b) *Why do you think one girl gets what she wants and the other girl doesn't?* WB p. 31/10

3 Role play: Meet halfway

a) *Make two lists from the Useful phrases box: the phrases that A can use to start the conversation, and the phrases that A* ***and*** *B can use.*

b) *Choose one of the situations below, or find your own situation. Do the role play this way:*

1. A starts and makes a suggestion.
2. B answers and does not like the idea.
3. A and B talk about the idea: What is good? What is not so good? What else is there?
4. A and B meet halfway.

Situation 1: Your class has earned some money at a school event. Now you want to spend it. A wants to give the money to a very poor family in your town, B wants to spend it on your class, e.g. for a class party or for the cinema.

Situation 2: A good friend of A wants a birthday present, but it costs 20 euros. That is a lot, but A wants to buy the present anyway. B thinks that this is too much and thinks a cheaper surprise present is a better idea. WB p. 31/11; 12

USEFUL PHRASES

Can we talk about … ?
What do you think … ?
How do you feel about … ?
I see …
I don't mind that, but …
You've got a point, but …
That's true, but …
I know, but …
I guess you're right.
I've got an idea. / Maybe …
Can we meet halfway?
OK, fine!

Chatroom messages

Amy is chatting online with someone new.
Her name is Tess.

Groups People Help

A Amy: Brilliant idea! But if we turned it into my room, then my parents would have to get rid of all their junk, like Mum's fitness bike and Dad's computer. What do you think?

B Amy: I wish I was an only child like you!

C Tess: No walls then! You wouldn't fight so much if you had your own bedrooms. Can't you turn your hobby room into your bedroom?

D Tess: Hm. Your sister would be jealous if you had a bigger room. If I were you, I'd talk to Mel first.

E Amy: Really, Tess? You wouldn't say that if you knew mine, especially my twin sister Mel.

F Amy: Yes, Mel and I even tried to build a wall through our bedroom, but it fell down.

G Tess: And I wish I had brothers or sisters like you.

H Tess: Don't be so horrible! Have you tried to sort out your problems with her?

Amy
Tess

Amy: |

1 Sort the messages

Put the chat messages in the right order. (Start with B: "I wish I …")

2 Match the parts

a) 1. Amy thinks: If Tess **knew** Jake and Mel,
2. If Mel and Amy had their own bedrooms,
3. If they used the hobby room as a bedroom,
4. If Amy had a bigger room than Mel,
5. If Mel and Amy tried to build another wall,
6. Tess says: If I were you, Amy, …

a) they'd have to get rid of some junk.
b) I'd talk to my sister about the idea first.
c) she **wouldn't want** brothers or sisters.
d) it would probably fall down again.
e) they wouldn't fight so much.
f) Mel would be jealous.

b) *Find the rule: Look at the sentences in a). What are the verb forms in the if-clause and the main clause? Translate the sentences into German.*

WB p. 32/13

TIP
she'd = she would
no, she wouldn't = no, she would not

(→ G13)

3 Amy on chat

a) *Put the verbs in the right form: simple past, or* ***would*** *+ infinitive.*

"If a friend of mine 1 (lend) me a camera and I 2 (break) it, I 3 (try) to mend it myself. If my friend 4 (not know) the difference, I 5 (not need) to tell my friend anything. If it 6 (be) a really expensive camera or if the shop 7 (not be able to) help me, I 8 (have) a real problem!"

WB p. 32/14

⟨b)⟩ *What would you do?* *Start:* If **I were** Amy, **I would** …

4 Imagine!

a) *Jake is imagining what he would do if he was lucky with money. Make sentences with* ***If …***

Example: 1. **If I saw** 2 p in the street, **I wouldn't pick** it **up**. I'd leave it there.

TIP
If the if-clause comes first, don't forget the comma after it.

(→ G13)

1. see 2 p in the street – not pick it up.
2. find £ 1 in a park – pick it up and keep it.
3. find someone's purse at school – give it to a teacher
4. get too much change from a shop assistant – tell him / her about it
5. win £ 10,000 – save half and buy a boat with the other half

WB p. 32/15

⟨b)⟩ *Ask each other what you would do in the same situation. (Change pounds to euros!)*

Example: What would you do if you saw 50 cents in the street? – I'd pick it up.

5 Would you ever do this?

kiss a policeman / policewoman | read your best friend's diary | do a bungee jump | eat cat food | paint your face green | learn to speak Chinese | travel to Alaska | spend €1000 on clothes

Example: I **would** only **kiss** a policewoman if she **was** my mum.

WB p. 33/16

6 Your turn: Give advice

TIP
You can say "If I **were** you" or "If I **was** you" when you give someone advice.

(→ G13)

a) *What advice would you give Jake and the twins?*

Start: 1. **If I were** you, Amy, **I'd** …

1. Amy: Mum doesn't know any recipes for vegetarians. 2. Mel: Amy always borrows my CDs, and she never asks me. 3. Jake: I'm always tired in the morning. I just can't get up! 4. Mel: My mum sometimes reads my diary. It makes me really angry.
5. Amy: My friends laugh at me because I don't wear the same trainers as them.
6. Amy and Mel: We often get the same birthday presents, or even presents to share!

⟨b)⟩ *Write down 2–3 problems or difficult situations. Ask each other for advice.*

7 Revision: If-clauses type 1

Look at Grandpa Patterson's wise words *on page 43. Say them another way with* ***If***.

Example: If you don't brush your teeth three times a day, they'll all fall out.

WB p. 33/17

8 ⟨A poem: I wish⟩

Write your own 'I wish' *poem.*
Think about:

- *what you wish you were;*
- *where you wish you lived;*
- *what you wish you could do.*

I wish I were rich,
But I'm poor.
I wish I were young,
But I'm old.
I wish I could live where it's sunny and hot,
But I live where it's rainy and cold.
I wish I could fly,
But I can't.
I wish that my wishes were more than just wishes,
But I'm sorry to say that they aren't.

A letter to an agony aunt

A reader wrote this letter to an 'agony aunt' in TEEN◆BUZZ magazine to ask for advice.

Dear Mary,
I need your help! My best mate Tina isn't talking to me and I don't know what to do. Her new boyfriend, Luke, is really bad for her. He went out with my sister, but they split up. My sister left him after I had told her about his other girlfriends. If I hadn't told her, they wouldn't have split up! Anyway, when I told Tina about all of Luke's girlfriends, she got really angry with me and ran out of the room. I talked to my mum about it, and then she told Tina's parents. They went crazy when they found out about Tina's 'secret boyfriend'. I hadn't known it was a secret! Now Tina has to stay at home next Saturday, and she's not allowed to see Luke again. Maybe if I hadn't said anything, she wouldn't have been so angry with me.
Linda

I understand your problem, Linda. But don't worry – you did the right thing. If you hadn't said anything to her, you wouldn't have been a real friend. But are the stories about Luke really true? If you had been more careful with your words, maybe Tina would have listened to you. If the boy is as bad as you say, she'll soon find out for herself without your advice.

1 Complete the sentences

Example: If Linda **hadn't told** her sister about Luke's other girlfriends, they **wouldn't have split up**. (Or: … her sister **wouldn't have left** him).

1. If Linda hadn't told Tina about Luke's other girlfriends, Tina … 2. If Linda hadn't told her mum about Tina, Linda's mum … 3. If Linda hadn't said anything to Tina, she … *(two endings!)* 4. If Linda had been more careful with her words, maybe …

WB p. 34/18

2 Find the rule

a) *Copy the grid and then complete it. The if-sentences in the two texts can help you.*

Type	verb form in if-clause	verb form in main clause	
1	*simple present*	*will + infinitive*	
	If I **go** to bed late tonight,	I **will be** tired tomorrow.	(or: **I'll** be)
2	?	?	
	If I **went** to bed late every night,	I **would be** tired all the time.	(or: **I'd** be)
3	?	?	
	If I … earlier last Monday,	I … tired on Tuesday.	(or: …)

b) *When do you use the three different types of if-sentences?*

3 Your turn: Your story

Write about important events in your life. How would things have been different if they hadn't happened?

Example: If we **hadn't moved** to Berlin last year, I **wouldn't have come** to this school. …

WB p. 34/19

LISTENING SKILLS

Telephone messages

Sometimes it is difficult to make a phone call or speak on an answerphone in a different language. But don't worry if you don't understand everything you hear. You can make notes, or the other person can repeat her / his sentence. These exercises will help you to use the telephone better.

1 Answerphones

What is good or not so good about answerphones or voice mail? Give two or more reasons.

2 Listening: Understand a message

Listen to three phone messages and write down:

- … who the caller is;
- … who the message is for;
- … what the caller wants from this person;
- … how this person can contact the caller.

3 Leave a message

Jake has left his skateboard helmet at a friend's house. When he calls, he hears this message:

> Hi, this is Don Newman's mobile. Sorry, but I can't take your call at the moment. If you leave your name and number after the tone, I'll phone you as soon as I can.

What message does Jake leave? WB p. 35/20

USEFUL PHRASES

Hello, this is …
I've got a message for …
I'm just calling to say that …
I'd like … / I'm afraid / Sorry, …
Could you call me back, please?
You can phone me at … *(phone number)*.
Hope to hear from you soon.
Thanks, and bye.

4 Role play: A phone message

Sometimes you give your message to a person, not a machine.

Work with a partner.

1. ***Decide who plays which role.*** *A calls and wants to speak to C, but B answers the phone because C is not at home. B writes down A's message.*
2. ***Use the Useful phrases.*** *Which of the Useful phrases on the right can A use, and which phrases can B use? Make lists. If you are A, you must think of a message, too.*
3. ***Act the phone call.*** WB p. 35/21; 22

USEFUL PHRASES

Hello, how can I help you?
Hi, this is … I'd like to speak to …
I'm afraid / Sorry, she / he isn't in at the moment.
Can I take a message?
Yes, please. Could you tell him / her that … ?
Could he / she call me back, please?
I'll give you my name and address.
Just a moment, I'll get a pen.
I'm sorry, I didn't understand your name.
Could you spell it for me, please?
Thanks a lot.
You're welcome. Bye!

Home alone

Cast list:

Amy	Mrs Patterson
Mel	Mr Patterson
Jake	Grandpa Patterson
	Friends of Mel and Amy (monsters)

Time: Saturday morning / afternoon / evening
Place: The Pattersons' house (living room next to hobby room) / Grandpa's flat / the Pattersons' car

Scene 1 Let's have a party!

(In the Pattersons' living room. Mel and Amy are playing cards. Jake is listening to music on his MP3 player and playing 'air guitar' to himself. Their parents enter the room.)

Mum: We're leaving now to see Grandpa. Will you be OK by yourselves? *(Mel and Amy go on playing cards.)* I said … *(shouts)* WILL YOU BE OK BY YOURSELVES??
Jake: You needn't shout, Mum. I'm 16, remember?
Dad: We're taking our mobiles, so if there's a problem, just call.
Mum: You'll look after the girls, won't you, Jake?
Jake: Sure. I'll make sure they brush their teeth and go to bed early.
Mel: Shut up, Jake. We're not babies!
Dad: Bye everyone, and *please* be nice to each other! *(Mr and Mrs Patterson leave.)*
Amy: *(makes a face)* Mmm! – Hey, we've got the whole house to ourselves!
Mel: Cool! Uh – what can we do now? Watch a DVD?
Amy: No, I've got a better idea. Let's have a party!
Mel: Shhh! Not so loud! *(The two girls run to the window and wave goodbye to their parents.)*
Amy: We could have a monster party, and wear monster and witch costumes. Let's phone our friends!
Jake: Have a little kids' party if you want! I'm going to my room to listen to music. *(leaves)*
Amy: Come on, Mel, let's plan this party now. *(They put their heads together.)*

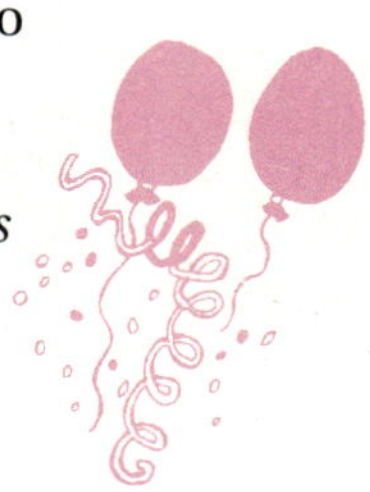

Scene 2 Never!

(In Grandpa's flat. He is in bed and is reading a newspaper. Mr and Mrs Patterson enter.)

Dad: Hello, Father. How are you?
Grandpa: Terry! Sally! What a surprise! Well, as you can see, I'm, uh, fine.
Mum: Hm. We heard about your problem. Richard, you can't look after yourself any more.
Grandpa: Has my cleaning lady called you about me again? Lies, all lies!
Dad: But we've got some good news! We've found a nice home for you, not far from where we live. The people there are very kind, and the gardens are beautiful. Look, here's a picture.

Grandpa: I'm *not* going into a home! *Never!* I can look after myself, thank you very much.

Dad: Father, you really must listen to us. You need help. If you saw the home, you'd love it.

Grandpa: OK, you can *show* me. But you'd bring me back here if I didn't like it, wouldn't you?

Mum: Of course we would! Don't worry. You don't have to do anything you don't want to.

Scene 3 How about that?

(In the Pattersons' car. Grandpa is there, too. He looks grumpy.)

Grandpa: I'm *not* going into that home! It was terrible!

Mum: You're right. That lunch they gave us … Yuk! I'm sure it was cat food!

Dad: Father, you know you can't manage on your own. But Sally and I have had a little talk.

Mum: After we'd seen the home, we made a decision. Would you like to come and live with us?

Grandpa: Oh – I must say, that's *very* kind of you. But, well, I'd get in the way, wouldn't I?

Dad: Don't worry! We could turn our old hobby room into your bedroom. How about that?

Grandpa: But what about the twins? If they had their own rooms, they wouldn't fight so much.

Scene 4 This is terrible!

Amy: *(In the hobby room)* Our friends will be here soon. *(phone rings)* Oh, hi, Mum … What? Now?! *(She runs to the window.)* I can't believe it! Mel! Come here, look! *(Mel runs to the window.)*

Mel: Oh, no! It's our car – with Grandpa! This is terrible! What can we do?

Amy: Mel, make sure they don't come in here, OK? *(Amy takes off her monster mask and runs into the living room.)* You tidy up, and I'll phone our friends. I hope it's not too late!

Scene 5 Important news

(Mum, Dad and Grandpa enter the living room. They kiss Amy and say their 'hellos'.)

Mum: We've got some important news to tell everyone.

Dad: First things first. Father, would you like to see the hobby room right now?

Grandpa: Oh, yes, fine.

Amy: *(stands in front of hobby room door)* No, don't come in here!

Mum: Amy! Why can't we go in there? And why are you wearing my black evening dress?

Amy: The room is a terrible mess. Why don't you sit down, Grandpa?

Grandpa: Don't worry about the mess. I'd like to see my new bedroom. This is exciting! *(All go into the hobby room.)*

Amy: New bedroom!? *(She puts her hands over her face and follows the others into the hobby room.)*

Mel: Uh, hi, Mum. Hi, Dad – hi, Grandpa. We can explain everything, really! *(doorbell rings)* Oh, no! Our friends are here. *(Mel runs out and opens the front door. Their friends hurry in.)*

Mum: What's going on? This room is like a dungeon! I wish we hadn't left you on your own!

Amy. It's just a little party, that's all. *(Jake comes downstairs.)* Hey, here's Jake. Help us, Jake!

Jake: It was your idea, girls.

Mel: *(to her friends)* Sorry, guys. We can't have a party after all.

Monsters: What's the problem? We want to have a good time. Where's the food?

Grandpa: Ooh, I love parties! And what an interesting room this is!

Amy: Do you really like it, Grandpa? Isn't it too scary?

Grandpa: It isn't as scary as the old people's home I've just visited. It was like a horror film! *(The monsters enter the hobby room.)*

Dad: Jake, Mel, Amy! I hope you can explain this, or there won't be any pocket money … ever!

Grandpa: I was young once, you know, Terry. The girls weren't so bad. Let's enjoy ourselves. *(Amy offers him a plate of crisps.)* Thank you, Mel … or is it Amy? *(Jake puts on music. The monsters start to dance. One by one, everyone else starts to dance. The lights go out.)*

1 Talk about the play

a) *Was the party a good or a bad idea? Did anyone make a mistake?*

b) *Work in groups. Talk about how the play ends. Is it too open, or too happy?*

c) *Your turn: Has a situation like this ever happened to you or to your friends? How did you or your / their parents react? Could you meet halfway?* WB p. 36/23; 24

2 How to: Put on a play

It is great fun to put on a play. *Every* person – not only the cast – is very important! Here is how you can put on a play.

1. **The people:** Decide who is going to play which character. Who is going to be the director? Who can do the make-up / the props / the costumes / the lights?
2. **The things:** Make or bring the costumes. Make or find the props. Bring the lights and the make-up.
3. **The programme:** Write an interesting programme for the play (see Ex. 3).
4. **The roles:** The actresses and actors must learn their roles.

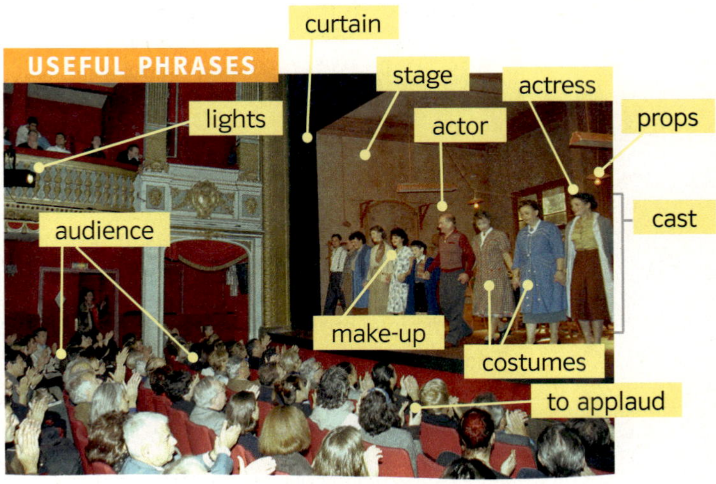

5. **Rehearsals:** Rehearse the play often. Listen to the director's advice.
6. Put it on!

WB p. 36/25

3 Writing texts: Write an interesting programme for the play

1. Write about the play you are going to put on: the title and author, the cast, the director. Can you put any pictures in the programme? 2. Then write about the play itself: What is it about? **Who** does **what when**? 3. What is special about the play? 4. When and where can the audience see the play?

WB p. 36/26

1 Describing people

a) *Find words with opposite meanings.*

tall, grumpy, slow, healthy, boring, cool, quiet, wise, calm, bad, kind, crazy, shy, rich, strong

silly, loud, normal, poor, excited, aggressive, selfish, happy, good, interesting, weak, nervous, ill, fast, short

b) *Which words describe what people* ***are like****? Which ones describe what they* ***look like****? Make a 'personal vocabulary' list with adjectives for your folder.*

c) *Which words describe the Pattersons? Can you find more words to describe them?*

WB p. 37/27

2 Sounds: Word stress

Put the words in groups to show where the stress is.

departure, official, message, rehearsal, antique, relax, government, themselves, commercial, colony, decision, swimsuit, laptop, audience, answerphone, assistant, compare

x X	X x	x X x	X x x
mis**take**	**feel**ing	po**lite**ness	**tele**phone
…	…	…	…

3 ⟨A song: Shiny happy people⟩

Shiny happy people laughing
Meet me in the crowd
People people
Throw your love around
Love me love me
Take it into town
Happy happy, put it in the ground
Where the flowers grow
Gold and silver shine

Shiny happy people holding hands
Shiny happy people laughing
Everyone around love them, love them
Put it in your hands
Take it take it
There's no time to cry
Happy happy, put it in your heart
Where tomorrow shines
Gold and silver shine

a) *Like a poem, a song can have words that sound the same at the end, words that begin with the same sound and words that are repeated. Find examples in the text.*

b) *A song can also have words that express a special kind of feeling. What kind of feeling does this song express? Which words in the song show this?*
If you want to know more about poems, read pages 120–122 in the Free section.

NOW YOU CAN

- ✓ Talk about family problems.
- ✓ Use reflexive pronouns.
- ✓ Meet people halfway.
- ✓ Use conditional forms (if-clauses).
- ✓ Give advice.
- ✓ Take and leave phone messages.
- ✓ Put on a play.
- ✓ Describe people.

1 Reflexive pronouns (→ G 11, 12)

buy turn off hurt kiss throw

Write what these people have just done to themselves or each other.

1

2

3

4

5

WB p. 38/30

2 Put in the correct verb form (→ G 13)

a) *Use if-clauses (type 2):*

1. If you [1] (wouldn't be / weren't) so selfish, Amy, you [2] (had / would have) more friends.
2. I [1] (didn't buy / wouldn't buy) frozen pizzas if I [2] (would have / had) time to make them myself.
3. If it [1] (is / was) my turn to make lunch, I [2] (cooked / would cook) just vegetables.
4. I [1] (drove / would drive) myself to school if I [2] (had / would have) my own car.

b) *Use if-clauses (type 3):*

1. If I [1] (not leave) a message on Mr Patterson's answerphone, he and his wife [2] (not visit) his father.
2. Our kids [1] (not have) a party if we [2] (not go) to visit my old dad.
3. If Mum and Dad [1] (stay) at home last weekend, we [2] (not have) a party and I [3] (not wear) Mum's evening dress. If I [4] (not wear) it, I [5] (not get) chocolate all over it and she [6] (not be) so angry with me.

WB p. 38/31; 32

c) *Who do you think said what?*

3 On the phone

You phone a friend, but his / her sister answers the phone. You leave a message.

First, think of a message and write it down. Then act the phone call with a partner. Exercise 4 on page 50 can help you.

4 Good advice

Your friend's brother always takes your friend's CDs and DVDs.

Give your friend some good advice. Act the dialogue with a partner. Exercise 6 on page 48 and 'Talkwise' on page 46 can help you.

〈Project〉 English and Biology

STEP 1: Look at breakfast in different countries

People from different countries eat different things in the morning, but wherever you go, breakfast is the first and most important meal of the day.

a) *Look at the pictures and say which breakfast you like best and why.*

b) *Have you ever had breakfast in another country? What did you have?*

English kids like cereal[1] with milk for breakfast. They sometimes eat eggs, bacon and sausages[2], or porridge[3]. They never eat cheese.

1

2

Japanese[4] people traditionally eat soup[5] for breakfast.

Mexicans[6] like to eat fruit for breakfast. They also have tortillas with meat, vegetables or eggs.

3

4

Swedish[7] kids like bread with butter[8], jam[9], cheese or fish. They also eat cornflakes with milk in the morning.

STEP 2: Find out about your own breakfast

a) *What do you have for breakfast? Make two groups. Write down on cards what you eat in the morning.*

b) *Collect the cards and sort them into groups (e.g. fruit, cereal, …). Then put them up on the board.*

STEP 3: Make a bar chart[10]

PROJECT SKILLS

When you are preparing a presentation, you will often find useful information in charts. You can also use a chart to show what you have found out if you have done a survey[11].

1. In your groups look at the cards on the board and count how many of you eat which food for breakfast (e.g. milk 20; eggs 15 …).
2. Now put the information you have found in a bar chart. Write the food on the x-axis[12] and the number of pupils who eat the food on the y-axis[13].
3. Draw the bars. Now you can see how many of you eat which food. Compare the two groups.

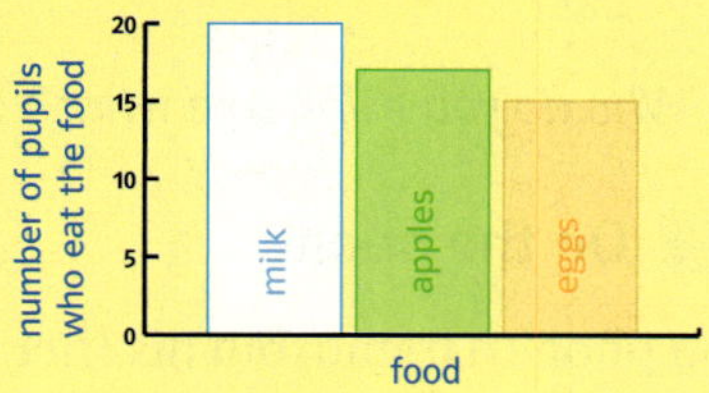

[1] **cereal** ['sɪəriəl] = Getreide (Cornflakes etc.) • [2] **sausage** ['sɒsɪdʒ] = Würstchen • [3] **porridge** ['pɒrɪdʒ] = Haferbrei • [4] **Japanese** [ˌdʒæp'ni:z] = japanisch • [5] **soup** [su:p] = Suppe • [6] **Mexican** ['meksɪkn] = Mexikaner / -in • [7] **Swedish** ['swi:dɪʃ] = schwedisch • [8] **butter** ['bʌtə] = Butter • [9] **jam** [dʒæm] = Marmelade • [10] **bar chart** ['bɑ: ˌtʃɑ:t] = Balkendiagramm • [11] **survey** ['sɜ:vei] = Studie, Umfrage • [12] **x-axis** [eks 'æksɪs] = X-Achse • [13] **y-axis** [waɪ 'æksɪs] = Y-Achse

STEP 4: Look at food and its contents[14]

We eat a lot of different things every day. Almost everything we eat contains[15] fats[16], proteins[17] and carbohydrates[18]. Some foods have more of these than others. If you want to eat healthily, you also need minerals[19], vitamins[20], fibre[21] and water.

Look at the chart on the right and compare it to what you have found out about breakfast in your class. Do you think you eat a healthy breakfast? Is breakfast in other countries healthier? Say why or why not.

STEP 5: Do a project: Healthy food

You have learned a lot about healthy food so far, and maybe you have found out that some of you eat the wrong things. Now it's your turn to inform the pupils at your school. Read about Jamie Oliver first.

JAMIE OLIVER is a famous TV cook. He is worried about the food British pupils eat at school and at home, and has cooked at different British schools to show kids how bad fast food is and how good healthy food can be. He has been to Thomas Tallis, too. At one school he threw a lot of chips, burgers and other fast food onto the floor to show how terrible the smell is.

Unhealthy food is not only a problem at British schools. Lots of German pupils eat the wrong things, too. Plan a healthy food campaign[22] for your next school project week. You could have an information stand[23] with posters and give a presentation in which you use charts. You could also sell healthy food.

1. Think of more ideas in class.
2. Get together in groups of four or five and decide what the different groups are going to do.
3. In your group, talk about what you have to do (e.g. find information in books, on the Internet, draw posters etc.). Decide who is going to do what and when. Make a plan.
4. After you have finished your group projects, plan the campaign with your teacher.

[14] **contents *(pl)*** ['kɒntents] = Inhalt • [15] **(to) contain sth** [kən'teɪn] = etw. beinhalten • [16] **fat** [fæt] = Fett • [17] **protein** ['prəʊti:n] = Protein • [18] **carbohydrate** [ˌkɑ:bə'haɪdreɪt] = Kohlenhydrat • [19] **mineral** ['mɪnrl] = Mineralstoff • [20] **vitamin** ['vɪtəmɪn] = Vitamin • [21] **fibre** ['faɪbə] = Ballaststoff • [22] **campaign** [kæm'peɪn] = Kampagne • [23] **information stand** [ˌɪnfə'meɪʃn ˌstænd] = Informationsstand

Unit 4 The UK on the move

Manchester

Windsor

Liverpool

North Wales

South Wales

VISIT BRITAIN Kids

The Britons are always on the move. On average, a British family will move house more often than a German family, for example. Imagine you have to move to another part of the UK, perhaps because one of your parents gets a job in another town. Wouldn't it be great if you could test the place before you go? To win a week with an exchange family at the other end of the country, e-mail us and tell us which region you'd like to visit and why. Good luck!

Maybe you'd like to see one of these places …

St. Anne's Square, Manchester

Modern Manchester

Does Manchester mean dirty factories and small, dark houses to you? Then you haven't been to one of Europe's most modern cities: The old industries are gone, and the city is now the pop cult capital of the UK.

→ Find out more …

Windsor, the royal city

Windsor is full of English tradition and history. Visit the Castle or walk in the beautiful Great Park. The town has lots of modern shops, too, and the UK's capital is only 40 minutes away by train …

→ Find out more …

Windsor Castle

1 Find the information

a) *Find all the places on the map at the front of the book.*

b) *Look at the photos. What contrasts can you see?*

Examples: buildings – landscape – modern – old-fashioned – …

c) *Read the texts and make two lists: 1) things you find interesting; 2) things you don't find interesting.*

⟨d⟩ *Compare your lists with a partner's. Which things are the same, which are different? Can you say why?* WB p. 40/1

DID YOU KNOW?

- No place in Britain is more than 74 miles from the sea.
- There are 2.9 million people in Wales – and 11 million sheep.
- It rains less in London than in Freiburg, Germany's sunniest city.

Manchester

Windsor

Liverpool

orth Wales

outh Wales

Liverpool, a city with a new face

Famous as the birthplace of the band *The Beatles* and home of Liverpool FC, Liverpool has recently had a facelift, and the city on the River Mersey is now one of the UK's most exciting places again.

→ Find out more …

Albert Dock, Liverpool

Near Mount Snowdon

North Wales

This part of Wales is famous for its wild landscape of mountains and lakes – and for the many speakers of Welsh. But the people here are just as proud of their traditional regional culture and their high-tech industries (the wings for the European Airbus plane come from here!).

→ Find out more …

South Wales

South Wales has a history of coal mines and heavy industry – and of male voice choirs! Some industry still exists, but today, cities like Cardiff and Swansea are great places for modern culture and technology.
The beaches here are great, too!

→ Find out more …

Wales Millennium Centre, Cardiff

2 Listening: Regional voices

a) *A reporter interviews people from three regions of Britain. Which regions are they, and what do you find out about them? Make notes (in three lists).*

b) *Listen to parts of the interviews again. What words do the people say differently to other speakers you have heard?*

Example: The first speaker says "… is ett", not "is it".

WB p. 40/2

3 Your turn: Your region

a) *What is special about the region of Germany where you live? Think of:*

landscape • culture • language • industry …

b) *Talk about your ideas in class.*

WB p. 40/3

Welsh relatives

Rhona Williams and her friend Shirin Khan are looking at the VISIT BRITAIN Kids website.

Shirin: Oh, you're so lucky, Rhona! Your family has always lived in Swansea; you've got lots of friends and are really at home here. We moved here a year ago, but I still don't have many friends. And I miss my aunts and uncles who still live in Manchester.

Rhona: So why did your family move here?

Shirin: Well, my father's an engineer; he lost his job in Manchester but then found one with a firm here. They work on projects for the poor in Pakistan, so Dad is really useful to them. And they're close, so he goes to work by bike and gets home for tea at six!

Rhona: Cool! Well, friendship is important, Shirin; the friendship we have is *very* important to me. But I'd rather have a big family like yours than lots of friends. I haven't got any brothers and sisters – or cousins! My mum's an only child, too. Dad's got one brother in North Wales, but *he* hasn't got any children.

Shirin: Hey, is your uncle bilingual, Welsh and English?

Rhona: Yes, he is! I think Welsh is a beautiful language, but it's hard to learn.

Shirin: Last week you hated Welsh lessons! Why are you suddenly … ? Oh, I know: It must be love! Come on, Rhona, tell me – that's what friends are for!

Rhona: OK – Do you remember that guy we saw at the National Waterfront Museum? Well, I met him on the bus into town after lunch the next day, and we … um … talked.

Shirin: Ooh! This is good news! Wasn't he wearing a pair of trendy glasses at the museum?

Rhona: Yes, weren't they great? He has great taste. He's into Welsh culture, especially music. And he plays rugby. His team is very good.

Shirin: Well of course! I expect you always go and watch them, too!

Rhona: No, I don't! Hey, he's not the love of my life, and a lot of the music he listens to is awful!

1 Friends or family?

Do you agree with Rhona? Which do you think is more important: friends or family?

2 Find the rule

a) *"A firm here had **work** for him." "**Life** got harder."*
"Work" and "life" are abstract nouns. Can you find more in the dialogue? Make a list.

b) *Look at the dialogue again and find examples of abstract nouns that have and haven't got a definite article ("the"). Find the rule: When do you need the definite article?*

⟨c)⟩ *Make eight more sentences with the nouns in your list from a), four with the definite article, four without.*

TIP

Abstract nouns often describe ideas, not things, e.g. **love, fun, luck.** Abstract nouns don't usually have a plural form.

(→ G14)

WB p. 41/4

3 Talk about people you know

Example: My dad's **a** bus driver. He goes **to work by car**. or bus
He sleeps **before tea**. after dinner

Job ...	Goes to work ...	Reads the newspaper / goes shopping / sleeps ...
bus driver baker doctor ...	bus car train bike ...	before / after / at breakfast / lunch / tea ... ...

WB p. 41/5

TIP
We often use articles in English and German differently:
My dad is **an** engineer.
He can go **to work by bike**.
I met David **after lunch**.

(→ G14)

4 You can use some adjectives as nouns

Example: They work on projects for **the poor**. (= for poor people)

young • famous • sick • rich • poor • old

a) *Finish these sentences.*

1. Doctors help ...
2. People sometimes collect money for ...
3. Reporters like to interview ...
4. DJs are very popular with ...
5. We can learn a lot from ...
6. People are often jealous of ...

b) *Make more sentences with:* weak • strong • lonely • disabled

WB p. 42/6

5 How to: Meet new people

Imagine you meet someone new after a film at the cinema. Use the Useful phrases to start a conversation. How much can you find out about each other in three minutes?

USEFUL PHRASES

Hi, haven't we met before? Hello. I like your sunglasses!	Where do you go to school? I'm at ... School.	Do you live near here? Did you enjoy the film?

WB p. 42/7

6 Revision: Possessive pronouns

his • theirs • mine • hers • yours • ours

Dear Cousin Tariq,

Rhona didn't meet the love of her life last weekend, but I met the love of [1]: The National Waterfront Museum – it's brilliant! But my old camera is terrible :-(You must lend me [2] soon!
I liked the photo you sent of your favourite band – thanks! Rhona's new boyfriend David invited us to a concert to see [3], but we didn't like them much: too traditional! They sing at the National Eisteddfod, too, which is a big festival of traditional Welsh music, so they must be somebody's taste – just not [4]! Anyway, I think David and his friends will like our music more than we like [5].
Lots of love from your favourite cousin Shirin. :-*

PS: Rhona thinks I'm writing to my new boyfriend – just because she thinks about [6] all day!!

WB p. 42/8

TALKWISE

Dealing with problems

1 Listening: Shall I do that for you?

It is Saturday, and Shirin wants to go to the city centre. On her way to the bus stop she meets Rhona's father, Gavin.

a) *Listen to the dialogue. What is Gavin's problem, and how does Shirin help him?*

b) *What can people say when they help someone? Start a list with these phrases and then listen again to find more.*

USEFUL PHRASES

You want to help someone	**Someone helps you**
Can I help?	That's very kind of you.
Shall I ...?	Could you ... for me?
Just take your time. ...	You've been a great help. ...

WB p. 43/9

2 Work with a partner

One of you has a problem, and the other wants to help. Make a dialogue. Use the phrases you collected in 1b).

You have a problem with yesterday's homework.

You want to have a voice mail message on your new mobile.

You want to buy a bus ticket into town at a machine.

3 Listening: Sorry!

Shirin has finished her shopping and is on her way home. When she arrives at the bus stop, Rhona is already there.

a) *Listen to the conversation. Shirin says something, and then she is sorry. What does she say, and why is she sorry?*

b) *What can people say when they apologize to someone? Start a list with these phrases and listen again to find more.*

WB p. 43/10

USEFUL PHRASES

You want to apologize	**Someone apologizes to you**
I apologize ...	Never mind. / No problem. /
I'm terribly sorry ...	Don't worry.
I didn't mean to be rude.	Be more careful next time. / ...

4 Role play: An embarrassing situation

"Katie never wears cool clothes."

"Sue always wants to borrow money."

"We don't want Max in our football team."

a) *In groups of three to four, prepare a dialogue: One of you is talking to a friend and says something rude about a third person. But the third person hears it. Look at the ideas on the left, and use the Useful phrases from exercise 3. Then act your role play.*

b) *Do you know an embarrassing situation from a magazine or a TV show? Tell the class about it.*

Up North

“I didn’t know you had so many relatives here,” Rhona said to Shirin quietly. She looked around the room at ten of Shirin’s aunts, uncles and cousins. They had come to help Aunt Zeba and her five sons to move house, and Shirin had invited Rhona to come and meet the rest of her family. Aunt Zeba put the sixth different kind of food on the table. “I know you feel hungry after the long trip,” she said, “so don’t be shy – eat!” The Asian food looked unusual to Rhona, but most things – especially the curries – smelt and tasted good, and she ate hungrily.

When Rhona listened to some of Shirin’s older relatives, she was surprised: They spoke a language she couldn’t understand. “That’s Punjabi,” Shirin’s cousin Tariq explained. “I don’t speak it very well. I understand it, but I usually answer in English. Mum gets angry about that. Has Shirin told you anything about Manchester?” he asked. “Yes, it sounds great,” replied Rhona. “But is it really the ‘pop cult capital’ of the UK?” she asked. “It gets more exciting every year,” Tariq answered. He told her excitedly about the cool clubs, and about bands which had become famous from one day to the next.

Two days later, after they had said good-bye to Aunt Zeba, the girls went to Liverpool with Shirin’s English mother. When they found out that she wanted to visit more relatives, the two girls looked sad. But first she took them to Albert Dock, and they seemed happier: There were shops and cafés, and they were able to listen to a busker, too. The girls felt much better. “You two don’t want to meet even more relatives, do you?” she said. “Look, there’s the *Beatles Story* exhibition over there. They would be your grandfather’s age now, but I thought you might be interested – they made Liverpool famous! I’ll meet you here at 5 o’clock, OK?”

1 Read the text and say …

1. … why Shirin’s family is in Manchester.
2. … why Rhona is not sure about the food.
3. … why Rhona is surprised.
4. … why Tariq’s mother gets angry.
5. … what band Liverpool is famous for.
6. … where the girls have to be at 5 o’clock.
7. … what three things in ‘Up North’ you find interesting, and why.

WB p. 44/11

2 Revision: Adjective or adverb?

‘In The City’ is a music event which happens 1 (regular) in Manchester every year. Bands give 2 (great) concerts in small clubs and fans queue 3 (excited) for tickets. Some of the bands are already 4 (famous). But others are 5 (new) – and 6 (nervous). Adam from Five Blue Mountains says, “At first it was really 7 (scary)! But the concert went 8 (good), and everyone applauded 9 (happy).” Fans should choose their concerts 10 (careful). If they’re 11 (lucky), maybe they’ll see the next great pop star.

WB p. 44/12

3 Verbs with adjectives

a) *You already know that adverbs describe the verb they follow. Find examples in the text on page 63.*

Example: Rhona **said** to Shirin **quietly**.

b) *Sometimes there is an adjective after the verb. Find sentences like this in the text.*

Example: I know you **feel hungry** after the long trip.

c) *Finish Rhona's letter to a friend in Swansea.*

GRAMMAR
verb + adjective

feel	hungry / cold / silly …
look	unusual / funny / tired …
taste	good / terrible / sweet …
smell	nice / awful / funny …

(→ G16)

WB p. 45/13

Dear Megan,
Went to *The Beatles Story* yesterday. It was more 1 (interesting) than I had expected; I must buy a CD! After that we walked 2 (slow) round Albert Dock. It was warm, but the wind felt 3 (cold), and Shirin bought a new scarf. It looks 4 (terrible), but don't tell her, she'd be 5 (angry)! We found a pizza place that seemed 6 (good). The pizza came 45 minutes later, but we waited 7 (patient). It smelt 8 (good), but tasted 9 (horrible), so Shirin's dad bought us a curry, which we ate 10 (hungry). He's 11 (wicked)! After one day in Liverpool, we had 12 (quick) learnt that Asian food is the best here! See you!
Lots of love, R.

d) *The verbs **be**, **get** and **become** tell you what something or someone **is** (good, exciting, famous, surprised …). What can you say about the other verbs in the text on page 63 that you use with adjectives?*

TIP

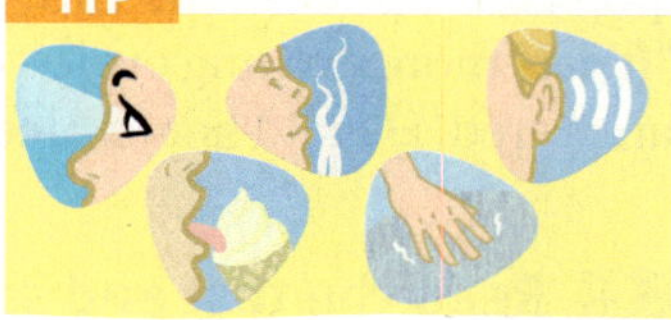

(→ G16)

4 ⟨A game: Sixth sense⟩

a) *Make groups of 3–4. Your teacher thinks of something but only tells you "It smells good", for example. In two minutes, think of and write down as many things as you can that "smell good".*

b) *After two minutes, you get a point for each thing. If you think of exactly the same thing as your teacher, you get five more points for your 'sixth sense'.*

5 Your turn: A new situation

a) *Think about how Rhona feels at Aunt Zeba's house: new faces, strange food, different language …*
Make notes with your ideas.

b) *Now think for a few minutes about a time when **you** had to meet new people or find your way in a strange place. Tell your partner about it.*

WB p. 45/14

6 Tariq's week

We're moving house tomorrow – it's going to be a crazy day! By tomorrow afternoon we'll have moved into the new house. I expect we'll have lost half of our things, and I won't have found all my CDs again yet – no Bhangra for me tomorrow! And will Shirin have gone back home, too? Yes, of course she will. I must remember to send her the CD she wanted – if I can find it …

What will Tariq do each day this week? What ***will he have done*** *by the end of the week?*

Example: He'll find Shirin's CD on Sunday. By the end of the week **he'll have sent** it to her.

Monday: get pocket money / spend it all

Tuesday: borrow books / not read any

Wednesday: buy a new CD / lose it

Thursday: write to Shirin / get a reply

WB p. 46/15

7 Listening: The Beatles Story

More than 40 years after they split up, The Beatles are still Liverpool's most famous sons. You can go on an audio tour of the exhibition on Albert Dock to find out about them.

a) *What do you know about The Beatles?*

b) *Listen to the tour and find the right answers.*

1. Rock and roll came to Liverpool from
   a) Hamburg. b) America. c) the City of London.
2. The Beatles' first name was
   a) The Quarrymen. b) Beatlemania. c) Mersey.
3. The Beatles arrived in the USA in a) 1961. b) 1964. c) 1973.
4. 'Apple' is the name of a) The Beatles' firm. b) a club. c) a Beatles record.
5. The Beatles split up when a) Paul married. b) John died. c) Paul left the band.

WB p. 46/16

8 ⟨A song: I wish I was back in Liverpool⟩

I wish I was back in Liverpool.
Liverpool town where I was born,
Where there ain't no trees, no scented breeze,
No fields of waving corn.

But there's lots of girls with peroxide curls,
And the Black and Tan flows free.
There's six in a bed by the old pier head,
And it's Liverpool town for me.

READING SKILLS

Factual texts

When you are doing research for a project, for example, you will often use factual texts, e. g. brochures, Internet pages, newspaper articles, etc. In *Green Line* 2, Unit 7 you learnt how the pictures and headings in a brochure can help you to read and understand it. The skills on this page will help you to get information from any factual text quickly.

1 Skimming

How can you find out easily what a text is about? You can **skim** a text to decide whether it is useful or interesting for you.

a) *Look through this text quickly. Do not read every word. Concentrate on keywords like nouns and verbs.*

b) *Now say in one or two sentences what the text is about. (An event in the past? A person?)*

2 Scanning

Imagine you are looking for information on topics a–f. Would this text help you? You can **scan** the text and find out.

Look at the text again. Do not read every word. Is there any information about these things? Say "yes" or "no".

a) famous people
b) going to London
c) heavy industry
d) free time activities
e) scary situations
f) spending money

How about a boat trip on the River Thames? Start in London, but don't go to the North Sea. Go west. Stop after 40 miles, and you're in Reading (say it like "redding"!). You won't find this town as a "must-see" place in all the guidebooks. But thousands of people think it's a great place to live and work. Reading is a regional centre in the UK's "Silicon Valley", so you will be able to guess where many people work – in computer technology and other kinds of high-tech jobs. You can see that from all the modern buildings and the names of the big international firms. There are also lots of jobs in Reading's city centre shops – all the famous ones are there –, as well as in the hotels where big firms have conferences and in the modern restaurants. (The restaurants are perfect for a quiet dinner, too!) Water is important for lots of leisure activities in and around Reading: For example, you can choose between rowing, a week on a houseboat (instead of a holiday flat) and fishing. If you would rather stay on land during your stay, you might want to try the Rivermead Leisure Complex – it's great for sports, but also for top concerts and festivals. Reading is very near to London, so if you can't find what you want in Reading, you can be in the capital for your concert or your shopping day in 40 minutes by train or one hour by bus on the M4 motorway.

3 Collect information

a) *Complete this list of topics from the text.*

- jobs (computers, shops, …)
- leisure (rowing, …)
- …
- …

b) *Now write down in a few sentences what the text tells you about life in Reading today.* WB p. 47/17

4 ⟨Write an e-mail⟩

Debbie, a girl from Canada, is going to stay with her relatives in Reading in the summer.

Write and tell her what she can do during her stay. Use your notes from exercise 3.

Changing places

1 Before you read

a) *Look at the photos on the pages that follow. Which place looks most interesting to you? Why?*

b) ***Skim** the texts and then make notes:*

1. Which places did the people visit?
2. What do you already know about these places?

2 Collect more information

***Scan** the texts. Find information about these things in the places that Wayne, Michael and Rhona visited:*

leisure activities · language · people · history · culture

Put the information in two lists: one for positive things, one for negative things.

WB p. 48/18; 19

Last month the readers of VISIT BRITAIN Kids had the chance to win a week with an exchange family in another part of the UK. Find out what our **three winners** said about their 'holidays' …

Wayne from London had an interesting time in **Swansea**, Wales.

"I looked at the city centre and thought: 'Oh no! The same shops as at home. This could be anywhere in Britain.' I had expected some differences, but the only one was that all the signs looked funny because they were in English and Welsh. ('Swansea' is 'Abertawe' – don't ask me why!) Nobody I met spoke Welsh, only English, and that was a pity. But the Welsh accent sounded cool."

We asked Wayne to choose his **top three places:** ✶✶✶

The Gower Coast ✶

"'One of the most beautiful parts of the UK coast' it says in the guidebook that VISIT BRITAIN Kids gave me. That sounded good to me, and I loved the beach at Rhossili – miles and miles of sand, great for a city kid like me! But I soon got tired of all that fresh air, and it was cold, so we went to the café on the hill to get warm again."

The National Waterfront Museum ✶

"I don't usually like museums but my Welsh exchange partner Rhodri wanted to go here, so I couldn't say no. (I'm a polite visitor, see?) But now I'm glad we went, because it wasn't boring at all. The whole place is really high-tech, and you can do a lot because it's all interactive. It was the first (and last?) time I found history interesting!"

Swansea Leisure Centre Skatepark ✶

"This isn't the only skatepark in Swansea (there are nine!), but it's the best I saw. Rhodri's mates are really good skaters. They showed me some wicked new tricks. I can't wait to show them to my friends at home!"

Find out more on the next page →

"It was funny to hear that Liverpool accent in real life – I quickly started to speak like that myself! I did the visitors' sightseeing tour – and I never want to hear the word 'Beatles' again! I know they're famous, and some tourists (the older ones!) go to Liverpool just for them, but I can't tell a lie: they're not my favourite band."

Michael from Leicester spent a few days in **Liverpool**.

Michael's **top three places** are: ✶✶✶

The ferry across the Mersey ✶

"If I lived in Liverpool, I'd go on a ferry trip with my friends every weekend – just for laughs! It's fun on the boat, you can see the docks and the waterfront, and it doesn't cost much. It's also a good way to meet people: We met some girls from Liverpool and found out a lot about the city from them – like where to eat, or get the best music. One of them gave me her address!"

The Williamson Tunnels ✶

"This must be the weirdest place in Liverpool! They're under normal streets. A rich man called Joseph Williamson built them in the 1820s – but nobody knows why! We went to the visitor centre and had a look. The funniest thing was, we met the girls from the Mersey ferry again, and chatted with them in the café!"

Anfield Road ✶

"That's the home of Liverpool Football Club, one of the most famous clubs in English football. I'm not really a football fan, but I enjoyed the match I went to on Saturday afternoon. The crowd sang the song 'You'll never walk alone' and cheered wildly every time Liverpool FC got the ball. But the Manchester fans drove me crazy: They looked (and sounded!) very aggressive, and some of them behaved like animals."

3 ⟨Would you like to live there?⟩

Tell your partner which place you would or would not like to live in, and explain why. Use the notes you made in exercises 1 and 2.

4 Writing texts: Your "top three places"

a) *Think of three things you would like to do on holiday in the UK. Write down some useful keywords that go with them.*

b) *Then use an Internet search engine or a guide to the UK: Look for a town where you can do at least two of the things you chose in a).*

Rhona from Swansea tried out life in **Reading**.

"People seemed richer here than at home. There are lots of big houses with gardens, and things in the shops were more expensive than in Swansea. Some kids made fun of my accent when I started to talk, but *they* didn't speak BBC English, and when I told them that, they stopped. Most people seemed nice."

Rhona's **top three places** in the Reading region: ✶✶✶

The Rivermead Leisure Complex ✶

"In the summer they have big open-air rock and folk festivals here. Sometimes they go on all weekend. I'd like to come back to one of them with my boyfriend in August – then I'll be able to show him what *good* folk music is! I also loved the leisure pool. You can swim there of course, but it's got all the extras, too: wave machine, lights under the water, music …"

The Reading Rowing Club ✶

"My exchange partner took me there, and I tried out rowing. It's a great feeling. You're moving very, very fast, but it's quiet. I'm quite fit, but my arms and shoulders hurt the next day! They have famous races on the Thames in the summer. I'd like to see that."

Windsor ✶

"No, I didn't see the Queen, I just had a look at her castle. (My exchange family from Reading paid quite a lot to get in!) It's a very big place – but I wouldn't like to live in ANY of those rooms, they're all far too old-fashioned! Windsor town centre is a good place to hang out in. There's the Thames again, like in Reading – and all the people who buy the rubbish in the tourist shops!"

c) *Use the reading skills you learnt on page 66 to find out more about the town you have found.*

d) *Now write about your own "top three places" for your holiday town. Say:*

- what the place is;
- why you like it;
- what you can do there;
- what is not so good about it.

e) *Remember to write down any useful new words you find in your 'personal vocabulary' list and put it in your English folder.*

WB p. 48/20

1 Mixed bag: An interesting idea

Did you hear about those kids w [1] won a week with an e [2] family in another part of the UK? The idea seemed i [3] because most people don't get a chance to test another r [4] before they move h [5]. Of course, the w [6] of the competition found out about the people and culture in the places they v [7]. One boy f [8] friendship on a Mersey ferry. A girl met people who made f [9] of her accent, but they soon had to agree that theirs might s [10] funny to other people, too! I would happily s [11] a week in a different town in the UK – but I'd r [12] live somewhere a bit more e [13] than Reading!

2 Singular or plural?

Some nouns only have a plural form, and some things are usually in pairs. If you want to say how many there are, you can say "a pair of" or "pairs of".

Example:
Have you seen my glasses? – I saw **a pair of glasses** in the kitchen. Are they yours?

Complete the text with "pair(s) of". WB p. 49/22

How many  have you got at home? Three? Or four? Pop stars must have big wardrobes: Some singers wear three  at one concert. British star Elton John owns 4,000 ! And when cult bands use fire on stage, each member of the band needs a . I know people who think they have to buy a  every time they see a shoe shop. And who steals my socks? I've got four  with one sock missing! Have you?

3 Sounds: One sound makes a difference

The *Queen Mary* isn't a sheep [iː] – it's a ship [ɪ].

a) *Listen and say which you hear: a) or b).*

1. a) prize b) price
2. a) bad b) bat
3. a) dog b) dock
4. a) man b) men
5. a) boat b) bought

WB p. 49/23

⟨b)⟩ *Test your partner: Choose a) or b) and say the word. Your partner writes down the word he/she hears. Does your partner understand what you say?*

4 Make adjectives

Lots of English adjectives have a main part which comes from a noun and an ending (or 'suffix') which makes an adjective.

Examples:

univers(e) + -al wonder + -ful wind + -y

Which suffixes can you add to these nouns? (Check the spelling in your dictionary.)

milk event pain help region tradition culture industry

NOW YOU CAN

- ✓ Talk about people and places in England and Wales.
- ✓ Use abstract nouns.
- ✓ Use the definite and indefinite articles.
- ✓ Meet new people.
- ✓ Offer help and make apologies.
- ✓ Use adjectives and adverbs.
- ✓ Use the future perfect.
- ✓ Get information from factual texts.

1 With or without *the*? (→ G14)

Starry magazine is very popular with 1 young in Britain. There are many articles about 2 pop culture (for example 3 music) and there is usually an interview with a star from 4 world of 5 sport. Last week there was an article about 6 success of Britain's disabled athletes. 'Marsha's page' is for people who have problems with 7 love – or with 8 life. Marsha gives 9 help to 10 sad and 11 lonely, and 12 help she gives is always very useful.

WB p. 50/24

2 *The, a / an,* or no article? (→ G14)

I bought 1 pair of DAZZ trainers at 2 weekend. I wanted to wear them to 3 school on 4 Monday, but Dad said no. I think that's silly: He's 5 teacher and he goes to 6 work by 7 car, so it's no problem if he wears shoes; I have to go by 8 bike and I think trainers would be better for that. I talked to Mum about it after 9 lunch, but she said I should ask Dad! I think that when I'm older I'll become 10 athlete – then I can wear trainers all 11 day!

3 Adjective or adverb? (→ G16)

1. "I feel so ▭ (excited) about the concert!"
2. "Here's the programme. The first band sounds ▭ (interesting)."
3. "I just can't wait for *Moonlight* – they sing so ▭ (beautiful)!"
4. "You needn't push – we'll ▭ (easy) get to our places before it starts."
5. "This is good. We can see ▭ (perfect) from here."
6. "Please don't eat your sandwich here. It doesn't smell ▭ (nice)."
7. "Have you seen the posters? The costumes look ▭ (cool)!"
8. "Yes! Do you think the man in the shop will give me one if I smile at him ▭ (sweet)?"

WB p. 50/26

4 Your turn: What can you say?

a) *Give an answer to these people. The Useful phrases on page 62 can help you.*

"Oh, this bag is so heavy!" • "Shall I mend it for you?" • "I'm the 'idiot' you were talking about …" • "Try again. You're doing fine." • "Sorry. I didn't mean to be rude." • "Did you kick this ball into my garden?"

b) *Choose two of the phrases from a) and imagine the whole situation. Write a short dialogue for each one.*

⟨Benny and Omar⟩

Benny Shaw's life is going to change very soon: His father – his 'da' – has to go and work in Tunisia, and he wants to take his family with him. If he does not go, he will lose his job. After difficult goodbyes and the first language problems at the airport in Tunisia, the Shaw family arrives at Marhaba village – a 'walled camp'[1] as Benny calls it – near the city of Sfax. On their first day in Marhaba, the village manager Talal Khayssi comes to give the Shaws – Benny, his father, his mother, and his little brother George – an introduction to their new life in Tunisia. There are many things that Benny has to learn about life in Tunisia – and about himself.

"Here in Africa, things are not the same as in Europe," said Mister[2] Khayssi. "There are certain things to be careful of. A scorpion sting[3], for example …"

"Excuse me?"

"A scorpion, Madam[4]. A small insect with a poisonous[5] sting. It lives in Africa."

"I know what a scorpion is, Mister Khayssi."

"Do not worry, Madam. In three years we have only seen one scorpion in Marhaba village. And never once a snake[6]."

Benny started to listen. "Snakes? Now, wait a minute!"

Talal Khayssi smiled. "Please, young man, let me continue. If – and this is a big if – you have a scorpion sting, you have more than one hour to get to a hospital."

"Oh, sure, that's great then."

"Benny! Sarcasm is not going to help us here."

"There is a nurse[7] at the factory. And I have here a paper which says 'I have been bitten by a scorpion' in French and Arabic."

"What about English?"

"I thought you spoke English, Mister Shaw. In any case, the nurse's English is not so good."

"That makes me feel better."

"You really need not worry about this, Mrs Shaw. The chances are very small."

"What about snakes then?" asked Da.

Talal Khayssi looked at his papers. "Snakes, as I say, have never been seen in the village. They do not like to climb walls." He laughed nervously. "Also, your children are too big: A snake could not eat them whole."

George looked ill. Benny knew he should say something sarcastic, but his stomach was turning somersaults[8] at the moment.

"A small snake might be able to get under the gate[9] at night. If a snake bites you, please

[1]**walled camp** [wɔːld 'kæmp] = von einer Mauer umgebenes Lager • [2]**Mister** ['mɪstə] = Herr • [3]**sting** [stɪŋ] = Stich; Stachel • [4]**Madam** ['mædəm] = gnädige Frau • [5]**poisonous** ['pɔɪznəs] = giftig • [6]**snake** [sneɪk] = Schlange • [7]**nurse** [nɜːs] = Krankenschwester • [8]**(to) turn a somersault** [ˌtɜːn ə 'sʌməsɔːlt] = einen Purzelbaum schlagen • [9]**gate** [geɪt] = Tor

remember the colour of the snake and go to the factory immediately."

"Is there any special colour we should worry about?"

"No, no, Mister Shaw. Except maybe black. Yes … worry about black. But, as I say, we have never seen snakes in the village. It has been months since anyone has died in Sfax."

Ma grabbed Khayssi's water and drank it all. "Do you have any good news, Khayssi?"

"Of course," smiled Talal Khayssi. "Your car has arrived. It is a Toyota Landcruiser."

Da tried not to smile, but lost. The scorpions and snakes didn't sound so bad now. Not with a big shiny jeep parked outside.

"There is a radio in the jeep. Always have it with you in the car. You are … ah … Zulu Three. Central is Bravo One. The locals[10] get angry if another local is hurt, even though it's usually the locals' fault[11]. The young people are very wild on their mobylettes[12]. If there is an accident, lock[13] your doors and drive straight to the station of the Garde Nationale."

"Or?"

"Or if a fundamentalist is watching, he may try to start a riot[14]."

"A riot! But this is a stable[15] country. They told us this!"

"It is, Madam," answered Khayssi. "I am only telling you about the worst things that could happen, but they probably[16] won't happen."

"I see."

The Tunisian saw that his glass was empty. He stood up to leave.

"Oh, and one more thing. Please be very careful when you cross the train tracks. The warning lights often do not work. We have lost one car already this year."

"Aah …" said Da. His jeep didn't look quite as good any more.

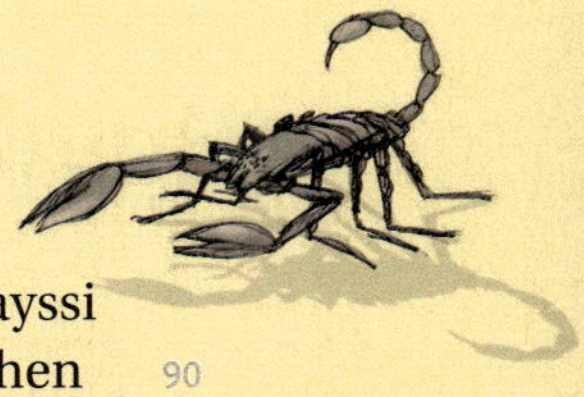

"If you need anything, call me at the office," said Khayssi.

Everyone shook hands and Talal Khayssi left. No-one said anything for a while, then Ma decided she needed to have a talk with her husband. In private. Benny suddenly felt the weight[17] of Africa on him. He pulled himself out of the chair and went for a sleep.

What he didn't know was that it wouldn't be a scorpion or a snake that got him that

afternoon. Instead, a tiny little mosquito got into his room, landed on Benny's forehead[18] and sucked[19] a few drops of blood out of him. This was a pity[20] because Benny was allergic to mosquitoes.

Benny has trouble with his new school, the other kids, the teachers and the rules. With everything about his new life. Then he meets Omar, a local boy who lives on the streets, and he begins to feel more at home. He learns about Omar's Tunisia – the real Tunisia, which is very different from the country Talal Khayssi knows.

adapted from:
Benny and Omar by Eoin Colfer

[10] **local** [ˈləʊkl] = Einheimische / -r • [11] **fault** [fɔːlt] = Schuld • [12] **mobylette** [ˌməʊbɪˈlet] = Mofa • [13] **(to) lock** [lɒk] = abschließen • [14] **riot** [ˈraɪət] = Unruhen, Aufstand • [15] **stable** [ˈsteɪbl] = stabil • [16] **probably** [ˈprɒbəbli] = wahrscheinlich • [17] **weight** [weɪt] = Gewicht • [18] **forehead** [ˈfɔːhed] = Stirn • [19] **(to) suck** [sʌk] = saugen • [20] **(to) be a pity** [bi ə ˈpɪti] = bedauerlich sein

⟨Revision for tests⟩ Unit 3–4

1 Mixed bag: British food

"Britons can't cook." Jim Villiers always gets a [1] when he hears this sentence. He is p[2] of British food, and last year he started work as a c[3] in a school cafeteria. In Britain most pupils h[4] lunch a[5] school, but many of them don't like it. They say the food tastes a[6]. But if Jim w[7] their school cook, they w[8] enjoy their meals. He believes that t[9] young eat too many c[10]. "If teenagers a[11] more vegetables, they w[12] feel healthier," Jim says. He has t[13] himself to cook Asian food, too, and that has b[14] very popular in his cafeteria recently. But even then, the pupils don't always b[15] themselves. "Sometimes they push e[16] other. One day a plate o[17] curry fell down and went all over a girl's new pair of j[18]! But it w[19] her mistake: If she hadn't t[20] around suddenly, it wouldn't h[21] happened."

2 Listening: Helping the family

A caller is telling *Rachel's Radio Show* about the jobs he does in and around the house.

a) *Listen, and put the pictures in the right order. One picture is wrong; which one is it?*

b) *There is no picture for one of Justin's jobs. What job is missing?*

3 An e-mail to friends in London

Last month Fiona and her family moved from London to a town in the North of England. Fiona wants to write to her old tutor group in London and tell them about her new home and how she feels about it.
Read the notes and write her e-mail.

- how the day we moved was (what a mess!)
- the new house: my own room :-) ...
- what's different here:
  neighbours :-) class :-) town :-(...
- what I miss most: ...
- see you all maybe???

4 Role play: Hey! What do you think you're doing?

Read about what happened to Nicola, then act the role play with a partner. Use the Useful phrases on page 62.

Nicola is on her way home from school on her bike. She almost hits a boy who is sitting in the road with his skateboard. She is angry at first, then she finds out about the boy's accident ... Both teenagers apologize, then Nicola wants to help the boy.

5 Good for business

a) ***Skim*** *this text and say in 2–3 sentences what it is about.*

b) ***Scan*** *the text. Does it give you any information about these things? (Say "yes" or "no".)*

- Diana's family
- people she works for
- British history
- the tourist industry

Diana comes from a small town in Wales not far from the sea. While she was still at school, she had a weekend job as a waitress in the café at Redstone Castle, the home of old Sir Clarence. His relatives built the castle centuries ago. "I didn't earn much," she says. "Sir Clarence always tells everybody how expensive life in an old castle is for him. But I think he's just a mean old man. He always wore an awful old school scarf that he had!"

A few tourists came to visit the castle, and after the tour people went to the café for tea. "I'm sure the guides weren't very good," laughs Diana, "because tourists often asked me questions about the castle. 'Is there a dungeon?' (Yes.) 'Is there a ghost?' (No.)" After she left school, Diana became an official guide at Redstone Castle and took tourists round the rooms herself.

One afternoon she was with a group of tourists in the Great Hall. Suddenly there was a loud shout from the back of the group. Diana went to see what had happened. A woman was lying on the floor. She looked scared. The only words she could say were: "A ghost!"

Diana was just getting her mobile out to call for help when there was more bad news for her: The woman's son was missing. Where was he? Some of the tourists had their own ideas.

"He's gone to get a doctor."

"The ghost has taken him away!"

The situation was getting difficult. Diana decided to phone Sir Clarence. "He sounded happy when I told him about the ghost," she remembers. "That surprised me."

A moment later Sir Clarence arrived in the Hall, then the missing boy came back and told his story: "I saw the ghost, too!" he cried. "It went through that door, so I opened it and tried to follow it." Then the boy showed everybody an old scarf which he had found on the floor and which the ghost had lost. Some people laughed, others took photos of the scarf.

Redstone Castle has now become very popular. "The visitors come to see the Redstone Ghost – that's what they pay for," Sir Clarence says. Diana has her own ideas about the Redstone Ghost, but she keeps them to herself.

c) *What does the text tell you about Sir Clarence?* ***Collect information*** *and make notes.*

For example: lives in Clarence Castle – mean old man – …

Then write a few sentences to describe him.

d) ***Writing texts:*** *Write a short play for lines 20 to 46 of the text.*

1. Make a list of the characters. (Are there roles for other people, too? – *1st tourist, …*)
2. Write the dialogues. (Some sentences are in the story. You must think of the rest.)
3. Write about the action. (Describe the scene at the beginning: The Great Hall, what the people are doing. Say what the characters do: *X comes in, Y opens …*).

Unit 5 Media messages

Check out your fave celebs and wear this year's hottest clothes! Copy them for your next party. Read this advice: YOU can wear celeb clothes, too!

Teenagers get tips and advice from magazines. *Shout* is the trendiest magazine for teenage girls today in the UK.
From 1978 to 2006 the magazine *Smash hits* was very popular, but the pop world changes fast, and in 2006 *Smash hits* had to finish.

THE TIMES
No. 68725 ▪ TUESDAY JUNE 13 2006 ▪ timesonline.co.uk
INTERNATIONAL EDITION
WORLD CUP SPECIAL
EVERY KICK EVERY PASS EVERY GOAL SPORT
Blair backs Israel on withdrawal
Al-Qaeda's new Iraq chief
Chinese exports
SuDoku
Pilots rescued
Graft at Games
TIMESONLINE SHARE PRICES
The heatwave ends
Brine helps wine
Islam rules city

There are 'quality' and 'popular' newspapers.
The Times is a high quality newspaper,
The Sun and *The Daily Mirror* are popular.
The Times started in 1785!

1 Media

a) *What kinds of media can you see in the pictures? Do you use them all?*

b) *What can people "get" from each medium? Work with a partner and make lists.*

⟨c)⟩ *Can you believe every media message? Give reasons.* WB p. 53/1

DID YOU KNOW?

- RCA made the first colour TVs in 1954. In today's prices, a 1954 TV cost £3,432 – or more!
- The BBC started in 1922. Its nickname is 'the Beeb'.
- Lycos was the first Internet search engine in 1993.
- The popular newspaper *The Sun* sells 3,145,000 copies every day, *The Times* 669,000.

Click here and listen to ***Arctic Monkeys'*** new single or download it to your mobile for only £1.99. Send a free music e-card to your friends!

Mobiles today are not only phones. They are becoming mobile Internet. Tim Berners-Lee created the first web browser in 1990. He also wrote HTML, the language of the Internet. The World Wide Web was ready for the public in 1991.

Before there was TV, radio was the main kind of entertainment in most homes. Radio started in the early 20th century. Now radio offers music, news and information, and sport.

The British soap opera *Coronation Street* started in 1960 and is still on TV today. Other popular soaps are *Neighbours*, *Emmerdale* and *EastEnders*. All the soaps try to be realistic about life with its happy times, its problems and some violence. The name "soap opera", or just "soap", goes back to radio dramas in the 1930s – the commercials were for housewives, and they advertised soap and other cleaning products.

2 Listening: On the radio

a) *Which word describes each programme best: information, entertainment, news? Why?*

b) *What is each programme about?*

c) *What can you say about the way the three radio people talk? Describe their voices and the phrases that they use.* WB p. 53/2

3 Your turn: You and the media

What are your favourite media? Why are they important for you?

Casting for a daily soap

Want to be a star? Want to be discovered? Not so fast! Before you can get anywhere, the programme has to "cast" you first. Have you ever been invited to do a casting? You haven't? Well, TEEN◆BUZZ tells you all about it. Matt Stirling from *EastEnders* can give you a few tips, too.

First, you talk to an agent and give him or her your photo. Then one day the agent is phoned by a Casting Director who is looking for a special character for a soap. She tells the agent who she needs. Let's call him "Justin". So the agent looks through his files and finds a photo of – *you*! Your photo is sent to the Casting Director, who looks at hundreds of photos for the right "Justin". She likes your face!

Matt: I was lucky. I was informed about my casting by my agent, and then the script was given to me. This script is called the "sides". Then I went to the casting. Was I nervous!

When you get to a casting, don't be surprised: About 30 people have been invited, and they're all there. Like Matt, you'll be too nervous to talk. You'll reread your "sides" and make sure you know the role well. Then you have to act the role. The Casting Director is a nice lady, but you're number 27, so don't get your hopes up too high.

Matt: I was lucky again. The Casting Director and her assistant liked the way I acted. Two days later, I was invited back. Now there were only ten people left.

The Casting Director might suggest different ways you should play the role – to see if you can act and follow directions. And if you're super-lucky and you're even better than the first time …

Matt: … I was chosen to act "Justin" in *EastEnders*! A week later, I signed my contract. Wow!

1 Soap stars

a) *How many things do you have to do to become a star? Start with:* Find an agent.

b) *Would you like to be a soap star? Why or why not?*

2 Find the rule

Look for passive forms in the TEEN◆BUZZ *text, and collect them in a grid like this. Find the rule about how the passive is made. What verb forms do you use?*

Present tense			Past tense			Present perfect		
Subject	'to be'	…	Subject	…	…	Subject	…	…
The agent	is	…	I	was	…	…		

3 How a daily soap is made

Use the words and write sentences in the present passive.

Example: A story idea **is** discuss**ed**.

1. discuss a story idea ✓
2. write script A script is written
3. cast actresses and actors
4. discuss script with cast
5. find place for the scenes
6. buy clothes
7. film the scenes
8. show the soap on TV

TIP

Is or **are**? Find the subject of the passive sentences first.

Example: story idea → **is**
clothes → **are**

WB p. 54/3

4 How did Matt get the role?

Write sentences about the pictures. Use the past passive.

Start: Matt **was** photograph**ed**.

WB p. 54/4

1

2

3

4

5

6

5 Don't watch this film!

is/are has/have been was/were

Put in the passive: simple present, present perfect or past tense. Look for the signal words. You need them in the passive, too.

Watch out: Don't watch this film! It 1 already 2 (call) the silliest film that 3 ever 4 (make) – and it's true. *Baby Terminator 7* 5 (write) in 2005 by Amanda Church and 6 (film) the same year by the great Micky Wendover. Great? Did I say 'great'? "The idea 7 (give) to me five years ago by Justin Clooney, and it was Amanda's job to write the script," says Micky. Poor Amanda, that's all *I* can say. But the actresses and actors who 8 (ask) to play the silly roles in 2005 had a more difficult job! In the film, people 9 (kill) when a baby alien says *"Goo!"*. Maybe the best role 10 (give) to him that year! The baby's secret 11 soon 12 (discover) and he must quickly learn to speak and, well, soon he forgets the word *"Goo!"*. Isn't that a silly story?

WB p. 54/5; 55/6

TIP

Past: last night, yesterday, a few days ago, in 2006
Present perfect: already, ever, not … yet, just, never

(→ G19)

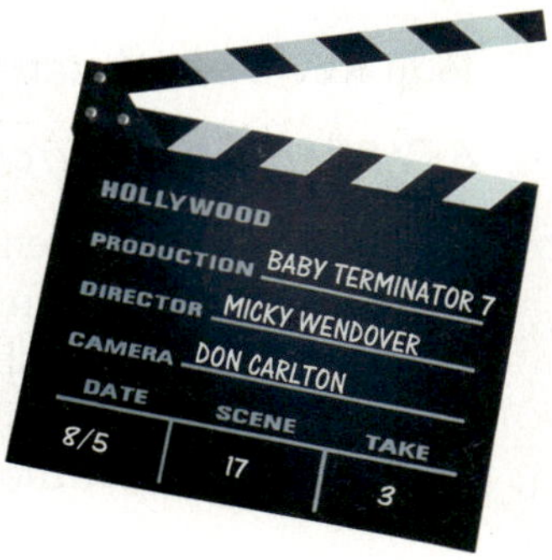

6 From active to passive

Put these active sentences into the passive.

TIP
A lot of people **read** popular newspapers.
Popular newspapers **are read by** a lot of people.

(→ G 20)

Example: 1. Teenagers buy TEEN◆BUZZ.
→ TEEN◆BUZZ **is bought by** teenagers.

2. RCA made the first colour TV in 1954. → The first colour TV **was** …
3. Too many people believe media messages. 4. Radio dramas advertised soap and cleaning products. 5. After the invention of TV in the 1950s, most people forgot the radio stars. 6. Everyone now saw the stars' faces! 7. Listeners call the BBC 'the Beeb'. 8. The script authors often write the script five or ten times! WB p. 55/7

7 Passive or not?

a) *Look at these examples. Say why the passive is or isn't used.*

TIP
The passive is often used when it is not important – or not clear – who does the action.

(→ G 19, 20)

1
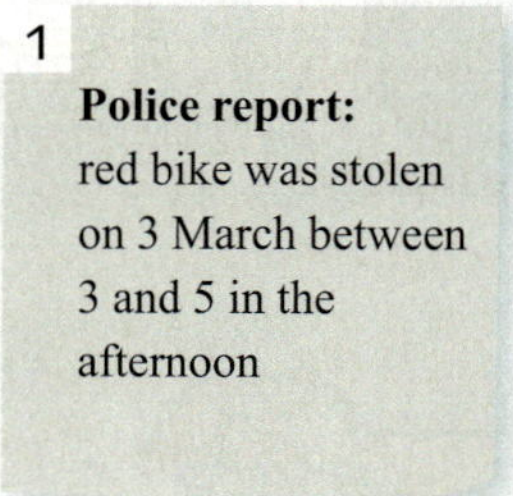

2

3

4
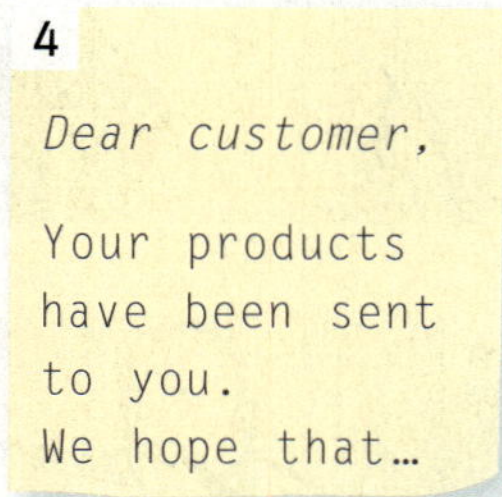

b) *Would you use active or passive forms in these situations? What would you say?*

1. You want to tell your dad who did more work in the garden.
2. You want to inform the police that your money is not in your locker any more.
3. You want to say you built the tree house – all alone.

WB p. 56/8

8 Your turn: Watching TV

a) *What are your favourite TV shows? What do you like about them?*

⟨b)⟩ *Act one short scene from a show – in English! Can the others guess which show it is?*

9 Revision: If-clauses (type 2 and 3)

A TV reporter is talking about a road accident. Find the right endings for the sentences.

1. If the driver had been driving more slowly, … … he wouldn't have accidents like this.
2. If the driver had seen the cow sooner, … … it wouldn't go onto the road so often.
3. If the van hadn't crashed … … he would have seen the cow on the road.
4. If the cow wasn't so silly, … … the van wouldn't have crashed.
5. If the driver drove more carefully … … the pigs wouldn't have fallen out.

WB p. 56/9

TALKWISE

Talk about media in your life

1 Couch potato?

a) *Look at the pictures and decide which one is most like you.*

magazine junkie

bookworm

super surfer

music maniac

couch potato

b) *Find a partner who has chosen the same picture. Talk about why you chose that one. Find a definition together.*

2 Listening: Interesting people

a) *Listen to these three people. They are talking about media in their lives. Write down the kinds of media they are talking about.*

b) *Listen again. Why are these media important for them?* WB p. 57/10

3 Collect phrases

There are lots of media words and phrases on the Check-in pages and in the TEEN◆BUZZ article on page 78.

Make your own Useful phrases box for your "personal media vocabulary". Put it in your English folder. WB p. 57/11

4 Your turn: Pros and cons of media

1. *Work in groups and choose two kinds of media.*
2. *Use your own Useful phrases box from exercise 3 and say: What do you think is good or bad about these two media? Give reasons for your pros and cons.*

WB p. 57/12

5 ⟨A cartoon⟩

Advertising

What do you think about this?
The text was written before the football star had even tried the product.
(But he will be asked to try the product soon.)

1 What's in an ad?

a) *What can you see in each picture? What are the two ads about?*

b) *Would you buy these products? Why or why not?*

c) *How do the ads try to make you interested in the products?*

TIP
had + been + past participle
(→ G 21)

2 Put in the past perfect passive

1. Music fans were waiting outside the studio. They ___ (ask) to act in an ad.
2. The sports star didn't know the name of the hair gel. He ___ (not inform)!
3. The singer didn't have time to try the make-up. The make-up ___ (not send) to her before the show.
4. The new car ad was much better than the old one. The text ___ (change).
5. I didn't get a poster with my *Shout* magazine. It ___ (forget).
6. And I didn't get any hair gel at the football match! It ___ (give) to the public by the Gizzette people before the game.

WB p. 58/13

3 You're on TV!

Imagine you are going to be on TV in your favourite show. Tell your friends about your new job.

Start like this: **I have been offered …**

GRAMMAR

Personal passive

Sentences in the personal passive start with the **person** and not with a thing.
Person as subject: I have been given a CD.
Thing as subject: The CD has been given **to** me.

(→ G 22)

1. They have offered me the role of the rock star. 2. The Casting Director has sent me all the information. 3. She has given me £ 1000 for new clothes. 4. The film people have promised me my own car. 5. One of the actors has shown me the studio. 6. Some of the actors have taught me how to dance. 7. They have told me crazy stories about the studio.

WB p. 58/14

4 Let's go to the studio

Ads and commercials are sometimes filmed in studios. These people are on a tour of the studio.

Use the words to make sentences in the will future passive.

Example: **Will** we **be taken** to the studio cafeteria?

WB p. 59/15

5 ⟨Put in the correct passive tense⟩

Did you know this about Reese Witherspoon, hot Hollywood actress? She **1** (be born) on March 22, 1976, in Louisiana. So she's from the sweet South! In 1990 she **2** (cast) for her first film near her home. The Casting Director was so happy with her that the 14-year-old Reese **3** (fly) to LA. She **4** (see) in many films. After she **5** (give) a role in *Sweet home Alabama*, she **6** (ask) to act in *Walk the line*. **7** she (give) any more great roles soon?
"I **8** (offer) so many roles so far," she said, "I'm not worried."
– Good luck, Reese!

6 Writing texts: An ad

a) *Think of something that you would like to sell on the Internet: CD, book, clothes, DVD …*

b) *Write your own advertisement like this:*

1. You need a **headline** to get people's attention.
2. Now you need a good / funny / exciting **colour picture**.
3. Write a **short text** about your product.
   - First collect adjectives, e. g. *great, exciting*.
   - Give all the important information.
   - Say why someone really needs your product.

WB p. 59/16

7 How to: Check each other's ad

a) *Give your ad to a partner, and look at your partner's ad. Go back to exercise 1 on page 82. Answer the questions for each other's ads.*

b) Pupil A: *Make some suggestions to improve the ad.*

c) Pupil B: *Do you agree with your partner's suggestions?*

USEFUL PHRASES

Pupil A: It would be better if you … / You should … / I don't understand this sentence. / If I were you, I would … / Could you write … ? / How about … ?

Pupil B: I know what you mean. / I'll change that. / But I think it's OK like this. / I'll think about what you said. / That's a good idea. / I think I'll do that. / Thanks!

8 Revision: Simple past and present perfect

Practise these sentences with a partner. One sentence or question should be in the simple past and the other in the present perfect.

Example: A: I **saw** the new ad for mobiles **yesterday**. – B: But I **haven't seen** it **yet**.

1. A: Have you seen Matt Stirling with his new hair style? – B: Yes, I … yesterday.
2. Have you ever been to Hollywood? – B: Yes, I …
3. A: I tried those new crisps last week. They were great! – B: I …
4. A: We went on the tour of the studio two months ago. – B: …
5. A: Have you seen the new 3-minute football ad yet? – B: Yes, …
6. A: My parents haven't given me my own TV yet. Have yours? – B: Yes, …

9 Your turn: Celebrities and ads

Think of ads or commercials you know with famous people.

a) *What are they advertising?*

b) *Do you like the ads? Why / why not?*

c) *Would the famous person help to sell the product to you?*

WRITING SKILLS

Writing a newspaper report

Headline – tells the readers what the article is about.

The **passive** is often used in newspaper reports – when you don't know who did the action or if it's not important.

Don't give your **opinion** in a newspaper report.

Computer party ends in violence

A LAN party in Dorchester ended in violence last Saturday. The party was attended by 75 teenagers, and was organised by a youth club. "We just wanted to raise some money for our club," said one boy. "We didn't want any problems."

After they had played for six hours, two players got angry with each other. One player was angry because he had lost the game. The argument soon became violent. Chairs, tables and computers were broken. At 10.45 the police were called by neighbours who had heard the noise. Two 15-year-old boys were taken to the police station and the party ended.

LAN parties are becoming very popular in England. The parties are usually attended by teenagers and sometimes violent computer games are played. The parties go on for one to three days. Often you must pay to join a party.

A hotline has been set up by the Dorchester Police Department. If you are organising a party and have questions or if you are worried about violence at LAN parties, please call 892 3487.

The beginning gives **basic information**: who, what, when, where.

Here you can give some more **interesting details**.

Here is some **background information** on the topic.

At the end you can give some **useful information**.

1 Violence in Dorchester

Dorchester is having more problems with violence.

Read these notes from a press conference. Use them to write a report. Look at the ideas in the report above. Think of a good headline and use the passive when you can.

teacher found mobile with violent film scenes on Friday at Redwood School / headmaster called police "I was shocked that this could happen at my school" / teenager filmed violent scenes in school and in playground / mobile of a Redwood pupil / show three pupils who hit a smaller pupil / all attend Redwood: ages 13–15, smaller pupil about 10 / violent scenes on mobiles are becoming a problem in England / film scenes are sent to friends' mobiles / it's cool to have more violent scenes than others / mobiles now not allowed at Redwood / the school doesn't want more violence / headmaster: "enough violence on TV, parents should check their children's mobiles"

2 A better report

a) *Exchange reports with a partner. Give your partner suggestions to improve his / her report. The Useful phrases in exercise 7 on page 84 can help you. Look at the tips for reports on this page, too. Has your partner used the passive?*

b) *Rewrite your report. Use your partner's suggestions if you agree with them.*

3 News in your town

Find an interesting article in your local newspaper. Take notes and write a report in English.

WB p. 60/17

No couch potatoes!

1 Before you read

Your parents have decided on a new rule: no TV in the house. Convince them that they should keep the TV. Write down as many positive things about TV as you can.

Mariah's media corner

We've all heard it a thousand times: "You watch too much TV!" and "You should read more!" But parents aren't always right and sometimes kids have to learn things for themselves. This month two of our readers share their media experiences with us.

Bill, age 13, Southampton

"Maybe you won't believe what I'm going to tell you and maybe you can explain it another way, but I believe it's all connected. This is the story of how I, Bill Burton, who never reads anything (not even the cereal box in the morning) read a long – and I mean *loooong* – book! It wasn't just *any* book, it was Harry Potter. The first book. My mum always said, "It'll take magic to get Bill to read a book." And she's right; it did.

My mum loves to read. She goes to the library about twice a week and always asks, "Shall I bring you a book, too?" I say yes to make her happy. Mum finishes her books, and mine stay in a pile on my desk, or fall off my desk or get lost under my bed.

One day my mates and I were skateboarding and we needed a higher ramp. I ran to my room to look for something and the last book on my desk (the other books had disappeared) was exactly the right size. We had a great time on the ramp that afternoon – until my skateboard cracked in two, I fell over and broke my leg.

Then I was taken to hospital and stayed there and hated it. The break was bad. "You'll have to stay three weeks or more," the doctor told me. Then I got a cold, I had to drink tea and there seemed to be Brussels sprouts AND spinach for lunch every day. My mates visited me and brought along part of the skateboard ramp – my library book. But it no longer looked like a library book should. I put it on my table and it stayed there. Of course all the nurses said, "Oh, that's a great book!"

And one day it happened. It was so boring at hospital that I actually opened the book and read. After I had finished the first chapter, my cold went away. After the fifth chapter, there was spaghetti for lunch – and no vegetables! And when I had finished the book, the doc said, "Your leg is much better. You can go home soon."

I admit that the book was really good; I could imagine the pictures in my head. But don't think this means I'm going to read the second one. And don't tell my mum!"

Mariah says: As soon as Bill had finished this article, he lost his pocket money, couldn't find his bike key and his mobile didn't work. The second Harry Potter book has been sent to him.

Janice, age 14, Manchester

"My parents believe that my favourite TV show *ER* (that is the hospital soap *Emergency Room*) isn't realistic. Wrong!

Last September I was walking home from school. Suddenly I heard a noise – someone or something was crying. I thought it was an animal, like a cat after a fight or something. But then I heard a weak 'Help!'. It was strange because I was walking past the old metal factory and it had been closed years before. I looked around a little, but couldn't see anything. Then I heard the voice again. It was coming from above me. I looked up into the sun and could see the outline of someone on the roof. There was a little boy up there and he was crying. "My leg is bleeding," he shouted down to me. He had chased after his cat on the roof and then cut his leg on some metal.

Watch out! This is where TV enters. I looked for a place to climb up to the roof. I saw a pipe at the corner, tested it and climbed right up. I saw that on *CSI: Miami* once.

When I got to the boy, I could see that he didn't look good. He had a big gash in his leg. There was lots of blood around and he looked quite white in the face. At first I was scared, but then I remembered my doctor's training – from TV. You know, I watch *ER* as often as I can so I know how to talk to patients and how to help them.

I asked the boy his name and tried to distract him. I even got him to laugh when I told him my favourite joke. Then I took off my T-shirt and used it as a bandage. It was my favourite ManU T-shirt, but this was an emergency and fashion couldn't get in the way. I tied it really tight. Ricky (that was the boy's name) shouted when I did that, but it had to be tight.

The next thing was the 999 call. I held Ricky's hand while we waited for the ambulance and I talked calmly to him like the doctors on the show.

After I had rescued Ricky, I was invited to tell my story everywhere – to the newspapers, on the TV news and now in this magazine. I was sent 12 new ManU T-shirts from all over England. And this whole thing has really helped me to decide about my future. When I grow up, I want to be a doctor – or an actress."

2 What do you think?

a) *Do you like the two stories? Why or why not?*

b) *Has anything like this ever happened to you or to a friend?*

WB p. 61/18; 19

3 Your turn: Books and TV

a) *What was the last book that you read? Why did you read it?*

b) *How could your favourite TV show be useful in* ***your*** *life? Or could it not?*

WB p. 61/20

4 ⟨A media survey⟩

a) *Work in groups of five.*

b) *Write 3–5 questions about media habits (which kinds of media, how much money is spent on them, how much time every week etc.).*

c) *Ask all the people in your group and then five adults. Write the answers down.*

d) *Report to your class. How will you show them the results? In a grid? Or in a chart?*

1 Find the polite answer

1. **Excuse me.**
   a) What do you want?
   b) How can I help you?
   c) Huh?

2. **I'm sorry. I can't find your CD!**
   a) Can't you do *anything* right?
   b) I'll never give you a CD again.
   c) Well – let's look for it together.

3. **Thanks for all your help.**
   a) What help?
   b) You're welcome.
   c) Forget it.

4. **Could you help me, please?**
   a) No.
   b) I only help nice people.
   c) I'd be glad to help you.

WB p. 62/21

2 Sounds: Strong and weak forms

Some short words can have strong and weak forms. Usually the weak form is used, but if the word is important or at the end of a sentence, you use the strong form.

Listen, and say these sentences:

1. There are some great computer games, but some can be boring, too. 2. Who's the costume for? Is it for you? 3. She wants to go to London, but I don't want to. 4. It was a crazy thing to do – it really was. 5. Can you help me, please? I hope you can.

3 ⟨A song: *Sk8er boi* by Avril Lavigne⟩

Read the text and listen to the song. What mistake did the girl make?

He was a boy
She was a girl
Can I make it any more obvious?
He was a punk
She did ballet
What more can I say?
He wanted her
She'd never tell
Secretly she wanted him as well
But all of her friends
Stuck up their nose
They had a problem with his
Baggy clothes

Chorus:
He was a skater boy
She said see you later, boy
He wasn't good enough for her
She had a pretty face
But her head was up in space
She needed to come back down to earth

Five years from now
She sits at home
Feeding the baby
She's all alone
She turns on TV
Guess who she sees?
Skater boy rockin' up MTV
She calls up her friends
They already know
And they've all got
Tickets to see his show
She tags along
Stands in the crowd
Looks up at the man that
She turned down …

NOW YOU CAN

- ✓ Talk about different kinds of media.
- ✓ Use the passive.
- ✓ Talk about media in your life.
- ✓ Write an advertisement.
- ✓ Check each other's work.
- ✓ Write a report.

1 Matt Stirling (→ G 19, 21)

Complete the sentences with the passive in the correct tense.

1. Matt ___ (see) in the UK on the soap *EastEnders* every week. 2. He ___ (discover) last year in a TV commercial. 3. Before that he ___ (not offer) any other TV roles, but he ___ (give) lots of jobs as a model. 4. After the casting, Matt ___ (ask) to play the role of "Justin" by the Casting Director. 5. "It's not so easy," Matt said. "Sometimes a scene ___ (film) ten or twenty times." 6. As an *EastEnders* star, he ___ (send) thousands of fan letters every month. 7. A poster of him ___ (put in) in next month's *Shout* magazine. The girls will go crazy!

WB p. 63/24

2 Put these sentences into the passive (→ G 20, 22)

1. After Bill's accident, an ambulance took him to hospital. 2. The people in hospital gave him Brussels sprouts and spinach every day! 3. But soon they brought him spaghetti. 4. "My mates visited me every day." 5. Janice rescued Ricky. 6. After Janice had rescued Ricky, TV, newspapers and a magazine invited Janice to tell her exciting story. 7. People and firms from all over England sent her new T-shirts. 8. Soon the BBC will ask her to tell her story, too.

WB p. 63/25

3 Your turn: A school magazine report

a) 1. *Choose one of these topics:*
the last school play • two boys fight in the school playground • a bike accident
2. *Write notes about the topic.*
3. *Write a short report about your topic. Remember to use the passive.*

b) *Check your partner's report. Remember the Useful phrases in exercise 7 on page 84.*

WB p. 63/26

4 Write an ad

Choose a product like this, or another product. Write an ad for it.
The ideas in exercise 6 on page 84 can help you.

⟨Project⟩ English and Geography

STEP 1: Find out about the weather

The Vikings[1] thought cats were a sign of heavy rain and that dogs were a sign of storms and wind. So 'It's raining cats and dogs' means a bad rainstorm[2]. The cartoon is funny because people think it rains a lot in the UK, but is that true?

a) *Look at these annual average rainfall totals[3] (mm) and find the places in your atlas[4].*

Fort William	1900	Manchester	800	Falmouth	1100
Glasgow	1200	Norwich	600	Newcastle	670

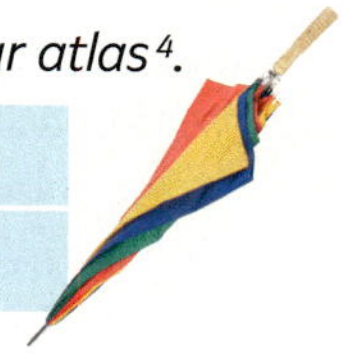

b) *Look at a relief[5] map in your atlas which shows the highland[6] and lowland[7] areas[8] of the UK. Where does it rain a lot? Where does it rain less? Can you explain why?*

STEP 2: Collect weather words

The weather is with us all the time – rain, snow, sun, wind. When we talk about weather we describe what the atmosphere[9] is like in one place at one time.

a) *Collect all the weather words you know and make a word web.*

b) *Now look out of the window and write a short weather report. The words in your word web will help you.*

Start like this: The weather in (place) (this morning) is …

STEP 3: Make a weather forecast[10]

a) *Listen to the weather forecast and find out what the weather will be like in Wales.*

b) *Look at the weather map and the weather symbols[11] on the next page. Find the regions on a map in your atlas.*

c) *Write a UK weather forecast for the TV news. These Useful phrases may help you.*

d) *Now do your weather forecast for a partner.*

USEFUL PHRASES

Here is the UK weather forecast for (Monday, 14th April);
It will be (dry, wet, cloudy, …) over (most of the country/…);
There will be (some sun, light[13]/heavy rain) in (the North/South/…);
That's all for now and now back to (Susan).

[1] **Viking** ['vaɪkɪŋ] = Wikinger/-in • [2] **rainstorm** ['reɪnstɔ:m] = starke Regenfälle • [3] **annual average rainfall total** [ˌænjuəl ˌævrɪdʒ 'reɪnfɔ:l ˌtəʊtl] = durchschnittliche Niederschlagsmenge pro Jahr • [4] **atlas** ['ætləs] = Atlas • [5] **relief** [rɪ'li:f] = Relief • [6] **highland** ['haɪlənd] = Hochland- • [7] **lowland** ['ləʊlənd] = Flachland- • [8] **area** ['eərɪə] = Gebiet, Region • [9] **atmosphere** ['ætməsfɪə] = Atmosphäre • [10] **forecast** ['fɔ:kɑ:st] = Vorhersage • [11] **symbol** ['sɪmbl] = Symbol • [12] **Met** [met] = (Abkürzung für) Meteorologie • [13] **light rain** [laɪt 'reɪn] = Nieselregen

The different regions on the weather map

→ Northern Scotland
→ Southern Scotland
→ Northern Ireland
→ Wales
→ North-east England
→ North-west England
→ South-east England
→ South-west England
→ The Midlands

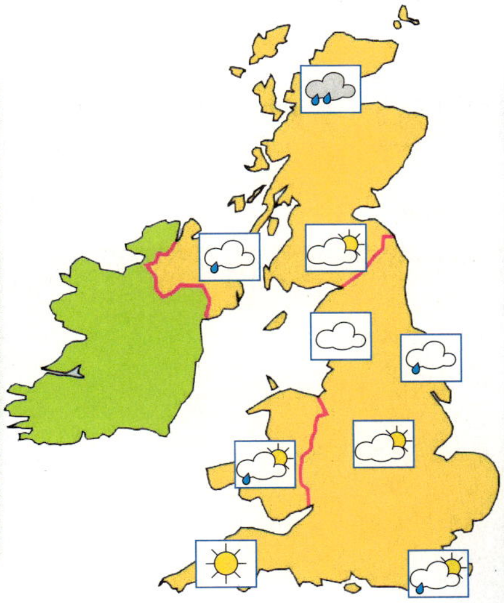

The symbols on the weather map

- sunny intervals
- light rain showers
- light rain
- heavy rain
- cloud / cloudy
- sun / sunny

STEP 4: Give a presentation

PROJECT SKILLS

If you have to prepare a presentation, you first look for important information. Then you must organize the information you have found. The ideas here will help you to present the information clearly.

1. **Start your presentation with an introduction[14].**
   The theme of today's presentation is …
   Firstly we are going to talk about … Secondly … Then …
   Our fourth and final part is …

2. **Now present your information:**
   To begin with, I'd like to look at …
   The next point / idea is …
   Let's have a look at / As you can see on the map …

3. **At the end of your presentation you can summarize[15] the main points and answer questions.**
   Before we finish, we'd like to summarize the main points.
   Well, that brings us to the end of our presentation.
   If you have got any questions, we'll try to answer them.

STEP 5: Do a project: Britain's climate[16]

Climate is the average weather over many years. In the UK the climate is a bit different in every region.

a) *Make groups. Each group looks at one of the five regions on the map.*

b) *Find out about the climate in your group's region. Look at:*
annual rainfall • average temperature • hours of sunshine[17].
(Remember the Project skills you learnt on page 23.)

c) *Now find out about the climate of the region where you live in Germany. Is the UK really wetter? Give a presentation.*

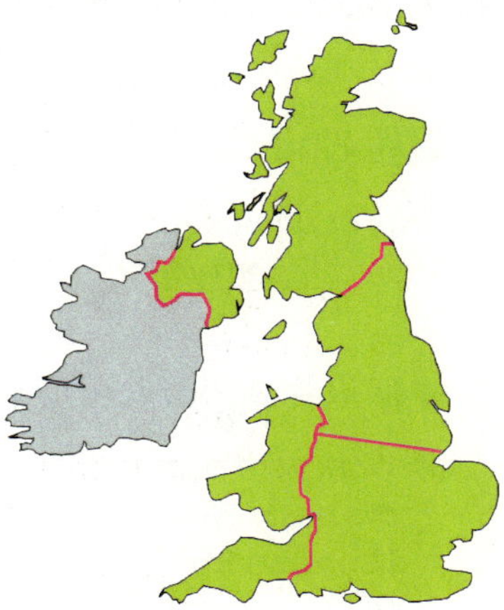

[14] **introduction** [ˌɪntrəˈdʌkʃn] = Einleitung • [15] **(to) summarize** [ˈsʌmraɪz] = zusammenfassen • [16] **climate** [ˈklaɪmət] = Klima • [17] **sunshine** [ˈsʌnʃaɪn] = Sonnenschein

Unit 6 Time to travel

A

B

1 Find headings for the photos

Look at photos A to E. Write down headings for them. Then compare your headings in class.

2 Talk about journeys

a) *Work with a partner. Why did people travel in the past? Why do they travel today? Use ideas from the photos and the texts about famous travellers, and also your own ideas.*

b) *How were journeys in the past different from journeys today? Think of: time, money, transport …*

WB p. 65/1

3 Listening: A trip to Australia

Find out …

1. … why Ryan's father is going to Australia.
2. … what he is not so happy about.
3. … what the journey to Australia was like in the days of Captain Cook.
4. … what Ryan is doing next month.

WB p. 65/2

C

D

E

Famous travellers and journeys:

- Italian *Marco Polo* (1254–1324) travelled through Asia for 24 years! He brought noodles back to Europe from China, and everyone wanted to read the book he wrote about his adventures.
- In 1770 *Captain Cook* discovered the east coast of Australia and took the land for Britain. He also made maps while he was sailing around the world.
- *Charles Darwin's* job on the ship 'Beagle' in the 1830s was to learn about plants and animals in other parts of the world. His new ideas about evolution explained where the different kinds of animals come from.
- In 1930 *Gladys Aylward* travelled from England to China to work as a missionary. When Japan attacked China in 1931 she helped 100 children to walk for 12 days through the mountains to safety.
- The first person on the moon was American *Neil Armstrong*. When he landed there in 1969, he said "That's one small step for a man, one giant leap for mankind."
- Britain's *Ellen MacArthur* loves a challenge! In 2005 she sailed 27,000 miles alone around the world. Her trip took 71 days, a new world record.

4 Your turn: See the world

Which part of the world would you like to visit? Collect photos and show them to the class. Explain why you want to go there. Give three or more reasons.

DID YOU KNOW?

English …

- … is the first language of more than 330 million people.
- … is an official language for another 400 million people – most of them in countries that were British colonies in the past.
- … is learnt by more people around the world than any other language.
- … is used for more than 85 per cent of all Internet messages.

To the ends of the earth

At the shops Ryan sees a girl from his class. She is coming out of a trendy clothes shop.

Ryan: Hi, Jade! Looking for something special you can wear for those boys in France during our school trip?

Jade: Ha ha, very funny! So, what are *you* doing here at the shops?

Ryan: I'm going to buy a new computer game with my birthday money. Ben said it was brilliant. He told me that he had borrowed it from Nick, and –

Jade: From Nick? You aren't talking about *To the ends of the earth*, are you?

Ryan: Yes – Ben said it was the most exciting adventure game he had ever played!

Jade: Did he? Well, Kelly told me that Nick had lent it to her, too.

Ryan: Yes, Ben mentioned that Nick had promised to lend it to someone else.

Jade: She thought it was really disappointing. She said that after a few minutes she had got bored with it and had gone back to the book she was reading.

Ryan: But Ben said I would love the game. He even told me he was going to buy it himself as soon as he could find the money! It isn't cheap … Hm. Now I'm not sure what I should do.

To the ends of the earth is brilliant! You go on an adventure journey and all kinds of scary things happen! It's the most exciting game I've ever played. I borrowed it from Nick. But I had to give it back because he had promised to lend it to someone else. I'm going to buy it myself as soon as I can find the money. If you want my advice, Ryan, get it. You'll love it!

Nick lent me his new computer game *To the ends of the earth*, but it was really disappointing. I usually enjoy computer games. But after a few minutes I got bored with it and went back to the book I'm reading. It's about Ellen MacArthur's world record trip, and it's much better than that game!

1 What do you think?

What should Ryan do now? What advice would you give him, and why?

2 Find the rule

a) *Which words change when Ryan and Jade report what Ben and Kelly said? Make a list.*

b) *How do tenses change when you report what someone said? Can you make a rule?*

direct speech	→	indirect speech
is	→	was
I	→	he
borrowed	→	…

c) *Collect phrases from the text that introduce indirect speech. Which verbs are used? Can you think of more verbs you could use? Be careful: What do you always need with the verb 'tell'?*

Ben said …
He told me …
…

3 An interview with Ellen MacArthur

a) *Kelly heard an interview with Ellen after her world record trip. What does she say to Jade? Use your rules from exercise 2.*

Start: Ellen **told** the reporter **she was** …
She **explained that** … *Go on, please.*

b) *Can you think of any interviews you have heard recently with people you like (sports stars, singers etc.)? What did they say?*

WB p. 66/3

I'm very tired after my trip. • I sailed through some terrible storms, so I didn't get the chance to sleep much. • I feel excited, and can't believe that I've broken the world record. • I'll never forget my welcome home because thousands of people came to see me. • I have no idea what my next challenge will be, and I don't even want to think about it yet. • The first thing I'm going to do is sleep!

4 An e-mail from Ryan's father

What does Ryan tell Ben? Use indirect speech. Look for words on the right to change the words in blue. Why do you need to change these words?

Start: My dad sent an e-mail from Australia last week.
He **said that it was** warm … *Go on, please.*

that day · take · go · two days earlier · the next day · there · that · the day before

WB p. 66/4; 67/5

Dear Ryan,
It's warm but not too hot here, because it's June and the winter is starting. Yesterday I was in the office, but today I've had time for sightseeing. This morning I took a boat round Sydney harbour and under the famous bridge. Tomorrow I'm planning to visit Bondi Beach, but I won't go swimming because two days ago someone saw a shark! I'm glad I remembered to bring a camera – I've got some great photos. One day you'll be able to come to Australia yourself!
Love, Dad

5 Role play: Around the world

a) A: *You are a celebrity on an exciting journey around the world. First make notes about where you are now, what you did last week, what you're going to do tomorrow etc. Then act a phone call to B.*

B: *You are a magazine reporter. Act a phone call to A and ask about his / her journey. Then report to the class what A told you.*

Example: "I interviewed … He / She **said she was** …"

b) *Change roles: B is the star and A is the reporter.*

⟨c)⟩ *At the end, talk about which interview you liked best, and why.*

TIP
When you report what people said, you needn't repeat every word. Just report the important information.

TALKWISE

Read the book, watch the film, play the game

1 What kind of books, films and games are these?

a) *Look at the titles and match them with the words on the right.*

Example: I think *Champion!* is a sports game.

battle game
science fiction film
biography
comedy
love story
action film
car game
thriller
sports game

b) *What other kinds of books, films and computer games are there?* WB p. 68/7

2 Collect phrases that give advice about things

First look for ideas in these two texts. Then think of other phrases you might use. Write your own list of Useful phrases.

"You should read *The Lord of the Rings*! It's a brilliant story – the best book I've ever read. It's very long, but it's really exciting. I'd recommend it to anyone. I'm sure you'd love it, too."

"If I were you, I wouldn't watch that old film about Gladys Aylward. You'll just fall asleep! Although there's some action in it, it's very old-fashioned. If you want my advice, forget it. Choose a different DVD."

3 What can you ask?

When people tell you about books, films or games, you often want to know more. Collect ideas for questions. Some questions can go in more than one group.

Books	Films	Computer games
What's it about?	What kind of film is it?	What do you have to do?
Is it easy to read?	Who's in it?	Is it exciting?
...	...	...

WB p. 68/8

4 Your turn: What would you recommend?

Talk in groups about books, films and computer games you know.

- *Say which ones you would or wouldn't recommend, and explain why.*
- *Try to find out more about the things your friends mention.*
  (Use your Useful phrases and questions from exercises 2 and 3.)

Emergency on the motorway

"I'm reporting from the M20 where there has been an accident between a lorry and a coach. The facts are not clear yet. A police officer is still asking both drivers what happened. But I have learnt that the coach was bringing pupils back from a school trip to France and that the lorry is carrying dangerous chemicals. After the accident the lorry driver warned everyone to get off the coach fast and run away. A few minutes ago two girls came out of a field behind me and asked if it was safe to come back. They are shocked, but say they are OK.

I can't give you much more information at the moment. All the emergency services are here, and there are two ambulances. I asked a paramedic whether anyone needed to go to hospital, but she said she didn't know yet. The firefighters have told people not to go near the lorry. They have closed the area around it and are checking whether there is a problem with the chemicals. Since the accident happened, lots of cars have stopped. Some people just want to look, while others want to know how they can help. But this is making the situation worse, so now police officers are advising people not to stop and are telling everyone to get back into their cars and leave."

1 What can you remember?

Close your books. What has happened on the M20? Describe what is happening now.

2 Report the police officer's words

a) *Two boys in a car stop on the M20. One of them jumps out, talks to a police officer, and then gets back into the car. What does he tell his friend?*

"That police officer **says we have to** leave again …
She says …"

Go on, please.

b) *Later the boys meet their girlfriends. How do they report the police officer's words to them?*

Start: "When we stopped, a police officer **told us we had to** leave …
She said that …" WB p. 69/9

TIP

When you report words right away, you often use the present tense to introduce indirect speech. Then the tenses of the verbs you report don't change.

Compare: She says we **have** to leave.
She said we **had** to leave.

(→ G 26)

3 What did the police officer ask?

The lorry driver phones his boss. How does he report what the police officer asked?

Example: "What do you remember?"
→ She **asked what I remembered.**

TIP
When you make indirect questions:
1. Keep the question word ('what', etc.).
2. Use normal word order (S-V-O).
3. Use normal verb forms (not question forms, so you don't need 'do / does / did').

(→ G 27)

1. How did the accident happen?
2. How far were you behind the coach?
3. Why didn't you see the brake lights?
4. What are you carrying on the lorry?
5. Where have you come from?
6. When did you start your journey?
7. How fast do you usually drive?
8. When was your last break?

4 What did the paramedic want to know?

When Ryan gets home, he tells his parents what a paramedic asked. What does he say?

TIP
When you report a question without a question word, use 'if' or 'whether'.

(→ G 27)

Start: She **asked if I was** OK. She **wanted to know whether** …
Go on, please.

Are you OK? • Does anything hurt? • Can you remember the accident? • Did you get a shock? • Did you hit your head? • Have you got a headache? • Do you feel sick? • Has anyone given you something to drink? • Do you want to sit in the ambulance? • (*Any more ideas for questions?*)

WB p. 69/10

5 Indirect commands

a) *Look again at the text on page 97. Find the sentences that report these commands.*

1. Lorry driver: Get off the coach fast and run away!
2. Firefighters: Don't go near the lorry.
3. Police officers: Please get back into your cars and leave.

GRAMMAR
indirect commands

	verb	object	(not) to + infinitive
She	asked	me	to drive.
He	told	them	not to worry.

(→ G 28)

b) *Put the indirect commands from a) into German. Can you always use the infinitive in German, too?*

c) *What did people tell Ben to do before the school trip to France?*

ask tell warn advise

Example: Teacher: Practise your French. Don't worry too much about mistakes.
→ His teacher **advised him to practise** his French.
But she **told him not to worry** too much about mistakes.

1. Mother: Watch out for traffic on the right. Don't have an accident in France!
2. Father: Don't lose your passport. Keep it somewhere safe. Look after your money, too.
3. Sister: Don't behave like an idiot with Ryan! Oh, and bring me a nice present back.
4. Grandma: Take some nice photos, Ben. Have fun – and enjoy your trip!

WB p. 69/11

6 Listening: Emergency calls

a) *Listen to the dialogues. Which picture is correct: A or B?*

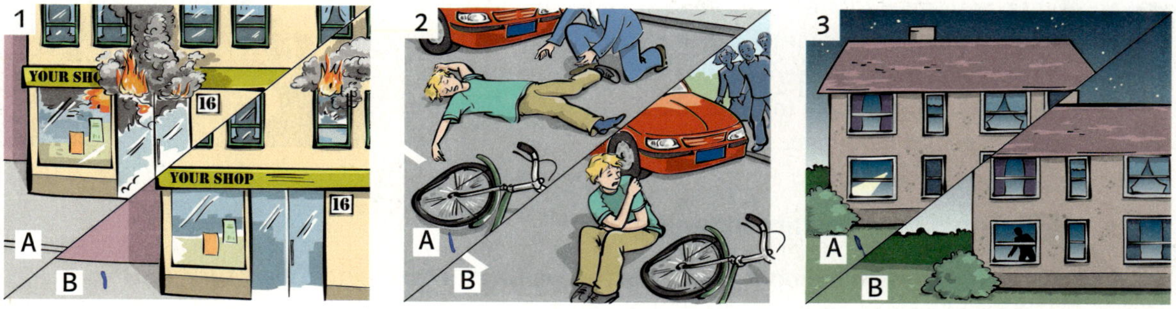

b) *Listen again. Who makes the best emergency call?*
Why do you think it is the best one?

WB p. 70/12

7 How to: Get help in an emergency

IN AN EMERGENCY
CALL **999** OR **112**
Fire Police Ambulance

- Say which service you need.
- Say where you are calling from.
- Give the important facts.
- Be ready to answer questions.
- Try to stay calm and speak clearly.

USEFUL PHRASES

The police / fire / ambulance service, please!
I'm calling from …
There has been / I've just seen an accident.
There's a fire / a burglar in / at …
A man / child … is hurt / trapped.
It looks really bad / dangerous / …
Sorry, I don't know / can't tell you that.

Practise emergency calls with a partner. Use your own ideas for the situations.

WB p. 70/13

8 Revision: Questions with prepositions

Who / What …

take a photo of
have problems with
spend money on
look for
talk to
laugh about

Take turns to ask and answer questions about Ben in France. Use the phrases on the right for the questions. Think of your own answers.

Start: 1. What is Ben having problems with?
– He's having problems with the French menu …

WB p. 70/14

9 Your turn: Good advice for a trip

Have people ever given you advice for a trip? What advice was it, and was it useful?

SPEAKING SKILLS

Small talk

When you travel to other countries, it's good if you can talk easily to people you meet. English is useful in many parts of the world because there are so many Commonwealth countries. Most people in these places speak English as a first or second language.

1 Show that you are listening

a) *The speakers on the right meet at an airport in South Africa. How do they show they are listening to what the other person says? Collect the words and phrases they use.*

Oh, I see.
...

A: Are you waiting for the flight to New York, too?
B: No, Toronto. I'm on my way home there.
A: Oh, I see. So you've been on holiday here, eh?
B: Yes, it was a prize I won in a competition.
A: Really? How fantastic! I expect you enjoyed it.
B: It was great. You say you're flying to New York, right?
A: Yes, but my flight is an hour late.
B: Oh no! It's so annoying when that happens, isn't it?
A: Yes, I know. But you just have to sit and wait, don't you?
B: Exactly. Oh, I have to go now. Well, nice to talk to you.
A: And you. Bye. Have a nice flight.

b) *Show that you are listening to these people. The words and phrases from a) can help.*

1. My passport was stolen.
2. I'm on a world trip.
3. I've been on a course here.
4. This café is expensive, isn't it?
5. I can speak ten languages.
6. There aren't enough check-in desks.

WB p. 71/15

2 Show that you are happy to talk

Look at the dialogue in exercise 1 again. How do the speakers show that they are happy to talk and that they want the conversation to continue? What signals do they use?

Example: A asks why B has been in South Africa.

3 Listening: Fillers

a) *When you talk, you often use extra words and phrases ('fillers') you wouldn't use when you write. Listen to the conversation and make a list.*

b) *Explain why people use phrases like this.*

4 A game: Small talk champion

Work with a partner. Imagine you meet in another part of the world. Choose a situation, then act a conversation and talk for as long as you can. The pair that talks the longest wins the game.

Ideas for situations:

- "Is this your first trip to the USA?"
- "It's very hot in Australia, isn't it?"
- "Excuse me. Is anyone sitting here?"
- "Which flight are you waiting for?"
- "…"

WB p. 71/16

My big adventure

1 Before you read

What might an adventure story be about? Collect ideas.

pirates? a dangerous storm? a trip to the moon? ...?

Every year there is a competition for schools in Commonwealth countries. This year the competition is: Write an adventure about yourself and the characters of a favourite book. This is what Jade wrote:

I felt so excited when we started to move! This was my big adventure. Three thousand, seven hundred and eighty-six miles, all the way from San Francisco to New York. The railway had been completed in 1869, and I had always wanted to make the journey. Now, three years later, I was a stewardess on the train!

We left the station at six o'clock in the evening. There were all kinds of passengers in the carriage I was looking after. One group of three looked especially interesting. While I was turning the seats into beds for the night, I talked to the younger of the two men in the group. He told me that his name was Passepartout and that he was French. He was the servant of the other man, Phileas Fogg, a rich Londoner. The beautiful young woman with them was Aouda, a princess whose life they had saved in India.

India! Maybe my big adventure wasn't as big as I had thought ...

The next morning we were in Nevada, and for a long time the railway track followed a river. Then the landscape changed, and we travelled over great prairies. Far away a long line of high mountains came into view.

Suddenly the train slowed down and stopped. There was a strong smell. Then a loud bellow. I almost jumped out of my skin! What was it?

Aouda stood up and looked out of the window. "Buffalo!" she cried. "Ten thousand of them! They're crossing the track."

"Oh no! We don't want any delays. Drive the train through those cows!" shouted Passepartout. Then he explained to me, "Mr Fogg has made a bet that he can travel around the world in eighty days. We mustn't arrive late in New York because the ship to England leaves on the same day. If we aren't back in London on the twenty-first of December, he'll lose twenty thousand pounds!"

The train tried to push the buffalo out of the way, but there were too many of them.

We had to wait until they had all gone, and it was dark before we were able to continue.

After Nevada came Utah, and then on the third day Wyoming, with the tall Rocky Mountains in front of us. Slowly we started to climb. Passepartout was worried that we might lose more time, but the train carried us over the mountains without any more delays.

"Now you can relax," I told him.

I had spoken too soon.

The train stopped again, although it was still a mile to the next station at Medicine Bow. A man had come on foot from there. He wanted to warn us not to cross the bridge over the river. It was not safe for a heavy train, he said.

Passepartout gasped. But it was not only Mr Fogg who had a problem. All the passengers wanted to go to New York. But how could they get there if the train couldn't cross the bridge?

The train driver was not ready to give up easily. "I think that if we go fast enough, we'll be OK," he said.

The man from Medicine Bow thought this was crazy. Did we all want to risk our lives? Of course not. But most of the passengers wanted to take the chance.

We went back to our seats. A minute later there was a loud whistle. We began to move. Fast, then faster. Everything began to shake. I was shaking, too. It felt like the train was going to leave the track!

Eighty miles an hour. Ninety. A hundred. Would we make it?

I didn't see the bridge. We flew over it. Then – crash! The bridge fell into the river. But we were already on the other side.

After the drama at the bridge I thought that we would be able to complete our journey to New York without any more trouble.

I was wrong!

Suddenly we heard loud bangs and screams from other parts of the train. A second later there were more bangs, and a window near me broke. Now people in our carriage started to scream, too. Hundreds of Sioux were attacking us! They were riding their horses next to the train. I could see their frightening faces.

Mr Fogg quickly took three guns out of his bag, one for himself and the other two for Passepartout and Aouda. The Sioux were shooting into the carriage, and we all had to fight for our lives. I ran and got a gun, too.

We fought hard. The smell of the guns burned my nose, and I could taste smoke in my mouth. Some of the Sioux were hit and fell from their horses. One or two passengers were also hit.

The train was going as fast as it could, but that was no problem for the Sioux. One of them made a giant leap from his horse onto the train. He threw open the door of the carriage and ran in with a knife in his hand.

The passenger nearest the door was Mr Fogg. But he was still shooting out of one of the windows, so he didn't see the danger.

Bang! I shot and the Sioux fell. I had saved Mr Fogg's life.

But the Sioux wasn't dead.

He threw the knife and it hit me. I felt the shock and sank to my knees. For a moment I saw stars in front of my eyes. Then everything was dark. No more pain. Nothing.

My story has to end here. I'm sorry, but I can't tell you any more.

Did the other people on the train survive? Did Mr Fogg get to London on time and win his bet? If you want to know the answers, you'll have to find out what famous book I got my ideas from …

2 Talk about the end of the story

a) *What happens at the end of the story? Do you think this is a good way to end or not? Say why.*

⟨b)⟩ *Can you answer Jade's questions at the end of the story?*

WB p. 72/17

3 ⟨Compare then with now⟩

a) *What problems are there on the journey in the story? Could these problems happen on the same train journey today?*

b) *What different problems might there be now? What nice things might be missing?*

4 Write and act a dialogue

Work with lines 58 to 75. The questions on the right can help you. You can start:

Man on foot: I've come from … You can't …
Passepartout: Oh no! This is …
Passenger: …

- What does the man on foot say?
- What does Passepartout think?
- What do you think the other passengers say?
- What does the train driver think?
- What do they all decide to do in the end?

WB p. 72/18

5 Writing texts: Make a story more interesting

a) *It can make a story more interesting if you describe what people can see, hear, smell, feel or taste. Look for phrases like this in Jade's story.*

Examples: a long line of high mountains *(line 26)* – a loud bellow *(line 30)*

b) *There are lots of different ways to make a story more exciting. Match the ideas in the box with the examples on the right. Maybe you can find more examples in the story.*

- Try to make the reader interested. Show that something else is going to happen.
- Show that the characters are nervous.
- Give the reader a shock. Go suddenly to a dangerous situation.
- Describe the action in short sentences.
- Use words that describe sounds.

We began to move. Fast, then faster. *(line 77)*

I had spoken too soon. *(line 57)*

But the Sioux wasn't dead. *(line 118)*

Crash! *(line 84)*

I almost jumped out of my skin! *(line 30)*

c) *Write your own adventure. Imagine yourself in a scene from a book or film you know. Look again at the ideas in a) and b), and try to use interesting and exciting words. Collect new words you find interesting for your 'personal vocabulary' and put them in your folder.*

WB p. 72/19

6 ⟨A song: Hit me with your rhythm stick⟩

In the desert of Sudan
And the gardens of Japan,
From Milan to Yucatan
Every woman, every man.

Hit me with your rhythm stick,
Hit me, hit me,
Je t'adore, ich liebe dich,
Hit me, hit me, hit me.

In the wilds of Borneo
And the vineyards of Bordeaux,
Eskimo, Arapaho
Move their body to and fro.

1 Guess new words

a) *Read the tips about how to guess new words. Then guess what the words in blue mean. Say which tip(s) helped you.*

TIP
Do you know another word from the same word family?
Does the context help you?
Is the word like one you know in another language?
(e.g. German, French)

Two adults and one child to Bristol, please. Is a return ticket cheaper than two singles?

My name is Ben Brown. I have a reservation for a room. My travel agency booked it for me.

We'd like to cook for ourselves, so we're looking for a self-catering flat. We don't want to be more than a short distance from the beach.

b) *Make dialogues for the situations in a). Take turns to play the different roles. Think of different things the people might ask or say.*

2 Listening: Sounds and spelling

a) *Sometimes two words with different spellings and different meanings have exactly the same sound.* *Example:* [hɪə] Can you **hear** me? Come **here**, please.

Listen and say which spelling is correct.

1. [rəʊd] a) road b) rode
2. [feə] a) fair b) fare
3. [ˈweðə] a) whether b) weather
4. [breɪk] a) brake b) break
5. [bɔːd] a) bored b) board
6. [wiːk] a) weak b) week

b) *Can you find two different spellings for these sounds?*

1. [siː] 2. [ðeə] 3. [nəʊ] 4. [miːt] 5. [wʊd]

WB p. 73/21

3 Mixed bag: Complete the missing words

The Smiths had to get to the a_____t before they could fly to America. They decided not to d___e there because it would be very expensive to p__k the car for two weeks. So they decided to use the r_____y and go by train. They only expected the j_____y to t__e forty-five minutes. But the train d____r got a phone call to w__n him about some cows on the t___k. Of course he did not want to have an a______t, so he had to s__w down and stop. There was a long d___y while the cows were taken away, and so the train was not on t__e. The Smiths thought they would a____e too l__e. But when they got to the check-in d__k they found out that their f____t was l__e, too. All the other p________s on the p___e found this very a_____g – but not the Smiths!

WB p. 73/22

NOW YOU CAN

- ✓ Talk about journeys.
- ✓ Report what people said or asked.
- ✓ Talk about different kinds of books, films and games.
- ✓ Use indirect commands.
- ✓ Get help in an emergency.
- ✓ Talk to people you meet on journeys .

1 Report a call from France

When Ryan called home from France his sister answered the phone. How does she tell her mother what Ryan said or asked?

Start: He said he …
He told me that …

WB p. 74/23

I arrived in Toulouse OK. Robert and his family are very nice. I haven't had time to see much yet. But I'm sure I'm going to love my time in France. … By the way, did Manchester United win yesterday? – I hope I'll get tickets for a game here tomorrow. … Have you heard from Dad? Is he enjoying his trip? … Oh, I must go now. Robert wants me. I'll call again soon. Maybe I can speak to Mum then. Bye!

2 Complete the dialogues at the airport

Complete what the second speakers say with indirect commands.

tell / not wear them – ask / get cheese – advise / get here early – remind / pack it – tell / bring yours – warn / not lose it

1. "I don't think I put my swimsuit in my bag." – "Are you sure? I reminded you to …"
2. "You won't be happy to hear this – but I can't find my passport." – "Oh no! I …"
3. "Here you are. A nice chicken sandwich." – "You didn't listen! I …"
4. "You've got your mobile with you, haven't you?" – "No. I …"
5. "Hm. I don't think it was a good idea to travel in white jeans." – "I know. I …"
6. "Look at that long queue!" – "Well, our friends …"

3 Improve the conversation

Write this conversation again. Show that the speakers are listening to the other person and want the conversation to continue.

A: I'm from Japan. This is my first time in London.
B: I'm Italian. There's a lot to see here.
A: It's difficult to decide which place you should visit first!
B: I want to go on the London Eye.
A: That's next to the Thames.
B: I've heard it's very expensive.
A: I'm sure there's a great view from the top.

4 Your turn: What do you think of Green Line 3?

In groups of 3 – 4 talk about which units you found interesting or not so interesting, and which texts you enjoyed or didn't enjoy. Make a list of your ideas and try to explain your opinions.

WB p. 74/24

⟨Treasure Island⟩

"Treasure Island", a book about pirates, sailing and adventure, was written by Robert Louis Stevenson and takes place[1] in the 18th century. A boy, Jim Hawkins, tells us the story. His mother and father run[2] the 'Admiral Benbow' inn[3] in Bristol. One day an old captain arrives with his sea-chest[4] and stays at the inn. This man drinks too much rum[5]. That is when he sings this song:

"Fifteen men on the dead man's chest – yo-ho-ho-, and a bottle of rum!
Drink[6] and the devil had done for the rest[7] – yo-ho-ho-, and a bottle of rum!"

One day a blind[8] beggar[9] comes to the inn and gives the captain a piece of paper with a black spot[10] and leaves. This is the sign among pirates that the person will be killed. The captain is very frightened and dies. What should Jim do now?

My mother and I knew that we were in a terrible situation. Some of the captain's money in his sea-chest belonged[11] to us because he hadn't paid for his room, but surely the blind beggar wouldn't give us any money. I couldn't go to find help and leave my mother alone in the house. And we couldn't stay in the house – everything we heard frightened[12] us. We were afraid that the awful blind beggar was still near and would come back to the inn again. We decided to go together to our neighbours and ask for help.

It was foggy when we left the inn. Sometimes we stopped and listened for strange sounds, but we didn't hear any. Soon we reached our neighbours' house and were happy to see the yellow candle-light in their doors and windows. But we soon found out that that was the best help we would get from them. None of the neighbours wanted to come back with us to the 'Admiral Benbow'. Some of the men had seen strangers[13] on the road. They were frightened to death of anyone who might be the captain's comrade[14].

Then my mother became angry and said: "I will not lose money that belongs to my fatherless boy." My father had died a day

before the captain. "If you are all afraid, Jim and I aren't. Back we will go, the way we came – with no thanks to you chicken-hearted[15] men. We'll have that sea-chest open if we die for it."

Of course I went with my mother. The full moon was rising[16] so we tried to stay hidden behind the bushes[17], and moved quickly and quietly. We were glad when we reached the 'Admiral Benbow' and locked the door behind us.

My mother got a candle. I drew[18] the curtains and we went into the room where the dead captain was. I had to find the key[19] to the sea-chest. I went down on my knees and found a piece of paper with a black spot on one side. On the other side of the paper were the words: 'You have until ten tonight.'

[1] **(to) take place** [teɪk 'pleɪs] = spielen • [2] **(to) run** [rʌn] = betreiben • [3] **inn** [ɪn] = Gasthaus • [4] **sea-chest** ['si: tʃest] = Seemannskiste • [5] **rum** [rʌm] = Rum • [6] **drink and the devil** [drɪŋk‿and ðə 'devl] = Alkohol und der Teufel • [7] **(to) do for the rest** [du: fə ðə 'rest] = jmdm. den Rest geben • [8] **blind** [blaɪnd] = blind • [9] **beggar** ['begə] = Bettler • [10] **spot** [spɒt] = Fleck, Punkt • [11] **(to) belong to sb** [bɪ'lɒŋ tə] = jmdm. gehören • [12] **(to) frighten** ['fraɪtn] = ängstigen, erschrecken • [13] **stranger** ['streɪndʒə] = Fremde/-r • [14] **comrade** ['kɒmreɪd] = Kamerad • [15] **chicken-hearted** ['tʃɪkn,hɑ:tɪd] = feige, ängstlich • [16] **(to) rise** [raɪz] = aufgehen • [17] **bush** [bʊʃ] = Busch • [18] **(to) draw** [drɔ:] *hier:* zuziehen • [19] **key** [ki:] = Schlüssel

"He had until ten, mother," said I; and just as I said it, our old clock struck[20]. This frightened us, but the news was good. It was only six.

"Now, Jim," she said, "that key." I felt in all his pockets, but I didn't find anything. My mother suggested his neck. I opened his shirt at the neck and there was the key on a string[21]. I cut[22] the string with the captain's knife and my mother unlocked[23] the sea-chest, and when she opened it, we smellt tobacco. On the very top were some very good clothes. Under that we found tobacco, some pistols[24], some silver[25] and an old Spanish watch. At the very bottom we found a bundle[26] tied up[27] in cloth[28], and a bag of coins.

"I'll take only the money that belongs to us and no more," my mother promised. She wanted to show that she was an honest[29] woman.

I suddenly put my hand on her arm because I heard in the quiet, cold air a sound that brought my heart into my mouth – the tap-tapping of the blind man's stick on the frozen road. It came closer and closer. We sat still. The stick hit the inn door and the beggar tried to open the door. It was quiet for a long time and then the tapping started again. The beggar was walking away.

"Mother," said I, "take everything and let's go. I'm sure he'll come back and not alone."

But my mother, even though she was frightened, wouldn't take more money than what belonged to her and wouldn't be happy with less. "It's not yet seven," she said. "We've still got time."

She was still arguing[30] with me when we heard a little whistle from the hill. That was enough, and more than enough, for both of us.

"I'll take what I have," she said and jumped to her feet.

"And I'll take this to make it fair," said I and picked up the cloth bundle.

We left the candle upstairs, felt our way down the steps, opened the door and ran away. It was not a moment too soon. The fog was rising and the moon was shining on the hills. We heard footsteps[31] and saw a light that went up and down.

"My dear," said my mother suddenly, "take the money and run. I'm going to faint[32]."

This was the end for both of us. Our neighbours were scared and my mother was too honest and greedy[33] at the same time! We stopped at a little bridge and I helped my mother to the edge[34] of the bank[35]. There she fell on my shoulder. I don't know how I did it, but I pulled[36] her down the bank and a bit under the bridge. I couldn't hide her better because the bridge was not high enough. So we had to stay there – my mother almost out in the open[37] and both of us so close to the inn that we could hear everything.

There was a treasure map in the cloth bundle. Jim sailed away to find the treasure – but he wasn't the only one. You can read the rest of the story in the "Easy Reader" book: "Treasure Island".

[20] **(to) strike** [straɪk] = schlagen (Uhr) • [21] **string** [strɪŋ] = Schnur • [22] **(to) cut** [kʌt] = (durch)schneiden, durchtrennen • [23] **(to) unlock** [ʌn'lɒk] = aufschließen • [24] **pistol** ['pɪstl] = Pistole • [25] **silver** ['sɪlvə] = Silber • [26] **bundle** ['bʌndl] = Bündel • [27] **(to) tie up** [taɪ 'ʌp] = festbinden, festschnüren • [28] **cloth** [klɒθ] = Tuch, Stoff • [29] **honest** ['ɒnɪst] = ehrlich, aufrichtig • [30] **(to) argue** ['ɑːgjuː] = sich streiten • [31] **footstep** ['fʊtstep] = Schritt • [32] **(to) faint** [feɪnt] = ohnmächtig werden • [33] **greedy** ['griːdi] = habgierig • [34] **edge** [edʒ] = Rand • [35] **bank** [bæŋk] = Ufer • [36] **(to) pull** [pʊl] = ziehen • [37] **out in the open** [aʊt‿ɪn ði‿'əʊpn] = im Freien

⟨Revision for tests⟩ Unit 5–6

1 Mixed bag: From Station Road to Hollywood

Max Finley became a TV [1] when he [2] given the role of Kevin in the daily [3] *Station Road*. Before that he [4] been seen in [5] for cars and mobile phones. After a year of *Station Road* Max decided that he wanted to [6] in films. His agent thought Max [7] too young for big film roles, [8] Max's friends told him not [9] give up. Last month a casting director asked Max [10] he [11] interested in a role in an American action film. Max was [12] the role of the hero. Max was [13] the script last week, and now the [14] has just [15] signed. Max has [16] told reporters where he [17] give his next interview: in Hollywood!

2 Eric Liddell – athlete and missionary

Eric Liddell was born in 1902 in China, where his Scottish parents worked as missionaries. Look at the pictures and write about his life. Remember to use connecting words and interesting vocabulary, and say what people see, feel etc.

3 Mediation: There's been an accident

A British police officer wants to ask a German tourist some questions, but the man doesn't speak much English. Help the police officer (A) and the tourist (B) to speak to each other.

A: Are you hurt?
You: Sind Sie … ?
B: Nein – ich hatte nur einen Schock.
You: He isn't … He …
A: Did you see what happened?
B: Nicht wirklich. Aber es sah schlimm aus!
A: Was the car driving very fast?
B: Es tut mir leid; das kann ich Ihnen nicht sagen. Ist jemand verletzt worden?
A: Yes. The driver of the car has been taken to hospital in an ambulance.
B: Oh – mir ist schlecht.
A: I'll ask a paramedic to look after you.
B: Vielen Dank.

4 Listening: Which film is right for Julie?

Read about Julie (14). Then listen and say which film is right for her: 1, 2 or 3?

Fave hobby: Taking photos
Big hope: To travel to other countries

Likes: Real adventure stories, History (sometimes), Her own website

Hates: Silly love stories, Brother's computer games

5 Who makes our footballs?

a) ***Before you read:*** *What jobs do children in Germany do? How much do they earn? Can jobs be a problem for children? Why or why not? Write answers in 8–10 sentences.*

"I'm twelve years old, and I live in a small town in Pakistan. My family is poor. My mother is very ill, and my father had to give up his job in the football factory to look after us. A few years ago I was a football stitcher[1], too. The work was hard, and I was too tired for school. I was given twenty rupees[2] for each ball, and I usually made two balls a day. But children aren't allowed to work in those factories any longer. Now I go to school every day. The classroom is always very full, but I try to sit near the front. I want to learn quickly. Maybe I'll be able to read soon! I'm sad that I can't earn money for the family, but my father goes back to work next month – I can help my mother now. I'll get a better job one day, when I can read and write."

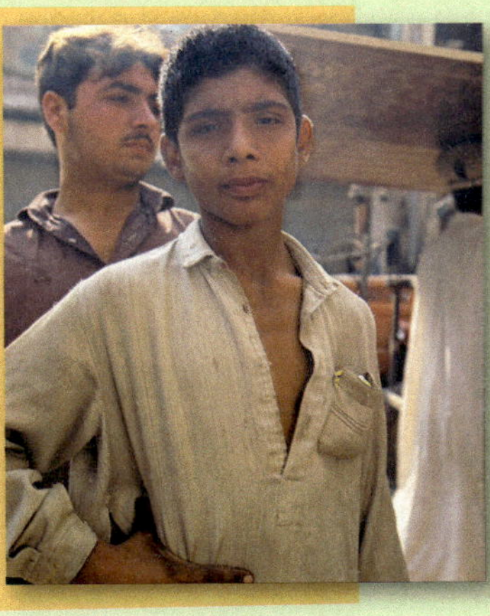

Pakistan
- 166 million people (more than Russia!)
- 70 % live in small towns or villages
- 54 % (or less) can read and write
- Only half of the children go to school
- About 20 % of the children go to work
- 68 rupees = 1 euro

The football industry – some facts

More than half the world's footballs are made in one region of Pakistan.

Children under 14 are not allowed to work in the Pakistan football industry.

A ball is made from 32 pieces.

A factory worker earns 40 rupees for a ball.

Many clubs in Europe buy only fair-trade[3] footballs.

b) ***Writing texts:*** *A report about football stitchers in Pakistan for your school newspaper.*

1. Decide which information from the texts is useful for your report. (What is interesting? Are any of the facts about Pakistan or the football industry linked to the boy's personal situation? If they are, can you say why?)
2. Make notes about what you want to say in each part of your report.
3. Write your report. Then read it again and try to improve it. (Remember the Writing skills you learned on page 85 in Unit 5).
4. Think of a heading for your report.

[1] **football stitcher** ['fʊtbɔ:l ˌstɪtʃə] = Fußballnäher • [2] **rupee** [ru:'pi:] = Rupie *(indische Währung)* •
[3] **fair-trade** [ˌfeə 'treɪd] = Fairer Handel

Mediation

MEDIATION SKILLS

Wenn du die Aufgabe erhältst, englische Texte oder Teile davon sinngemäß ins Deutsche zu übertragen, sieht das auf den ersten Blick häufig kompliziert aus. Es ist aber gar nicht schwer, wenn du folgende Arbeitsschritte beachtest:

1. Überlege, welche Informationen wichtig sind und notiere dir Stichpunkte.
2. Überlege, ob du dafür die deutschen Vokabeln kennst, oder wie man gegebenenfalls denselben Sachverhalt umschreiben könnte. Versuche nicht gleich Wort für Wort zu übersetzen.
3. Denke an die richtige englische Satzstellung.
4. Arbeite mit einfachen, kurzen Sätzen. Lass alles Unwichtige weg.
5. Ganz wichtige fehlende Wörter kannst du im Wörterbuch nachschlagen.

UNIT 1 American Football

Dein Bruder Jan ist ganz verrückt nach American Football. Er spielt mit seinen Freunden schon seit Jahren in einer „normalen“ Fußballmannschaft, möchte mit ihnen aber nun American Football ausprobieren – vielleicht kommen die Freunde auch auf den Geschmack! Im Internet habt ihr eine Website gefunden, die die Sportart zusammenfasst. Das wird deinem Bruder helfen, seinen Teamkameraden nach dem nächsten Fußballspiel einiges über diese Sportart zu erklären – aber auf Deutsch, da einige in der Mannschaft nicht so gut Englisch können.

AMERICAN FOOTBALL

Hi, I'm Justin Walden from Manchester in the UK. I'm 16, and I'm a huge fan of American football. I play in a team here in Manchester. Over the years, many people have told me they just don't understand American football. So I thought I could build a website where my friends – or anyone else who's interested! – can learn a bit about my favourite sport.

A FEW BASICS

- ★ **First,** let's not forget that Americans don't call their sport 'American football'; it's just 'football'. They call our football here in Europe 'soccer', like many people in the UK, too.
- ★ **Number of players:** An American football team has 11 players on each side, so that's like our football, too.
- ★ **The field:** A football field is just a bit bigger than a soccer field: 100 'yards' (91.44 metres), and it has two halves. But that's where the similarities with our kind of football end …
- ★ **Game time:** A game of American football is only 60 minutes. There are four 15-minute 'quarters', with a half-time of only 12 minutes. Our soccer is a 90-minute game, of course, with a half-time of 15 minutes.
- ★ **The ball:** The **'ball'** isn't really a ball, when you think about it. It's oval-shaped.

A FEW RULES

- ★ **Aim of game:** The main aim of the game is to get a member of your team into the other team's **'end zone'** (the part of the field behind the goal posts) with the ball in his hands or under his arm. But it isn't easy to get to the end zone: There are 11 very big guys from the other team who will do anything to stop you!
- ★ **Point system:** When a player gets into the other team's end zone with the ball, the player scores a **'touchdown'** (6 points). Directly after a touchdown, his team can score one extra point if the team's **'kicker'** is able to kick the football through the goalposts. (The kicker can also score three points for a **'field goal'** at any time in the game.)
- ★ **Important playing positions:** There are lots of different positions in American football, but let's just talk about the most important ones:
  a) The **'quarterback'** is always the star of any football team. He's a player on the attacking side, and he's the one who throws the ball to the other players, who try to get it into the end zone.
  b) The person who usually catches the ball is the **'wide-receiver'**. The fastest way for your team to get into the other team's end zone is for the quarterback to throw the football as far as he can to the wide-receiver. This way, your players needn't fight through the line of the other team's players.
- ★ Oh, and let's not forget the **cheerleaders!** NO football game is complete without cheerleaders on the sidelines! They cheer and dance for their team – and they look nice, too. (Well, sometimes …)

Lies dir die Football-Übersicht aus dem Internet durch. Hilf deinem kleinen Bruder Jan, eine kurze Zusammenfassung der Sportart für seine Freunde zu erstellen. Notiere dir nur die wichtigsten Informationen zu den Grundlagen des Spiels und zu den Hauptregeln. Du musst nicht jedes Wort verstehen.

UNIT 2 Einen Besuch zum Tower of London planen

Deine Klasse plant eine Reise nach London. Jeder in der Klasse übernimmt eine Aufgabe für die Organisation der Reise. Du sollst den Besuch im Tower of London planen. Dein Lehrer hat dir diese Broschüre gegeben. Ihr habt vor, am Dienstag, den 4. April, um 17.00 Uhr dort zu sein. Bevor du die Eintrittskarten für alle 25 Schüler und zwei Lehrer bestellst, stellst du fest, dass du noch Fragen hast, die weder die Broschüre noch der Webauftritt des Towers beantworten können.

THE TOWER OF LONDON
Planning your visit

Opening hours
1 March–31 October
Tues–Sat: 09.00–18.00
Sun–Mon: 10.00–18.00
Last admission: 17.00
1 November–29 February
Tues–Sat: 09.00–17.00
Sun–Mon: 10.00–17.00
Last admission: 16.00

Admission charges
Adults: £14.50
Students (with ID) and senior citizens (60+): £10.50
Children 5–16: £9.50
(Children under 5: Free)
Family ticket: £37.50
(up to 2 adults and 3 children)
Group discount (15 or more):
Adults £13.00, children £8.55
Information:
booking.confirmations@hrp.org.uk

Groups should not join the main queue. There is a special group ticket office where you can collect your tickets. Then just follow the signs to the group entrance. All coach drivers and Blue Badge Guides bringing groups to the Tower are admitted free of charge.

Stelle in einer E-Mail deine Fragen an das Informationsbüro des Tower of London:

- Beginne deine E-Mail mit einer passenden Anrede.
- Erkläre, wer ihr seid, und dass ihr in sechs Wochen in London sein werdet.
  1. Frage: Muss man die Eintrittskarten jetzt schon bezahlen? Wenn ja, wie?
  2. Frage: Wo genau bekommt man die reservierten Karten?
  3. Frage: Du schreibst, an welchem Tag und zu welcher Uhrzeit ihr euren Besuch im Tower geplant habt, dass euer Terminplan aber sehr eng ist. Du weißt, dass an Dienstagen im April der letzte Einlass um 17.00 Uhr ist. Ihr habt eine Reservierung für das London Eye für 14.00 Uhr und ihr seid sicher, dass ihr rechtzeitig um 17.00 Uhr beim Tower sein werdet. Falls ihr aber doch etwas zu spät kommt, werdet ihr trotzdem noch hineingelassen?
  4. Frage: Du möchtest wissen, was ein 'Blue Badge Guide' ist; das hast du in der Broschüre gesehen.
- Du bedankst dich für die Auskünfte und verabschiedest dich.

UNIT 2 Eine Unterhaltung im V&A

Du bist in London auf einer Sprachschule. Nach dem Unterricht gehst du mit einer deutschen Freundin, Janine, die ebenfalls Sprachschülerin ist, ins berühmte Victoria and Albert Museum – „the V and A". Janine will die historischen Kostüme dort sehen. In der Kostümabteilung bleibt ihr vor einem besonders prächtigen Kleid stehen. Eine junge britische Modestudentin, Ruby, sitzt am Boden und zeichnet das Kleid ab. Ihr kommt mit Ruby ins Gespräch. Du unterhältst dich mit ihr auf Englisch, aber Janine hat Schwierigkeiten, sie zu verstehen.

Du hast die Aufgabe, für Janine zu dolmetschen.

Janine: Was für ein schönes Kleid – ein Traum! All die Perlen und Juwelen!
You: Ja, aber das schwere Ding tragen?! Vergiss es, ein Albtraum wäre das! Nein, lieber Jeans und T-Shirts. … Ach, schau mal – das Mädchen da macht eine Skizze von dem Kleid.

(*zum Mädchen*) Er, excuse me – that's a wonderful drawing there.

Ruby: Oh, thanks a lot. I'm in my first year at the London College of Fashion. I love to draw historical costumes, and this one is one of my favourites. I also love the history of the costumes.

Janine: Was sagt sie?

You:

Janine: Was ist die Geschichte dieses Kleids? Da stehen ganz viele Informationen auf Englisch, aber das ist noch zu schwer für mich.

You:

Ruby: This dress here? One thing that you have to know about historical clothing is that after three or four centuries it can be very difficult to find out who the dress or costume belonged to. But with this wonderful piece here we know that it was Elizabeth I who once wore it!

You:

Janine: War es wirklich ein Kleid von Königin Elizabeth?

You:

Ruby: Yes, it was. And we know exactly when she wore it. It was a present from the Queen of France, who was hoping to arrange a marriage[1] for her son, the Duke of Alençon, with Elizabeth. The Duke brought the dress to England on a state visit[2], and Elizabeth loved it. So she kept it – but she didn't keep the Duke!

You:

Janine: Sehr intelligent von Elizabeth – die Geschichte gefällt mir gut!

You:

Ruby: Yes, Elizabeth loved the attention[3] from all the European princes. They all wanted to marry her – and get the throne of England. But Elizabeth never married. She felt that she was 'married to England'. Maybe it was better for her that way – and better for England.

You:

Janine: Hey, das war so viel interessanter als alles, was in meinem Reiseführer über dieses Museum steht! Danke schön! Es war nett, mit dir zu reden.

You:

UNIT 3 Ein Brief an eine Jugendzeitschrift

Du hast ein Problem und würdest gern um Rat bei deinem Lieblingsjugendmagazin bitten, traust dich aber nicht: Denn auch wenn du einen anderen Namen angeben würdest, hättest du das Gefühl, dass deine Freunde wissen könnten, wer den Brief geschrieben hat. Aber dann fällt dir etwas Besseres ein: Du kaufst ab und zu das britische Jugendmagazin TEEN◆BUZZ und findest es ganz cool, besonders den Ratgeber-Teil – die Ratschläge sind immer ganz vernünftig. Du traust dir zu, dein Problem auf Englisch zu schildern und Mary, die *agony aunt* von TEEN◆BUZZ, in einem Brief anzuschreiben.

- Begrüße Mary. Vergiss nicht, deine Adresse anzugeben.
- Schildere dein Problem (z. B.: – Ärger in der Familie / in der Schule – du fühlst dich körperlich nicht fit – du bist mit deinem Aussehen nicht zufrieden – …).
- Frage Mary, was du tun sollst.
- Bedanke dich bei ihr und verabschiede dich freundlich.

[1]**to arrange a marriage** [əˌreɪndʒ‿əˈmærɪdʒ] = eine Heirat arrangieren • [2]**state visit** [ˌsteɪt ˈvɪsɪt] = Staatsbesuch • [3]**attention** [əˈtenʃn] = Aufmerksamkeit

UNIT 4 Neu in der Nachbarschaft

Die Familie Madison aus Liverpool ist vor einer Woche in das Haus direkt neben deinem gezogen. Mark Madison, dem 16jährigen Sohn, bist du schon einmal kurz begegnet. Aber jetzt kommt er vorbei, um sich deiner Familie vorzustellen. Mark kann noch gar kein Deutsch, und deine Mutter kann kaum Englisch.

Du sollst im Gespräch dolmetschen.

Mark: Hey, how are you? Nice to see you again. And hello, Frau Wilhelm.
You: Hi, Mark. Nice to see you, too!
Mum: Hello, Mark. How are you? Leider reicht mein Englisch nicht weiter, tut mir Leid!
You:
Mark: I'm fine. And don't worry about your English, Frau Wilhelm – my German is much worse!
You:
Mum: Wie ist es hier nach einer Woche?
You:
Mark: Oh, everyone's nice. But I miss the chippie – I mean the fish-and-chip shop – at the corner of our street in Liverpool!

You:
Mum: Mark, warum habt ihr England verlassen, wenn ich fragen darf?
You:
Mark: My dad is an engineer. He lost his last job three months ago and couldn't find a new one anywhere in the UK. Finally, he found a firm here in Germany that was looking for somebody like him. So here we are.
You:
Mum: Das muss interessant sein. Eine neue Stadt, neue Sprache, neue Freunde!
You:
Mark: Well, yes and no. This neighbourhood is nice. And we're happy about Dad's new job.
You: That sounds great. What's the problem then? *(Du dolmetschst für deine Mutter, bevor Mark fortfährt.)*
Mark: Well, this is the third time in six years that we've moved house. I'm sick of it, really. But we have to go where Dad finds work. The problem is that I go to a new school and make new friends, and then we have to leave again because Dad's contracts are usually for only two years. And then the whole thing starts again.
You:
Mum: Ach, verstehe. Das klingt nicht so toll. Vermisst du deine Freunde?
You:
Mark: Yes, I do. I miss my football mates. But I really miss my girlfriend, Sophie …
You:
Mum: Oje, Fußball-Kumpels und Freundinnen – ich glaube, es ist Zeit, dass ich ins Haus gehe. Ihr zwei könnt hier draußen bleiben und weiterreden. Viel Spaß!
You:

UNIT 5 Ein Filmabend

Dein Cousin Jordan, der in Kanada aufgewachsen ist, ist zu Besuch bei dir und deiner Familie. Er kann etwas Deutsch, aber nicht so viel, dass er einen Spielfilm auf Deutsch richtig verstehen könnte. Ihr seid in einer Videothek und du hast zwei DVDs gefunden, die du Jordan vorschlagen möchtest. Er kennt beide Filme nicht.

MEDIATION SKILLS

Erinnerst du dich an *skimming*? Meist enthalten Texte mehr Informationen als du gerade brauchst. Überfliege deshalb zuerst die beiden Texte und mache dir Notizen zu den wichtigsten Informationen, die darin stehen. Du wirst sehen, dass du keine Wörter nachschlagen musst, wenn du nur die wesentlichen Dinge herausfilterst.

Komödie **Der rosarote Panther**
(Originaltitel: *The Pink Panther*)
Ein Fußballmanager wird ermordet. Er sitzt mitten in einem voll besetzten Stadion, wo ihm der berühmteste – und wertvollste – Ring der Welt geklaut wird: der rosarote Panther. Inspektor Clouseau (Steve Martin) soll ermitteln. Sein Chef Dreyfus (Kevin Kline) verzweifelt an seinem Mitarbeiter und gibt ihm den Detektiv Ponton (Jean Reno) zur Seite. Als die Polizisten bei ihren Ermittlungen auf Xania (Beyoncé Knowles) stoßen, die schöne Freundin des Toten, beginnt die Arbeit Spaß zu machen.

Komödie **Girls Club**
(Originaltitel: *Mean Girls*)
Cady (Lindsay Lohan) ist in Afrika aufgewachsen und hatte Privatlehrer. Daher hat sie keine Ahnung, was auf sie zukommt, als sie zum ersten Mal in den USA eine öffentliche Schule besucht. Schnell findet sie ihre ersten Freunde: die Außenseiter Jan und Damien. Cady merkt bald, dass Jan und Damien die Mädchen der elitären Clique „The Plastics" hassen. Die Außenseiter stacheln ihre neue Freundin Cady an, diese Mädchenbande auszuspionieren und über ihre miesen Machenschaften zu berichten.

a) *Fasse für Jordan kurz auf Englisch zusammen, worum es in beiden Filmen geht.*
b) *Schreibe auf Englisch eine ähnliche Zusammenfassung deines Lieblingsfilms.*

UNIT 6 Durchsagen am Flughafen

MEDIATION SKILLS

Auf Flughäfen werden wichtige Informationen häufig über Lautsprecher weitergegeben. Das ist für ausländische Besucher manchmal nicht ganz einfach:

- Die Ansagen kommen oft unerwartet.
- Manchmal sind Hintergrundgeräusche sehr störend.
- Die Ansagen enthalten häufig auch unbekannte Wörter.
- Man kann die Durchsagen nur 1–2 Mal hören. Konzentriere dich deshalb auf wichtige Wörter wie Personen- und Ortsnamen, Zahlen- und Zeitangaben, Substantive und Verben als Schlüsselwörter. Versuche damit, den Sinn der Ansage zu erschließen.

Du bist mit deiner Familie am Londoner Flughafen Heathrow. Nach einem Urlaub in Großbritannien wartet ihr jetzt auf euren Rückflug nach Berlin. Ihr fliegt mit British Airways, die Flugnummer lautet BA0982. Eure Abflugzeit ist für 9.15 Uhr angesetzt und ihr seid momentan in der Wartehalle, wo ihr darauf wartet, die richtige Gate-Nummer zu erfahren. Ihr hört eine Reihe von Durchsagen. Welche betreffen euch, welche nicht?

Fasse jeweils den Inhalt für deine Familie auf Deutsch zusammen, damit sie richtig informiert ist.

⟨The Spaniards[1] are coming!⟩ (after Unit 2)

A I am an old man now, but I will never forget that hot evening in July, 1588. I remember every minute! And every minute is a picture full of life – and adventure.

All was quiet at Plymouth harbour where the English fleet[2] lay at anchor[3]. Everyone in England had heard that the Spaniards wanted to attack us with the greatest fleet in the world. They called it the Great Armada. The only question was: When would they come? The Spaniards had a large army in the Netherlands[4], and they wanted to bring it *here*, to England. Our ships had been ready for weeks.

On that evening Sir Francis Drake and a few other officers[5] had gone to play bowls[6] on a hill above the town. I was a very young officer and had to take care of[7] Sir Francis's ship when he was gone. Suddenly I heard the shouts of our men on land[8].

I ran to the side of the ship and looked down. "What is it?" I asked.

"The Spaniards, sir," a sailor[9] shouted. "Some of our men have seen their ships in the English Channel. Over a hundred!"

Over a hundred! There was only one thing to do. I left the ship and ran all the way through the town to the bowling-green[10]. Sir Francis and Lord Howard, the commander[11] of the English fleet, were standing with a group of officers. I ran up to them.

[1]**Spaniard** ['spænɪəd] = Spanier / -in • [2]**fleet** [fli:t] = Flotte • [3]**(to) lie at anchor** [ˌlaɪ‿ət 'æŋkə] = vor Anker liegen • [4]**Netherlands** ['neðələndz] = Niederlande • [5]**officer** ['ɒfɪsə] = Offizier • [6]**(to) play bowls** [pleɪ 'bəʊlz] = bowlen • [7]**(to) take care of** [teɪk 'keə‿əv] = *hier:* bewachen • [8]**on land** [ɒn 'lænd] = an Land • [9]**sailor** ['seɪlə] = Matrose, Seemann • [10]**bowling-green** ['bəʊlɪŋ gri:n] = Rasenfläche zum Bowlen • [11]**commander** [kə'mɑ:ndə] = Kommandant

"My Lord Howard! Sir Francis!" I said. "The Spaniards are coming up the Channel! The Armada is almost here!"

Lord Howard threw down his bowl, and all the other officers – but not Drake – looked very worried.

"Back to your ships, gentlemen," said Lord Howard. "There is no time to lose!"

"One moment, my Lord," Drake said quietly. "There is time to finish the game and defeat the Spaniards, too. Let the Spaniards go by[12], and with the help of God we can follow them and defeat them. We'll finish the game first."

That was the way of Sir Francis Drake. He never became excited or worried. He smiled, took his bowl, which he still held in his hands, and continued the game.

B When we left the harbour we soon sighted[13] the Armada. The heavy ships were sailing up the Channel in the shape[14] of a great half-moon. I had never seen so many ships in my life. I heard later that there were 130 of them, with 30,000 men on them.

Our little ships were not even half the size of the big Spanish ships. But we could sail much faster. As Drake had planned, we attacked them from behind[15]. First we fired off[16] our cannon balls[17], then we turned away before the Spaniards could fire theirs.

This is the way we followed the Armada up the Channel, until the Spaniards turned towards the French coast and entered the harbour of Calais. It was difficult to attack them there, but Drake, as always, knew what to do. We filled six of our oldest ships with pitch[18] and tar[19]. Then, in the night, we set fire to[20] them and let them drift[21] towards the Spanish fleet.

It was terrible to see those burning Spanish ships in the night. We could hear the shouts of the Spaniards as they tried to sail off[22].

That was the chance we had been waiting for. We surrounded[23] a few of the largest ships and sank them. The rest of the ships sailed out into the North Sea. We followed them and fired off our cannons again and again. Soon, we had no more cannon balls, and then we turned back.

C Before we got home, a great storm had come up. The ships of the Armada had to sail farther[24] and farther north. We heard no more of them for a long time until Lord Howard told us that they had sailed round the north of Scotland. The Spaniards had lost most of their ships on the coast of Scotland and Ireland, and only 54 out of 130 returned to Spain.

There was great joy[25] in all of Queen Elizabeth's land. When we returned to England, bonfires[26] were burning, church bells[27] were ringing, and all the people were dancing in the streets. Everyone was celebrating the greatest victory[28] in English history. I was a very young officer, so I danced on the deck with the other men. Sir Francis stood there and watched us, and I could see that he was smiling.

[12] **(to) go by** [gəʊ ˈbaɪ] = vorbeiziehen • [13] **(to) sight** [saɪt] = sichten • [14] **shape** [ʃeɪp] = Form • [15] **from behind** [frɒm bɪˈhaɪnd] = von hinten • [16] **(to) fire off** [ˌfaɪə‿ˈɒf] = abfeuern • [17] **cannon ball** [ˈkænən bɔːl] = Kanonenkugel • [18] **pitch** [pɪtʃ] = Pech • [19] **tar** [tɑː] = Teer • [20] **(to) set fire to** [set ˈfaɪə tə] = in Brand stecken • [21] **(to) drift** [drɪft] = driften • [22] **(to) sail off** [seɪl‿ˈɒf] = davonsegeln • [23] **(to) surround** [səˈraʊnd] = umstellen, umzingeln • [24] **farther** [ˈfɑːðə] = weiter • [25] **joy** [dʒɔɪ] = Freude • [26] **bonfire** [ˈbɒnfaɪə] = Freudenfeuer • [27] **bell** [bel] = Glocke • [28] **victory** [ˈvɪktri] = Sieg

⟨Authentic Britain⟩ (after Unit 3)

Got a worry you want to share? Write to **Cathy, A Problem Shared, *Shout* Magazine.**
If you'd prefer a personal reply, please enclose a stamped envelope addressed to yourself.

The *Only* Mag To Write Back!

a problem shared

High School Blues

When I started high school, I thought it would be great. I was so wrong! Ever since I started I've been really stressed and I have completely taken it out on my parents. I've heard my mum crying about it and I hate that, because I don't mean to be so nasty. It's making me really sick and down.

Whatever it is about high school that's making you so stressed and unhappy, you need to tell someone. Right now you're taking your misery out on your family, which isn't fair, so it's time to come clean and tell them exactly why you're so moody and sad. Once things are out in the open, they can help you. Good luck.

My Parents Are Divorcing

My mum and my dad are getting divorced. Now I live with my mum and grandparents. I've had to leave my school and I hate my new one. I really miss all the mates I've left behind. I spoke to my mum about how I feel but all she says is, "This is the worst six months of our lives." What can I do, Cathy? I feel so down.

Your mum is feeling lost herself just now, but you did the right thing to talk to her. Tell your guidance tutor at school how you're feeling, but try to make new friendships, too. It takes time, but it will happen. Your mum's right, this is a very tough time for you all, but things will get better, I promise.

I Don't Get On With My Mum

I need some advice on how to get on with my mum. I argue with her nearly every day but I love her and she loves me. My best mates don't have this problem with their mums, so why do I? I need your help, Cathy.

These fights may be down to a personality clash, or even just the fact that you're growing up, but they won't go on forever. Tell your mum how much you love her and make a big effort not to get angry. Take time to do fun stuff together, like clothes shopping or watching a funny DVD. Gradually, you'll work out ways to avoid the fights. What you're going through happens to lots of mums and daughters, so you're not alone, and you can get through it.

PROBLEMS

She Hangs Around

My sister is 16 and has no social life. She hangs around with me and my mates and it drives me crazy. She ruins everything we like doing. We're only 11. I feel like telling her to get a life. What should I do?

Make sure you see your mates in town or away from your house once in a while, so you get some time together alone. When you're at your house, make an effort to make your sister feel included — ask her to give you make-overs or tell you about high school. Don't make her feel unwelcome. She's clearly shy, but she'll make her own friends and build her own social life when she's ready. Until then be friendly and understanding and spend some time with her.

I Miss My Dog

My dog died a few weeks ago. I'd had him all my life. I can't stop thinking about him and the whole family is very upset. I can't believe he's gone. Can you give me some advice, Cathy?

For many young people, losing a pet is their first experience of death. A pet can be a best friend and part of the family. Share your memories, look at photos and think of the good times. Your dog had a good life and you loved him. You'll always miss him, but the hurt will fade. Nothing can replace your pet, but there are many unwanted, unloved dogs in the world. Perhaps one day your family will be ready to share their home with one of them … I reckon your old dog would approve!

⟨Poems⟩ (after Unit 3 or Unit 4)

Poems use very few words to say a lot. For that reason, they are often difficult to understand. But very often, they suddenly help you to see something clearly. And many poems are beautiful and say old things in a new way.

- Poems often use **symbols**[1] (poem C: "waves in the sea").
- They also use language in a very special way, so sometimes the last word in a line **rhymes**[2] with another last word (poem D: "drink – brink[3]").
- There is often a special **metre**[4] to the lines. You will hear the rhythm of the sounds – that is the 'metre': (poem C: "WHEN he LOOKS at ME / I SHAKE like LEAVES[5] on a TREE.").

In modern poems the writer is free to use rhymes or metre as she / he wants.

1 Images[6]

Poems often use "pictures" or "images" in a new way. Images in poems help you to "see" things while you read the poem.
Look at this picture. What does this tell you about how the person feels?

2 Read poems A to D

A

I'm just finding a way back
Into my dream
When my mum's loud voice
Leaves me no choice[8].

What does she want?
What's all the fuss[9] …?
"You'd better get up –
Or you'll miss your bus!"

I'm drifting along
Like a cloud of smoke
But the sun's sudden glare[10]
Is now everywhere.

What does she want?
What the heck[11] …?
"You'd better wake up –
You look like a wreck[12]!"

I'm just trying hard
To forget last night
And my stupid[13] head
Feels as heavy as lead[14].

What does she want?
Is this a joke?
"Get up right now
Or you'll give me a stroke[15]!"

I'm just doing my best …
… To get up!

Leroy Glenn, 13

[1]**symbol** ['sɪmbl] = Symbol • [2]**(to) rhyme** [raɪm] = (sich) reimen • [3]**brink** [brɪŋk] = *hier:* Anschlag • [4]**metre** ['mi:tə] = Versmaß, Metrum • [5]**leaf pl. leaves** [li:f, li:vz] = Blatt • [6]**image** ['ɪmɪdʒ] = Bild • [7]**(to) drift along** [drɪft ə'lɒŋ] = sich treiben lassen • [8]**choice** ['tʃɔɪs] = Wahl • [9]**fuss** [fʌs] = Aufregung, Getue • [10]**glare** [gleə] = grelles Licht • [11]**What the heck … ?** [ˌwɒt ðə 'hek] = Was zum Teufel … ? • [12]**wreck** [rek] = Wrack • [13]**stupid** ['stju:pɪd] = blöd, dumm • [14]**lead** [led] = Blei • [15]**stroke** [strəʊk] = Schlaganfall • [16]**That's that!** [ðæts 'ðæt] = Basta! • [17]**there's no harm** [ˌðeəz nəʊ 'hɑ:m] = es wird niemandem schaden • [18]**(to) add** [æd] = hinzufügen • [19]**(to) have a fit** [ˌhæv‿ə 'fɪt] = einen Anfall bekommen, Zustände kriegen • [20]**(to) get into a state** [get ˌɪntə ə 'steɪt] = durchdrehen • [21]**(to) choke** [tʃəʊk] = ersticken • [22]**glee** [gli:] = Freude • [23]**(to) swerve** [swɜ:v] = schlittern • [24]**curve** [kɜ:v] = Kurve • [25]**alive** [ə'laɪv] = lebendig, lebend

B

He said: No tattoo and that's that[16]!
Oh, Dad, I said, there's no harm[17],
What do you mean, no harm?!
And to that Mum added[18],
Now, dear, stay calm!

No is no, get that into your head
But Dad, I said, Tony's got one …
What's Tony got to do with it!
Be quiet, Mum said,
Stop having a fit[19]!

But I say, it's not fair
I don't think they really care
How it feels when you have to wait.
It's such a tiny little thing
And they get into such a state[20]!

David Jones, 16

C

When he looks at me,
I shake like leaves on a tree.
When he smiles at me,
I'm all waves in the sea.
When he stands next to me,
I go weak in the knees.
When he talks to me,
I could choke[21] with glee.[22]
Please help me – please!
How can I tell him
What he means to me?

Lauren Akodu, 14

D

Why
did he drink
to the brink?
Why
did Ann leave
with Steve?
Why
did he swerve[23]
in the curve[24]?
Why
didn't he see
the tree?
Why
didn't they arrive
alive[25]?

Mark Wilkins, 16
(For my sister Ann)

3 Match these images

Match these images with the right phrases from the poems.

Example:

1. to choke with glee – poem C

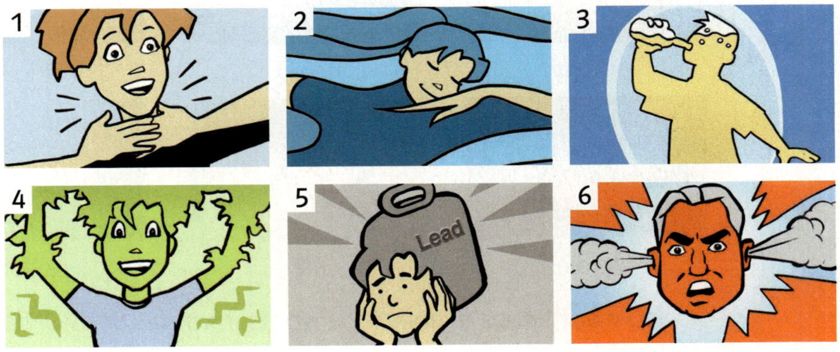

4 The title helps

a) *Look at the titles on the right. Which one goes with which poem?*

b) *Think of your own titles for the poems. Which is better? What does your partner think?*

Help! | Such a tiny little thing | Monday morning, 6 am | Why?

5 How to: Talk about poems

Choose one of the poems and talk about it in your group.

1. What is it about?
2. Who likes it? Who does not like it? Why?

USEFUL PHRASES

I think poem … is about … It describes how the person feels when … We know this because in line … he/she says … I (don't) like it because …	He/She feels … angry/mad sad tired happy/glad nervous worried excited unhappy …

6 Present the poem

1. *One person in your group reads the poem your group has chosen (from exercise 5) to the class.*
2. *One of you explains it to the class. Start like this:*

   The poem … tells you about … and … The author wants to say: …
3. *One of you says why it is or is not interesting. Say what is good about the poem (and maybe: what is not so good about it).*

7 Writing texts: Write a poem yourself

1. *Think of a **topic**[26] **or a situation** and collect ideas about it. Make notes. What do you want to say in the poem?*
2. *Do you want to use **images**? Look at exercises 1 and 3 for help.*
3. *Do you want to use **symbols**? If you do, start with easy symbols, e.g. rose[27] = (to) love, sun = happy etc. These symbols can help you:*

happy

heavy

I'm blue = sad

free

to die

life

trouble

love

4. *Do you want to use **rhymes**? The words from this box will help you:*

[ɪə]	[u:]	[aɪn]	[eɪt]	[i:t]	[æd]	[əʊ]	[aɪk]
ear	blue	fine	create	complete	add	go	bike
hear	do	line	date	feet	bad	grow	hike
here	new	mine	late	meet	glad	know	like
near	shoe	nine	mate	street	mad	no	
year	true	shine	plate	sweet	sad	show	
	view	wine	skate			snow	
			wait				

5. *Think of a short but good **title** for the poem.*
6. *Read your poem to your group or to your class, and put it in your folder.*
7. *Discuss the poems in class. Say why the poems are good or why you don't like them.*

[26] **topic** ['tɒpɪk] = Thema • [27] **rose** [rəʊz] = Rose

⟨Working with films⟩ (after Unit 5)

1 Important film questions

a) *First choose a film together with your teacher. Then watch a scene from that film and answer the questions:*

- Who are the people in the film?
- Where are the people?
- What are they doing?
- How do they feel?
- What is the film about?

TIP
The people in a film are the **characters**.
The place where they are is the **setting**.
The **action** is what happens in the film.
The **plot** is the story that the film tells.

b) *Now work in groups. Watch another scene from that film. Take notes and find out as much as you can about the characters, the setting, the action and the plot. Talk about your ideas in class and say what you think about the film.*

2 Let's work with films

Get another DVD or video to do this exercise.

a) *Play one or more scenes from a film* ***without sound***[1]*. What can you see in the pictures? How many people are there? What are they saying? Then listen to the sound and discuss your answers.*

b) *Now play* ***only the sound*** *of one or more other scenes. What is happening? What are the people doing? Then look at the film and discuss your answers.*

c) *Play* ***part of a scene*** *and then* ***stop*** *it. What do you think the people are going to do or say next?*

3 Writing texts: A film scene

a) *Work in groups. Choose one of the settings on the right.*

b) *Write a short scene with characters from* ***Green Line****.*

c) *Role play: Act your scene.*

d) *If possible, record it, for example on video. Make a film poster for your film.*

1. On the bus
2. In the shop
3. At home
4. At a birthday party

[1] **sound** [saʊnd] = Ton

Grammar

Liebe Schülerin, lieber Schüler,
dieser Grammatikteil ist dir mittlerweile vertraut.
Er fasst die Regeln zusammen, die dir helfen können,

- wenn du etwas nicht verstanden hast
- wenn du ein paar Stunden gefehlt hast
- wenn du etwas wiederholen möchtest
- wenn du Hausaufgaben machst
- wenn du für eine Klassenarbeit übst.

Jedes Grammatikkapitel hat eine Nummer, z. B. G 2 , und eine große Überschrift. Die Seitenangabe rechts neben dieser Überschrift zeigt dir, auf welcher Seite der neue Grammatikstoff in der Unit eingeführt wird.
Wo ein **!** steht, musst du besonders aufpassen. Ein **(R)** bedeutet Revision – also Wiederholung.

Da du die englische Sprache jetzt schon recht gut beherrschst, kannst du nun auch auf Englisch über grammatische Regeln sprechen. Dabei helfen dir die kurzen englischen Zusammenfassungen nach jedem Pensum: **ENGLISH SUMMARY**
Unter ***Grammatical terms*** findest du wieder eine Liste der grammatischen Begriffe, die in diesem Buch vorkommen.

Grammatical terms

English term	English example	Deutsche Bezeichnung / Übersetzung
abstract nouns G14	**Life** is too short.	Abstrakte Nomen
adjectives after certain verbs G16	That doesn't **sound good**.	Adjektive nach bestimmten Verben
adjectives used as nouns G15	I like to read about **the rich** and **famous**.	Adjektive als Nomen
conditional sentences G13	**If** I **won** a lot of money, I **would go** on a world tour. **If** you **had asked** me, I **would have helped** you.	Bedingungssätze

English term	English example	Deutsche Bezeichnung / Übersetzung
defining relative clauses G5 bis G7	Is this the girl **who knows so many skateboard tricks**?	Notwendige Relativsätze
contact clauses G5	That is the trick **I like best**.	Notwendige Relativsätze ohne Relativpronomen
definite article G14	We must catch **the** train to Windsor.	Bestimmter Artikel
each other G12	They often help **each other**.	sich (gegenseitig)
future tenses G1 **(R)** bis G4, G17		Futurzeiten
future perfect G17	I **will have finished** the job by tomorrow.	Futur II
going to future **(R)** G1	He**'s going to watch** the match.	*Going to* Futur
will future **(R)** G1	I think England **will win**.	*Will* Futur
will for spontaneous decisions G4	I**'ll carry** that for you.	*Will* für spontane Enscheidungen
simple present G2	The concert **starts** at 7.30.	Einfache Form der Gegenwart (*'timetable future'*)
present progressive G3	She **is meeting** Rob tomorrow.	Verlaufsform der Gegenwart (zukünftiger Gebrauch)
indefinite article G14	Her father is **a** doctor.	Unbestimmter Artikel
indirect speech G23 bis G28	She said **that she had read the book**.	Indirekte Rede
modal auxiliaries G8 **(R)** G9		Modale Hilfsverben
can, be able to G9	He **wasn't able to do** the exercise.	können / nicht können
can / may, mustn't, be allowed to G9	I **wasn't allowed to go** to the party.	dürfen / nicht dürfen
must, needn't, have to G9	She **didn't have to** phone me.	müssen / nicht müssen
pair words G18	I've got a new **pair of trousers**.	Paarwörter
passive G19 bis G22	He **was given** the role.	Passiv
past perfect (simple) G10	After William **had won** at Hastings, he went to London.	Vorvergangenheit / Plusquamperfekt
reflexive pronouns G11	We can see **ourselves** in the photo.	Reflexivpronomen
-self / -selves **pronouns** G11	Dad repaired the TV **himself**.	Pronomen auf *-self / -selves*

Unit 1

IN DIESER UNIT LERNST DU

- als Wiederholung: wie man verschiedene Zukunftsformen verwendet. G1
- wie du mit dem *simple present* über feststehende Termine in der Zukunft sprechen kannst. G2
- wie du mit dem *present progressive* ausdrücken kannst, dass etwas in der nahen Zukunft vereinbart ist. G3
- wie du mit dem *will future* spontane Entscheidungen ausdrücken kannst. G4
- wie du mit notwendigen Relativsätzen Personen und Dinge näher bestimmen kannst. G5 G6 G7

G1 Wiederholung: Die Wiedergabe der Zukunft

Revision: How to express the future

Seite 10–11

Im Englischen kannst du das, was in der Zukunft geschieht, auf verschiedene Weise ausdrücken. Welche dieser Formen man wählt, hängt davon ab, was man besonders betonen möchte.

Revision

Du kennst schon zwei dieser Futurformen: das *going to future* und das *will future*. Zur Erinnerung:

Going to future	
I'**m going to watch** *Match of the Day* on TV this evening.	▶ Du verwendest das ***going to future***, wenn du sagen willst, dass du vorhast, in der Zukunft etwas zu tun. Du hast einen **Plan** oder eine **Absicht**.
It's 6:2, 5:1. Harry'**s going to win** easily.	▶ Du kannst es auch verwenden, wenn du sicher bist, dass etwas geschehen wird, weil es schon **Anzeichen** dafür gibt.

Will future	
It's my sister's birthday this Sunday. She'**ll be** 17.	▶ Du verwendest das ***will future***, wenn du ausdrücken möchtest, dass etwas in der Zukunft geschehen wird, auf das du keinen Einfluss hast.
I hope she'**ll like** the present.	▶ Das ***will future*** steht auch, wenn du ausdrücken möchtest, dass du etwas vermutest, z. B. nach ***I hope, I think, I'm sure, I promise*** usw.

"I hope she'**ll like** it."

G2 Das *simple present* zur Wiedergabe der Zukunft
The simple present to express the future

Seite 10

- The match **starts** at 15.30.
- When **does** our train **leave**?
- It **leaves** at 12.25. Platform 6.
  And it **arrives** in Brighton at 13.58.

▶ Du kannst das ***simple present*** verwenden, wenn es sich um **feste Termine** in der Zukunft handelt.
Meist sind dies **genaue Zeitangaben aus Fahrplänen, Programmen usw.** Deshalb wird diese Verwendung des ***simple present*** auch als *timetable future* bezeichnet. Es wird häufig mit den Verben *arrive, leave, start* und *end* gebraucht.

!

Im Deutschen gebraucht man sehr häufig das Präsens für die Zukunft:
*Ich **schaue** mir morgen das Spiel **an**.*
Im Englischen wird das ***simple present*** jedoch nur **sehr selten** verwendet, um über die Zukunft zu sprechen: nur im *timetable future*! In den meisten Fällen verwendet man andere Zukunftsformen, z. B. **I'm going to** watch the match tomorrow.

G3 Das *present progressive* zur Wiedergabe der Zukunft
The present progressive to express the future

Seite 11

What **are** you **doing** at the weekend, Laura?
– Well, tomorrow afternoon we'**re making** a video for our partner school.
On Saturday morning we'**re visiting** my grandma in hospital and in the afternoon I'**m playing** in that volleyball match.
But on Sunday we can do something together.

▶ Mit dem ***present progressive*** kannst du ausdrücken, dass jemand etwas für die Zukunft fest geplant hat. Es handelt sich um **Vereinbarungen** *(arrangements)*.
Um Verwechslungen mit der Gegenwart zu vermeiden, steht es oft mit Zeitbestimmungen der Zukunft wie *tomorrow, at the weekend, on Sunday, next week* usw.

G4 Das *will future* zum Ausdruck von spontanen Entscheidungen
The will future to express spontaneous decisions

Seite 11

Will you **look** at this exercise, please?
– Is it difficult? OK, I'**ll help** you with it.

▶ Das ***will future*** kann auch ausdrücken, dass jemand um Hilfe bittet oder **spontan** seine Hilfe anbietet, ohne dies vorher geplant zu haben.

ENGLISH SUMMARY

You can use different forms when you want to talk about the future in English:
- You use the **going to future** when you have a plan to do something in the future.
- You use the **will future** to talk about events in the future. The speaker cannot control these events (like *the weather*).
- You can also use the **will future** to ask for help or when you want to help someone.
- You can use the **simple present** for *'timetable' information* in the future (*train times* etc.).
- You can use the **present progressive** when you want to talk about arrangements for the future. (You often use it with future adverbials like *next Saturday, tomorrow* etc.)

G5 Notwendige Relativsätze
Defining relative clauses

Seite 13–15

Notwendige Relativsätze bestimmen das Wort, auf das sie sich beziehen (in diesem Beispiel *the girl)*, näher:

sentence	
main clause	defining relative clause
This is **the girl**	**who broke the school record.**

- Der Relativsatz beschreibt das Mädchen näher. Ohne ihn wäre der Sinn des Hauptsatzes unklar.
- Anders als im Deutschen steht zwischen dem Hauptsatz und dem notwendigen Relativsatz **kein Komma.**
- Beim Sprechen macht man im Englischen **keine Pause** zwischen Hauptsatz und notwendigem Relativsatz.

a) Die Relativpronomen *who, which* und *that* als Subjekt des Relativsatzes

Für Personen:	who / that		
	subject		
The player	**who / that**	scores most goals in the competition will win a prize.	… der Spieler, **der** …
We're looking for people	**who / that**	want to help on sports day.	… Leute, **die** …

Für Dinge:	which / that		
	subject		
Cricket is a game	**which / that**	is very popular in Britain, but not in Germany.	… ein Spiel, **das** …
Where are the tennis balls	**which / that**	were on this chair only a minute ago?	… die Tennisbälle, **die** …

- ***Who, which*** und ***that*** werden sowohl für den Singular als auch für den Plural verwendet.
- ***Who*** bezieht sich nur auf Personen. ***Which*** bezieht sich nur auf Dinge.
- ***That*** kann sich auf Dinge und Personen beziehen.

b) Die Relativpronomen *who, which* und *that* als Objekt des Relativsatzes – *Contact clauses*

Nach dem Objekt eines Satzes fragst du mit **wem** oder **wen** oder **was**:
Wen sieht man da im Bild? – *The man **who/that** you can see …*

	object	subject		
The man	**who / that**	**you**	can see in the picture is a famous American football star.	… der Mann, **den** …
The man	→	**you**	can see in the picture is a famous American football star.	… der Mann, **den** …
Is that the equipment	**which / that**	**cricket players**	use?	… die Ausrüstung, **die** …
Is that the equipment	→	**cricket players**	use?	… die Ausrüstung, **die** …

- Wenn das Relativpronomen **Objekt** des Relativsatzes ist, wird es häufig weggelassen.
- Solche Relativsätze ohne Relativpronomen nennt man ***contact clauses***, da sie direkt an das Bezugswort (*the man, the equipment*) angehängt werden. Es gibt also ohne das Relativpronomen einen direkten ‚Kontakt' zwischen Hauptsatz und Relativsatz (*the man you …*).
- ***Contact clauses*** sind vor allem in der Umgangssprache gebräuchlich.

!

Du darfst das Relativpronomen nicht weglassen, wenn es Subjekt des Relativsatzes ist.

subject	This is a list of all the people	**who**	want to join the skateboard group.
Aber:	This is a list of all the people	–	**Laura** has written down so far.

wenn hinter who ein Nomen steht kann man who weglassen

G6 Relativsätze mit *whose*
Relative clauses with *whose*

Seite 13–14

Relativsätze können auch durch ***whose*** + **Nomen** eingeleitet werden:

I met a **girl** ←	**whose**	grandmother played at Wimbledon.	… ein Mädchen, **dessen Großmutter** …
There are a few **athletes** ←	**whose**	names I've never heard before.	… einige Athleten, **deren Namen** …
I don't know any **towns** ←	**whose**	skateparks are as good as ours.	… keine Städte, **deren Skateboardanlagen** …

- ***Whose*** drückt Besitz oder Zugehörigkeit aus: im Deutschen **dessen** oder **deren**.
- Es kann für Personen und Dinge verwendet werden, und zwar im Singular und Plural.

!

whose = dessen, deren
who's = who is = wer ist

G7 Präpositionen im notwendigen Relativsatz
Prepositions in defining relative clauses

Seite 14

This is a tennis racket	**–**	Roger Federer played **with**.	… ein Tennisschläger, **mit dem** …
	that	Roger Federer played **with**.	
	which	Roger Federer played **with**.	
	with which	Roger Federer played.	
Most of the boys	**–**	I was talking **to** are Liverpool fans.	Die meisten der Jungen, **mit denen** …
	that	I was talking **to** are Liverpool fans.	
	who	I was talking **to** are Liverpool fans.	
	to whom	I was talking are Liverpool fans.	

- Im notwendigen Relativsatz steht die Präposition (*with, to*) meist hinter dem Verb.
- Das Relativpronomen wird häufig weggelassen: ***contact clause!***
- In diesen ***contact clauses*** steht die Präposition immer hinter dem Verb.
- Im förmlichen Stil steht die Präposition auch vor dem Relativpronomen. Als Relativpronomen stehen in diesem Fall nur ***which*** oder ***whom*** (***with which, to whom***).

ENGLISH SUMMARY

- A defining relative clause gives you important information about a noun.
- You use the relative pronoun **who** for people and the relative pronoun **which** for things. You can use **that** for people and things.
- When the relative pronoun is the **object** of the relative clause, you can leave it out *(weglassen)*. A relative clause without a relative pronoun is a **contact clause**.
- When people or things belong together *(zusammengehören)*, you can use the relative pronoun **whose**.
- If the verb in a defining relative clause has a preposition (*play with, talk to*), put the preposition after the verb.

Unit 2

IN DIESER UNIT LERNST DU

- ✓ als Wiederholung, wie man die modalen Hilfsverben *can, may, must* und ihre Verneinungen gebraucht. G8
- ✓ wie du mit den modalen Hilfsverben und ihren Ersatzformen Fähigkeit, Erlaubnis, Notwendigkeit und Verbot ausdrücken kannst. G9
- ✓ wie du mit dem *past perfect* ausdrücken kannst, dass sich ein Ereignis vor einem anderen in der Vergangenheit abgespielt hat. G10

G8 Wiederholung: Die modalen Hilfsverben

Revision: Modal auxiliaries

Seite 26–27

Du kennst schon die modalen Hilfsverben ***can***, ***may*** und ***must*** und ihre Verneinungen ***can't***, ***may not***, ***mustn't*** und ***needn't***.
Zur Erinnerung noch einmal eine Übersicht über die bejahten und verneinten Formen:

can (können)	**can't (nicht können)**
She **can** speak German and English.	But she **can't** speak Italian. She **couldn't** understand much when they were in Italy last year.
can / may (dürfen)	**can't / mustn't (nicht dürfen)**
Can / may we use dictionaries in the test?	Yes, but you **can't / mustn't** use your mobiles.
must (müssen)	**needn't (nicht müssen / nicht brauchen)**
I really **must** finish my English homework.	But I **needn't** do any Maths today.

- ▶ Die modalen Hilfsverben ***can***, ***may*** und ***must*** und ihre Verneinungen können nur im ***simple present*** verwendet werden. (Die einzige Ausnahme ist die Form ***could***, die im ***past tense*** gebraucht wird.)
- ▶ Sie stehen immer mit der Grundform des Verbs ohne ***to***.
- ▶ Sie sind für alle Personen gleich, haben also kein ***s*** in der dritten Person Singular.
- ▶ ***May*** klingt sehr förmlich und wird vorwiegend in höflichen Fragen verwendet:
  May *I ask you a question, please?* Gebräuchlicher sind Fragen mit ***can*** oder ***could***:
  Could *you tell me the way to Madame Tussaud's?* (Könnten …)
  May not benutzt man vor allem in Kurzantworten: ***May*** *we use … ? – No, you* ***may not***.
  Als Verneinung von ***may*** steht ansonsten ***mustn't***.

ENGLISH SUMMARY

- ▶ **Can**, **may**, **must** and their negative forms **can't**, **may not**, **mustn't** and **needn't** are **modal auxiliaries**.
- ▶ You always use them with the infinitive of a main verb.
- ▶ There is no 'to' between the auxiliary and the main verb.
- ▶ The present tense forms have no **s** in the 3rd person singular.

G 9 Die modalen Hilfsverben und ihre Ersatzverben
Modal auxiliaries and their substitutes

Seite 26–28

Da die modalen Hilfsverben meist nur im ***present tense*** verwendet werden können, benutzt man für die anderen Zeitformen die ‚Ersatzverben' ***be able to***, ***be allowed to*** und ***have to***.

a) *can* und *be able to* (können)

Present tense	Visitors	**can see / are able to see**	lots of famous people at the wax museum.
	But you	**can't see / aren't able to see**	all the modern pop stars.
Past tense	We	**could** only **spend / were** only **able to spend**	an hour at the museum when we were in London.
	So we	**couldn't see / weren't able to see**	everything.
Will future	I hope I	**'ll be able to go**	to London again soon.
	But maybe I	**won't be able to save**	enough money for the trip.

- ▶ Mit ***can*** und der Ersatzform ***be able to*** kannst du ausdrücken, dass jemand in der Lage ist oder fähig ist, etwas zu tun.
- ▶ Im ***present tense*** gebraucht man meistens ***can*** oder ***can't***, im ***past tense*** gibt es die Form ***could*** / ***couldn't***.
- ▶ In den anderen Zeiten verwendet man ***be able to***, das man auch im ***present*** und ***past tense*** benutzen kann.

b) *can / may, mustn't* und *be allowed to* (dürfen)

Present tense	You	**can take / may take / are allowed to take**	photos of Elizabeth I.
	But you	**cannot get / mustn't get / aren't allowed to get**	too near her dress.
Past tense	Francis Drake	**was allowed to attack**	the Spanish ships because the Queen wanted to get rich.
	So, of course, he	**wasn't allowed to keep**	all the gold.
Will future	Do you think we	**'ll be allowed to go**	to "The Sir Francis"?
	I'm afraid we	**won't be allowed to stay**	very long.

- Mit ***can***, ***may*** und dem ‚Ersatzverb' ***be allowed to*** kannst du ausdrücken, dass jemand etwas tun darf.
- Die verneinten Formen ***can't***, ***may not***, ***mustn't*** und ***not allowed to*** drücken ein Verbot aus.
- ***May*** und ***mustn't*** können nur im ***present tense*** verwendet werden, ***could / couldn't*** auch im ***past tense***.
- Für die anderen Zeiten gebraucht man ***(not) be allowed to***, das auch im ***present tense*** und ***past tense*** benutzt werden kann.

!

Die deutschen Sätze *Es ist verboten, das zu tun.* bzw. *Es ist nicht erlaubt, das zu tun.* darfst du nicht wörtlich übersetzen.
Im Englischen musst du sagen: You **aren't allowed** to do that.
You aren't allowed to smoke in this restaurant. *Es ist verboten / Es ist nicht erlaubt, in diesem Restaurant zu rauchen.*

c) *must, needn't* und *have to* (müssen, nicht brauchen)

Present tense	We	**must leave / have to leave**	early. There are always long queues at Madame Tussaud's.
	You	**needn't worry / don't have to worry.**	The bus will collect us at 9 o'clock.
Past tense	I	**had to stand**	in a queue for over an hour when I went to Madame Tussaud's.
	But we	**didn't have to wait**	long at the London Eye.
Present perfect	She	**has had to learn**	a lot about Shakespeare.
	But she	**hasn't had to learn**	*everything* about him to be a Globe guide.
Will future	We	**'ll have to get**	tickets today. *The Queen's Pirate* is a very popular musical.

- Mit ***must*** kannst du ausdrücken, dass etwas notwendig ist.
- Mit ***needn't*** drückst du aus, dass etwas nicht notwendig ist.
- ***Must*** und ***needn't*** können nur im ***present tense*** verwendet werden.
- Für die anderen Zeiten gebraucht man ***have to*** (für **must**) und ***not have to*** (für ***needn't***). Diese Ersatzverben können auch im ***present tense*** stehen.

!

To have to ist ein Vollverb. Deshalb wird es in Fragen mit ***do / does*** und ***did*** und in verneinten Sätzen mit ***don't / doesn't*** und ***didn't*** umschrieben:

Must she **go** home now? – **Does** she **have to go** home now?
You **needn't** worry. – You **don't have to worry**.

ENGLISH SUMMARY

- You use **can / can't** to say that someone **is** or **is not able to do** something.
- You can use **can / can't** in the present tense and **could / couldn't** in the past. You can use **be able to** in all tenses.
- **Can / may** show that someone is allowed to do something. Their negative forms **can't**, **may not** and **mustn't** say that someone is not allowed to do something.
- You can use **can / can't**, **may / mustn't** in the present tense and **could / couldn't** in the past. You can use **be allowed to** in all tenses.
- **Must** shows that someone has to do something. The negative form **needn't** says that you mustn't do something.
- You can use **must** und **needn't** in the present tense only. You can use **have to** in all tenses.

G10 Das Plusquamperfekt The simple past perfect

Seite 30–31

Wenn du über Dinge berichten möchtest, die sich in der Vergangenheit ereignet haben, nimmst du das ***past tense***:

Francis Drake **sailed** all round the world from 1577 to 1580.
After that Elizabeth I **thanked** him.

Wenn du jedoch betonen möchtest, dass sich ein Ereignis **vor** einem anderen in der Vergangenheit abgespielt hat, verwendest du das ***simple past perfect***.

1577–1580 — Zuvor: *past perfect*

1580 — Damals: *past tense*

After Francis Drake **had sailed** all round the world,
Nachdem Francis Drake um die ganze Welt **gesegelt war** / die ganze Welt **umsegelt hatte**, …

Elizabeth I **thanked** him and he **became** Sir Francis Drake.
dankte ihm Elizabeth I. und er **wurde** Sir Francis Drake.

- Das ***simple past perfect*** wird gebildet aus ***had*** und dem ***past participle***.
- Es ist für alle Personen gleich.
- Das ***past perfect*** steht fast immer in der Nähe von ***past tense***-Formen.
- Sehr häufig wird das ***past perfect*** in Nebensätzen der Zeit mit ***when***, ***after*** oder ***as soon as*** und in Nebensätzen des Grundes mit ***because*** verwendet:

As soon as William **had become** King of England, he built strong castles all over the country.
When the Empire **had come** to an end, lots of British colonies joined the Commonwealth.
Stephen Hoskins was only allowed to do very simple jobs **because** he **hadn't done** any training.

ENGLISH SUMMARY

- You use the **past perfect** if you want to say that something happened **before** another action in the past.
- You almost always use it together with **past tense** forms.
- The **past perfect** very often is in clauses with **after**, **when**, **as soon as** and **because**.

Unit 3

IN DIESER UNIT LERNST DU

- wie du reflexive Pronomen im Englischen verwendest. G11
- wie du mit den Pronomen auf *-self / -selves* betonen kannst, dass jemand etwas selbst tut. G11
- wie du mit *each other* ausdrückst, dass zwischen Personen etwas wechselseitig geschieht. G12
- wie du mit verschiedenen Bedingungssätzen (*if*-Sätzen) ausdrücken kannst, was geschehen könnte oder was hätte geschehen können. G13

G11 Die Pronomen auf *-self / -selves* (Reflexivpronomen)
Self-pronouns (Reflexive pronouns)

Seite 44–45

Die *-self / -selves*-Pronomen kommen als Reflexivpronomen und als verstärkende Pronomen vor.

a) Reflexiver Gebrauch

I'm hungry. **I**'ll make	**myself**	something to eat.	… mache **mir** …
Can **you** see	**yourself**	in the photo, Mel?	… du **dich** … sehen?
Poor Jake. **He**'s hurt	**himself**	at football.	… hat **sich** … verletzt.
Amy only thinks of	**herself.**		… denkt nur an **sich**.
Look at that cat. **It**'s washing	**itself.**		… wäscht **sich** (selbst).
We've taught	**ourselves**	how to cook.	… haben **uns** (selbst) … beigebracht.
Why can't **you** behave	**yourselves?**		… ihr **euch** nicht benehmen?
The two girls are looking at	**themselves**	in a video.	… schauen **sich** … an.

- Mit den Reflexivpronomen kannst du ausdrücken, dass jemand etwas **für sich selbst** oder auf sich bezogen tut.
- Die Singularformen enden auf *-self (herself)*, die Pluralformen auf *-selves (themselves)*.
- Den Reflexivpronomen im Englischen entspricht im Deutschen **mich / mir (selbst), dich / dir (selbst), sich (selbst)** usw.
- Die Reflexivpronomen sind Objekt im Satz und beziehen sich zurück auf das Subjekt: *myself* → *I*.

b) Deutsch: reflexiv – englisch: nicht reflexiv

Jake has	**changed**	a lot.	Jake hat **sich** sehr **verändert**.
The twins	**relax**	at the weekend.	Die Zwillinge **entspannen sich** am Wochenende.

- Das Reflexivpronomen kommt im Englischen viel seltener vor als im Deutschen. Vielen Verben, die im Deutschen mit **sich** gebildet werden, entspricht im Englischen ein nicht reflexives Verb:

sich (ver)ändern	**to change**	sich erinnern	**to remember**
sich anziehen	**to get dressed**	sich fühlen	**to feel**
sich beeilen	**to hurry**	sich öffnen	**to open**
sich bewegen	**to move**	sich (hin)setzen	**to sit down**
sich entscheiden	**to decide**	sich treffen	**to meet**
sich entspannen	**to relax**	sich trennen	**to split up**
sich ereignen	**to happen**	sich verirren	**to get lost**

c) Verstärkender Gebrauch

Shall I call Charlie for you, Amy?	No, thank you. **I** can call him	**myself.**
Can you help me with this exercise?	Why don't **you** try to do it	**yourself?**
Hey, this is a cool song!	Yes, my **brother** wrote it	**himself.**
Mel's dress looks nice.	Imagine. **She** made it	**herself.**
Do you think Dad should help us?	I think **we** can build the wall	**ourselves.**
We won't be there tomorrow.	**You**'ll have to make lunch	**yourselves.**
Did Jake tell you about Amy's and Mel's party?	No, **they** told us	**themselves.**

▶ Mit den Pronomen auf ***-self/-selves*** kannst du betonen, dass jemand etwas **selbst** tut. Diese Pronomen stehen meist am Satzende.

!

Beachte den Unterschied:

You did it **yourself**. – **Du** hast es selbst gemacht.
You did it **yourselves**. – **Ihr** habt es selbst gemacht.

G12 *Each other*

Seite 45

Jake and Miriam often talked to	**each other.**		… miteinander …
And they sometimes helped	**each other**	with their homework.	… sich (gegenseitig) …
But now they haven't seen	**each other**	for some time.	… sich …

▶ Wenn du ausdrücken möchtest, dass zwischen Personen etwas wechselseitig geschieht, so kannst du ***each other*** verwenden.

▶ Im Deutschen kann ***each other*** mit **sich, einander** oder **gegenseitig** wiedergegeben werden.

Amy and Mel are looking at **themselves** in the mirror.

Amy and Mel are looking at **each other**.

ENGLISH SUMMARY

▶ The singular forms of the **self-pronouns** end in **-self** (**myself**), the plural forms end in **-selves** (**ourselves**).

▶ You can use the **self-pronouns** reflexively: (**He** hurt **himself**.). The **object** (**himself**) and the **subject** (**he**) are the same person.

▶ You can also use the **self-pronouns** to stress that someone has done something **herself / himself**.

▶ You use **each other** to say that there is an 'exchange' (*Interaktion*) between people: 'I help you and you help me: We help **each other**'.

G13 Bedingungssätze Conditional sentences

Seite 47–49

Wie du schon weißt, besteht ein Bedingungssatz aus einem ***if***-Satz (***if-clause***) und einem Hauptsatz (***main clause***). Der ***if***-Satz beschreibt eine Bedingung und der Hauptsatz drückt aus, was passieren wird oder passieren könnte, wenn diese Bedingung erfüllt wird. Es gibt drei Grundtypen von Bedingungssätzen:

Typ 1	Typ 2	Typ 3

a) Typ 1 (Revision)

Dieser Typ von Bedingungssätzen ist dir schon bekannt. Der Sprecher hält die Bedingung für realistisch. Sie scheint erfüllbar zu sein.

Erfüllbare Bedingung im *if*-Satz: *simple present*	Folge im Hauptsatz: *will future*
If Jake **goes** to bed late,	he **will be** tired tomorrow.
If we **build** a wall through our bedroom,	we'**ll have** two rooms.
If that **doesn't work**,	we **can** turn the hobby room into a bedroom.
If you **need** some help,	ask Dad.

- Im ***if***-Satz verwendest du das ***simple present***. Im Hauptsatz steht meist das ***will future***.
- Neben dem ***will future*** werden im Hauptsatz häufig auch die modalen Hilfsverben ***can***, ***must***, ***needn't*** verwendet oder der Imperativ (…, *ask Dad.* – …, frage Papa!)
- Bedingungssätze können entweder mit dem ***if***-Satz oder dem Hauptsatz beginnen:

If you need some help, ask Dad. → Komma vor dem Hauptsatz.
Ask Dad if you need some help. → Kein Komma vor dem ***if***-Satz.

!
Im ***if***-Satz steht das ***simple present***, nie das ***will future***.

b) Typ 2

Diesen Typ verwendest du, wenn du daran zweifelst, dass die Bedingung erfüllbar ist oder wenn du genau weißt, dass sie nicht erfüllt werden kann.

Nur theoretisch erfüllbare Bedingung im *if*-Satz: *simple past*	Folge im Hauptsatz: *conditional (would + infinitive)*
If Amy and Mel **had** their own rooms,	there **wouldn't be** any trouble.
Wenn Amy und Mel ihre eigenen Zimmer **hätten**,	**gäbe** es keine Schwierigkeiten / **würde** es keine Schwierigkeiten **geben**.
If the twins **didn't fight** all the time,	the Pattersons **could enjoy** their meals more.
Wenn die Zwillinge sich nicht dauernd **streiten würden**,	**könnten** Pattersons ihre Mahlzeiten mehr **genießen**.
If I **were** you, Amy,	I'**d talk** to your sister about your problems.
Wenn ich an deiner Stelle **wäre**, Amy,	**würde** ich mit deiner Schwester über eure Probleme **sprechen**.

- Im *if*-Satz steht das ***simple past***. Das ***simple past*** drückt hier nicht aus, dass die Handlung in der Vergangenheit stattfand, sondern beschreibt eine unwahrscheinliche oder unmögliche Bedingung (*If I **were** you …* – Wenn ich du **wäre** …).
- Neben dem ***conditional (would + infinitive)*** kannst du im Hauptsatz auch ***could/ might + infinitive*** gebrauchen: *If I **had** lots of money, I **could travel** round the world.* – Wenn ich eine Menge Geld **hätte**, **könnte** ich um die Welt reisen.
  *If Dad **had** more time, he **might take** us on trips more often.* – Wenn Papa mehr Zeit **hätte**, **würde** er **vielleicht** mehr Ausflüge mit uns gemeinsam machen.
- Wenn du jemandem einen Rat geben möchtest, kannst du das mit ***If I were you*** … oder ***I if was you*** … tun: *If I **were/was** you, I wouldn't do that.* – Wenn ich an deiner Stelle **wäre**, **würde** ich das nicht tun.

!

Anders als im Deutschen darf im *if*-Satz nie das ***conditional*** (Konditional) stehen.
→ Kein ***would*** im *if*-Satz! **If** I **were** you, I would go home.

c) Typ 3

Bei diesen Bedingungssätzen weiß der Sprecher, dass die Bedingung nicht mehr erfüllt werden kann, weil es sich um eine Situation handelt, die in der Vergangenheit liegt und vorbei ist. *(If they **had asked** their father … → But they **didn't ask** their father.)*

Nicht mehr erfüllbare Bedingung im *if*-Satz: *past perfect*	Folge im Hauptsatz: *conditional perfect (would + have + past participle)*
If the girls **had asked** their father,	he **would have helped** them.
Wenn die Mädchen ihren Vater **gefragt hätten**,	**hätte** er ihnen geholfen.
If Jake **hadn't come** home so late,	he **wouldn't have been** so tired the next day.
Wenn Jake nicht so spät nach Hause **gekommen wäre**,	**wäre** er am nächsten Tag nicht so müde **gewesen**.
If Jake **had been** nicer to Miriam,	they **wouldn't have split up**.
Wenn Jake netter zu Miriam **gewesen wäre**,	**hätten** sie sich nicht **getrennt**.
If people **had known** about the party earlier,	they **could have bought** some costumes.
Wenn die Leute früher von der Party **gewusst hätten**,	hätten sie Kostüme **kaufen können**.

- Im ***if***-Satz steht das ***past perfect***, im Hauptsatz das ***conditional perfect*** (***would + have + past participle***) oder ***could + have + past participle***.
- Dem ***past perfect*** im englischen ***if***-Satz entspricht im Deutschen eine Konditionalform: gefragt hätten, gekommen wäre, gewesen wäre, gewusst hätten:
  *If Jake **had known** more about girls, he **would have been** nicer to Miriam.*
  Wenn Jake mehr über Mädchen **gewusst hätte**, **wäre** er zu Miriam netter gewesen.

!

Bei den Kurzformen musst du aufpassen:

'd kann die Kurzform von ***had*** und von ***would*** sein.
Der Zusammenhang macht dir klar, um welche Form es sich handelt.
I'**d** have phoned if I'**d** known your mobile number. =
I **would** have phoned if I **had** known your mobile number.

ENGLISH SUMMARY

- A **conditional sentence** has two parts, an **if-clause** and a **main clause**.
- There are three types of conditional sentences:
  - In type 1 (possible conditions) you use the **simple present** in the **if-clause** and the **will future** in the **main clause**.
  - In type 2 (theoretical conditions) you use the **simple past** in the **if-clause** and the **conditional** in the **main clause**.
  - In type 3 (impossible conditions) you use the **past perfect** in the **if-clause** and the **conditional perfect** in the **main clause**.

Careful: You mustn't use **will** and **would** in the **if-clauses**.

Unit 4

IN DIESER UNIT LERNST DU

- ✓ wie du den bestimmten und den unbestimmten Artikel im Englischen verwendest. G14
- ✓ wie du mit Adjektiven, die du als Nomen benützt, eine gesamte Gruppe von Menschen beschreibst (*the rich*). G15
- ✓ dass du nach bestimmten Verben (wie *get, feel, taste* usw.) ein Adjektiv verwenden musst. G16
- ✓ wie du mit dem *future perfect* ausdrücken kannst, dass eine Handlung zu einem bestimmten Zeitpunkt in der Zukunft abgeschlossen sein wird. G17
- ✓ wie du Paarwörter (*trousers, jeans*) benützt. G18

G14 Der bestimmte und der unbestimmte Artikel

Seite 60–61

The definite and the indefinite article

a) Der bestimmte Artikel

- Der bestimmte Artikel ***the*** zeigt an, dass etwas näher bestimmt ist. Der Artikel steht nicht, wenn von Personen oder Dingen ganz allgemein gesprochen wird.
- Im Englischen gibt es für bestimmte Gruppen von Nomen Regeln, die dir sagen, wann der bestimmte Artikel verwendet wird. Dazu gehören abstrakte Begriffe, Verkehrsmittel und Mahlzeiten. Beachte die Unterschiede zum Deutschen!

Abstrakte Begriffe:

ohne Artikel	mit Artikel
Life is too short. **Das Leben …**	I'm reading a book about **the life** of Francis Drake.
Time goes very quickly. **Die Zeit …**	I'll always remember **the time** we spent together.

- ***Music, life, time, love, work*** usw. sind abstrakte Begriffe. Wenn sie im allgemeinen Sinn verwendet werden, stehen sie ohne Artikel. Wenn sie durch eine ***of-phrase*** (*of Francis Drake*) oder durch einen Relativsatz (*we spent together*) näher bestimmt werden, stehen sie **mit dem bestimmten Artikel**.

Verkehrsmittel:

ohne Artikel	mit Artikel
I usually go to work by **bus**. … mit **dem Bus**.	I saw her on **the bus** yesterday.
We can go to Windsor by **train**. … mit **der Bahn**.	**The train** to Windsor leaves at 11.35.

▶ Wenn man an ein Verkehrsmittel allgemein denkt, steht kein Artikel. Wenn ein ganz bestimmtes Fahrzeug oder eine bestimmte Verbindung gemeint ist (*the train to Windsor*), steht der Artikel.

Mahlzeiten:

ohne Artikel	mit Artikel
Rhona often cooks **lunch** herself. … **das Mittagessen**.	**The lunch** we had at that restaurant was nice.
We sometimes watch TV after **tea**. … nach **dem Abendessen**.	I enjoyed **the tea** on Shirin's birthday.

▶ Wenn von Mahlzeiten allgemein gesprochen wird, steht **kein Artikel**. Ist eine ganz bestimmte Mahlzeit gemeint (*the tea on Shirin's birthday*), steht der **Artikel**.

b) Der unbestimmte Artikel

Im Englischen wird der unbestimmte Artikel ***a / an*** meistens genauso verwendet wie in den deutschen Entsprechungen. Nur in einigen wenigen Fällen, die du z. T. schon kennst, unterscheidet sich der Gebrauch:

Berufsbezeichnungen:

Shirin would like to be **a doctor**.	… möchte gern **Ärztin** werden.
In the holidays she worked as **a shop assistant**.	… arbeitete sie als **Verkäuferin**.

Bestimmte Redewendungen:

Poor Rhona. She has **a headache** and **a temperature**.	… sie hat **Kopfschmerzen** und **Fieber**.
Sorry, I can't talk to you. I'm in **a hurry**.	… ich bin in **Eile**.

G15 Das Adjektiv als Nomen
Adjectives used as nouns

Seite 60–61

Im Englischen können Adjektive – anders als im Deutschen – nur in bestimmten Fällen als Nomen verwendet werden.

the + adjective	adjective + noun
We're collecting money for **the blind**. … für **Blinde** / … für **die Blinden**.	**A blind man** was waiting in the queue. **Ein blinder Mann … / Ein Blinder …**
Doctors look after **the sick**. … **Kranke** / … **die Kranken**.	They took **the sick woman** to hospital. … **die kranke Frau** … / … **die Kranke** …

- Wenn ein Adjektiv als Nomen gebraucht wird, bezieht es sich auf eine gesamte Gruppe von Menschen: ***the rich*** = die Reichen allgemein, alle Reichen.
- Obwohl die Adjektive keine Pluralendung haben, werden sie wie Pluralformen verwendet und stehen mit Verben und Pronomen im Plural: ***The famous aren't*** *always happy.* ***They*** *have* ***their*** *problems, too.*
- Wenn man von einzelnen Personen oder von bestimmten Gruppen spricht, muss das Adjektiv durch ein Nomen wie ***person, man, woman, people*** oder das Stützwort ***one/ones*** ergänzt werden.
- Man kann nicht wie im Deutschen das Adjektiv für sich allein verwenden: **die Kleine** = ***the little girl.***

ENGLISH SUMMARY

- You use the **definite article** when you talk about certain people or things. You don't usually use the definite article when you talk about people or things in general.
- With some nouns (**abstract nouns**, **transport** and **meals**) you use the **definite article** differently in English and in German.
- You must use the **indefinite article** when you talk about a person's job.
- You can use **the + adjective** when you mean a whole group of people (**the** blind = **all** blind people).

G16 Adjektive nach bestimmten Verben

Adjectives after certain verbs

Seite 63–64

Du weißt, dass Adjektive ein Substantiv näher bestimmen. Das Adjektiv gibt an, **wie** eine Person oder eine Sache **ist**. Es steht entweder vor einem Nomen (*There are* ***cool clubs*** *in Manchester.*) oder nach dem Verb ***to be*** (*This club* ***is cool.***). Adverbien dagegen gehören zum Verb und geben an, **wie** jemand etwas **tut** oder wie etwas **geschieht** (*How did Rhona* ***eat****? – She* ***ate hungrily****. How did Tariq* ***talk*** *to Shirin? – He* ***talked*** *to her* ***excitedly***).

Es gibt jedoch eine Reihe von Verben, die nicht eine Tätigkeit, sondern einen Zustand beschreiben. Diesen Verben folgt ein Adjektiv:

be, seem, feel, stay	
Rhona **was** a little **shy** at first. Everything **seemed** so **strange** to her. But soon she **felt better**. And she **stayed calm** when they all started to speak Punjabi.	Rhona war zuerst ein wenig schüchtern. Alles erschien ihr so seltsam. Aber bald fühlte sie sich besser. Und sie blieb ruhig, als …

- Die Verben ***be, seem, feel*** und ***stay*** verweisen auf einen **Zustand** oder eine **Eigenschaft**. Deshalb steht nach ihnen ein Adjektiv.

become, get	
Some bands **have become famous** in Manchester. I'm **getting tired** of this music.	Einige Bands sind in Manchester berühmt geworden. Ich habe diese Musik langsam satt.

▶ ***Become*** und ***get*** entsprechen dem deutschen **werden**. Ihnen folgt ein Adjektiv.

look, smell, sound, taste	
The Asian food **looked interesting**. It **smelled good** and **tasted great**. Some of the names **sounded unusual**.	Das asiatische Essen sah interessant aus. Es roch gut und schmeckte großartig. Einige der Namen klangen ungewöhnlich.

▶ ***Look***, ***smell***, ***sound*** und ***taste*** drücken **Sinneswahrnehmungen** aus. Auch nach ihnen steht ein Adjektiv.

ENGLISH SUMMARY

- ▶ Usually adjectives describe nouns and adverbs describe verbs. But there are some English verbs that do not describe an activity, but show what something or someone is like.
- ▶ You use an adjective after **be**, **seem**, **feel**, **stay**, **get** and **become**.
- ▶ You also use an adjective after **look**, **sound**, **smell** and **taste** when these verbs describe the way things are.

G17 Das Futur II The future perfect

Seite 65

Du kennst schon eine Reihe von Zukunftsformen. Das ***future perfect*** ist eine weitere Möglichkeit, zukünftiges Geschehen auszudrücken.

By the end of next week Tariq **will have finished** his report. But he **won't have read** many of the books he borrowed from the library.	Tariq **wird** seinen Bericht bis Ende nächster Woche **geschrieben haben**. Aber er **wird** nicht viele der Bücher, die er sich aus der Bibliothek ausgeliehen hat, **gelesen haben**.

▶ Das ***future perfect*** wird gebildet aus ***will/won't*** + ***have*** + ***past participle***. Es ist für alle Personen gleich.

▶ Mit dem ***future perfect*** kannst du ausdrücken, dass eine Handlung zu einem bestimmten Zeitpunkt in der Zukunft abgeschlossen sein wird. Dieser Zeitpunkt wird häufig durch eine Zeitangabe wie ***by the end of next week***, ***by Friday***, ***by July*** etc. festgelegt.

ENGLISH SUMMARY

- ▶ You use the **future perfect** to talk about events or actions that will have come to an end by a certain time in the future.
- ▶ You often use it with adverbials like **by next week**, **by Friday**, **by July** etc.

G18 Paarwörter Pair words

Seite 70

Have you seen **my glasses**? I can't find **them**. **Your new trousers** look really nice. Where did you buy **them**? I've got **a pair of trousers** just like that.	Hast du **meine Brille** gesehen? Ich kann **sie** nicht finden. **Deine neue Hose** sieht wirklich gut aus. Wo hast du **sie** gekauft? Ich habe genauso **eine**.

- Paarwörter wie ***trousers***, ***jeans***, ***glasses*** usw. bezeichnen Dinge, die aus zwei Teilen bestehen (z. B. zwei Hosenbeinen). Deshalb werden sie im Englischen nur im Plural verwendet.
- Wenn du die Anzahl der Paarwörter genau angeben willst, verwendest du ***pair of*** für die Einzahl und ***pairs of*** für die Mehrzahl:
  Tariq owns more than **five pairs of sunglasses**. = Tariq besitzt mehr als fünf Sonnenbrillen.

ENGLISH SUMMARY

- You always use the plural with **pair words**.
- If you speak of the exact number of pair words, you use **pair of / pairs of**.

Unit 5

IN DIESER UNIT LERNST DU

- ✓ wie du verschiedene Zeitformen des Passivs verwendest. G19 G21
- ✓ wie du Sätze vom Aktiv ins Passiv setzt. G20
- ✓ wie du Passivsätze mit Verben bilden kannst, die zwei Objekte haben. G22

G19 Das Passiv The passive

Seite 78–80

Aktivsätze betonen, **wer** etwas tut. Passivsätze jedoch betonen, was getan wird. Die Handlung selbst steht im Vordergrund und nicht derjenige, der etwas tut.

Active	Passive
The Casting Director **interviewed** all the actors.	All the actors **were interviewed**.

- In dem Aktivsatz ist *The Casting Director* Subjekt und daher betont, während im Passivsatz die Betonung auf *All the actors* liegt.
- Sehr häufig wird in Passivsätzen der Verursacher einer Handlung nicht genannt, weil er entweder unwichtig, ganz offensichtlich oder unbekannt ist.
- Passivsätze findet man vor allem in Zeitungsberichten, historischen Texten und technischen Beschreibungen.

Die Zeitformen des Passivs *(simple present, simple past, present perfect)*

- Die passiven Verbformen werden aus einer Form von ***to be*** und dem ***past participle*** gebildet.
- Passivsätze können in verschiedenen Zeitformen vorkommen. Dabei wird die Form von ***to be*** der jeweiligen Zeitstufe angepasst.
- Die Zeitformen des Passivs werden nach denselben Regeln verwendet wie die aktiven Verbformen:

Simple present	
am / is / are + past participle	Every day millions of newspapers **are sold** in Britain. ... werden ... verkauft. The popular papers **are read** by lots of people. ... werden ... gelesen.

- Das ***simple present*** wird verwendet, wenn etwas regelmäßig geschieht oder wenn es sich um eine Tatsache handelt.
- Signalwörter für das ***simple present*** sind: ***every day***, ***often***, ***never***, ***regularly*** etc.

Simple past	
was / were + past participle	The first colour TVs **were made** in 1954. ... wurden ... hergestellt. The early soap operas **were used** to advertise cleaning products. ... wurden benutzt ...

- Das ***simple past*** betont, dass eine Handlung in der Vergangenheit abgeschlossen wurde und vorbei ist.
- Signalwörter für das ***simple past*** sind: ***in 1954***, ***yesterday***, ***some years ago***, ***last night*** etc.

Present perfect	
have been / has been + past participle	**Have** the actors **been phoned** yet? Sind ... angerufen worden? The script for the soap **has** already **been written.** ... ist ... geschrieben worden.

- Das ***present perfect*** verwendet man, wenn man betonen will, dass eine Handlung, die in der Vergangenheit stattfand, in der Gegenwart noch spürbar ist.
- Signalwörter für das ***present perfect*** sind: ***yet***, ***already***, ***ever***, ***just now*** etc.
- Adverbien wie ***already***, ***ever***, ***never*** usw. stehen nach dem ersten Hilfsverb (***has** already been written*).

G 20 Vom Aktiv ins Passiv

From active to passive

Seite 80

Will man einen Aktivsatz in einen Passivsatz umwandeln, muss man Folgendes beachten:

- Das Objekt des Aktivsatzes wird zum Subjekt im Passivsatz.
- Meist wird in Passivsätzen der Verursacher einer Handlung – also das Subjekt des Aktivsatzes – nicht genannt. Möchte man jedoch besonders betonen, von **wem** etwas getan wird, kann man ihn mit Hilfe der Präposition ***by*** (auf Deutsch: **von**) am Satzende anfügen. Dieser Verursacher der Handlung wird ***by-agent*** genannt.
- Das Aktivverb wird zum Passivverb. Die Zeit bleibt in beiden Sätzen gleich. Im Passivsatz verändert sich die Form von ***to be*** je nach der Zeit:

He finds her. → She **is found**. He found her. → She **was found**.

Active	subject Matt Stirling	plays	object the role of 'Justin'.
Passive	The role of 'Justin' subject	is played	by Matt Stirling. by-agent

G 21 Weitere Zeitformen des Passivs

Other tenses of the passive

Seite 82–83

Past perfect	
had been + past participle	*Smash hits* **had been read** by millions of teenagers before the magazine finished. … war … gelesen worden … The first scenes **had** already **been filmed** when Matt came to the studio. … waren … gedreht worden …

- Das ***past perfect*** beschreibt Handlungen oder Ereignisse, die vor anderen Handlungen in der Vergangenheit stattfanden.
- Es steht fast immer zusammen mit dem ***past tense*** (***gave up***, ***came***, …).
- Signalwörter für das ***past perfect*** sind: ***after***, ***when***, ***as soon as*** etc.

Will future	
will be + past participle	A great new daily soap **will be filmed** in this studio from next week. … wird … gefilmt werden … But the story **won't be told** before it is shown on TV. … wird nicht verraten werden …

- Das ***will future*** beschreibt zukünftige Ereignisse, die nicht von eigenen Entscheidungen abhängen. Es kann auch Vermutungen über die Zukunft ausdrücken.
- Signalwörter für das ***will future*** sind: ***next week***, ***tomorrow*** und Ausdrücke wie ***I hope***, ***I'm sure*** etc.

ENGLISH SUMMARY

- Active sentences tell you **who / what does something**.
- Passive sentences stress **what is done**. Often you do not know who / what has done the action, or you think this is not important.
- You form the passive with a form of **to be** and the **past participle**.
- If you want to say who / what does something in a passive sentence, you use the **by-agent**.
- You use the same tense in the passive sentence as in the active sentence.

G 22 Das Passiv bei Verben mit zwei Objekten

Verbs with two objects in passive sentences

Seite 82–83

- Viele englische Verben werden (ganz ähnlich wie ihre deutschen Entsprechungen) mit zwei Objekten verwendet. Zu ihnen gehören: ***give***, ***offer***, ***promise***, ***send***, ***show*** usw. Vergleiche: They've offered **him the role**.– Sie haben **ihm die Rolle** angeboten.
- Beide Objekte des Aktivsatzes können zum Subjekt im Passivsatz werden:

Active	Object 1 (Person) An assistant showed **the actors**	Object 2 (Sache) **the studio**.
Passive	**The actors** were shown the studio. Subject 1 (Passive 1)	**The studio** was shown **to** the actors. Subject 2 (Passive 2)

- Anders als im Deutschen kann das Objekt, das eine Person beschreibt, zum Subjekt im Passivsatz werden. Man spricht hier vom **persönlichen Passiv**, dem ***personal passive***. Übersetzt werden diese Sätze meist mit dem deutschen **man** oder **jemand** + **Aktiv**: **Matt** was given the role of ‚Justin'. → **Man** gab Matt die Rolle des ‚Justin'.

Es gibt also grundsätzlich zwei Möglichkeiten, Sätze, die Verben mit zwei Objekten enthalten, ins Passiv zu setzen:

Passive 1 (personal passive)	Passive 2
Everyone was sent a brochure with a lot of useful information.	A brochure with a lot of useful information **was sent to everyone in the group.**
Allen wurde eine Broschüre … geschickt / Man / Jemand hat allen (…) eine Broschüre … geschickt.	
The people were given all the information.	All the information **was given to the people who had come to the casting.**
Man gab den Leuten (…) die gesamte Information.	

- Das **persönliche Passiv** ist die gebräuchlichere der beiden Passivarten.

- Die Person wird mit der Präposition *to* am Satzende genannt.
- Diese Konstruktion ist weniger gebräuchlich. Sie wird vorwiegend dann verwendet, wenn dieses Objekt besonders lang ist oder betont werden soll: ***to me*** / ***to us***.

ENGLISH SUMMARY

- Verbs like **give**, **offer**, **promise**, **send**, **show** etc. can have two objects: They gave **her a CD**.
- If you want to stress **who** is given or offered something, you can use the **personal passive**: **She** was given a CD.
- If a "thing" (the CD) becomes the subject of the passive sentence, the person is put at the end of the passive sentence with the preposition **to**: The CD was given **to her**.

Unit 6

IN DIESER UNIT LERNST DU

- ✓ die Unterschiede zwischen direkter und indirekter Rede kennen. G 23 G 26
- ✓ wie du die Zeitformen veränderst, wenn du direkte in indirekte Rede überträgst. G 24
- ✓ wie du Zeitangaben in der indirekten Rede machst. G 25
- ✓ wie du indirekte Fragen stellst und indirekte Aufforderungssätze bildest. G 27 G 28

G 23 Direkte und indirekte Rede Direct and indirect speech

Seite 94–95

Wenn du wiedergeben möchtest, was jemand gesagt hat, verwendest du die indirekte Rede.

Direct speech	Indirect speech
Ryan's father said: "**I have** to go to Australia for a few weeks. **I'll fly** a day after **your** birthday."	My father said that **he had** to go to Australia for a few weeks. He said **he would** fly a day after **my** birthday.

- Die direkte Rede ist ein direktes Zitat. Sie steht in Anführungszeichen.
- Die indirekte Rede besteht aus einem Einleitungssatz (*My father said …*) und einem Folgesatz (*… that he had to go to Australia …*).

- Das einleitende ***that*** des Folgesatzes kann weggelassen werden: *He said he would fly …*
- Wie im Deutschen müssen Personalpronomen und Possessivbegleiter verändert werden, wenn sie dem neuen Standpunkt nicht mehr entsprechen: ***I*** → ***he***, ***your*** → ***my*** etc.
- Anders als im Deutschen steht zwischen dem Einleitungssatz und der indirekten Rede **kein** Komma.

G 24 Indirekte Rede mit Zeitverschiebung
Indirect speech with tense shift

Seite 94–95

Wenn man einen Satz von der direkten Rede in die indirekte Rede umwandelt, kommt es meist zu einer Verschiebung der Zeiten im Folgesatz.

- Steht das einleitende Verb (***said***, ***told***) in der Vergangenheit, tritt im Folgesatz eine Verschiebung der Zeiten auf. Das einleitende Verb selbst bleibt im ***past tense*** stehen.

Direct speech	Indirect speech
"I **have** to go to Australia." simple present →	Ryan's father told him / said that he **had** to go to Australia. simple past
"I'**m getting** everything ready." present progressive →	He said that he **was getting** everything ready. past progressive
"I'**ve** already **bought** a new camera." present perfect →	Ryan's father said that he **had** already **bought** a new camera. past perfect
"Captain Cook **discovered** Australia. They **didn't know** anything about Australia in those days." simple past →	Ryan said that Captain Cook **had discovered** Australia and that they **hadn't known** anything about Australia in those days. past perfect simple
"They **hadn't seen** all the strange animals before." past perfect →	He said that they **hadn't seen** all the strange animals before. past perfect
"It **will be** warm." will →	He told Ryan that it **would be** warm. would
"I'm sorry. But you **can't come** with me." can →	He explained that he was sorry but that Ryan **couldn't go** with him. could

- Das ***past perfect*** in der direkten Rede bleibt ***past perfect*** in der indirekten Rede, da es keine noch weiter in die Vergangenheit zurückreichende Verbform gibt.
- Auch ***could***, ***would*** und ***should*** werden nicht verändert.

!

Say und ***tell***: My boss **said** that I would have to go to Australia.
My boss **told me** that I would have to go to Australia.

Nach ***tell*** folgt immer ein Objekt (die Person, mit der jemand spricht).

ENGLISH SUMMARY

- If you want to report something that you've heard to another person, you use indirect speech.
- Usually you introduce a sentence in indirect speech with a clause with **say** or **tell**. This clause is followed by a **that**-clause with indirect speech.
- If the verb that introduces the **that**-clause is in the past tense, you have to change the verb forms in indirect speech (**present** → **past**, **present perfect** → **past perfect**, **past** → **past perfect**, **will** → **would**).

G 25 Zeitangaben in der indirekten Rede

Expressions of time in indirect speech

Seite 95

Monday, June 9th (in the morning)	Monday, June 9th (in the afternoon)	Friday, June 13th
I'll give you the CD **tomorrow**.	Nick said he would give me the CD **tomorrow**.	He promised he would give me the CD **the next day**.

- Zeitangaben wie ***today***, ***this month***, ***this year*** usw. werden in der indirekten Rede beibehalten, wenn man noch am gleichen Tag, im gleichen Monat oder Jahr berichtet, was jemand gesagt hat. Wenn der Tag (der Monat, das Jahr) jedoch vorbei ist, verändern sich diese Zeitangaben in der indirekten Rede:

today	→ **that day**	tonight	→ **that night**
tomorrow	→ **the next day / the following day**	this evening	→ **that evening**
yesterday	→ **the day before**	three days ago	→ **three days before / earlier**
next year	→ **the following year**	last week / year	→ **the week / year before**

- Neben diesen Zeitangaben müssen manchmal auch weitere Wörter verändert werden, um sie dem Standpunkt des Berichtenden anzupassen. Zum Beispiel: ***here*** → ***there***, ***this*** → ***that***, ***come*** → ***go*** und ***bring*** → ***take***.

It's quite cold over **here**. **This** is unusual for the time of year. So when you **come**, you shouldn't forget to **bring** some warm clothes. See you soon. Ciao,
François

ENGLISH SUMMARY

- If you report something on the same day or in the same week, month etc., you needn't change the adverbials of time (**today** = **today**, **this week** = **this week** etc.).
- But if you report it later (the next day or the next month, for example), you must change these adverbials (**today** → **that day**, **yesterday** → **the day before**, **tomorrow** → **the following day** etc.).
- Sometimes you have to change other words, too, like: **here** → **there**, **this** → **that**, **come** → **go** and **bring** → **take**.

G 26 Die indirekte Rede mit Einführungssatz im Präsens

Seite 97

Indirect speech with reporting verb in the present

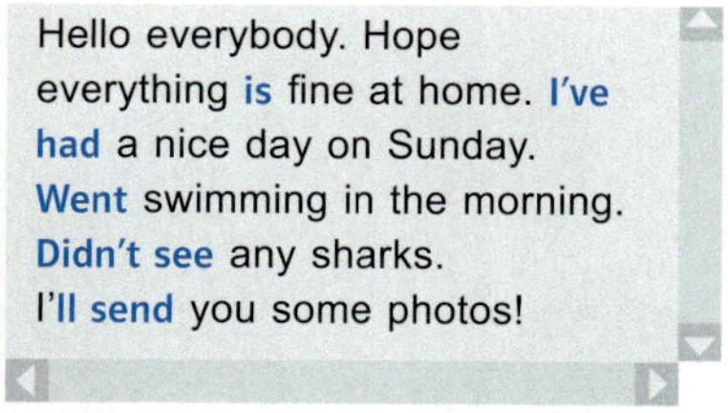

- Wenn du direkt wiedergibst, was jemand sagt oder geschrieben hat, so verwendest du für die indirekte Rede einen Einleitungssatz im *present tense* (*hopes, says, promises*).
- In diesem Fall werden die Zeitformen der direkten Rede in der indirekten Rede beibehalten: *is* → *is*, *have had* → *has had* etc.

ENGLISH SUMMARY

- If you report at once what someone says or writes, you use a reporting verb in the **present tense**.
- The verb forms in direct speech and in indirect speech stay the same.

G 27 Fragen in der indirekten Rede

Seite 97–98

Indirect questions

Direct speech	Indirect speech
Jade: "**What did** you **watch** last night, Ryan?"	Jade asked Ryan **what** he **had watched** the night before.
"**When was** it on?"	She wanted to know **when** it **had been** on.
"**Who are** the actors in that film?"	She asked him **who** the actors in that film **were**.

- Steht in der direkten Rede ein Fragewort (*what, when, who*), wird es in der indirekten Rede beibehalten.

Ryan: "**Have** you ever **seen** an action film like that, Jade?"	Ryan wanted to know **whether** Jade **had** ever **seen** an action film like that.
"**Did** you **enjoy** it?"	He **asked** her **if** she **had** enjoyed it.
"Do you **like** love stories better?"	He wanted to know **whether** she **liked** love stories better.

- ▶ In indirekten Fragen gelten dieselben Regeln der Zeitenfolge, die du schon aus dem indirekten Aussagesatz kennst.
- ▶ Steht in der indirekten Rede kein Fragewort, wird der Folgesatz in der indirekten Rede mit ***if*** oder ***whether*** eingeleitet (im Deutschen: …, **ob** …).
- ▶ ***Do***, ***does*** und ***did*** werden in indirekten Fragen nicht verwendet.
- ▶ Die Wortstellung in indirekten Fragesätzen ist dieselbe wie in Aussagesätzen:

	subject	Verb	object
"Did you like the film, Ryan?" – Jade asked Ryan whether	**he**	**had liked**	**the film.**

G 28 Indirekte Aufforderungssätze

Seite 97–98

Indirect commands

Direct speech	Indirect speech				
		verb	object	infinitive	
Police: "Please **drive on**."	The police	**told**	people	**to drive on.**	
"**Don't stop** here."	They	**warned**	them	**not to stop**	there.
"If you want to find out more, **read** the newspapers tomorrow."	They	**advised**	everybody	**to read**	the newspapers the next day.

!

Beachte die Übersetzung und Satzstellung bei ***warn***: Matt's father **warned him not to lose** his passport. … warnte ihn davor, …

- ▶ Aufforderungssätze werden in der indirekten Rede meist als Infinitivkonstruktion mit ***to*** oder ***not to*** wiedergegeben.
- ▶ Neben den Verben ***tell***, ***warn*** und ***ask*** können sie auch durch ***remind*** eingeleitet werden.

ENGLISH SUMMARY

- ▶ If you report questions with question words, you use **ask / want to know + question word**.
- ▶ If there is no question word in the direct question, you use **if** or **whether** in the indirect question.
- ▶ You do not use **do**, **does** or **did** in indirect questions.
- ▶ The word order in indirect questions is the same as in statements (subject - verb - object).
- ▶ You usually use the infinitive with **to** or **not to** in indirect commands.
- ▶ You use **ask**, **tell** or **warn** to introduce indirect commands.

Vocabulary

Wie du schon von Band 1 und 2 weißt, findest du im ***Vocabulary*** alle neuen englischen Wörter und Redewendungen. Sie stehen in der Reihenfolge, in der sie im Buch vorkommen. Das *Vocabulary* ist in drei Spalten aufgeteilt:

- Links stehen die englischen Wörter und Sätze. In Klammern ist das Wort in Lautschrift aufgeführt. Sie zeigt dir, wie du das Wort aussprichst. Die Erklärung der Lautschrift findest du am Ende dieser Seite.
- In der Mitte steht die deutsche Übersetzung.
- Rechts findest du Bilder, Beispielsätze, Erklärungen oder Hinweise auf Besonderheiten (siehe →). Neu in diesem Band sind Verweise auf verwandte Wörter in Französisch oder Latein.

Die **fett** gedruckten Wörter musst du lernen und anwenden können. Normal gedruckte Wörter sind nur zum Verständnis bestimmter Texte oder Übungen nötig.
In den Units und in der *Free Section* findest du manchmal neue Wörter in Fußnoten unten auf der Seite. Auch diese helfen dir, die Texte zu verstehen. Du musst sie nicht lernen.

Auf das *Vocabulary* folgt dann ab Seite 183 das ***Dictionary (English–German)***. Falls du ein Wort vergessen hast, kannst du einfach in dieser alphabetischen Wortliste nachsehen. Englische Begriffe wie *open-air*, die du auch im Deutschen verwendest, stehen nicht im *Vocabulary*. Du kannst ihre Aussprache und Übersetzung aber im *Dictionary* nachschlagen. Das gleiche gilt für Wörter, die auf Englisch und Deutsch fast gleich geschrieben und ausgesprochen werden, wie z. B. *tennis*.
Eine Liste der unregelmäßigen Verben findest du hinten im Buch auf Seite 210/211, das ***Dictionary (German–English)*** ab S. 217.

Abkürzungen und Zeichen

pl.	Plural	jmdn.	jemanden	*Lat.*	Latein
sing.	Singular	etw.	etwas	5	In dieser Übung kommen die Wörter vor.
sth	*something*	***f***	feminin/weiblich	!	Achtung!
sb	*somebody*	***m***	maskulin/männlich	↔	ist das Gegenteil von
adj	*adjective*	***n***	neutrum/sächlich	→	ist verwandt mit
jmdm.	jemandem	*Fr.*	Französisch	=	entspricht

Englische Laute

Mitlaute (Konsonanten)

[b]	**bed**	[p]	**picture**
[d]	**day**	[r]	**red**
[ð]	**the**	[s]	**six**
[f]	**family**	[ʃ]	**she**
[g]	**go**	[t]	**ten**
[ŋ]	**morning**	[tʃ]	**lunch**
[h]	**house**	[v]	**video**
[j]	**you**	[w]	**we, one**
[k]	**can, milk**	[z]	**easy**
[l]	**letter**	[ʒ]	**revision**
[m]	**man**	[dʒ]	**page**
[n]	**no**	[θ]	**thank you**

Selbstlaute (Vokale)

[ɑː]	**car**
[æ]	**apple**
[e]	**pen**
[ə]	**again**
[ɜː]	**girl**
[ʌ]	**but**
[ɪ]	**it**
[i]	**happy**
[iː]	**teacher**
[ɒ]	**dog**
[ɔː]	**ball**
[ʊ]	**book**
[u]	**January**
[uː]	**too, two**

Doppellaute

[aɪ]	**I, my**
[aʊ]	**now, mouse**
[eɪ]	**name, they**
[eə]	**there, pair**
[ɪə]	**here, idea**
[əʊ]	**hello**
[ɔɪ]	**boy**
[ʊə]	**sure**

[ː] der vorangehende Laut ist lang, z. B. *you* [juː]
[‿] der Bindebogen zeigt, dass zwei Wörter in der Aussprache verbunden werden
[ˈ] die folgende Silbe zeigt den Hauptakzent
[ˌ] die folgende Silbe zeigt den Nebenakzent
Alle anderen Zeichen werden genauso ausgesprochen, wie sie geschrieben werden, z. B. [b], [j], [l] usw.

Unit 1: The world of sport

VOCABULARY SKILLS

Erinnerst du dich noch an die *Vocabulary Skills* aus den letzten beiden Bänden? Auch in diesem Jahr können sie dir wieder beim Vokabellernen helfen:

- Führe deine Vokabelkartei fort. Markiere Wörter, die du dir nicht so leicht merken kannst, mit einem farbigen Punkt: gelb für Ausspracheschwierigkeiten, blau für Rechtschreibschwierigkeiten und rot für Schwierigkeiten mit der Betonung.
- Nimm dir jeden Tag kleine Lernportionen von 10–15 Wörtern vor. Lerne und wiederhole sie drei Mal täglich je 5–10 Minuten und schau sie dir noch einmal vor dem Einschlafen an.
- Stelle für jedes neue Wort einen Zusammenhang her. Lerne vor allem schwierige Wörter möglichst in einem ganzen Satz oder mit anderen, schon bekannten Wörtern aus der gleichen Wortfamilie.
- Lerne immer alle drei Formen der unregelmäßigen Verben, z. B. *shake, shook, shaken*
- Um Verwechslungen mit anderen Fremdsprachen, die du lernst, zu vermeiden, solltest du Folgendes beachten: Lerne zuerst die Vokabeln der einen Fremdsprache, mache dann Hausaufgaben in z. B. Mathematik und lerne schließlich für die andere Fremdsprache. So kannst du die einzelnen Sprachen besser auseinanderhalten. Und denk daran: Auch die Lernpausen dazwischen sind wichtig!

Check-in

oval ['əʊvl]	oval, eiförmig →	an *oval* ball 
pitch [pɪtʃ]	Spielfeld, Platz	
referee [ˌrefə'riː]	Schiedsrichter/-in	
to **control** [kən'trəʊl]	kontrollieren →	! The referee *controls* the football game. ↔ The teacher checks the pupil's homework.
baseball ['beɪsbɔːl]	Baseball →	*Baseball* is very popular in the USA.
ice [aɪs]	Eis →	! *ice* = Eis ↔ ice-cream = Eis(creme)
stick [stɪk]	Stock, Schläger	
base [beɪs]	Base *(beim Baseball)*	
field [fiːld]	Feld, Spielfeld	
bat [bæt]	Schläger *(beim Tischtennis, Baseball)* →	a *bat* 
cricket ['krɪkɪt]	Kricket →	*Cricket* is very popular in Australia, England, India, New Zealand, Pakistan and South Africa.
to **go on** [gəʊ‿'ɒn]	(an)dauern →	The game was from 11 am to 4 pm. It *went on* for 5 hours.
athletics [æθ'letɪks]	Leichtathletik →	! *Athletics* **is** an important part of PE in British schools.
rugby ['rʌgbi]	Rugby	
track [træk]	Bahn, Laufbahn; Weg	
skateboarding ['skeɪtbɔːdɪŋ]	Skateboardfahren	
American [ə'merɪkən]	Amerikanisch; amerikanisch →	She is from the USA. She is *American*.
helmet ['helmət]	Helm →	When you ride a bike you must wear a *helmet*.
racket ['rækɪt]	Schläger *(Tennis-)* →	a *racket* 
umpire ['ʌmpaɪə]	Schiedsrichter/-in →	An *umpire* controls a tennis match.
court [kɔːt]	Spielfeld →	! a tennis *court* ↔ a football field
ice hockey ['aɪs ˌhɒki]	Eishockey	
race [reɪs]	Wettlauf, Rennen	
brake [breɪk]	Bremse →	The car crashed into another car because the *brakes* did not work.

Language 1: A new trick

	event [ɪ'vent]	Ereignis, Veranstaltung →	There are a lot of interesting *events* in our town every month. *Lat. eventum* ***n***
	chance [tʃɑ:ns]	Chance; Gelegenheit, Möglichkeit →	She lost the race because the others were too fast. She did not have a *chance*.
	arrangement [ə'reɪndʒmənt]	Abmachung, Vereinbarung; Plan →	*arrangement* = plan *Fr. l'arrangement* ***m***
	feeling ['fi:lɪŋ]	Gefühl →	*feeling* → to feel
	not until [nɒt ʌn'tɪl]	erst (dann), wenn	
4	to **open** ['əʊpn]	eröffnen →	! He *opened* the new museum yesterday. He opened the door.
6	**situation** [ˌsɪtju'eɪʃn]	Situation →	! Achtung Aussprache *Fr. la situation*

Talkwise: Is it important to win?

	talkwise ['tɔ:kwaɪz]	„redegewandt"	
	agreeing [ə'gri:ɪŋ]	Zustimmen	
	disagreeing [ˌdɪsə'gri:ɪŋ]	Widersprechen →	agreeing ↔ *disagreeing*
1	**wheelchair** ['wi:ltʃeə]	Rollstuhl →	*wheelchair* → chair
2	**once** [wʌns]	einmal	
	to **agree** [ə'gri:]	zustimmen →	Yes, you're right. I *agree*.
	exactly [ɪg'zæktli]	genau →	*Exactly*! That's what I think, too. It's my 13th birthday today – I'm *exactly* 13 years old.
	rubbish ['rʌbɪʃ]	Unsinn, Quatsch; Müll; Gerümpel →	*Rubbish*! That's not true!
3	**luck** [lʌk]	Glück →	*luck* → to be lucky

USEFUL PHRASES

Do you agree or not? These phrases are useful for a discussion.

I agree.	I don't agree.
You're right.	Sorry, but you're wrong.
Exactly!	Don't be silly!
That's what I think, too.	Rubbish!
That's true.	I don't think that's true.

Language 2: Did you know?

relative clause [ˌrelətɪv 'klɔ:z]	Relativsatz	
which [wɪtʃ]	der, dem, den, die, das *(Relativpronomen)* →	The shop *which* opened in Church Street last week has got really cool clothes.
American football [əˌmerɪkən 'fʊtbɔ:l]	American Football	
half pl. **halves** [hɑ:f; hɑ:vz]	(die) Hälfte; Halbzeit →	Did you like the film? – Well, the first *half* was OK, but the second *half* was really boring.
channel ['tʃænl]	Kanal; Programm →	BBC1 is a British TV *channel*.
that [ðæt]	der, dem, den, die, das *(Relativpronomen)* →	Is Scott the boy *that* comes from Canada?

commercial break [kəˌmɜːʃl ˈbreɪk]	Werbepause →	I don't like *commercial breaks*. They're boring.
commercial [kəˈmɜːʃl]	Werbespot	
who [huː]	der, dem, den, die *(Relativpronomen)* →	Scott is the boy *who* comes from Canada.
also [ˈɔːlsəʊ]	auch →	I like football and I *also* like baseball. = I like football and I like baseball, too.
unusual [ʌnˈjuːʒl]	ungewöhnlich	
bobsleigh [ˈbɒbsleɪ]	Bob	
snow [snəʊ]	Schnee →	There was a lot of *snow* last winter.
whose [huːz]	dessen, deren *(Relativpronomen)* →	David has got a sister *whose* name is Mary.

Explaining words you don't know

You can explain or describe a word you don't know like this:

- **a person** X is a person / man / woman / someone **who** …
- **a place** X is a place / town / city / country **where** / **which** …
- **a thing** X is something **which** / **that** …
- **an activity** X is an activity **where** …
- **an event** X is an event **which** / **that** …

rowing [ˈrəʊɪŋ]	Rudern	
the lungs *(pl.)* [lʌŋz]	die Lunge	
swimming [ˈswɪmɪŋ]	Schwimmen →	*swimming* → to go swimming
scientist [ˈsaɪəntɪst]	Wissenschaftler/-in →	*scientist* → science
disabled [dɪˈseɪbld]	behindert	
athlete [ˈæθliːt]	(Leicht)Athlet/-in →	! Achtung Schreibung und Aussprache *Fr. l'athlète* ***m***; *Lat. athleta* ***m***
gold medal [ɡəʊld ˈmedl]	Goldmedaille →	The team has already won two *gold medals*.
record [ˈrekɔːd]	Rekord →	! Achtung Schreibung und Aussprache *Fr. le record*
marathon [ˈmærəθn]	Marathon →	! Achtung Aussprache
love [lʌv]	null *(Tennis)*	
2 **relative pronoun** [ˌrelətɪv ˈprəʊnaʊn]	Relativpronomen →	You can learn more about relative clauses and *relative pronouns* in G5–G7.

Football

There are different kinds of football in the English-speaking world. Football, American football and rugby are the most popular ones. Some of the rules are the same, some are different.

	Football	**American football**	**Rugby**
time	2 x 45 min.	4 x 15 min.	2 x 40 min.
players in a team	11	11	15
ball	round	oval	oval
how to move the ball	kick head throw	kick carry throw	kick carry throw

3 **sweat** [swet]	Schweiß	
oddity [ˈɒdɪti]	Eigenartigkeit, Kuriosität	
4 **definition** [ˌdefɪˈnɪʃn]	Definition →	! Achtung Aussprache *Fr. la définition*

6 **contact clause** ['kɒntækt ˌklɔ:z]	*Relativsatz ohne Relativpronomen* →	A *contact clause* is a relative clause **without** a relative pronoun: I really like the book I got for my birthday.
9 **exact** [ɪg'zækt]	genau, exakt	

Text: Eddie the Eagle

eagle ['i:gl]	Adler	
glasses *(pl.)* ['glɑ:sɪz]	Brille →	! *glasses* steht immer im Plural: My *glasses* **are** broken. I need new ones.
ski jump ['ski: dʒʌmp]	Skispringen	
ski [ski:]	Ski	
jump [dʒʌmp]	Sprung →	a *jump* → to jump
press conference ['pres ˌkɒnfrns]	Pressekonferenz →	At a *press conference* reporters can ask a lot of questions.
to **mist up** [mɪst‿'ʌp]	(sich) beschlagen	
goggles *(pl.)* ['gɒglz]	Skibrille, Schwimmbrille →	The children are wearing *goggles*. 
ski jumper ['ski: ˌdʒʌmpə]	Skispringer	
van [væn]	Lieferwagen, Transporter →	car – pick-up – *van* – lorry
tradition [trə'dɪʃn]	Tradition →	! Achtung Aussprache Tennis has got a very long *tradition* in Europe. It is almost 400 years old. *Fr. la tradition; Lat. traditio* ***f***
far [fɑ:]	weit →	You can't walk to the train station. It's too *far*.
might [maɪt]	könnte(n) →	Maybe he will play well in the match. He *might* even win it!
to **slide, slid, slid** [slaɪd, slɪd, slɪd]	gleiten; rutschen →	He *slid* down the hill.
to **flap** [flæp]	flattern, *(mit den Flügeln)* schlagen	
place [pleɪs]	Platz →	They won the race. They got first *place*. *Fr. la place*
to **wave** [weɪv]	winken →	The star *is waving* to the fans. 
6 to be afraid (of) [bi:‿ə'freɪd‿əv]	(sich) fürchten (vor), Angst haben (vor)	
the dark [dɑ:k]	Dunkelheit	
golden ['gəʊldn]	golden	
silver ['sɪlvə]	silbern	
lark [lɑ:k]	Lerche	
to walk on [wɔ:k‿'ɒn]	weitergehen, weiterlaufen	
though your dreams be tossed and blown [ðəʊ jɔ: 'dri:mz bi 'tɒst‿ənd 'bləʊn]	auch wenn deine Träume zerschlagen werden	

Skills: Vocabulary skills – Using a German-English dictionary

context ['kɒntekst]	Kontext, Zusammenhang →	**TIP** A word can have different meanings in different *contexts*. Other parts of the sentence or text are the *context* of the word and give you the correct meaning.  *Fr. la contexte; Lat. contextus* ***m***

Unit 2: Once upon a time …

VOCABULARY SKILLS

Warte mit dem Vokabellernen nicht bis zum letzten Moment! Verteile die zu lernenden Vokabeln möglichst gleichmäßig auf die Zeit, die dir zur Verfügung steht. Überlege dir, wann du besonders gut lernen kannst.

Bist du zu bestimmten Zeiten eher müde (z. B. nach dem Mittagessen)? Dann suche dir eine günstige Zeit aus, in der du „fit" bist. Nutze diese „Spitzenzeiten" aus.

Check-in

Once upon a time … ['wʌns‿əˌpɒn‿ə 'taɪm]	Es war einmal … →	*Once upon a time* there was a young and beautiful, but very sad queen. …
elephant ['elɪfənt]	Elefant	
steel [sti:l]	Stahl →	a *steel* bridge 
AD (= Anno Domini) [eɪ'di:]	nach Christus	
Salve! *(lat. Begrüßung)* ['sælveɪ]	Sei gegrüßt!	
to **keep out** [ki:p‿'aʊt]	draußen halten; draußen bleiben →	The enemies could not come into the city. The soldiers *kept* them *out*.
century ['sentʃri]	Jahrhundert →	We live in the 21st *century*.
invention [ɪn'venʃn]	Erfindung →	*Fr. l'invention **f**; Lat. inventio **f***
wood [wʊd]	Holz →	You use *wood* to make a fire.
Valete! *(lat. Gruß zum Abschied)* [və'leɪti]	Es soll Euch gut gehen!	
heir [eə]	Erbe, Erbin →	When a king dies his *heir* becomes king or queen.
to **attack** [ə'tæk]	angreifen →	The army *attacked* the city. There was a big battle.
Bonjour! *(frz. Begrüßung)* [bɒŋ'ʒʊə]	Guten Tag!	
Norman ['nɔ:mən]	Normanne, Normannin; normannisch →	The *Normans* came to Britain from France.
knight [naɪt]	Ritter →	! Achtung Aussprache! Das 'k' wird nicht gesprochen. a *knight* 
Saxon ['sæksn]	Sachse, Sächsin; sächsisch	
to **hate** [heɪt]	hassen, nicht mögen →	*to hate* ↔ to love
Bonjour, mes petits. *(Fr.)* [bɒŋ'ʒʊə me pəˌti:]	Guten Tag, meine Kleinen.	
Catholic ['kæθlɪk]	Katholik/-in; katholisch →	Most people in Italy are *Catholics*.
Protestant ['prɒtɪstnt]	Protestant/-in; protestantisch →	*Protestant* ↔ Catholic
gold [gəʊld]	Gold →	*Gold* is beautiful and expensive.
fave *(Abkürzung für* favourite) [feɪv]	Lieblings- →	*fave* = favourite
Hasta luego! *(Sp.)* [ˌʌstə lʊ'eɪgəʊ]	Bis später! *(Spanisch)*	
to **defeat** [dɪ'fi:t]	besiegen →	They won the battle. They *defeated* their enemies.
Elizabethan [ɪˌlɪzə'bi:θn]	elisabethanisch	
age [eɪdʒ]	Zeitalter; Alter →	The Elizabethan *age* is the time when Elizabeth I was Queen of England.

poet ['pəʊɪt]	Dichter/-in →	She is a famous *poet*. She writes beautiful poems. *Fr. le poète; Lat. poeta* ***m***
Romeo, wherefore art thou Romeo? ['rəʊmiəʊ ˌweəfɔ: 'ɑ:t ðaʊ 'rəʊmiəʊ]	Romeo, warum musst du nur Romeo sein?	
Industrial Revolution [ɪnˌdʌstriəl revˈlu:ʃn]	Industrielle Revolution →	The *Industrial Revolution* started in Britain at the end of the 18th century.
factory ['fæktri]	Fabrik; Werk →	A *factory* is a large building or a group of buildings where things are made.
steam engine ['sti:m ˌendʒɪn]	Dampfmaschine →	The *steam engine* was the most important invention of the 18th century.
power ['paʊə]	Strom, Elektrizität, Energie	
workshop ['wɜ:kʃɒp]	Werkstatt; Workshop →	*workshop* → work → to work
empire ['empaɪə]	Reich; Kaiserreich →	A lot of countries all round the world were part of the British *Empire* in the 19th and 20th centuries.
colony ['kɒləni]	Kolonie →	India was a British *colony* until 1947.
World War II [ˌwɜ:ld ˌwɔ: 'tu:]	der Zweite Weltkrieg	
independent [ˌɪndɪ'pendənt]	unabhängig →	India became *independent* in 1947.
European Union [ˌjʊərəˌpi:ən 'ju:njən]	Europäische Union	

Language 1: Visit the World Stage

Briton ['brɪtn]	Brite, Britin →	! Britain = Großbritannien a *Briton* = ein Brite, eine Britin
stage [steɪdʒ]	Bühne →	In a play the actors act on the *stage*.
wax [wæks]	Wachs	
dress [dres]	Kleid →	Trousers for women were not in fashion until the 1960s. Before that, women usually wore *dresses* and skirts.
to **be able to** (do sth) [bi‿'eɪbl tə]	können, fähig sein (zu) →	They didn't know what to do. They *weren't able to* help him.
No way! [ˌnəʊ 'weɪ]	Was?!/Echt?!/Nie im Leben! →	*No way*! I can't believe that!
to **be allowed to** (do sth) [bi:‿ə'laʊd tə]	dürfen →	Children *aren't allowed to* drive cars.

Modal auxiliaries and their substitutes

	present tense	past tense	will future
can / be able to	She **can** / **is able to** play the piano.	She **couldn't** / **wasn't able to** play the piano two years ago.	She **will be able to** play in a concert next year.
can / may / be allowed to	**May** I / **Can** I / **Am** I **allowed to** go to the party? – No, you **may not**. / No, you **can't** / **aren't allowed to** go.	He **wasn't allowed to** go to the party last Saturday.	He **will be allowed to** go next time.
must / have to / needn't	You **must** / **have to** do your homework. You **needn't** / **don't have to** bring your dictionary. You **mustn't** copy your partner's homework.	You **had to** do a lot of homework yesterday, didn't you?	You **won't have to** do any homework tomorrow.

	modern ['mɒdn]	modern →	! Achtung Aussprache
	action ['ækʃn]	Handlung; Action →	There was a lot of *action* in the play. = A lot of things happened in the play.
	to **have to** ['hæv tə]	müssen →	Sorry, I can't go swimming this afternoon. I *have to* do lots of homework.
7	**negative** ['negətɪv]	Verneinungsform	
8	**the following** ['fɒləʊɪŋ]	folgende/-r/-s	

USEFUL PHRASES

You might want to ask a lot of questions when you visit a museum.

How much are the tickets?
Are there special prices for pupils/schools …?
Where can I get souvenirs/a brochure …?
Can you show/tell me the way to …, please?
May I take a photo of …/ask a question about …?
Are we allowed to use mobile phones/eat in …?

Talkwise: Planning a special event

	making suggestions [ˌmeɪkɪŋ sə'dʒestʃnz]	Vorschläge machen	
3	**suggestion** [sə'dʒestʃn]	Vorschlag →	Can I make a *suggestion*? Let's go to the cinema tonight. *Fr. la suggestion; Lat. suggestio **f***
	to **suggest** [sə'dʒest]	vorschlagen →	*to suggest* → suggestion *Fr. suggérer*
	ought to ['ɔːt_tə]	sollte(n) →	I think we *ought to* talk about it. = I think we should talk about it.
4	**open day** [ˌəʊpn 'deɪ]	Tag der offenen Tür →	Our school is having an *open day* next week.
	to **prepare** [prɪ'peə]	vorbereiten; zubereiten →	Dad is making lunch today. He is *preparing* lunch right now.

Language 2: Get the facts: Victorian Britain

	Victorian [vɪk'tɔːriən]	viktorianisch; Viktorianer/-in	
	hot [hɒt]	heiß; gefragt	
	reign [reɪn]	Herrschaft →	Queen Victoria's *reign* was from 1837 to 1901.
	throne [θrəʊn]	Thron →	*Lat. thronus **m***
	raw material [ˌrɔː mə'tɪəriəl]	Rohstoff →	Oil is an expensive *raw material*.
	empress ['emprəs]	Kaiserin	
	farmer ['fɑːmə]	Farmer/-in, Landwirt/-in →	*farmer* → farm
	slum [slʌm]	Slum, Elendsviertel	
	clean [kliːn]	sauber →	*clean* ↔ dirty
	floor [flɔː]	Fußboden →	The girl is sitting on the *floor*.
	government ['gʌvnmənt]	Regierung →	*Fr. le gouvernement*
	free [friː]	kostenlos →	It doesn't cost anything. It's *free*.
2	**past perfect** [ˌpɑːst 'pɜːfɪkt]	Plusquamperfekt →	
3	**fortress** ['fɔːtrəs]	Festung	
	prison ['prɪzn]	Gefängnis →	*prison* → prisoner *Fr. la prison*
	tower ['taʊə]	Turm	

Skills: Reading skills – A historical story

TIP
When you read for the *gist* of a story, you look for information about who is in it or the action of the story.
When you look for the *details* in a text, you look at the text very carefully.

	to **get ready** [get 'redi]	sich vorbereiten; sich fertig machen	
	gist [dʒɪst]	das Wesentliche →	
	detail ['di:teɪl]	Detail, Einzelheit →	
1	**pre-reading** [pri:'ri:dɪŋ]	vor dem Lesen	
	to **be about** [bi ə'baʊt]	gehen um, handeln von →	What *is* the book *about*? = What is the subject of the book?
3	to **be connected** [bi kə'nektɪd]	zusammenhängen, in Zusammenhang stehen	
	connecting line [kə'nektɪŋ ˌlaɪn]	Verbindungslinie	
4	**close** [kləʊs]	genau; nahe →	! Achtung Aussprache: *close* [s] ↔ to close [z]

Text: The diary

girlfriend ['gɜ:lfrend]	Freundin *(in einer Paarbeziehung)* →	Sarah is Bob's new *girlfriend*.
jewellery ['dʒu:əlri]	Schmuck	
old-fashioned [əʊld'fæʃnd]	altmodisch →	*old-fashioned* ↔ modern
lord [lɔ:d]	Lord, Herr	
lady ['leɪdi]	Dame; Frau	
middle name ['mɪdl ˌneɪm]	zweiter Vorname →	My name is Colleen Amy Carter. My *middle name* is Amy.
to **joke** [dʒəʊk]	scherzen →	Don't worry, it's not true. I'm only *joking*!
servant ['sɜ:vnt]	Bedienstete/-r; Diener/-in →	Queen Victoria had a lot of *servants*.
to **feed** [fi:d]	ernähren →	I work in the factory because I have to *feed* my family. ↔ Did you feed the dog this morning?
lonely ['ləʊnli]	einsam →	I'm often alone, but I don't feel *lonely*.
to **reply** [rɪ'plaɪ]	antworten, erwidern, entgegnen →	*to reply* = to answer
to **shine**, **shone**, **shone** [ʃaɪn, ʃɒn, ʃɒn]	scheinen; glänzen →	The weather is beautiful, the sun *is shining*.
curious ['kjʊəriəs]	neugierig →	My little brother wants to know everything we talk about. He's very *curious*. *Fr. curieux, curieuse; Lat. curiosus*
to **clean** [kli:n]	säubern, reinigen →	When you *clean* something, it becomes clean.
fountain ['faʊntɪn]	Springbrunnen →	a *fountain* 
strange [streɪndʒ]	merkwürdig, seltsam; fremd	
odd [ɒd]	seltsam, komisch →	*odd* = strange
vision ['vɪʒn]	Vision →	! Achtung Aussprache
telegram ['telɪgræm]	Telegramm →	! Achtung Schreibung und Aussprache
to **drown** [draʊn]	ertrinken; ertränken →	The boat sank and a lot of people *drowned*.
to **gasp** [gɑ:sp]	tief einatmen, tief Luft holen; keuchen →	"Oh dear! That's terrible!" she *gasped*.
such [sʌtʃ]	solche/-r/-s →	That's scary! Don't tell me *such* things!
sixth sense [ˌsɪksθ 'sents]	sechster Sinn	
to **continue** [kən'tɪnju:]	weiterreden; weitermachen →	*to continue* ↔ to stop *Fr. continuer; Lat. continuare*
to **nod** [nɒd]	nicken →	*to nod* ↔ to shake your head
to **wonder** ['wʌndə]	sich fragen →	I *wonder* what it was like to live in the 16th century.

	ghost [gəʊst]	Geist →	Some people believe that there are *ghosts* in old houses or castles.
	great-great-grandmother [ˌgreɪtgreɪt'grænmʌðə]	Ururgroßmutter →	The mother of my mother's grandmother is my *great-great-grandmother.*
	whoever [hu:'evə]	wer auch immer →	*Whoever* started the fight should sort it out.
	wherever [weə'revə]	wo(hin) auch immer, egal wo(hin) →	*Wherever* you go, I'll come with you.
	metal ['metl]	Metall →	*Fr. le métal; Lat. metallum **n***
	flying ['flaɪɪŋ]	fliegend, Flug-	
	actually ['æktʃuəli]	tatsächlich, wirklich; eigentlich →	A lot of the things he saw *actually* happened. = A lot of the things he saw really happened.
	click [klɪk]	Klicken; Klick	
	line [laɪn]	(Telefon)leitung	
	to **have no idea** [hæv ˌnəʊ‿aɪ'dɪə]	keine Ahnung haben →	I *have no idea*! = I really don't know!
2	**ending** ['endɪŋ]	Schluss, Ende	
	paragraph ['pærəgrɑ:f]	Paragraph, Absatz →	word – sentence – *paragraph* – text

Wordwise

2	**stress** [stres]	Betonung	
	to **stress** [stres]	betonen, hervorheben →	When you *stress* something, it shows that you think it is very important.
4	Alas [ə'læs]	O weh	
	to do wrong [du: 'rɒŋ]	Unrecht tun	
	to cast off [kɑ:st‿'ɒf]	wegstoßen, zurückstoßen	
	discourteously [dɪ'skɜ:tiəsli]	grob	
	for [fɔ:; fə]	denn	
	to delight in [dɪ'laɪt‿ɪn]	Vergnügen empfinden bei	
	company ['kʌmpəni]	Gesellschaft	
	joy [dʒɔɪ]	Freude, Vergnügen	
	delight [dɪ'laɪt]	Vergnügen, Entzücken	
	and who but … [ənd hu: 'bʌt]	und wer, wenn nicht …	

Unit 3: Living together

VOCABULARY SKILLS

Achte beim Lernen neuer Wörter auf die Betonung – vor allem wenn sie besonders lang oder zusammengesetzt sind. Schau dir also auch immer die Lautschrift genau an. Nimm z. B. das Wort *Industrial Revolution* [ɪnˌdʌstriəl rev'lu:ʃn]:

- Das Zeichen ['] zeigt an, dass auf der nachfolgenden Silbe die Hauptbetonung liegt. Das Zeichen [ˌ] zeigt an, dass auf der nachfolgenden Silbe die Nebenbetonung liegt.
- Sprich ein neues Wort anfangs mit überdeutlicher Unterscheidung zwischen betonter und unbetonter Silbe aus und klopfe bei der betonten Silbe auf den Tisch.
- Unterstreiche auf deinen Karteikarten die betonten Silben.
- Achte besonders bei Vokabeln, die deutschen Wörtern ähneln, auf die Aussprache. Oft liegt die Betonung auf einer anderen Silbe, wie z. B. bei *modern* ['mɒdn].
- Vorsicht auch bei Substantiven, Adjektiven und Verben aus einer Wortfamilie. Meist werden unterschiedliche Silben betont: *alphabet* ['ælfəbet] → *alphabetical* [ˌælfə'betɪkl].

Check-in

	to **meet** [mi:t]	kennenlernen →	Do you know the Smiths? – Yes, we *met* them at the party on Saturday.
	wise [waɪz]	weise, klug	
	to **brush one's teeth** [brʌʃ wʌnz ˈti:θ]	(seine) Zähne putzen →	You should *brush your teeth* three times a day.
	or [ɔ:]	sonst →	You'll have to train much harder *or* you won't win the competition.
	pip [pɪp]	Kern →	My sister always eats the whole apple, even the *pips*.
	to **grow, grew, grown** [grəʊ, gru:, grəʊn]	wachsen →	All kinds of flowers *grow* in our garden.
	to **eat up** [i:t ˈʌp]	aufessen →	*Eat up* your lunch and go back to the classroom.
	crust [krʌst]	Kruste, Rinde	
	to **go curly** [gəʊ ˈkɜ:li]	sich kräuseln →	When my hair gets wet it *goes curly*.
	to **marry** [ˈmæri]	heiraten →	And then he asked her: "Darling, will you *marry* me?"
	bad luck [bæd ˈlʌk]	Pech, Unglück →	*bad luck* ↔ luck
	hat [hæt]	Hut	
	to **tell a lie** [ˌtel‿ə ˈlaɪ]	lügen →	It's not true! He *told a lie*!
	lie [laɪ]	Lüge	
	(not) any more [nɒt ˌeni ˈmɔ:]	(nicht) mehr →	He finished school last month. He *doesn't* go to school *any more*.
	vegetarian [ˌvedʒɪˈteəriən]	Vegetarier/-in →	I'm a *vegetarian*. I don't eat meat.
	to **split up, split, split** [splɪt‿ˈʌp, splɪt, splɪt]	sich trennen →	I can't believe that Fiona and David *split up* last week.
	to **get on** [get‿ˈɒn]	auskommen →	The two brothers fight a lot. They don't *get on* well.
	to **behave** [bɪˈheɪv]	sich benehmen, sich verhalten →	You're silly! You *behave* like a little child.
	twin [twɪn]	Zwilling, Zwillings- →	 *twins*
	to **drive someone crazy** [draɪv ˌsʌmwʌn ˈkreɪzi]	jmdn. verrückt machen →	Turn off that music! It's *driving me crazy*.
	selfish [ˈselfɪʃ]	selbstsüchtig →	She never does anything for other people. She is very *selfish*.
	to **tidy (up)** [taɪdi ˈʌp]	aufräumen, in Ordnung bringen →	What a mess! Please *tidy up* your room!
	2L8 (= too late) [tu: ˈleɪt]	zu spät *(Abkürzung in SMS oder E-Mail)*	
	UR (= you are) [ju: ˈɑ:]	du bist *(Abkürzung in SMS oder E-Mail)*	
	I don't care! [aɪ ˌdəʊnt ˈkeə]	Das ist mir egal! →	Guess who went to the cinema with Jamie yesterday. – *I don't care!*
	microwave [ˈmaɪkrəʊweɪv]	Mikrowelle	
	frozen [ˈfrəʊzn]	(tief)gefroren →	Ice is *frozen* water.
	Brussels sprout [ˌbrʌslz ˈspraʊt]	Rosenkohl	
	DIY (= Do-it-yourself) [ˌdi:aɪˈwaɪ]	Heimwerken →	*DIY* shops became very popular in the 1980s.
1	**scene** [si:n]	Szene →	*Fr. la scène; Lat. scaena* **f**
	in [ɪn]	aus, von, jede/-r/-s (zweite/dritte …) →	One *in* two children in the UK watches TV for more than 25 hours a week.

2	**each other** [iːtʃ‿ˈʌðə]	einander, sich (gegenseitig) →	The boys are looking at the girls. The girls are looking at *each other*.
4	**telephone** [ˈtelɪfəʊn]	Telefon →	*telephone* = phone
	cleaning lady [ˈkliːnɪŋ ˌleɪdi]	Putzfrau	
	answerphone [ˈɑːnsəfəʊn]	Anrufbeantworter →	I phoned Tim but he wasn't at home. I left a message on the *answerphone*.

Language 1: Sunday lunch

	to **enjoy oneself** [ɪnˈdʒɔɪ]	Spaß haben; sich amüsieren →	*Enjoy yourself*! = Have fun!
	himself [hɪmˈself]	er (selbst), sich (selbst); selber →	He's old enough to look after *himself*.
	to **help oneself (to)** [help wʌnˈself tə]	sich bedienen →	Everything is on the table. Just *help yourself*!
	themselves [ðəmˈselvz]	sie/sich (selbst); selber →	Everyone helped *themselves* to food and drink.
	to **decide** [dɪˈsaɪd]	(sich) entscheiden →	Which skirt do you like better? – I don't know. I can't *decide*. *Fr. (se) décider; Lat. decidere*
	yourself [jɔːˈself]	du/dir/dich/Sie/sich (selbst); selber →	Tell me something about *yourself*.
	extra [ˈekstrə]	mehr →	I'd like some *extra* sprouts, please. = I'd like some more sprouts, please.
	to **stand** [stænd]	ertragen, ausstehen →	I can't *stand* him. ↔ I like him a lot.
	myself [maɪˈself]	ich/mir/mich (selbst); selber →	I bought a pair of shoes for my daughter and a pair for *myself*.
	yourselves [jɔːˈselvz]	ihr/euch/Sie/sich (selbst); selber →	Did you enjoy *yourselves*? – Oh yes, the party was really great.
	to **get dressed** [get ˈdrest]	sich anziehen →	What should I wear today? – I don't care, just hurry up and *get dressed*.
	old people's home [əʊld ˈpiːplz həʊm]	Altersheim →	An *old people's home* is a place for old people who cannot look after themselves any longer.
	to **relax** [rɪˈlæks]	(sich) entspannen, (sich) ausruhen; sich beruhigen →	Are you worried? Just *relax*, everything will be OK.
	ourselves [aʊəˈselvz]	wir (selbst), uns (selbst); selber →	We looked so funny that we had to laugh at *ourselves*.
3	**reflexive** [rɪˈfleksɪv]	reflexiv	
	herself [hɜːˈself]	sie (selbst), sich (selbst); selber →	She looked at *herself* in the mirror.
	to **turn off** [tɜːn‿ˈɒf]	abschalten, ausschalten →	Please *turn off* the TV. It's time to go to bed.
	itself [ɪtˈself]	sich (selbst); selber →	The poor animal has hurt *itself*.
4	to **call** [kɔːl]	anrufen →	*to call* → a call

Self-pronouns (Reflexive pronouns)

I'll buy **myself** an ice-cream.	… mir …
Do you often talk to **yourself**?	… dir (selbst) …
My grandmother taught **herself** how to work with a computer.	… sich (selbst) …
Have you looked at **yourselves**? Your clothes are a mess.	… euch …
They hurt **themselves**.	… sich (selbst) …

Emphatic pronouns

Thanks, I don't need your help. I can do it **myself**.	… selbst/selber …
Did you build it **yourself**?	… selbst/selber …
Sarah made all those cakes **herself**.	… selbst/selber …
You have to sort out that problem **yourselves**.	… selbst/selber …
I won't tidy up their room. They have to do it **themselves**.	… selbst/selber …

Watch out!

Many words are used with a reflexive pronoun in German, but not in English.

sich anstrengen	to **try hard**	sich fühlen	to **feel**
sich anstellen	to **queue**	sich an etw. gewöhnen	to **get used to sth**
sich anziehen	to **get dressed**	sich Notizen machen	to **take notes**
sich etw. ausdenken	to **think of sth**	sich (hin)setzen	to **sit down**
sich etw. ausleihen	to **borrow sth**	sich um etw. Sorgen machen	to **worry about sth**
sich beeilen	to **hurry**	sich treffen	to **meet**
sich benehmen	to **behave**	sich trennen	to **split up**
sich bewegen	to **move**	sich verbessern	to **improve**
sich entscheiden	to **decide**	sich verirren	to **get lost**
sich entspannen	to **relax**	sich verlieben	to **fall in love**
sich an etw. erinnern	to **remember sth**	sich verstecken	to **hide**
sich fragen	to **wonder**	sich vorstellen	to **imagine**

Talkwise: Meet halfway

	to **meet halfway** [miːt hɑːfweɪ]	(sich auf halbem Weg) entgegenkommen →	I don't agree! But I don't want to fight, so let's *meet halfway.*
1	to **feel sorry for** [fiːl 'sɒri]	Mitleid haben mit; bedauern →	Tim couldn't go to the concert because he had the flu. I *felt sorry for* him.
	difference ['dɪfrns]	Unterschied →	*difference* → different
3	to **earn** [ɜːn]	verdienen →	She has got a good job and *earns* a lot of money.
	I see. [aɪ 'siː]	Ich verstehe./Aha! →	**TIP** You use "*I see*" when you understand what sb says or what sth means. If you say "Oh, *I see*!" it means 'Aha!'.
	to **mind** [maɪnd]	etwas dagegen haben; einem etwas ausmachen →	Do you *mind* if I open the window? – No, I don't *mind.* Are you sure you want to help us? It's a lot of work. – That's OK, I don't *mind.*
	You've got a point. [juːv gɒt‿ə 'pɔɪnt]	Da ist was dran. →	*You've got a point.* I hadn't thought about it that way.

Language 2: Chatroom messages

type [taɪp]	Typ, Art, Sorte →	*Fr. le type; Lat. typus **m***
to **chat** [tʃæt]	chatten; plaudern →	My grandmother loves to *chat* with her neighbours when she meets them in the street.
to **turn into** [tɜːn‿'ɪntə]	(sich) verwandeln in; werden →	He *has turned into* a real bully. = He has become a real bully.
to **get rid of** [get 'rɪd‿əv]	loswerden →	I don't like my old mobile any longer. I want to *get rid of* it.
junk [dʒʌŋk]	Gerümpel; Ramsch →	We have to tidy up the garage. There's too much *junk* in it.
to **wish** [wɪʃ]	(sich) wünschen →	**!** You use the past tense after the verb '*to wish*': I ***wish*** I **lived** in a big city. When I was young, I ***wished*** I **lived** in a big city. Now I am happy that I live in a small town.
jealous (of) ['dʒeləs‿əv]	neidisch; eifersüchtig →	*Fr. jaloux, jalouse*

	especially [ɪ'speʃli]	besonders, vor allem →	Susan likes sport, *especially* tennis.
2	**probably** ['prɒbəbli]	möglicherweise, wahrscheinlich	
	to **translate** [trænz'leɪt]	übersetzen →	What does this mean? Can you *translate* it for me, please?
3	**on chat** [ɒn 'tʃæt]	im Chat, beim Chatten	
4	**purse** [pɜ:s]	Portemonnaie, Geldbeutel →	I can't buy anything. I forgot my *purse*.
	comma ['kɒmə]	Komma →	! Achtung Schreibung
6	**advice** [əd'vaɪs]	Rat, Ratschlag →	! I really don't know what to do. – Let me give you **some** *advice*. …
	difficult ['dɪfɪklt]	schwierig	
8	wish [wɪʃ]	Wunsch	

Language 3: A letter to an agony aunt

	agony aunt ['ægəni ˌɑ:nt]	Kummerkastentante →	She did not want to talk about her problem with her friends or her family. So she wrote a letter to her favourite magazine's *agony aunt*.
	boyfriend ['bɔɪfrend]	Freund *(in einer Paarbeziehung)* →	*boyfriend* ↔ girlfriend
	to **go out with** [gəʊ‿'aʊt wɪð]	(aus)gehen mit →	Mary is my girlfriend. We*'re going out with* each other.
	to **go crazy** [gəʊ 'kreɪzi]	ausflippen, durchdrehen →	It's driving me crazy. I'll *go crazy* soon.
	secret ['si:krət]	geheim →	It's a secret. = It's *secret*.
	to **listen to** ['lɪsn tə]	hören auf →	I often give my little sister advice, but she never *listens to* me.

Skills: Listening Skills – Telephone messages

	difficult ['dɪfɪklt]	schwierig →	easy ↔ *difficult*
1	**voice mail** ['vɔɪs meɪl]	Voicemail; Mailbox	
2	**caller** ['kɔ:lə]	Anrufer/-in →	*caller* → a call → to call
	to **contact** ['kɒntækt]	(telefonisch) erreichen, sich in Verbindung setzen →	You can *contact* me on my mobile. *Fr. contacter*
3	to **leave** [li:v]	hinterlassen →	I called her and *left* a message on the answerphone.
	to take a call [ˌteɪk‿ə 'kɔ:l]	(Telefon) abheben, einen Anruf entgegennehmen →	The telephone is ringing. Can you *take the call*, please?
	tone [təʊn]	(Signal)ton →	Please leave a message after the *tone*.
	I'm afraid [aɪm ə'freɪd]	leider →	*I'm afraid* I can't take your call at the moment. = Sorry, I can't take your call at the moment.
4	to **be in** [bi:‿'ɪn]	da sein →	I'm sorry, Brian *isn't in*. He's just gone shopping.

USEFUL PHRASES

It can be more difficult to speak English on the phone than to talk to someone. These phrases will help you to ask for someone or to leave a message on an answerphone.

Hello, this is … .
I'd like to speak to …
Could I leave a message, please?
Could you tell him/her that …, please?
Could he/she call me back, please?
I'll give you my name and address.

Hi, this is … . I'm just calling to say that …
I'd like … / I'm afraid … / Sorry …
Could you call me back, please?
You can phone me at … (+ phone number)
Hope to hear from you soon.
Thanks, and bye.

Text: Home alone

	Home alone. [həʊm ə'ləʊn]	Allein zu Hause.	
	cast [kɑ:st]	Besetzung, Ensemble →	What a great *cast*! A lot of famous actors acted in the film.
	Shut up! [ʃʌt‿'ʌp]	Halt die Klappe! →	**TIP** It's not nice to say "*Shut up!*". It's better to use "Be quiet, please!"
	witch [wɪtʃ]	Hexe	
	costume ['kɒstju:m]	Kostüm	
	grumpy ['grʌmpi]	mürrisch, schlecht gelaunt →	Leave me alone! – Why are you so *grumpy* today?
	to **manage** (to do sth) ['mænɪdʒ]	(es) schaffen (etw. zu tun) →	Thanks, I don't need your help. I can *manage*.
	on one's own [ɒn wʌnz‿'əʊn]	(ganz) allein(e) →	Her friends didn't want to go to the cinema, so she went *on her own*.
	talk [tɔ:k]	Gespräch, Unterhaltung; Unterredung →	a *talk* → to talk
	to **make a decision** [ˌmeɪk‿ə dɪ'sɪʒn]	eine Entscheidung treffen →	*to make a decision* = to decide
	decision [dɪ'sɪʒn]	Entscheidung →	*decision* → to decide
	to **get in the way** [ˌget‿ɪn ðə 'weɪ]	stören, im Weg stehen	
	to **make sure** [meɪk 'ʃɔ:]	sichergehen →	Please *make sure* he gets the letter. It's very important.
	mask [mɑ:sk]	Maske	
	First things first. [ˌfɜ:st θɪŋz 'fɜ:st]	Das Wichtigste zuerst.	
	doorbell ['dɔ:bel]	Türklingel →	I rang the *doorbell* three times but nobody heard me.
	What's going on? [wɒts ˌgəʊɪŋ‿'ɒn]	Was ist denn hier los? →	*What's going on?* What are you doing?
	guy [gaɪ]	Typ, Kerl; *pl.:* Leute →	Our new classmate is a really cool *guy*.
	to **offer** ['ɒfə]	(an)bieten →	Can I *offer* you a drink? = Would you like a drink?
	one by one [ˌwʌn baɪ 'wʌn]	eine/-r/-s nach dem/der anderen →	Don't come in all at once. Please come in *one by one*.
1	to react [ri:'ækt]	reagieren	
2	to **put on (a play)** [ˌpʊt‿ɒn‿ə 'pleɪ]	(ein Theaterstück) aufführen →	Last year we *put on* "Robin Hood" at school.
	director [dɪ'rektə]	Regisseur/-in →	The *director* of a film tells everyone what to do.
	props *(pl.)* [prɒps]	Requisiten	
	lights *(pl.)* [laɪts]	Beleuchtung	
	programme ['prəʊgræm]	Programmheft →	You can find information about the play in the *programme*.
	actress ['æktrəs]	Schauspielerin →	*actress* ↔ actor
	rehearsal [rɪ'hɜ:sl]	Probe	
	to **rehearse** [rɪ'hɜ:s]	proben →	*to rehearse* → rehearsal
	curtain ['kɜ:tn]	Vorhang →	At the end of a play the *curtain* falls.
	audience ['ɔ:diəns]	Publikum →	The people who watch a play are the *audience*. *Lat. audiens* ***m***
	to **applaud** [ə'plɔ:d]	applaudieren →	The audience loved the play. They *applauded* for a long time.
3	author ['ɔ:θə]	Autor/-in	

Wordwise

2	**official** [əˈfɪʃl]	offiziell →	*Fr. officiel,le*
3	shiny [ˈʃaɪni]	glänzend	
	crowd [kraʊd]	Menschenmenge	
	ground [graʊnd]	Boden	
	silver [ˈsɪlvə]	Silber	
	to sound [saʊnd]	klingen	
	to express [ɪkˈspres]	ausdrücken	

Unit 4: The UK on the move

VOCABULARY SKILLS

Englische Vokabeln kannst du auch „nebenbei" im Alltag lernen. Achte z. B. im Supermarkt, beim Fernsehen, in Büchern, auf Werbeplakaten und auf Bahnhofs- oder Flughafenschildern auf englische Wörter: Du wirst erstaunt sein, wie oft du darauf stößt. Um dir die Wörter einzuprägen, trägst du sie am besten direkt vor Ort in ein kleines Notizbuch ein, das du dir extra für diesen Zweck zulegst und immer bei dir hast, vor allem dann, wenn du verreist. Schreibe für die Wörter, die du bereits kennst, gleich die deutsche Übersetzung mit auf. Die unbekannten Vokabeln kannst du zu Hause in einem Wörterbuch nachschlagen. Da du auf diese Weise mit jedem Wort eine kleine Geschichte oder bestimmte besondere Umstände verbindest („Ach ja! Dieses Wort habe ich am Bahnhof in … gesehen/im Kino gehört" …), wirst du es dir leicht merken können!

Check-in

to **be on the move** [bi: ɒn‿ðə ˈmu:v]	unterwegs sein →	He has to travel a lot in his job. He *is* always *on the move*.
on average [ɒn‿ˈævrɪdʒ]	durchschnittlich, im Durchschnitt	
to **move (house)** [mu:v ˈhaʊs]	umziehen →	When you *move house*, you leave your old home and go to live in a different house.
exchange [ɪksˈtʃeɪndʒ]	Austausch →	In an *exchange* between schools from different countries, pupils and teachers visit each other's schools for a few days or weeks.
region [ˈri:dʒn]	Region; Gegend →	Which *region* in England do you live in? – I live in the North West, near Manchester. *Fr. la région; Lat. regio* ***f***
industry [ˈɪndəstri]	Industrie, Industrieanlage →	! Achtung Schreibung und Aussprache
cult [kʌlt]	Kult →	Some MP3 players have become *cult* objects. = They have become very popular and a lot of people find them really cool.
birthplace [ˈbɜ:θpleɪs]	Geburtsort →	His *birthplace* is Birmingham. = He was born in Birmingham.
recently [ˈri:sntli]	kürzlich, vor kurzem, neulich; in letzter Zeit →	*recently* = not long ago
facelift [ˈfeɪslɪft]	Lifting, *hier:* Renovierung, Verschönerung	
landscape [ˈlændskeɪp]	Landschaft →	I love the *landscape* here with its beautiful hills and green fields. 

Welsh [welʃ]	walisisch; Walisisch →	*Welsh* people are from Wales. A quarter of them speak *Welsh*.
to **be proud (of)** [biː ˈpraʊd‿əv]	stolz sein (auf) →	Colleen has won the photo competition at school. She *is* very *proud of* herself.
regional [ˈriːdʒnl]	regional →	*regional* → region
culture [ˈkʌltʃə]	Kultur →	! Achtung Schreibung und Aussprache *Fr. la culture; Lat. cultura* **f**
wing [wɪŋ]	Flügel →	A bird has got *wings*.
coal mine [ˈkəʊl maɪn]	Kohlenbergwerk, Kohlengrube	
heavy industry [ˌhevi ˈɪndəstri]	Schwerindustrie →	There is no *heavy industry* in our town any more. All the factories are gone.
male voice choir [ˌmeɪl vɔɪs ˈkwaɪə]	Männerchor	
to **exist** [ɪgˈzɪst]	existieren, bestehen	
1 **contrast** [ˈkɒntrɑːst]	Kontrast, Unterschied →	The landscape in Scotland is very different from the landscape in Cornwall. There are a lot of *contrasts* between the two regions.
less [les]	weniger →	*less* ↔ more

United Kingdom, Great Britain or England?

Here is a map of the United Kingdom of Great Britain and Northern Ireland. (Or, as a lot of people call it, "the UK" or "Britain".) Four countries – England, Scotland, Wales and Northern Ireland – are part of the United Kingdom. Every country has its own culture, and the people there are very proud of it. So be careful when you talk about "England": You might really mean "the UK" or "Britain"!

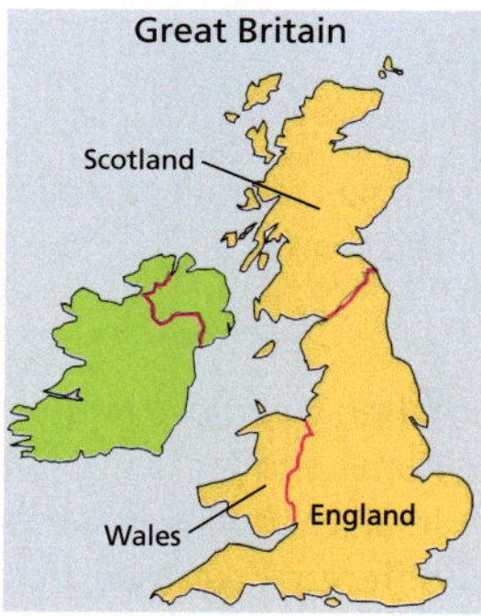

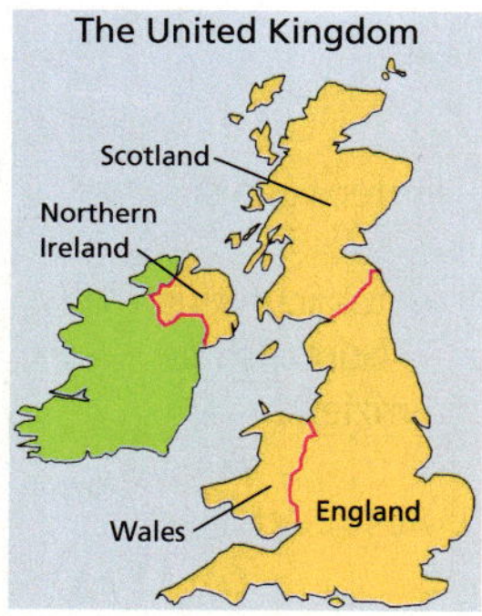

Language 1: Welsh relatives

abstract [ˈæbstrækt]	abstrakt →	! Achtung Schreibung und Aussprache
article [ˈɑːtɪkl]	Artikel →	! Achtung Schreibung und Aussprache
relative [ˈrelətɪv]	Verwandte/-r →	Aunts, uncles, cousins etc. are *relatives*.
engineer [ˌendʒɪˈnɪə]	Ingenieur/-in →	My father builds bridges. He's an *engineer*.
firm [fɜːm]	Firma →	My mother works for a very big *firm*.
the poor [ðə ˈpɔː]	die Armen	
tea [tiː]	(frühes) Abendessen →	breakfast – lunch – *tea*
friendship [ˈfrendʃɪp]	Freundschaft →	I've got lots of friends. I think *friendship* is very important.
I'd rather [aɪd ˈrɑːðə]	ich würde lieber →	Would you like to have bacon and eggs for breakfast? – No thanks, *I'd rather* have toast.
bilingual [baɪˈlɪŋgwl]	zweisprachig →	I speak English and German perfectly. I'm *bilingual*.
love	Liebe	

a pair of [ə 'peər‿əv]	ein Paar →	*a pair of ...*
taste [teɪst]	Geschmack →	I like her clothes. She's got good *taste*. I don't like this food. It's got a strange *taste*.
to **be into sth** [biː 'ɪntə]	an etwas interessiert sein →	*to be into sth* = to be interested in sth
awful ['ɔːfl]	schrecklich, furchtbar →	*awful* = terrible
2 **definite** ['defɪnət]	bestimmt	
indefinite [ɪn'defɪnət]	unbestimmt →	*indefinite* ↔ definite

Talkwise: Dealing with problems

helping ['helpɪŋ]	Helfen	
apologizing [ə'pɒlədʒaɪzɪŋ]	Entschuldigen	
dealing with problems [ˌdiːlɪŋ wɪð 'prɒbləmz]	Schwierigkeiten bewältigen	
to **deal with, dealt, dealt** ['diːl wɪð, delt, delt]	sich befassen mit, umgehen mit →	When you *deal with* a problem you try to sort it out.
1 **Take your time.** [ˌteɪk jɔː 'taɪm]	Lass dir Zeit. →	Sorry, I'm not ready yet. – No problem, *take your time*.
3 to **apologize** [ə'pɒlədʒaɪz]	sich entschuldigen →	*to apologize* = to say "I'm sorry!"
I didn't mean to ... [aɪ‿ˌdɪdnt 'miːn tə]	Ich wollte nicht ... →	Sorry! *I didn't mean to* be rude.
rude [ruːd]	unhöflich; unverschämt →	*rude* ↔ polite *Fr. rude; Lat. rudis*
Never mind! [ˌnevə 'maɪnd]	Macht nichts.; Mach dir nichts draus!; Schon gut. →	I'm really sorry. – *Never mind!*

USEFUL PHRASES

Use these phrases to help someone or to apologize to someone.

Can I help you?	That's very kind/nice of you, thanks.
Shall I ...?	Could you ... for me?
Just take your time. ...	You've been a great help. ...
I'm terribly/really sorry.	Never mind. / No problem. /
I didn't mean to be rude.	Don't worry.
I apologize ...	Be more careful next time. ...

Language 2: Up North

up North [ʌp 'nɔːθ]	im Norden →	They live *up North*, in Liverpool.
Asian ['eɪʃn]	asiatisch; Asiate, Asiatin	
curry ['kʌri]	Curry *(Gewürz oder Gericht)* →	I like Indian food, especially chicken *curry*.
to **smell, smelt, smelt** [smel, smelt, smelt]	riechen; duften →	*to smell* → a smell
to **taste** [teɪst]	schmecken →	*to taste* → taste
Punjabi [pʌn'dʒɑːbiː]	Pandschabi; pandschabisch	
to **sound** [saʊnd]	klingen →	*to sound* → a sound
to **seem** [siːm]	scheinen →	What was wrong with you yesterday? You *seemed* very unhappy.
exhibition [ˌeksɪ'bɪʃn]	Ausstellung →	I love to go to art *exhibitions* in museums and galleries. *Fr. l'exhibition **f***
by	(spätestens) bis	
Bhangra	Bhangra	
reply	Antwort	
audio	Audio -	

Adjectives after verbs

Anne **was angry**. But she **stayed calm**.	Anne war wütend. Aber sie blieb ruhig.
She **felt sick** and could not go to the party.	Sie fühlte sich krank und konnte nicht auf die Party gehen.
Her friend **seemed sad**, too.	Ihre Freundin schien auch traurig (zu sein).
This restaurant has **become expensive**.	Dieses Restaurant ist teuer geworden.
He **got angry**.	Er wurde wütend.
The food **smelt awful**.	Das Essen roch furchtbar.
But the drinks **tasted nice**.	Aber die Getränke schmeckten gut.
The singer **looked beautiful**.	Die Sängerin sah schön aus.
But her voice **sounded strange**.	Aber ihre Stimme hörte sich komisch an.

6 **by** [baɪ] — *(spätestens)* bis → — *by* tomorrow morning = not later than tomorrow morning

by / until

Get up **by** 8 am.	= **before or at** 8 am	Stehe spätestens **um** 8 Uhr auf.	= irgendwann zwischen jetzt und spätestens diesem Zeitpunkt
Wait **until** 8 pm.	= **before and at** 8 pm	Warte **bis** 20 Uhr.	= die ganze Zeit ab jetzt bis zu diesem Zeitpunkt
Don't call **until** 8 pm.	= **not earlier than** 8 pm	Ruf **erst** um/**nicht vor** 20 Uhr an.	= nicht vor diesem Zeitpunkt

Bhangra ['bæŋgrə] — Bhangra *(Musikstil, der Bestandteile der indischen und westlichen Musik in sich vereint)*

reply [rɪ'laɪ] — Antwort → — *reply* = answer

7 **audio** ['ɔ:diəʊ] — Audio-, Hör- → — ! Achtung Aussprache *Fr. audio-; Lat. audire*

8 ain't *(= isn't/aren't)* [eɪnt] — ist nicht, sind nicht

scented ['sentɪd] — duftend

breeze [bri:z] — Brise

waving [weɪvɪŋ] — wogend

corn [kɔ:n] — Getreide

peroxide [pə'rɒksaɪd] — Peroxyd *(Bleichmittel für Haare); mit Peroxid gebleicht*

curl [kɜ:l] — Locke

to flow [fləʊ] — fließen

Skills: Reading Skills – Factual texts

factual text [ˌfæktʃʊəl 'tekst] — Sachtext → — A text in a brochure or in a guide book etc. is a *factual text*.

research [ri:'sɜtʃ] — Untersuchung → — When you do *research*, you look for information about sth.

1 **skimming** ['skɪmɪŋ] — Überfliegen

to skim [skɪm] — überfliegen

to **concentrate** ['kɒnsntreɪt]	(sich) konzentrieren	
keyword ['ki:wɜ:d]	Stichwort; Schlüsselbegriff →	A *keyword* is an important word in a text. It gives information about the subject of a text.
2 **scanning** ['skænɪŋ]	Durchsuchen nach Details; Abtasten	
to **scan** [skæn]	durchsuchen, abtasten →	

TIP

When you skim a text you look at it very quickly and try to get the main ideas. When you *scan* a text you look at it quickly to find the details or information you want.

topic ['tɒpɪk]	Thema →	*topic* = subject
a must-see [ə ˌmʌst 'si:]	… muss man gesehen haben →	The new film with Orlando Bloom is *a must-see.*
conference ['kɒnfrns]	Konferenz, Tagung →	*Fr. la conférence*
dinner ['dɪnə]	Abendessen →	Last night they went to a very nice restaurant for *dinner.*
leisure ['leʒə]	Freizeit, Freizeit- →	*leisure* = free time
on land [ɒn 'lænd]	an Land →	I felt sick on the boat. I'm glad we're *on land* again.
during *(+ noun)* ['djʊərɪŋ]	während *(+ Substantiv)* →	! You always use *during* with a noun: *during* the journey = while we were travelling
motorway ['məʊtəweɪ]	Autobahn →	a *motorway*

Text: Changing places

changing places [ˌtʃeɪndʒɪŋ 'pleɪsɪz]	Ortswechsel	
It's a pity. [ˌɪts‿ə 'pɪti]	Das ist schade./ Es ist schade … →	*It's a pity* that you can't come to my party!
accent ['æksnt]	Akzent →	It can be difficult to understand a person who speaks with a strong *accent.* *Fr. l'accent* ***m****; Lat. accentus* ***m***
to **get tired of** [get 'taɪəd‿əv]	etwas satt bekommen →	How was your trip to London? – Awful, it rained all day. I *got* really *tired of* the weather.
interactive [ˌɪntər'æktɪv]	interaktiv →	! Achtung Schreibung und Aussprache
for laughs [fə 'lɑ:fs]	zum Spaß →	*for laughs* = for fun
waterfront ['wɔ:təfrʌnt]	Hafenviertel; Ufer	
weird [wɪəd]	merkwürdig, seltsam →	*weird* = strange
crowd [kraʊd]	Menschenmenge →	a *crowd* = a lot of people
to **cheer** [tʃɪə]	(zu)jubeln, anfeuern →	Everyone *cheered* when he scored a goal.
to **try out** [traɪ‿'aʊt]	ausprobieren →	I've never done orienteering. I'd like to *try* it *out.*
to **make fun of** [ˌmeɪk 'fʌn‿əv]	sich lustig machen über →	They *made fun of* our new classmate and said rude things about him.
quite [kwaɪt]	ziemlich; ganz, völlig →	Andreas only started to learn English last year. He already speaks *quite* well. I'm *quite* sure. = I'm 100% sure.
to **hang out (with), hung, hung** [ˌhæŋ 'aʊt wɪð, hʌŋ, hʌŋ]	sich treffen (mit); rumhängen (mit) →	When you *hang out* with friends, you meet them and spend time with them.
4 **search engine** ['sɜ:tʃ ˌendʒɪn]	Suchmaschine →	When you look for information on the Internet, it is best to use a *search engine.*
at least [ət 'li:st]	wenigstens, mindestens	

Unit 5: Media messages

VOCABULARY SKILLS

Wörter aus einem Themenbereich (z. B. *media*) kannst du spielerisch lernen, indem du aus ihnen eine Wortkette bildest. Verbinde hierzu die einzelnen Wörter in ihren Anfangs- und Endbuchstaben, z. B.

NEWSOAPUBLIC
oder
PROGRAMMENTERTAINMENTV

Ihr könnt euch diese Ketten auch gemeinsam in einer Gruppe ausdenken und aufschreiben und diese dann mit einer anderen Gruppe austauschen. Versucht die Wortketten der anderen zu knacken und schreibt alle Wörter heraus, die ihr entdeckt.

Check-in

medium pl. **media** ['miːdiəm, 'miːdiə]	Medium, Medien →	! *Media* steht meist im Plural: The *media* **are** full of stories about stars.
celeb(rity) [sə'lebrɪti]	berühmte Persönlichkeit →	*celeb(rity)* = famous person
to **copy** ['kɒpi]	nachmachen	
to **change** [tʃeɪndʒ]	(sich) verändern →	You look different! You've *changed* a lot. *Fr. changer*
quality ['kwɒləti]	Qualität; Qualitäts- →	*Fr. la qualité; Lat. qualitas **f***
popular newspaper [ˌpɒpjələ 'njuːsˌpeɪpə]	Boulevardzeitung	
newspaper ['njuːsˌpeɪpə]	Zeitung →	A newsagent sells lots of different *newspapers*.
to **create** [kri'eɪt]	(er)schaffen →	*Fr. créer; Lat. creare*
the public [ðə 'pʌblɪk]	die Öffentlichkeit →	Stars sometimes want to hide from *the public*. *Fr. le public; Lat. publicum **n***
studio ['stjuːdiəʊ]	Studio →	! Achtung Aussprache
concert ['kɒnsət]	Konzert →	! Achtung Schreibung und Aussprache
awesome ['ɔːsəm]	super, spitze; beeindruckend →	*awesome* = great
main [meɪn]	Haupt- →	What are your *main* subjects at school? – Maths, German, English and French.
entertainment *(no pl.)* [ˌentə'teɪnmənt]	Unterhaltung →	They always go to the cinema on Saturdays. The cinema is their favourite form of *entertainment* for the weekend.
soap (opera) ['səʊp ˌɒprə]	Seifenoper, Soap	
realistic [ˌrɪə'lɪstɪk]	realistisch →	*realistic* → real
violence *(no pl.)* ['vaɪəlns]	Gewalt →	*Fr. la violence; Lat. violentia **f***
housewife pl. **housewives** ['haʊswaɪf]	Hausfrau	
to **advertise** ['ædvətaɪz]	Werbung machen (für), werben; anpreisen; inserieren →	Have you heard about that new mobile? They *advertise* it a lot on TV.
soap *(no pl.)* [səʊp]	Seife →	I'd like to wash my hands, but there's no *soap* in the bathroom.
cleaning product ['kliːnɪŋ ˌprɒdʌkt]	Reinigungsmittel, Putzmittel	
nickname ['nɪkneɪm]	Spitzname →	A lot of people call the BBC 'the Beep'. 'The Beep' is its *nickname*.

	copy ['kɒpi]	Exemplar →	I'd like two *copies* of that book, please.
2	**programme** ['prəʊgræm]	Programm; Sendung →	There's an interesting *programme* about Australia on TV tonight. *Fr. le programme*

Language 1: Casting for a daily soap

	passive ['pæsɪv]	Passiv →	
	to **discover** [dɪ'skʌvə]	entdecken →	*to discover* = to find sth for the first time; to find sth out
	to **cast**, **cast**, **cast** [kɑ:st, kɑ:st, kɑ:st]	jmdm. eine Rolle (in einem Film) geben →	Fiona wanted to get a role in her favourite soap. So she went to a casting and they really *cast* her!
	agent ['eɪdʒnt]	Agent/-in →	! Achtung Aussprache
	file [faɪl]	Akte →	A *file* is a folder where information about something or somebody is kept.
	script [skrɪpt]	Drehbuch, Skript →	The actor didn't want to act in the film because he didn't like the *script*.
	sides [saɪdz]	Skript beim Casting	
	to **reread**, **reread**, **reread** [ri:'ri:d, ri:'red, ri:'red]	noch einmal lesen →	*to reread* = to read again
	Don't get your hopes up too high. [dəʊnt get jɔ: ˌhəʊps ʌp tu: 'haɪ]	Mach dir nicht zu viele Hoffnungen. →	I hope I will win the competition. – *Don't get your hopes up too high*, it's quite difficult.
	assistant [ə'sɪstnt]	Assistent/-in →	! Achtung Schreibung und Aussprache
	to **sign** [saɪn]	unterschreiben →	Please *sign* the letter and take it to the post office. *Fr. signer; Lat. signare*
	contract ['kɒntrækt]	Vertrag →	*Fr. le contrat; Lat. contractus*
	super ['su:pə]	super →	! Achtung Aussprache
3	to **discuss** [dɪ'skʌs]	diskutieren →	*to discuss* = to talk about sth
	to **film** [fɪlm]	filmen, drehen →	*to film* → a film
4	to **photograph** ['fəʊtəgrɑ:f]	fotografieren →	*to photograph* = to take a photo
6	**active** ['æktɪv]	Aktiv →	! Achtung Aussprache
	by [baɪ]	von →	The film was seen *by* more than one million people.

False friends

Do you remember what false friends are? They are words which look or sound like German words, but have a different meaning in English. So watch out for these nouns and verbs!

action	Handlung	**note**	Notiz
art	Kunst	**personal**	persönlich
(to) **become**	werden	(to) **photograph**	fotografieren
city	Großstadt	**rock**	Fels, Stein
map	Stadtplan, Landkarte	**sea**	Meer, die See
meaning	Bedeutung	(to) **spend**	ausgeben
menu	Speisekarte	**trainers**	Turnschuhe

Talkwise: Talk about media in your life

	discussing [dɪ'skʌsɪŋ]	Diskutieren	Discuss the role of computers in today's world.
	pros and cons *(pl.)* [ˌprəʊz‿n 'kɒnz]	Pro und Kontra →	Think of *pros and cons*.
	couch potato ['kaʊtʃ pəˌteɪtəʊ]	Fernsehglotzer/-in, Couchpotato →	At the weekend she watches TV all day. She's a real *couch potato*.
1	**maniac** ['meɪniæk]	Verrückte/-r, Wahnsinnige/-r →	He's got a fast car and drives like a *maniac*.
	bookworm ['bʊkwɜ:m]	Bücherwurm →	I love books. I'm a *bookworm*.

Language 2: Advertising

	advertising *(no pl.)* ['ædvətaɪzɪŋ]	Werbung, Reklame →	*advertising* → to advertise
	to **be worth** [bi 'wɜ:θ]	wert sein	
	smooth [smu:ð]	glatt →	Feel this wood – it's really *smooth*.
	look [lʊk]	Aussehen →	*look* → to look
	tube [tju:b]	Tube →	! Achtung Aussprache
	soccer ['sɒkə]	Fußball →	*soccer* = football
	product ['prɒdʌkt]	Produkt, Erzeugnis	! Achtung Schreibung und Aussprache
1	**ad(vertisement)** [əd'vɜ:tɪsmənt]	Anzeige; Werbespot →	*ad(vertisement)* → advertising → to advertise
6	**headline** ['hedlaɪn]	Schlagzeile →	The large words that start an article are called a *headline*.
	to **get attention** [get ə'tenʃn]	jmdn. auf sich aufmerksam machen →	Rachel likes our new classmate a lot. She always tries to *get* his *attention*.

USEFUL PHRASES

It always helps to check each other's work and to give each other advice on how to do things differently.

It would be better if you …
You should …
I don't understand this sentence.
If I were you, I would …
Could you write …?
How about …?

I know what you mean.
I'll change that.
But I think it's OK as it is.
I'll think about what you said.
That's a good idea.
I think I'll do that. Thanks!

Skills: Vocabulary Skills – Writing a newspaper report

	LAN *(Local Area Network)* [læn; ˌləʊkl ˌeəriə 'netwɜ:k]	LAN →	Are you going to the *LAN* party tomorrow?
	beginning [bɪ'gɪnɪŋ]	Anfang; Beginn →	*beginning* ↔ ending, end
	basic ['beɪsɪk]	grundlegend, Grund-; einfach →	*basic* = simple
	to **attend** [ə'tend]	teilnehmen, besuchen →	Did you *attend* the conference? = Were you at the conference?
	to **organise** ['ɔ:gənaɪz]	organisieren →	*Fr. organiser*
	youth [ju:θ]	Jugend →	Is there a *youth* club in your town?

	to **raise money** [reɪz 'mʌni]	Geld sammeln, Geld aufbringen →	Charities *raise money.*
	argument ['ɑ:gjəmənt]	Auseinandersetzung, Streit →	The boys didn't agree with each other. They had a big *argument.*
	violent ['vaɪələnt]	gewalttätig →	*violent* → violence *Fr. violent,e; Lat. violentus*
	noise [nɔɪz]	Lärm, Krach; Geräusch →	What a *noise!* Please turn off the music.
	background ['bækgraʊnd]	Hintergrund →	

TIP

If you want to understand the context of a story better, you should get more *background* information about it.

	police department [pə'li:s dɪˌpɑ:tmənt]	Polizeidienststelle	
	to **give one's opinion** [ˌgɪv wʌnz ə'pɪnjən]	seine Meinung äußern →	*to give your opinion* = to say what you think about sth
	opinion [ə'pɪnjən]	Meinung	
1	to **allow** [ə'laʊ]	erlauben, gestatten →	*to allow* → to be allowed to (do sth)
2	to **exchange** [ɪks'tʃeɪndʒ]	austauschen	
	to **rewrite** [ri:'raɪt]	umschreiben; neu schreiben →	to write → *to rewrite*

Text: No couch potatoes!

to **convince** [kən'vɪns]	überzeugen →	We couldn't *convince* her. She didn't believe us. *Fr. convaincre; Lat. convincere*
cereal *(no pl.)* ['sɪəriəl]	Frühstückszerealie, Getreideprodukt *(z. B. Cornflakes oder Müsli)* →	Many people in Britain have *cereal* for breakfast.
magic ['mædʒɪk]	Magie, Zauberei →	*Fr. la magie*
to **get sb to do sth** ['get ˌsʌmbədi tə 'du: ˌsʌmθɪŋ]	jmdn. dazu bewegen, etwas zu tun →	Bill hates horses. You would never *get him to* ride a horse.
pile [paɪl]	Stapel, Haufen →	a *pile* of books
to **fall off** [fɔ:l 'ɒf]	herunterfallen, (hinunter)fallen →	I *fell off* my horse last week.
ramp [ræmp]	Rampe	
to **disappear** [ˌdɪsə'pɪə]	verschwinden →	I can't find my MP3 player. It *has disappeared.*
to **crack** [kræk]	(zer)brechen; (zer)springen	
cold [kəʊld]	Erkältung →	I'm ill. I've got a *cold.*
spinach *(no pl.)* ['spɪnɪtʃ]	Spinat	
to **admit** [əd'mɪt]	zugeben →	If you have done something wrong or silly, it is not always easy to *admit* it. *Lat. admittere*
to **walk past** [wɔ:k 'pɑ:st]	vorbeigehen, vorbeilaufen	
above [ə'bʌv]	oben, über, oberhalb	
outline ['aʊtlaɪn]	Umriss, Silhouette →	the *outline* of a church
roof [ru:f]	Dach	
to **cut, cut, cut** [kʌt, kʌt, kʌt]	(sich) schneiden →	He *cut* his finger with a knife.
pipe [paɪp]	Rohr	
gash [gæʃ]	tiefe Schnittwunde →	She had been attacked by someone with a knife. There was a *gash* in her arm.
blood [blʌd]	Blut →	*blood* → to bleed
patient ['peɪʃnt]	Patient/-in →	There are a lot of *patients* in this hospital.
to **distract** [dɪ'strækt]	ablenken →	I didn't hear what our teacher said because my friend *distracted* me.

	bandage ['bændɪdʒ]	Verband →	Can I have a *bandage* for this patient, please?
	emergency [ɪ'mɜ:dʒnsi]	Notfall, Notlage →	In an *emergency*, call the doctor or the police.
	to **tie** [taɪ]	binden, zubinden	
	tight [taɪt]	fest, eng →	I can't wear this skirt. It's too *tight*.
	ambulance ['æmbjələns]	Krankenwagen →	*Fr. l'ambulance f*
	to **rescue** ['reskju:]	retten →	There was a ferry accident, but everybody *was rescued*.
4	survey ['sɜ:veɪ]	Umfrage; Studie	
	habit ['hæbɪt]	Gewohnheit	
	to report [rɪ'pɔ:t]	berichten	
	result [rɪ'zʌlt]	Ergebnis, Resultat	

Wordwise

3	obvious ['ɒbviəs]	offensichtlich	
	ballet ['bæleɪ]	Ballett	
	to stick up one's nose [ˌstɪk‿ʌp wʌnz 'nəʊz]	die Nase rümpfen	
	baggy clothes [ˌbægi 'kləʊðz]	weite Kleidung	
	space [speɪs]	Weltraum	
	now [naʊ]	heute	
	all alone [ˌɔ:l‿ə'ləʊn]	ganz allein	
	to rock [rɒk]	rocken	
	to tag along ['tæg ə'lɒŋ]	hinterherlaufen, hinterhertrotten	
	to turn down [tɜ:n 'daʊn]	abweisen	

Unit 6: Time to travel

VOCABULARY SKILLS

Sprich Englisch so oft wie möglich! Vielleicht ist in deiner Nachbarschaft jemand, mit dem du dich nur auf Englisch unterhalten kannst. Oder du hast im Urlaub Gelegenheit, Englisch zu sprechen. Nimm an einem Schüleraustausch teil, wenn du kannst. Und hab vor allem keine Angst vor Fehlern. Man wird dich trotzdem verstehen. Außerdem: Wenn dir etwas mal nicht einfällt, dann kannst du es sicher mit Hilfe anderer Wörter oder Wendungen umschreiben.

Höre Englisch so oft wie möglich! Englische Musik und englisches Radio und Fernsehen bieten dazu gute Möglichkeiten. Versuche einzelne Wörter herauszuhören und ihre Bedeutung zu erschließen oder ungefähr zu erraten. Schau dir Filme, die du schon kennst, noch einmal auf Englisch an. Du wirst staunen, was du alles verstehst. Oft haben Bibliotheken englische Videos oder eine Auswahl an DVDs.

Lies Englisch so oft wie möglich! In vielen Bibliotheken kannst du dir englische Bücher ausleihen oder englische Zeitschriften und Zeitungen lesen. Vielleicht gibt es dort ja ein englisches Buch über dein Hobby? Beginne am besten mit kürzeren Texten – Comics sind immer gut geeignet – und gib vor allem nicht bei den ersten unbekannten Wörtern auf. Meist lassen sie sich aus dem Zusammenhang erschließen.

Schreibe Englisch so oft wie möglich! Wie wäre es mit einer Brieffreundschaft? Frag doch mal deine Lehrerin oder deinen Lehrer oder knüpfe Kontakte über das Internet. Vielleicht kannst du deinen Brieffreund oder deine Brieffreundin später auch mal besuchen.

Check-in

traveller ['trævlə]	Reisende/-r →	*traveller* → to travel
journey ['dʒɜ:ni]	Reise →	On our *journey* through England we met a lot of nice people.
noodle ['nu:dl]	Nudel →	I think Italian *noodles* are the best!
plant [plɑ:nt]	Pflanze →	My grandmother has got a lot of different *plants* in her garden. *Fr. la plante; Lat. planta **f***
evolution [ˌi:və'lu:ʃn]	Evolution, Entwicklung →	! Achtung Aussprache The *evolution* of life on Earth started millions of years ago.
missionary ['mɪʃnri]	Missionar/-in →	*Fr. le missionaire*
moon [mu:n]	Mond →	You can see the *moon* best at night.
step [step]	Schritt, Stufe →	It's only a few more *steps* to their house.
giant [dʒaɪənt]	Riesen-, riesig →	*Fr. géant,e*
leap [li:p]	Sprung, Satz →	With a giant *leap* the cat jumped down from the tree.
mankind [mæn'kaɪnd]	Menschheit →	*Mankind* must remember to look after the Earth.
challenge ['tʃælɪndʒ]	Herausforderung →	His new job was a real *challenge*.
to **take** [teɪk]	dauern, (Zeit) brauchen →	It *takes* two hours to get from here to Edinburgh by train.
first language ['fɜ:st ˌlæŋgwɪdʒ]	Muttersprache →	My *first language* is German.
per cent [pə 'sent]	Prozent	

Language 1: To the ends of the earth

	reporting what someone said [rɪˌpɔ:tɪŋ wɒt sʌmwʌn 'sed]	wiedergeben, was jemand gesagt hat	
	to **mention** ['menʃn]	erwähnen →	Don't *mention* school. I'm enjoying my weekend right now.
	disappointing [ˌdɪsə'pɔɪntɪŋ]	enttäuschend →	How was the concert? – It was very *disappointing*. The band only played for 45 minutes!
	to **get bored** [get 'bɔ:d]	sich langweilen →	I always *get bored* when I read love stories.
2	to **report** [rɪ'pɔ:t]	berichten, wiedergeben →	Please *report* what the man told you word for word.
	to **introduce** [ˌɪntrə'dju:s]	einführen, einleiten →	*Lat. introducere*
	direct speech [ˌdɪrekt 'spi:tʃ]	direkte Rede	
	indirect speech [ˌɪndɪrekt 'spi:tʃ]	indirekte Rede →	
3	**welcome** ['welkəm]	Empfang →	Her friends gave her a great *welcome* after she had come back from her trip around the world.
4	**two days earlier** [ˌtu: deɪz 'ɜ:liə]	vor zwei Tagen, zwei Tage zuvor →	"I met him two days ago." = She said she had met him *two days earlier.*
	the day before [ðə ˌdeɪ bɪ'fɔ:]	am Tag vorher, am Tag zuvor →	"I went to London yesterday." = He said he had gone to London *the day before*.

Talkwise: Read the book, watch the film, play the game

	giving advice [ˌgɪvɪŋ əd'vaɪs]	einen Rat geben	
1	**biography** [baɪ'ɒgrəfi]	Biografie →	❗ Achtung Schreibung und Aussprache
	comedy ['kɒmədi]	Komödie →	I like *comedies*. They're funny. *Fr. la comédie*
2	to **recommend** [ˌrekə'mend]	empfehlen →	In a restaurant you can ask the waiter or waitress: "Excuse me, what can you *recommend* today?" *Fr. recommander*
3	**Who's in it?** [hu:z 'ɪn‿ɪt]	Wer spielt mit? →	This film sounds good. *Who's in it?*

Language 2: Emergency on the motorway

	coach [kəʊtʃ]	Reisebus →	A *coach* is a big bus for holidays or long trips.
	police officer [pəˌli:s 'ɒfɪsə]	Polizeibeamte/-r →	A *police officer* is a man or woman in the police.
	dangerous ['deɪndʒrəs]	gefährlich →	*dangerous* ↔ safe
	chemical ['kemɪkl]	Chemikalie	
	to **warn sb** [wɔ:n]	jmdn. warnen; jmdn. ermahnen →	They expected bad weather. So they *warned* us not to go on the hike.
	service ['sɜ:vɪs]	Service, Dienst; Verbindung *(Zug, Bus)* →	There's a good bus *service* into town, so we don't often go by car. *Fr. le service; Lat. servitium* ***n***
	paramedic [ˌpærə'medɪk]	Sanitäter/-in →	They called the ambulance service and the *paramedics* arrived three minutes later.
	whether ['weðə]	ob →	*whether* = if (in indirect speech)
	firefighter ['faɪəˌfaɪtə]	Feuerwehrmann, Feuerwehrfrau →	A lot of young boys say they want to become *firefighters* one day.
	area ['eəriə]	Areal; Fläche; Gebiet →	The *area* around the harbour is very beautiful. *Lat. area* ***f***
	to **advise (sb to do sth)** [əd'vaɪz]	(jmdm.) raten (etw. zu tun) →	❗ *to advise* → advice
5	**command** [kə'mɑ:nd]	Befehl →	"Come here at once!" is a *command*. *Fr. la commande*
	to **ask sb to do sth** ['ɑ:sk]	jmdn. bitten, etw. zu tun →	She *asked me to park* my car somewhere else.
7	**burglar** ['bɜ:glə]	Einbrecher/-in →	a *burglar*
	to **be trapped** [bi: 'træpt]	in der Falle sitzen →	The river was behind us, the tiger in front – we *were trapped*!

USEFUL PHRASES

When you make an emergency call it is important to give clear information. With these phrases you can get help quickly.

The police/fire/ambulance service, please!
My name is … and I'm calling from …
There has been an accident./I've just seen an accident.
There's a fire/a burglar in/at …
A man/child … is hurt/trapped.
It looks really bad/dangerous/ …
Sorry, I don't know/can't tell you that.

Skills: Speaking Skills – Small talk

	second language ['seknd ˌlæŋgwɪdʒ]	Zweitsprache	
	fantastic[fæn'tæstɪk]	fantastisch, großartig →	Surfing is *fantastic*. I love it. *Fr. fantastique*
	Right? [raɪt]	Stimmt's?/Nicht wahr? →	It's your birthday tomorrow, *right?* = It's your birthday tomorrow, isn't it?
	annoying [ə'nɔɪɪŋ]	ärgerlich; lästig →	It's so *annoying* that I have to take my little brother with me all the time during our holidays.
	And you. [ənd 'ju:]	Gleichfalls. →	Good night, sleep well. – Thanks, *and you.*
3	**filler** ['fɪlə]	Füllwort →	'Um', 'er', 'hm' etc. are *fillers.*
	extra ['ekstrə]	zusätzlich	

Text: My big adventure

railway ['reɪlweɪ]	Eisenbahn →	People often travelled by *railway* when there were no cars.
to **complete** [kəm'pli:t]	fertig stellen →	After ten years the director finally *completed* the film.
seat [si:t]	Sitz, Sitzplatz →	a *seat* → to sit
princess [prɪn'ses]	Prinzessin →	*Fr. la princesse*
to **save** [seɪv]	retten →	*to save* = to rescue *Fr. sauver; Lat. salvare*
track [træk]	Gleis; Spur →	They crossed the railway *tracks* and followed the path down to the river.
prairie ['preəri]	Prärie →	! Achtung Aussprache *Fr. la prairie*
to **slow down** [sləʊ 'daʊn]	langsamer werden →	*Slow down*, please, there are children in the street.
bellow ['beləʊ]	Gebrüll →	There was a loud *bellow* – then they saw the monkeys.
to **jump out of one's skin** [ˌdʒʌmp‿aʊt‿əv wʌnz 'skɪn]	sich zu Tode erschrecken	
skin [skɪn]	Haut; Fell	
buffalo pl. **buffalo** ['bʌfləʊ]	Büffel →	 *buffalo*
delay [dɪ'leɪ]	Verzögerung, Verspätung →	The train is half an hour late. We apologize for the *delay.*
bet [bet]	Wette →	I was sure that my team would win the match, but they didn't. I lost the *bet.*
to **continue** [kən'tɪnju:]	weitergehen, -fahren, -reisen →	*Fr. continuer; Lat. continuare*
on foot [ɒn 'fʊt]	zu Fuß →	There was no bus to the village, so they went *on foot.*
to **take the chance** [ˌteɪk ðə 'tʃɑ:ns]	es darauf ankommen lassen, das Risiko eingehen	
whistle ['wɪsl]	Pfiff, Pfeifen →	Did you hear the *whistle*? It's the end of the match.
to **make it** ['meɪk‿ɪt]	es schaffen →	They wanted to get home before dark, but they didn't *make it.*
side [saɪd]	Seite	
scream [skri:m]	Schrei →	They heard a *scream* and ran to help.

to **scream** [skri:m]	schreien, kreischen →	*to scream* → a scream Don't *scream* so loud!

Verbs and nouns with the same form

(to) **drink**	trinken	(to) **milk**	melken
drink	Getränk	**milk**	Milch
(to) **end**	enden	(to) **paint**	(an)malen, streichen
end	Ende	**paint**	Farbe
(to) **fight**	kämpfen	(to) **plan**	planen
fight	Kampf	**plan**	Plan
(to) **film**	filmen	(to) **rain**	regnen
film	Film	**rain**	Regen
(to) **help**	helfen	(to) **scream**	schreien, kreischen
help	Hilfe	**scream**	Schrei
(to) **hope**	hoffen	(to) **smell**	riechen
hope	Hoffnung	**smell**	Geruch
(to) **interview**	interviewen	(to) **taste**	schmecken
interview	Interview	**taste**	Geschmack
(to) **look**	aussehen	(to) **work**	arbeiten
look	Aussehen	**work**	Arbeit

Sioux pl. **Sioux** [su:, su:z]	Sioux-Indianer	
frightening ['fraɪtnɪŋ]	furchterregend →	*frightening* = scary I think thunderstorms are *frightening*.
gun [gʌn]	Schusswaffe	
to **shoot**, **shot**, **shot** [ʃu:t, ʃɒt, ʃɒt]	schießen, schoss, geschossen →	They *shot* the enemy with their guns.
danger ['deɪndʒə]	Gefahr →	*danger* → dangerous *Fr. le danger*
on time [ɒn 'taɪm]	pünktlich →	When you arrive *on time*, you arrive exactly at the right time.

3 then [ðen] — damals
now [naʊ] — heute
6 rhythm ['rɪðm] — Rhythmus
desert ['dezət] — Wüste
the wilds [ðə 'waɪldz] — die Wildnis
vineyard ['vɪnjəd] — Weinberg
Arapaho [ə'ræpəhəʊ] — Arapaho-Indianer
to and fro [tə ənd 'frəʊ] — hin und her, vor und zurück

Dictionary (English–German)

In dieser alphabetischen Wortliste findest du das gesamte Vokabular von *Green Line* 1, 2 und 3 mit Ausnahme der Wörter, die nicht zum Lernwortschatz von Band 1 und 2 gehören. Namen stehen in einer extra Liste am Ende des ***Dictionary***. Einträge, die aus mehreren Wörtern bestehen, kannst du meist unter verschiedenen Stichwörtern nachschlagen. So ist z. B. *all day* unter *all* und unter *day* eingetragen.
Die Fundstellen stehen immer hinter dem jeweiligen Wort und zeigen dir an, wo es zum ersten Mal vorkommt, z. B.
curious ['kjʊəriəs] neugierig **III U2**, 33 kommt zum ersten Mal vor in Band III, Unit 2, Seite 33.
U = Unit
Bei Wörtern, die nicht zum Lernwortschatz zählen, steht die Fundstelle in Spitzklammern, z. B.
desert ['dezət] Wüste ⟨III U6, 103⟩.
Die mit * gekennzeichneten Verben sind unregelmäßige Verben. Eine Zusammenstellung der unregelmäßigen englischen Verben findest du hinten im Buch auf Seite 210/211.

A

a, an [ə; ən] ein/e **I**
  a day [ə 'deɪ] pro Tag **II**
  a lot of [ə 'lɒt‿əv] viel/-e, eine Menge **I**
  a pair of [ə 'peər‿əv] ein Paar **III U4**, 60
aargh! [ɑ:g] Grrrr! **I**
*to be **able to (do sth)** [bi‿'eɪbl tə] können, fähig sein (zu) **III U2**, 26
about [ə'baʊt] über **I**
  to be about [bi ə'baʊt] gehen um, handeln von **III U2**, 32
above [ə'bʌv] oben, über, oberhalb **III U5**, 87
abseiling ['æbseɪlɪŋ] Abseilen **II**
abstract ['æbstrækt] abstrakt **III U4**, 60
accent ['æksnt] Akzent **III U4**, 67
accident ['æksɪdnt] Unfall **II**
to **act** [ækt] spielen **I**
action ['ækʃn] Handlung; Action **III U2**, 26
active ['æktɪv] Aktiv **III U5**, 80
activity [æk'tɪvəti] Aktivität **I**
actor ['æktə] Schauspieler **II**
actress ['æktrəs] Schauspielerin **III U3**, 53
actually ['æktʃuəli] tatsächlich, wirklich; eigentlich **III U2**, 35
AD (= Anno Domini) [eɪ'di:] nach Christus **III U2**, 24
to **add** [æd] etw. (zu etw.) hinzufügen **II**
addicted (to) [ə'dɪktɪd tə] süchtig **II**
address [ə'dres] Adresse **I**
  address book [ə'dres ˌbʊk] Adressbuch **I**
adjective ['ædʒɪktɪv] Adjektiv, Eigenschaftswort **I**
to **admit** [əd'mɪt] zugeben **III U5**, 86
adult ['ædʌlt] Erwachsene/-r **III U6**, 104
adventure [əd'ventʃə] Abenteuer **I**
adverb ['ædvɜ:b] Adverb **II**
to **advertise** ['ædvətaɪz] Werbung machen (für), werben; anpreisen; inserieren **III U5**, 77
ad(vertisement) [əd'vɜ:tɪsmənt] Anzeige; Werbespot **III U5**, 82
advertising *(no pl.)* ['ædvətaɪzɪŋ] Werbung, Reklame **III U5**, 82
advice [əd'vaɪs] Rat, Ratschlag **III U3**, 48
  giving advice [ˌgɪvɪŋ əd'vaɪs] einen Rat geben **III U6**, 96
to **advise (sb to do sth)** [əd'vaɪz] (jmdm.) raten (etw. zu tun) **III U6**, 97
aerobics [eə'rəʊbɪks] Aerobic **II**
*I'm **afraid** [aɪm ə'freɪd] leider **III U3**, 50
  to be afraid (of) [bi:‿ə'freɪd‿əv] (sich) fürchten, Angst haben (vor) ⟨**III U1**, 18⟩
after ['ɑ:ftə] nach; nachdem **I**
  after that ['ɑ:ftə ðət] danach **I**
afternoon [ˌɑ:ftə'nu:n] Nachmittag **I**
again [ə'gen] wieder, noch einmal, nochmal **I**
  again and again [ə'gen‿ənd‿ə'gen] immer wieder **II**
against [ə'genst] gegen **I**
age [eɪdʒ] Zeitalter; Alter **III U2**, 25
travel **agency** ['trævl ˌeɪdʒnsi] Reisebüro **III U6**, 104
agent ['eɪdʒnt] Agent/-in **III U5**, 78
aggressive [ə'gresɪv] aggressiv **II**
ago [ə'gəʊ] vor *(zeitlich)* **II**
agony aunt ['ægəni ˌɑ:nt] Kummerkastentante **III U3**, 49
to **agree** [ə'gri:] zustimmen **III U1**, 12
air [eə] Luft **I**
  open-air [ˌəʊpn'eə] Openair-, Freilicht-, im Freien **III U2**, 26
  to end in thin air [ˌend‿ɪn θɪn‿'eə] im Nichts enden **II**
airport ['eəpɔ:t] Flughafen **II**
alarm clock [ə'lɑ:m ˌklɒk] Wecker **I**
Alas [ə'læs] O weh ⟨**III U2**, 36⟩
alien ['eɪliən] Außerirdische/-r, außerirdisches Wesen **II**
all [ɔ:l] alle/-s; ganz **I**
  all alone [ˌɔ:l‿ə'ləʊn] ganz allein ⟨**III U5**, 87⟩
  all day [ɔ:l 'deɪ] den ganzen Tag **II**
  all of it ['ɔ:l‿əv‿ɪt] alle/-s (davon); ganz **II**
  all the time [ˌɔ:l ðə 'taɪm] die ganze Zeit **II**
allergic to [ə'lɜ:dʒɪk tə] allergisch auf **I**
to **allow** [ə'laʊ] erlauben, gestatten **III U5**, 85
  to be allowed to (do sth) [bi:‿ə'laʊd tə] dürfen **III U2**, 26
almost ['ɔ:lməʊst] fast, beinahe **II**
alone [ə'ləʊn] allein **I**
  all alone [ˌɔ:l‿ə'ləʊn] ganz allein ⟨**III U5**, 87⟩
  Leave him alone! [ˌli:v hɪm‿ə'ləʊn] Lass ihn in Ruhe! **II**
alphabet ['ælfəbet] Alphabet **I**
alphabetical [ˌælfə'betɪkl] alphabetisch **I**
already [ɔ:l'redi] schon, bereits **I**
also ['ɔ:lsəʊ] auch **III U1**, 13
although [ɔ:l'ðəʊ] obwohl **II**
always ['ɔ:lweɪz] immer **I**
am [ˌeɪ'em] vormittags *(Uhrzeit)* **I**
ambulance ['æmbjələns] Krankenwagen **III U5**, 87
American [ə'merɪkən] Amerikanisch; amerikanisch, aus Amerika **III U1**, 9
  American football [əˌmerɪkən 'fʊtbɔ:l] American Football **III U1**, 13
and [ænd; ənd] und **I**
  And you. [ənd 'ju:] Gleichfalls. **III U6**, 100

angry ['æŋgri] wütend, zornig, verärgert **II**
animal ['ænɪml] Tier **I**
animal home ['ænɪml həʊm] Tierheim **II**
announcement [ə'naʊnsmənt] Ankündigung; Durchsage **II**
annoying [ə'nɔɪɪŋ] ärgerlich; lästig **III U6,** 100
anorak ['ænəræk] Anorak **II**
another [ə'nʌðə] noch ein/-e; ein/-e andere/-r/-s **I**
answer ['ɑ:nsə] Antwort **I**
to **answer** ['ɑ:nsə] (be)antworten **I**
answerphone ['ɑ:nsəfəʊn] Anrufbeantworter **III U3,** 43
antique [æn'ti:k] Antiquität **II**
any ['enɪ] irgendein/-e/-er; irgendwelche **I**
(not) any longer [nɒt ˌeni 'lɒŋgə] (nicht) mehr, (nicht) länger **II**
(not) any more [nɒt ˌeni 'mɔ:] (nicht) mehr **III U3,** 43
anybody ['eniˌbɒdi] irgendjemand; jeder (beliebige) **II**
anyone ['eniwʌn] irgendjemand; jeder (beliebige) **II**
anything ['eniθɪŋ] irgendetwas **II**
anyway ['eniweɪ] trotzdem; jedenfalls, sowieso **II**
anywhere ['eniweə] irgendwo; überall (egal, wo) **II**
to **apologize** [ə'pɒlədʒaɪz] sich entschuldigen **III U4,** 62
to **applaud** [ə'plɔ:d] applaudieren **III U3,** 53
apple ['æpl] Apfel **I**
April ['eɪprl] April **I**
arcade games *(pl.)* [ɑ:'keɪd ˌgeɪmz] Spielautomaten **I**
area ['eəriə] Areal; Fläche; Gebiet **III U6,** 97
argument ['ɑ:gjəmənt] Auseinandersetzung, Streit **III U5,** 85
arm [ɑ:m] Arm **II**
army ['ɑ:mi] Armee **II**
around [ə'raʊnd] herum, umher **II**
arrangement [ə'reɪndʒmənt] Abmachung, Vereinbarung; Plan **III U1,** 10
arrival [ə'raɪvl] Ankunft **II**
to **arrive** [ə'raɪv] ankommen **II**
art [ɑ:t] Kunst **II**
arts and crafts (pl.) [ˌɑ:ts‿ənd 'krɑ:fts] Kunsthandwerk **II**
article ['ɑ:tɪkl] Artikel, Bericht *(in einer Zeitschrift, Zeitung)* **II**; Artikel **III U4,** 60
as [æz; əz] als **II**
as ... as [əz ... əz] so ... wie **II**
as soon as [əz 'su:n‿əz] sobald **II**
Asian ['eɪʃn] asiatisch; Asiate, Asiatin **III U4,** 63
to **ask** [ɑ:sk] fragen **I**
to ask sb to do sth ['ɑ:sk] jmdn. bitten, etw. zu tun **III U6,** 98
to ask for ... ['ɑ:sk fə] nach ... fragen **I**
asleep [ə'sli:p] schlafend **I**
to fall asleep [fɔ:l‿ə'sli:p] einschlafen **I**
assembly [ə'sembli] Versammlung; Morgenappell **II**
assistant [ə'sɪstnt] Verkäufer/-in **I**; Assistent/-in **III U5,** 78
shop assistant ['ʃɒp‿əˌsɪstnt] Verkäufer/-in **II**
at [æt; ət] in, auf, bei, an **I**
at first [ət 'fɜ:st] zuerst; zunächst **II**
at half past (three) [ət ˌhɑ:f pɑ:st 'θri:] um halb (vier) **I**
at home [æt 'həʊm] zu Hause **I**
at least [ət 'li:st] wenigstens, mindestens **III U4,** 68
at my house [ət 'maɪ haʊs] bei mir zu Hause **I**
at once [ət 'wʌns] auf einmal; sofort **I**
at the front [æt ðə 'frʌnt] vorn(e) **II**
at the front of [æt ðə 'frʌnt‿əv] an der Spitze (von), im vorderen Bereich **II**
at the weekend [æt ðə ˌwi:k'end] am Wochenende **I**
athlete ['æθli:t] (Leicht)Athlet/-in **III U1,** 13
athletics [æθ'letɪks] Leichtathletik **III U1,** 8
to **attack** [ə'tæk] angreifen **III U2,** 25
to **attend** [ə'tend] teilnehmen, besuchen **III U5,** 85
*to **get attention** [get ə'tentʃn] jmdn. auf sich aufmerksam machen **III U5,** 84
audience ['ɔ:diəns] Publikum **III U3,** 53
audio ['ɔ:diəʊ] Audio-, Hör- **III U4,** 65
to **audition** [ɔ:'dɪʃn] vorsingen, vorspielen; vortanzen; vorsprechen **II**
August ['ɔ:gəst] August **I**
aunt [ɑ:nt] Tante **I**
agony aunt ['ægəni ˌɑ:nt] Kummerkastentante **III U3,** 49
author ['ɔ:θə] Autor/-in ⟨**III U3,** 53⟩
autumn ['ɔ:təm] Herbst **I**
on **average** [ɒn‿'ævrɪdʒ] durchschnittlich, im Durchschnitt **III U4,** 58
away [ə'weɪ] weg **I**
right away [raɪt‿ə'weɪ] sofort **II**
awesome ['ɔ:səm] super, spitze; beeindruckend **III U5,** 77
awful ['ɔ:fl] schrecklich, furchtbar **III U4,** 60

B

back [bæk] Rückseite; Rücken **II**
like the back of my hand [laɪk ðə ˌbæk‿əv maɪ 'hænd] wie meine Westentasche, in- und auswendig **II**
back [bæk] zurück **I**
to get back [get 'bæk] zurückkommen **II**
background ['bækgraʊnd] Hintergrund **III U5,** 85
bacon ['beɪkn] (Schinken)speck **I**
bad [bæd] schlecht; böse **I**
bad luck [bæd 'lʌk] Pech, Unglück **III U3,** 43
bag [bæg] Tasche **I**
a bag of ... [ə 'bæg‿əv] eine Tüte ... **I**
baggage *(sing.)* ['bægɪdʒ] (Reise)Gepäck **II**
baggy clothes [ˌbægi 'kləʊðz] weite Kleidung ⟨**III U5,** 87⟩
bagpipes *(pl.)* ['bægpaɪps] Dudelsack **II**
baker ['beɪkə] Bäcker/-in **II**
ball [bɔ:l] Ball **I**
rubber ball [ˌrʌbə 'bɔ:l] Gummiball **I**
ballet ['bæleɪ] Ballett ⟨**III U5,** 87⟩
band [bænd] Band, Musikgruppe **I**
boy band ['bɔɪ ˌbænd] Boygroup **I**
bandage ['bændɪdʒ] Verband **III U5,** 87
bang [bæŋ] Knall, Schlag **I**
to **bang** [bæŋ] knallen, schlagen **I**
snack **bar** ['snæk bɑ:] Café **II**
to **bark** [bɑ:k] bellen **I**
to bark at ['bɑ:k‿ət] anbellen **I**
base [beɪs] Base *(beim Baseball)* **III U1,** 8
baseball ['beɪsbɔ:l] Baseball **III U1,** 8
basic ['beɪsɪk] grundlegend, Grund-; einfach **III U5,** 85
basketball ['bɑ:skɪtbɔ:l] Basketball **I**
bat [bæt] Schläger *(beim Tischtennis, Baseball)* **III U1,** 8
to **bat** [bæt] schlagen *(einen Ball)* **III U1,** 20
bathroom ['bɑ:θru:m] Bad(ezimmer) **I**
battle ['bætl] Schlacht, Kampf **II**
*to **be** [bi:; bi] sein **I**
ain't *(= isn't/aren't)* [eɪnt] ist/sind nicht ⟨**III U4,** 65⟩
How are you? [ˌhaʊ‿ɑ: 'jə] Wie geht es dir/Ihnen? **I**

I'm afraid [aɪm əˈfreɪd] leider **III U3,** 50
I'm fine. [ˌaɪm ˈfaɪn] Mir geht es gut. **I**
I'm sorry. [aɪm ˈsɒrɪ] Es tut mir leid. **I**
It's none of your business! [ɪts ˌnʌn‿əv jə ˈbɪznɪs] Das geht dich nichts an! **II**
this is ... [ˈðɪs‿ɪz] hier ist ... *(am Telefon)* **I**
to be a pain [bi‿ə ˈpeɪn] einem auf die Nerven gehen **I**
to be able to (do sth) [bi‿ˈeɪbl tə] können, fähig sein (zu) **III U2,** 26
to be about [bi əˈbaʊt] gehen um, handeln von **III U2,** 32
to be afraid (of) [biː‿əˈfreɪd‿əv] (sich) fürchten, Angst haben (vor) ⟨**III U1,** 18⟩
to be allowed to (do sth) [biː‿əˈlaʊd tə] dürfen **III U2,** 26
to be born [biː ˈbɔːn] geboren werden **II**
to be connected [bi kəˈnektɪd] zusammenhängen, in Zusammenhang stehen **III U2,** 32
to be fed up (with) [bi fed‿ˈʌp wɪð] sauer sein, die Nase voll haben (von) **I**
to be fun [bi ˈfʌn] Spaß machen; witzig sein **I**
to be gone [biː ˈɡɒn] verschwunden sein, weg sein **II**
to be good at [bi ˈɡʊd‿ət] gut sein in/bei **I**
to be good with [bi ˈɡʊd wɪð] gut umgehen können mit **I**
to be in [biː‿ˈɪn] da sein **III U3,** 50
to be in a hurry [bi ɪn‿ə ˈhʌri] es eilig haben, in Eile sein **I**
to be into sth [biː ˈɪntə] an etwas interessiert sein **III U4,** 60
to be late [bi ˈleɪt] zu spät kommen, spät dran sein **I**
to be lost [bi ˈlɒst] sich verirrt haben **II**
to be lucky [bi ˈlʌki] Glück haben **I**
to be on the move [biː ɒn‿ðə ˈmuːv] unterwegs sein **III U4,** 58
to be out of luck [ˌbiː aʊt‿əv ˈlʌk] kein Glück haben **III U1,** 19
to be proud (of) [biː ˈpraʊd‿əv] stolz sein (auf) **III U4,** 59
to be right [bɪ ˈraɪt] Recht haben **I**
to be scared for [bi ˈskeəd fə] Angst haben um **I**
to be shocked [biː ˈʃɒkt] geschockt sein **II**
to be trapped [biː ˈtræpt] in der Falle sitzen **III U6,** 99
to be unlucky [ˌbiː ʌnˈlʌki] Pech haben **III U1,** 19
to be with ... [bi ˈwɪð] bei ... sein **I**
to be wrong [bi ˈrɒŋ] Unrecht haben, sich irren **I**
Who's in it? [huːz ˈɪn‿ɪt] Wer spielt mit? **III U6,** 96
beach [biːtʃ] Strand **I**
beach holiday [ˈbiːtʃ ˌhɒlədeɪ] Strandurlaub **I**
on the beach [ɒn ðə ˈbiːtʃ] am Strand **I**
to **beam** [biːm] beamen **II**
beautiful [ˈbjuːtɪfl] schön; wunderbar **I**
because [bɪˈkɒz] weil, da **I**
*to **become** [bɪˈkʌm] werden **II**
bed [bed] Bett **I**
to go to bed [ɡəʊ tə ˈbed] ins Bett gehen **I**
bedroom [ˈbedruːm] Schlafzimmer **I**
before [bɪˈfɔː] bevor **I**; bis (zu), vor **I**
the day before [ðə ˌdeɪ bɪˈfɔː] am Tag vorher, am Tag zuvor **III U6,** 95
*to **begin** [bɪˈɡɪn] beginnen, anfangen **II**
beginning [bɪˈɡɪnɪŋ] Anfang; Beginn **III U5,** 85
to **behave** [bɪˈheɪv] sich benehmen, sich verhalten **III U3,** 43
behind [bɪˈhaɪnd] hinter **I**
to **believe** [bɪˈliːv] glauben **I**
He can't believe his eyes. [hi ˌkɑːnt bɪˌliːv hɪz ˈaɪz] Er traut seinen Augen nicht. **I**
bellow [ˈbeləʊ] Gebrüll **III U6,** 101
best [best] beste/-r/-s **I**
bet [bet] Wette **III U6,** 101
better [ˈbetə] besser **II**
between [bɪˈtwiːn] zwischen **II**
big [bɪɡ] groß **I**
bike [baɪk] Fahrrad **I**
mountain bike [ˈmaʊntɪn baɪk] Mountainbike **II**
bilingual [baɪˈlɪŋɡwl] zweisprachig **III U4,** 60
bill [bɪl] Rechnung **II**
biography [baɪˈɒɡrəfi] Biografie **III U6,** 96
bird [bɜːd] Vogel **I**
birthday [ˈbɜːθdeɪ] Geburtstag **I**
birthday party [ˈbɜːθdeɪ ˌpɑːti] Geburtstagsfeier **I**
Happy Birthday! [ˌhæpi ˈbɜːθdeɪ] Alles Gute zum Geburtstag! **I**
birthplace [ˈbɜːθpleɪs] Geburtsort **III U4,** 59
black [blæk] schwarz **I**
*to **bleed** [bliːd] bluten **II**
blood [blʌd] Blut **III U5,** 87
blue [bluː] blau **I**
board [bɔːd] Tafel; Brett **I**
boarding school [ˈbɔːdɪŋ ˌskuːl] Internat **II**
boat [bəʊt] Boot, Schiff **I**
bobsleigh [ˈbɒbsleɪ] Bob **III U1,** 13
body [ˈbɒdi] Körper **II**
book [bʊk] Buch **I**
address book [əˈdres ˌbʊk] Adressbuch **I**
exercise book [ˈeksəsaɪz ˌbʊk] Heft **I**
to **book** [bʊk] buchen, reservieren **III U6,** 104
bookworm [ˈbʊkwɜːm] Bücherwurm **III U5,** 81
boot [buːt] Stiefel **II**
golden boots [ˌɡəʊldn ˈbuːts] goldene Stiefel, Zauberstiefel **II**
*to get **bored** [ɡet ˈbɔːd] sich langweilen **III U6,** 94
boring [ˈbɔːrɪŋ] langweilig **I**
*to be **born** [biː ˈbɔːn] geboren werden **II**
to **borrow** [ˈbɒrəʊ] (sich) ausleihen **II**
boss [bɒs] Boss, Chef **II**
both [bəʊθ] beide **II**
bottle [ˈbɒtl] Flasche **I**
bottom [ˈbɒtəm] unteres Ende, Boden **I**
on the bottom [ɒn ðə ˈbɒtəm] unten **I**
bowl [bəʊl] Schüssel **I**
box [bɒks] Box, Kasten, Kästchen, Schachtel **I**
a box of ... [ə ˈbɒks‿əv] eine Schachtel ..., ein Karton ... **I**
boy [bɔɪ] Junge **I**
boy band [ˈbɔɪ ˌbænd] Boygroup **I**
boyfriend [ˈbɔɪfrend] Freund *(in einer Paarbeziehung)* **III U3,** 49
brake [breɪk] Bremse **III U1,** 9
bread [bred] Brot **II**
break [breɪk] Pause **II**
commercial break [kəˌmɜːʃl ˈbreɪk] Werbepause **III U1,** 13
*to **break** [breɪk] (zer)brechen, kaputtgehen **I**
breakfast [ˈbrekfəst] Frühstück **I**
to have breakfast [hæv ˈbrekfəst] frühstücken **I**
breeze [briːz] Brise ⟨**III U4,** 65⟩
bridge [brɪdʒ] Brücke **I**
brilliant [ˈbrɪliənt] toll, prima; glänzend **II**
*to **bring** [brɪŋ] (mit)bringen **I**
British [ˈbrɪtɪʃ] britisch **I**
Briton [ˈbrɪtn] Brite, Britin **III U2,** 26
brochure [ˈbrəʊʃə] Broschüre **I**
broken [ˈbrəʊkn] gebrochen, kaputt **II**
brother [ˈbrʌðə] Bruder **I**

brown [braʊn] braun **I**
web **browser** ['web ˌbraʊzə] Webbrowser **III U5,** 77
to **brush one's teeth** [brʌʃ wʌnz 'ti:θ] (seine) Zähne putzen **III U3,** 43
buffalo pl. **buffalo** ['bʌfləʊ] Büffel **III U6,** 101
*to **build** [bɪld] bauen **I**
building ['bɪldɪŋ] Gebäude **II**
bully ['bʊli] Rabauke, Rüpel, Tyrann **II**
to **bump into** [bʌmp‿'ɪntə] zusammenstoßen (mit) **II**
burger ['bɜ:gə] Hamburger **II**
burglar ['bɜ:glə] Einbrecher/-in **III U6,** 99
*to **burn** [bɜ:n] (ver)brennen **II**
bus pl. **buses** [bʌs; bʌsɪz] Bus **I**
bus stop ['bʌs ˌstɒp] Bushaltestelle **I**
It's none of your **business!** [ɪts ˌnʌn‿əv jə 'bɪznɪs] Das geht dich nichts an! **II**
busker ['bʌskə] Straßenmusikant/-in **II**
busy (with) ['bɪzi ˌwɪð] beschäftigt (mit) **I**
but [bʌt] aber **I**
*to **buy** [baɪ] kaufen **I**
by [baɪ] *(spätestens)* bis **III U4,** 65; von **III U5,** 80
by (Underground) [baɪ] mit (der U-Bahn), per **I**
bye [baɪ] tschüss **I**

C

café ['kæfeɪ] Café **I**
jazz café ['dʒæz ˌkæfeɪ] Jazzcafé **I**
cafeteria [kæfə'tɪəriə] Cafeteria **I**
cake [keɪk] Kuchen, Torte **I**
(phone) **call** ['fəʊn ˌkɔ:l] (Telefon)anruf **I**
to take a call [ˌteɪk‿ə 'kɔ:l] (Telefon) abheben, einen Anruf entgegennehmen **III U3,** 50
to **call** [kɔ:l] rufen, schreien **I**; nennen **I**; anrufen **III U3,** 45
caller ['kɔ:lə] Anrufer/-in **III U3,** 50
calm [kɑ:m] ruhig, friedlich **I**
camera ['kæmrə] Fotoapparat, Kamera **I**
campsite ['kæmpsaɪt] Campingplatz, Zeltplatz **II**
can [kæn; kən] können, dürfen **I**
can't *(=cannot)* [kɑ:nt; 'kænɒt] nicht können **I**
candle ['kændl] Kerze **I**
canoe [kə'nu:] Kanu **II**
capital ['kæpɪtl] Hauptstadt **II**
captain ['kæptɪn] Kapitän **I**
car [kɑ:] Auto **I**
card [kɑ:d] Karte, Spielkarte **I**; Chip, Speicherkarte *(für Digitalkameras)* **I**
e-card ['ɪ:kɑ:d] E-Card **III U5,** 77
top-up card ['tɒp‿ʌp kɑ:d] Aufladekarte *(fürs Handy)* **II**
I don't **care!** [aɪ ˌdəʊnt 'keə] Das ist mir egal! **III U3,** 43
careful ['keəfl] vorsichtig; sorgfältig **II**
caretaker ['keəteɪkə] Hausmeister/-in **I**
carriage ['kærɪdʒ] Wagen, Wagon **II**
to **carry** ['kæri] tragen; befördern **II**
cartoon [kɑ:'tu:n] Cartoon **III U1,** 12
cast [kɑ:st] Besetzung, Ensemble **III U3,** 51
*to **cast** [kɑ:st] jmdm. eine Rolle (in einem Film) geben **III U5,** 78
to cast off [kɑ:st‿'ɒf] wegstoßen, zurückstoßen ⟨**III U2,** 36⟩
casting ['kɑ:stɪŋ] Casting, Rollenbesetzung **III U5,** 78
castle ['kɑ:sl] Burg, Schloss **I**
sand castle ['sænd ˌkɑ:sl] Sandburg **I**
cat [kæt] Katze **I**
cat food ['kæt ˌfu:d] Katzenfutter **I**
*to **catch** [kætʃ] nehmen *(Bus, Zug)* **I**
cave [keɪv] Höhle **II**
CD [ˌsi:'di:] CD **I**
to **celebrate** ['seləbreɪt] feiern **II**
celeb(rity) [sə'lebrɪti] berühmte Persönlichkeit **III U5,** 76
centre ['sentə] Zentrum, Center **I**
information centre [ˌɪnfə'meɪʃn 'sentə] Touristeninformation **I**
century ['sentʃri] Jahrhundert **III U2,** 24
cereal *(no pl.)* ['sɪəriəl] Frühstückszerealie, Getreideprodukt *(z. B. Cornflakes oder Müsli)* **III U5,** 86
chair [tʃeə] Stuhl **I**
challenge ['tʃælɪndʒ] Herausforderung **III U6,** 93
champion ['tʃæmpiən] Gewinner/-in, Sieger/-in; Champion **II**
chance [tʃɑ:ns] Chance; Gelegenheit, Möglichkeit **III U1,** 10
to take the chance [ˌteɪk ðə 'tʃɑ:ns] es darauf ankommen lassen, das Risiko eingehen **III U6,** 102
change [tʃeɪndʒ] Münzgeld, Wechselgeld **II**
to **change** [tʃeɪndʒ] umsteigen; wechseln **II**; (sich) verändern **III U5,** 76
changing places [ˌtʃeɪndʒɪŋ 'pleɪsɪz] Ortswechsel **III U4,** 67
changing room ['tʃeɪndʒɪŋ ru:m] Umkleidekabine **II**
channel ['tʃænl] Kanal; Programm **III U1,** 13
character ['kærəktə] Charakter; Figur **II**
charity ['tʃærɪti] Wohltätigkeitsverein **II**
flow **chart** ['fləʊ ˌtʃɑ:t] Flussdiagramm **II**
charts [tʃɑ:ts] Hitparade **II**
to **chase** [tʃeɪs] verfolgen **I**
on **chat** [ɒn 'tʃæt] im Chat, beim Chatten **III U3,** 47
to **chat** [tʃæt] chatten; plaudern **III U3,** 47
chatroom ['tʃætrʊm] Chatroom **III U3,** 47
cheap [tʃi:p] billig, preiswert **I**
to **check** [tʃek] (über)prüfen; kontrollieren **II**
check-in ['tʃekɪn] Einchecken **I**
check-out ['tʃekaʊt] Auschecken **I**
to **cheer** [tʃɪə] (zu)jubeln, anfeuern **III U4,** 68
cheese [tʃi:z] Käse **I**
chemical ['kemɪkl] Chemikalie **III U6,** 97
chemistry set ['kemɪstri set] Chemiekasten **I**
chicken ['tʃɪkɪn] Huhn; Hähnchen, Hühnchen **I**
child pl. **children** ['tʃaɪld; 'tʃɪldrn] Kind **I**
only child [ˌəʊnli 'tʃaɪld] Einzelkind **I**
chips *(pl.)* [tʃɪps] Pommes frites **II**
fish and chips [ˌfɪʃ‿n‿'tʃɪps] Fisch und Pommes frites **II**
chocolate ['tʃɒklət] Schokolade **I**
male voice **choir** [ˌmeɪl vɔɪs 'kwaɪə] Männerchor **III U4,** 59
*to **choose** [tʃu:z] (aus)wählen **I**
Christmas ['krɪsməs] Weihnachten **II**
church [tʃɜ:tʃ] Kirche **I**
cinema ['sɪnəmə] Kino **I**
city ['sɪti] Großstadt **I**
to **clap** [klæp] klatschen **I**
class [klɑ:s] (Schul-)Klasse **I**
class trip [ˌklɑ:s 'trɪp] Klassenfahrt, Klassenausflug **I**
classmate ['klɑ:smeɪt] Klassenkamerad/-in **II**
classroom ['klɑ:srʊm] Klassenzimmer **I**
classroom phrases *(pl.)* ['klɑ:srʊm ˌfreɪzɪz] Redewendungen für den Unterricht **I**
contact **clause** ['kɒntækt ˌklɔ:z] Relativsatz ohne Relativpronomen **III U1,** 14
if-clause ['ɪfklɔ:z] if-Satz **II**
main clause ['meɪn klɔ:z] Hauptsatz **II**
relative clause [ˌrelətɪv 'klɔ:z] Relativsatz **III U1,** 13
to **clean** [kli:n] säubern, reinigen **III U2,** 34
clean [kli:n] sauber **III U2,** 30
cleaning lady ['kli:nɪŋ ˌleɪdi] Putzfrau **III U3,** 43

cleaning product ['kli:nɪŋ ˌprɒdʌkt] Reinigungsmittel, Putzmittel **III U5,** 77
to **clear the table** [ˌklɪə ðə 'teɪbl] den Tisch abräumen **II**
clear [klɪə] klar, verständlich **I**
clever ['klevə] schlau, klug, intelligent **II**
cliché ['kli:ʃeɪ] Klischee **II**
click [klɪk] Klicken; Klick **III U2,** 35
to **click on** ['klɪk‿ɒn] anklicken **I**
to **climb** [klaɪm] (hinauf)steigen, hinaufklettern, erklimmen **I**
rock **climbing** ['rɒk ˌklaɪmɪŋ] Klettern **II**
clock [klɒk] Uhr **I**
alarm clock [ə'lɑ:m ˌklɒk] Wecker **I**
o'clock [ə'klɒk] Uhr (*Zeitangabe bei vollen Stunden*) **I**
to **close** [kləʊz] schließen, zumachen **I**
close [kləʊs] genau; nahe **III U2,** 32
clothes *(pl.)* [kləʊðz] Kleidung, Kleider **I**
baggy clothes [ˌbægi 'kləʊðz] weite Kleidung ⟨**III U5,** 87⟩
cloud [klaʊd] Wolke **II**
cloudy ['klaʊdi] wolkig **II**
club [klʌb] Klub, Verein **I**
computer club [kəm'pju:tə ˌklʌb] Computerklub **I**
cooking club ['kʊkɪŋ ˌklʌb] Kochklub **I**
coach [kəʊtʃ] Reisebus **III U6,** 97
coal mine ['kəʊl maɪn] Kohlenbergwerk, Kohlengrube **III U4,** 59
coast [kəʊst] Küste **I**
cold [kəʊld] Erkältung **III U5,** 86
cold [kəʊld] kalt **I**
to **collect** [kə'lekt] sammeln, einsammeln **I**
colony ['kɒləni] Kolonie **III U2,** 25
colour ['kʌlə] Farbe **I**
*to **come** [kʌm] kommen **I**
Come on! [kʌm‿'ɒn] Komm schon!/ Komm jetzt! **I**
to come in [kʌm 'ɪn] hereinkommen **I**
to come over [kʌm 'əʊvə] herüberkommen, vorbeischauen **I**
to come up to [kʌm‿'ʌp tə] zukommen auf **II**
comedy ['kɒmədi] Komödie **III U6,** 96
comic ['kɒmɪk] Comic(heft) **III U2,** 25
comma ['kɒmə] Komma **III U3,** 48
command [kə'mɑ:nd] Befehl **III U6,** 98
comment ['kɒment] Kommentar **II**
commercial [kə'mɜ:ʃl] Werbespot **III U1,** 13
commercial break [kəˌmɜ:ʃl 'breɪk] Werbepause **III U1,** 13
communication skills [kəˌmju:nɪ'keɪʃn ˌskɪlz] Sprechfertigkeiten, Kommunikationsfertigkeiten **I**
company ['kʌmpəni] Gesellschaft ⟨**III U2,** 36⟩
comparative [kəm'pærətɪv] Komparativ **II**
to **compare (with/to)** [kəm'peə] vergleichen (mit) **II**
comparison [kəm'pærɪsn] Vergleich **II**
compass ['kʌmpəs] Kompass **II**
competition [ˌkɒmpə'tɪʃn] Wettbewerb **I**
to **complete** [kəm'pli:t] vervollständigen **I**; fertig stellen **III U6,** 101
compound ['kɒmpaʊnd] Kompositum *(zusammengesetztes Wort)* **II**
computer [kəm'pju:tə] Computer **I**
computer club [kəm'pju:tə ˌklʌb] Computerklub **I**
computer shop [kəm'pju:tə ˌʃɒp] Computergeschäft **I**
to **concentrate** ['kɒnsntreɪt] (sich) konzentrieren **III U4,** 66
concert ['kɒnsət] Konzert **III U5,** 77
conference ['kɒnfrns] Konferenz, Tagung **III U4,** 66
press conference ['pres ˌkɒnfrns] Pressekonferenz **III U1,** 16
*to be **connected** [bi kə'nektɪd] zusammenhängen, in Zusammenhang stehen **III U2,** 32
connecting [kə'nektɪŋ] verbindend **II**
connecting line [kə'nektɪŋ ˌlaɪn] Verbindungslinie **III U2,** 32
pros and **cons** *(pl.)* [ˌprəʊz‿n 'kɒnz] Pro und Kontra **III U5,** 81
contact clause ['kɒntækt ˌklɔ:z] Relativsatz ohne Relativpronomen **III U1,** 14
to **contact** ['kɒntækt] (telefonisch) erreichen, sich in Verbindung setzen **III U3,** 50
context ['kɒntekst] Kontext, Zusammenhang **III U1,** 19
to **continue** [kən'tɪnju:] weiterreden; weitermachen **III U2,** 34; weitergehen, -fahren, -reisen **III U6,** 101
contract ['kɒntrækt] Vertrag **III U5,** 78
contrast ['kɒntrɑ:st] Kontrast, Unterschied **III U4,** 58
to **control** [kən'trəʊl] kontrollieren; steuern **III U1,** 8
conversation [ˌkɒnvə'seɪʃn] Konversation, Gespräch, Unterhaltung **II**
to **convince** [kən'vɪns] überzeugen **III U5,** 86
cook [kʊk] Koch, Köchin **I**
to **cook** [kʊk] kochen **II**
cooking club ['kʊkɪŋ ˌklʌb] Kochklub **I**
cool [ku:l] cool, super **I**
copy ['kɒpi] Exemplar **III U5,** 76
to **copy** ['kɒpi] abschreiben, abmalen **I**; nachmachen **III U5,** 76
corn [kɔ:n] Getreide ⟨**III U4,** 65⟩
corner ['kɔ:nə] Ecke **II**
to **correct** [kə'rekt] korrigieren, berichtigen **I**
correct [kə'rekt] richtig **I**
corridor ['kɒrɪdɔ:] Gang, Flur, Korridor **II**
*to **cost** [kɒst] kosten **II**
costume ['kɒstju:m] Kostüm **III U3,** 51
couch potato ['kaʊtʃ pəˌteɪtəʊ] Fernsehglotzer/-in, Couchpotato **III U5,** 81
could [kʊd] konnte(n) **II**
could you [kʊd ju:] Könnten Sie/ Könntest du … ? **II**
to **count** [kaʊnt] zählen **I**
country ['kʌntri] Land **II**
course [kɔ:s] Kurs **II**
of course [əv 'kɔ:s] natürlich, selbstverständlich **I**
court [kɔ:t] Spielfeld **III U1,** 9
cousin ['kʌzn] Cousin, Cousine **I**
cow [kaʊ] Kuh **I**
to **crack** [kræk] (zer)brechen; (zer)springen **III U5,** 86
arts and **crafts** *(pl.)* [ˌɑ:ts‿ənd 'krɑ:fts] Kunsthandwerk **II**
craftspeople *(pl.)* ['krɑ:ftsˌpi:pl] Handwerker *(Pl.)* **II**
crash [kræʃ] Zusammenstoß **III U1,** 20
to **crash** [kræʃ] aufprallen, zusammenstoßen **I**
crazy ['kreɪzi] verrückt **II**
to drive someone crazy [draɪv ˌsʌmwʌn 'kreɪzi] jmdn. verrückt machen **III U3,** 43
to go crazy [gəʊ 'kreɪzi] ausflippen, durchdrehen **III U3,** 49
to **create** [kri'eɪt] (er)schaffen **III U5,** 77
credit ['kredɪt] Guthaben **II**
cricket ['krɪkɪt] Kricket **III U1,** 8
crisp [krɪsp] Kartoffelchip **I**
chocolate **crispies** *(pl.)* ['tʃɒklət ˌkrɪspɪz] Schokoplätzchen **I**
to **cross** [krɒs] überqueren, über … gehen **I**
crow's nest ['krəʊz ˌnest] Ausguck, Krähennest **I**
crowd [kraʊd] Menschenmenge **III U4,** 68; ⟨**III U3,** 54⟩
home crowd ['həʊm ˌkraʊd] heimisches Publikum **II**

crust [krʌst] Kruste, Rinde **III U3,** 43
to **cry** [kraɪ] weinen; schreien, rufen **II**
crystal ['krɪstl] Kristall **I**
CU ['si: ju:] bis bald *(Abkürzung in SMS oder E-Mail)* **I**
cult [kʌlt] Kult **III U4,** 58
culture ['kʌltʃə] Kultur **III U4,** 59
cup [kʌp] Tasse **II**
  a cup of [ə 'kʌp‿əv] eine Tasse … **I**
cupboard ['kʌbəd] Schrank **I**
curious ['kjʊəriəs] neugierig **III U2,** 33
curl [kɜ:l] Locke ⟨**III U4,** 65⟩
*to go **curly** [gəʊ 'kɜ:li] sich kräuseln **III U3,** 43
curry ['kʌri] Curry *(Gewürz oder Gericht)* **III U4,** 63
curtain ['kɜ:tn] Vorhang **III U3,** 53
customer ['kʌstəmə] Kunde, Kundin **I**
customs *(sing.)* ['kʌstəmz] Zoll **II**
*to **cut** [kʌt] (sich) schneiden **III U5,** 87
cyberpet ['saɪbəpet] virtuelles Haustier **I**

D

dachshund ['dækshənd] Dackel **II**
dad [dæd] Papa, Vati **I**
daily ['deɪli] täglich **I**
to **dance** [dɑ:ns] tanzen **I**
dancer ['dɑ:nsə] Tänzer/-in **II**
dancing lessons *(pl.)* ['dɑ:nsɪŋ ˌlesnz] Tanzunterricht, Tanzstunden **I**
danger ['deɪndʒə] Gefahr **III U6,** 102
dangerous ['deɪndʒrəs] gefährlich **III U6,** 97
the **dark** [dɑ:k] Dunkelheit ⟨**III U1,** 18⟩
dark [dɑ:k] dunkel **I**
date [deɪt] Datum **I**
daughter ['dɔ:tə] Tochter **II**
day [deɪ] Tag **I**
  a day [ə 'deɪ] pro Tag **II**
  all day [ɔ:l 'deɪ] den ganzen Tag **II**
  days of the week *(pl.)* [ˌdeɪz‿ɒv ðə 'wi:k] Wochentage *(pl.)* **I**
  open day [ˌəʊpn 'deɪ] Tag der offenen Tür **III U2,** 29
  the day before [ðə ˌdeɪ bɪ'fɔ:] am Tag vorher, am Tag zuvor **III U6,** 95
  two days earlier [ˌtu: deɪz 'ɜ:liə] vor zwei Tagen, zwei Tage zuvor **III U6,** 95
dead [ded] tot **I**
*to **deal with** ['di:l wɪð] sich befassen mit, umgehen mit **III U4,** 62
dear [dɪə] Schatz **I**; Lieber …, Liebe … *(Anrede in Briefen)* **II**
  Oh dear! [əʊ 'dɪə] Oje! **II**
December [dɪ'sembə] Dezember **I**

to **decide** [dɪ'saɪd] (sich) entscheiden **III U3,** 44
decision [dɪ'sɪʒn] Entscheidung **III U3,** 52
  to make a decision [ˌmeɪk‿ə dɪ'sɪʒn] eine Entscheidung treffen **III U3,** 52
to **defeat** [dɪ'fi:t] besiegen **III U2,** 25
definite ['defɪnət] bestimmt **III U4,** 60
definition [ˌdefɪ'nɪʃn] Definition **III U1,** 14
delay [dɪ'leɪ] Verzögerung, Verspätung **III U6,** 101
deliberate [dɪ'lɪbrət] bewusst, absichtlich **II**
delight [dɪ'laɪt] Vergnügen, Entzücken ⟨**III U2,** 36⟩
to **delight in** [dɪ'laɪt‿ɪn] Vergnügen empfinden bei ⟨**III U2,** 36⟩
department store [dɪ'pɑ:tmənt ˌstɔ:] Kaufhaus **I**
  police department [pə'li:s dɪˌpɑ:tmənt] Polizeidienststelle **III U5,** 85
departure [dɪ'pɑ:tʃə] Abflug, Abreise **II**
to **describe** [dɪ'skraɪb] beschreiben **I**
desert ['dezət] Wüste ⟨**III U6,** 103⟩
desk [desk] Schreibtisch **I**; Schalter **II**
detail ['di:teɪl] Detail, Einzelheit **III U2,** 32
diabetes [ˌdaɪə'bi:ti:z] Diabetes, Zuckerkrankheit **II**
dialogue ['daɪəlɒg] Dialog **I**
nine of **diamonds** [naɪn‿əv 'daɪəməndz] Karoneun *(beim Kartenspiel)* **I**
diary ['daɪəri] Tagebuch **I**
dictionary ['dɪkʃnri] Wörterbuch **I**
to **die** [daɪ] sterben **I**
difference ['dɪfrns] Unterschied **III U3,** 46
different ['dɪfrnt] anders, unterschiedlich **I**
difficult ['dɪfɪklt] schwierig **III U3,** 50; ⟨**III U3,** 48⟩
dinner ['dɪnə] Abendessen **III U4,** 66
dinosaur ['daɪnəsɔ:] Dinosaurier **II**
direct speech [ˌdɪrekt 'spi:tʃ] direkte Rede **III U6,** 94
director [dɪ'rektə] Regisseur/-in **III U3,** 53
dirty ['dɜ:ti] dreckig, schmutzig **I**
disabled [dɪ'seɪbld] behindert **III U1,** 13
to **disappear** [ˌdɪsə'pɪə] verschwinden **III U5,** 86
disappointing [ˌdɪsə'pɔɪntɪŋ] enttäuschend **III U6,** 94
Discman ['dɪskmæn] Discman **I**
disco ['dɪskəʊ] Disco, Diskothek **III U2,** 28

discourteously [dɪ'skɜ:tiəsli] grob ⟨**III U2,** 36⟩
to **discover** [dɪ'skʌvə] entdecken **III U5,** 78
to **discuss** [dɪ'skʌs] diskutieren **III U5,** 79
discussing [dɪ'skʌsɪŋ] Diskutieren **III U5,** 81
dishwasher ['dɪʃwɒʃə] Spülmaschine **II**
distance ['dɪstns] Distanz, Entfernung **III U6,** 104
to **distract** [dɪ'strækt] ablenken **III U5,** 87
divorced from [dɪ'vɔ:st frəm] geschieden von **I**
DIY (= Do-it-yourself) [ˌdi:aɪ'waɪ] Heimwerken **III U3,** 43
DJ ['di: ˌdʒeɪ] DJ, Discjockey **I**
*to **do** [du:; də; du] machen, tun **I**
  to do the shopping [ˌdu: ðə 'ʃɒpɪŋ] Einkäufe machen, Besorgungen machen **II**
  to do wrong [du: 'rɒŋ] Unrecht tun ⟨**III U2,** 36⟩
  to get sb to do sth ['get ˌsʌmbədi tə 'du: ˌsʌmθɪŋ] jmdn. dazu bewegen, etwas zu tun **III U5,** 86
dock [dɒk] Dock **III U4,** 68
doctor ['dɒktə] Arzt, Ärztin **II**
dog [dɒg] Hund **I**
  hot dog ['hɒt dɒg] Hot Dog *(Würstchen im Brötchen)* **II**
doghouse ['dɒghaʊs] Hundehütte **I**
dog-tired [dɒg'taɪəd] hundemüde **I**
door [dɔ:] Tür **I**
  next door [nekst 'dɔ:] nebenan **II**
doorbell ['dɔ:bel] Türklingel **III U3,** 52
down [daʊn] herunter, hinunter, nach unten, hinab **I**
to **download** ['daʊnləʊd] herunterladen **II**
downstairs [daʊn'steəz] unten, im Untergeschoss **I**
drama ['drɑ:mə] Theater; Drama **II**
in a **draw** [ɪn‿ə 'drɔ:] unentschieden **III U1,** 19
*to **draw** [drɔ:] zeichnen **I**
dream [dri:m] Traum **I**
*to **dream** [dri:m] träumen **III U1,** 20
dress [dres] Kleid **III U2,** 26
*to get **dressed** [get 'drest] sich anziehen **III U3,** 44
drink [drɪŋk] Getränk **I**
*to **drink** [drɪŋk] trinken **I**
*to **drive** [draɪv] fahren **I**
  to drive someone crazy [draɪv ˌsʌmwʌn 'kreɪzi] jmdn. verrückt machen **III U3,** 43
driver ['draɪvə] Fahrer/-in **I**

to drown [draʊn] ertrinken; ertränken **III U2**, 34
drummer ['drʌmə] Schlagzeuger/-in **II**
drums *(pl.)* [drʌmz] Schlagzeug **I**
dungeon ['dʌndʒn] Verlies **II**
during *(+ noun)* ['djʊərɪŋ] während **III U4**, 66
duty ['dju:ti] Pflicht **I**
to dye [daɪ] färben **II**

E

each [i:tʃ] jede/-r/-s **II**
each other [i:tʃ_'ʌðə] einander, sich (gegenseitig) **III U3**, 43
eagle ['i:gl] Adler **III U1**, 16
ear [ɪə] Ohr **I**
early ['3:li] früh **I**
to earn [3:n] verdienen **III U3**, 46
earth [3:θ] (Erd)Boden, Erde; die Erde **II**
earthquake ['3:θkweɪk] Erdbeben **II**
east [i:st] Osten **I**
east of ['i:st_əv] östlich von **I**
easy ['i:zi] leicht, einfach **I**
easy-peasy [ˌi:zi'pi:zi] babyleicht **I**
*__to eat__ [i:t] essen **I**
*__to eat up__ [i:t 'ʌp] aufessen **III U3**, 43
eatery ['i:tri] Kantine, Restaurant **I**
e-card ['ɪ:kɑ:d] E-Card **III U5**, 77
education [edʒʊ'keɪʃn] Erziehung, Bildung **II**
egg [eg] Ei **I**
Eh? [eɪ] Was? Nicht wahr? **I**
eight [eɪt] acht **I**
eighteen [ˌeɪ'ti:n] achtzehn **I**
eighty ['eɪti] achtzig **I**
elephant ['elɪfənt] Elefant **III U2**, 25
eleven [ɪ'levn] elf **I**
Elizabethan [ɪˌlɪzə'bi:θn] elisabethanisch **III U2**, 25
else [els] sonst **II**
what else [ˌwɒt_'els] was (sonst) noch **II**
e-mail ['i:meɪl] E-Mail **I**
e-mail address ['i:meɪl əˌdres] E-Mail-Adresse ⟨**III P1**, 23⟩
embarrassing [ɪm'bærəsɪŋ] peinlich **II**
emergency [ɪ'm3:dʒnsi] Notfall, Notlage **III U5**, 87
empire ['empaɪə] Reich; Kaiserreich **III U2**, 25
empress ['emprəs] Kaiserin **III U2**, 30
empty ['emti] leer **I**
end [end] Ende, Schluss **II**
to end [end] enden **I**
to end in thin air [ˌend_ɪn θɪn_'eə] im Nichts enden **II**
ending ['endɪŋ] Schluss, Ende **III U2**, 35
enemy ['enəmi] Feind/-in **II**
search engine ['s3:tʃ ˌendʒɪn] Suchmaschine **III U4**, 68
steam engine ['sti:m ˌendʒɪn] Dampfmaschine **III U2**, 24
engineer [ˌendʒɪ'nɪə] Ingenieur/-in **III U4**, 60
English ['ɪŋglɪʃ] Englisch **I**; englisch, aus England **I**
in English [ɪn_'ɪŋglɪʃ] auf Englisch **I**
English-speaking ['ɪŋglɪʃ ˌspi:kɪŋ] englischsprachig **II**
to enjoy [ɪn'dʒɔɪ] genießen **I**
to enjoy oneself [ɪn'dʒɔɪ] Spaß haben; sich amüsieren **III U3**, 44
enough [ɪ'nʌf] genug, genügend **II**
to enter ['entə] einreisen; hineingehen, hereinkommen; betreten **II**
entertainment *(no pl.)* [ˌentə'teɪnmənt] Unterhaltung **III U5**, 77
entrance ['entrəns] Eingang **II**
equipment [ɪ'kwɪpmənt] Ausstattung, Ausrüstung **II**
er [3:] äh **I**
escalator ['eskəleɪtə] Rolltreppe **II**
especially [ɪ'speʃli] besonders, vor allem **III U3**, 47
etc. (= et cetera) [ɪt'setrə] usw. (= und so weiter) **I**
euro ['jʊərəʊ] Euro *(Währung)* **II**
European [jʊərə'pi:ən] europäisch, aus Europa **I**
European Union [jʊərəˌpi:ən 'ju:njən] Europäische Union **III U2**, 25
even ['i:vn] sogar, selbst **I**
not even [nɒt 'i:vn] (noch) nicht einmal **I**
evening ['i:vnɪŋ] Abend **I**
in the evening [ɪn ði_'i:vnɪŋ] abends **I**
one evening [wʌn_'i:vnɪŋ] eines Abends **I**
event [ɪ'vent] Ereignis, Veranstaltung **III U1**, 10
ever ['evə] jemals **II**
every ['evri] jede/-r/-s **I**
every ten minutes [ˌevri ten 'mɪnɪts] alle zehn Minuten **I**
everybody ['evribɒdi] jeder; alle **II**
everyone ['evriwʌn] jeder **I**
everything ['evriθɪŋ] alles **I**
everywhere ['evriweə] überall **I**
evolution [ˌi:və'lu:ʃn] Evolution, Entwicklung **III U6**, 93
exact [ɪg'zækt] genau, exakt **III U1**, 15
exactly [ɪg'zæktli] genau **III U1**, 12
to examine [ɪg'zæmɪn] untersuchen, kontrollieren **II**
example [ɪg'zɑ:mpl] Beispiel **I**
exchange [ɪks'tʃeɪndʒ] Austausch **III U4**, 58
to exchange [ɪks'tʃeɪndʒ] austauschen **III U5**, 85
excited [ɪk'saɪtɪd] aufgeregt, begeistert **I**
exciting [ɪk'saɪtɪŋ] spannend, aufregend **II**
Excuse me. [ɪk'skju:s mi] Entschuldigung./Entschuldigen Sie. **I**
exercise ['eksəsaɪz] Übung **I**
exercise book ['eksəsaɪz ˌbʊk] Heft **I**
exhibition [ˌeksɪ'bɪʃn] Ausstellung **III U4**, 63
to exist [ɪg'zɪst] existieren, bestehen **III U4**, 59
to expect [ɪk'spekt] erwarten **II**
expensive [ɪk'spensɪv] teuer **I**
to explain [ɪk'spleɪn] erklären **I**
to express [ɪk'spres] ausdrücken ⟨**III U3**, 54⟩
extra ['ekstrə] Extra, Zusatz **III U4**, 69
extra ['ekstrə] zusätzlich **III U6**, 100
extra large (XL) ['ekstrə ˌlɑ:dʒ] besonders groß **I**
extra ['ekstrə] mehr **III U3**, 44
eye [aɪ] Auge **I**
He can't believe his eyes. [hi ˌkɑ:nt bɪˌli:v hɪz 'aɪz] Er traut seinen Augen nicht. **I**

F

face [feɪs] Gesicht **I**
to make a face [meɪk ə 'feɪs] ein Gesicht ziehen **II**
facelift ['feɪslɪft] Lifting; *(hier:)* Renovierung, Verschönerung **III U4**, 59
fact [fækt] Fakt, Tatsache **II**
factory ['fæktri] Fabrik; Werk **III U2**, 24
factual text [ˌfæktʃʊəl 'tekst] Sachtext **III U4**, 66
fair [feə] gerecht, fair **I**
*__to fall__ [fɔ:l] (hin)fallen **I**
to fall asleep [fɔ:l_ə'sli:p] einschlafen **I**
to fall in love [ˌfɔ:l_ɪn 'lʌv] sich verlieben **II**
to fall off [fɔ:l 'ɒf] herunterfallen, (hinunter)fallen **III U5**, 86
to fall over [fɔ:l 'əʊvə] umfallen, hinfallen **I**
false [fɔ:ls] falsch **II**
family ['fæmli] Familie **I**
family fun ['fæmli ˌfʌn] Spaß für die ganze Familie **I**

family tree ['fæmli ˌtri:] Familienstammbaum **I**
host family ['həʊst ˌfæmli] Gastfamilie **II**
famous ['feɪməs] berühmt **I**
fan [fæn] Fan, Anhänger/-in **II**
fantastic [fæn'tæstɪk] fantastisch, großartig **III U6,** 100
far [fɑ:] weit **III U1,** 17
so far ['səʊ fɑ:] bis jetzt **II**
fare [feə] Fahrpreis **II**
farm [fɑ:m] Bauernhof **I**
farmer ['fɑ:mə] Farmer/-in, Landwirt/-in **III U2,** 30
farmhand ['fɑ:mhænd] Landarbeiter/-in **I**
fashion ['fæʃn] Mode **II**
fashion model ['fæʃn ˌmɒdl] Model, Mannequin **II**
fast [fɑ:st] schnell **I**
father ['fɑ:ðə] Vater **I**
fave *(Abkürzung für* favourite*)* [feɪv] Lieblings- **III U2,** 24
favourite ['feɪvrɪt] Lieblings- **I**
February ['februri] Februar **I**
*to **feed** [fi:d] füttern **I**; ernähren **III U2,** 33
to be fed up (with) [bi fed‿'ʌp wɪð] sauer sein, die Nase voll haben (von) **I**
*to **feel** [fi:l] (sich) fühlen **II**
to feel sorry for [fi:l 'sɒri] Mitleid haben mit; bedauern **III U3,** 46
feeling ['fi:lɪŋ] Gefühl **III U1,** 10
ferris wheel ['ferɪs ˌwi:l] Riesenrad **I**
ferry ['feri] Fähre **II**
festival ['festɪvl] Fest, Festival **I**
kite festival ['kaɪt ˌfestɪvl] Drachenfest **I**
a **few** [ə 'fju:] ein paar, einige; wenige **I**
science **fiction** [ˌsaɪəns 'fɪkʃn] Sciencefiction **II**
field [fi:ld] Wiese, Weide, Acker **I**; Gebiet, Bereich **II**; Feld, Spielfeld **III U1,** 8
fifteen [fɪf'ti:n] fünfzehn **I**
fifty ['fɪfti] fünfzig **I**
fight [faɪt] Kampf, Streit **II**
*to **fight** [faɪt] kämpfen; sich streiten **I**
to fight over [faɪt‿'əʊvə] sich streiten um **I**
file [faɪl] Akte **III U5,** 78
to **fill in** [fɪl‿'ɪn] ausfüllen **I**
filler ['fɪlə] Füllwort **III U6,** 100
film [fɪlm] Film **I**
to **film** [fɪlm] filmen, drehen **III U5,** 79
finally ['faɪnli] schließlich, endlich, zum Schluss **I**

*to **find** [faɪnd] finden **I**
finding the way [ˌfaɪndɪŋ ðə 'weɪ] den Weg finden **I**
to find out [faɪnd‿'aʊt] herausfinden **II**
fine [faɪn] in Ordnung, gut **I**
I'm fine. [ˌaɪm 'faɪn] Mir geht es gut. **I**
finger ['fɪŋgə] Finger **II**
to **finish** ['fɪnɪʃ] (be)enden, fertig stellen **I**
fire ['faɪə] Feuer **II**
firefighter ['faɪəˌfaɪtə] Feuerwehrmann, Feuerwehrfrau **III U6,** 97
firm [fɜ:m] Firma **III U4,** 60
first [fɜ:st] zuerst, als Erstes **I**; erste/-r/-s **I**
at first [ət 'fɜ:st] zuerst; zunächst **II**
first language ['fɜ:st ˌlæŋgwɪdʒ] Muttersprache **III U6,** 93
First things first. [ˌfɜ:st θɪŋz 'fɜ:st] Das Wichtigste zuerst. **III U3,** 52
fish pl. **fish** [fɪʃ] Fisch **I**
fish and chips [ˌfɪʃ‿n‿'tʃɪps] Fisch und Pommes frites **II**
fishing ['fɪʃɪŋ] Fischerei; Angeln, Fischen **II**
fit [fɪt] fit, in Form **II**
to keep fit [ki:p 'fɪt] fit bleiben **II**
fitness ['fɪtnəs] Fitness **II**
five [faɪv] fünf **I**
to **flap** [flæp] flattern, *(mit den Flügeln)* schlagen **III U1,** 17
flat [flæt] Wohnung **I**
flavour ['fleɪvə] Geschmack, Geschmacksrichtung, Aroma, Sorte **I**
flight [flaɪt] Flug **II**
floor [flɔ:] Fußboden **III U2,** 30
flour [flaʊə] Mehl **I**
flow chart ['fləʊ ˌtʃɑ:t] Flussdiagramm **II**
to **flow** [fləʊ] fließen ⟨**III U4,** 65⟩
flower [flaʊə] Blume **I**
flu [flu:] Grippe **II**
*to **fly** [flaɪ] fliegen **I**
to fly a kite [flaɪ ə 'kaɪt] einen Drachen steigen lassen **I**
flying ['flaɪɪŋ] fliegend, Flug- **III U2,** 35
fog [fɒg] Nebel **II**
foggy ['fɒgi] neblig **II**
folder ['fəʊldə] Ordner, Mappe **I**
to **follow** ['fɒləʊ] hinterhergehen; (be)folgen **II**
the **following** ['fɒləʊɪŋ] folgende/-r/-s **III U2,** 28
food [fu:d] Essen, Nahrung, Nahrungsmittel **I**
cat food ['kæt ˌfu:d] Katzenfutter **I**
foot pl. **feet** [fʊt; fi:t] Fuß **I**
on foot [ɒn 'fʊt] zu Fuß **III U6,** 102

football ['fʊtbɔ:l] Fußball **I**
American football [əˌmerɪkən 'fʊtbɔ:l] American Football **III U1,** 13
for [fɔ:; fə] für **I**; denn ⟨**III U2,** 36⟩
for (many) hours [fə ˌmeni 'aʊəz] stundenlang **I**
for laughs [fə 'lɑ:fs] zum Spaß **III U4,** 68
for (many) years [fə ˌmeni 'jɪəz] jahrelang **I**
*to **forget** [fə'get] vergessen **I**
fork [fɔ:k] Gabel **II**
form [fɔ:m] Form **I**; Art **II**
fortress ['fɔ:trəs] Festung **III U2,** 31
forty ['fɔ:ti] vierzig **I**
fountain ['faʊntɪn] Springbrunnen **III U2,** 34
four [fɔ:] vier **I**
four of them ['fɔ:r‿əv ðəm] vier davon *(Personen, Tiere …)* **I**
fourteen [fɔ:'ti:n] vierzehn **I**
fox [fɒks] Fuchs **I**
free [fri:] frei **II**; kostenlos **III U2,** 30
free time ['fri: ˌtaɪm] Freizeit **I**
French [frenʃ] Französisch; französisch **II**
fresh [freʃ] frisch **I**
Friday ['fraɪdeɪ] Freitag **I**
friend [frend] Freund **I**
to make friends [ˌmeɪk 'frendz] Freundschaft schließen **II**
friendly ['frendli] freundlich, nett **II**
in a friendly way [ɪn‿ə ˌfrendli 'weɪ] freundlich *(Adverb)* **II**
friendship ['frendʃɪp] Freundschaft **III U4,** 60
frightening ['fraɪtnɪŋ] furchterregend **III U6,** 102
Frisbee ['frɪzbi] Frisbeescheibe **II**
from [frɒm; frəm] aus, von **I**; von … entfernt **I**
from … to ['frəm tə] von … bis **I**
Where are you from? [ˌweər‿ə jə 'frɒm] Woher kommst du? **I**
at the **front** [æt ðə 'frʌnt] vorn(e) **II**
at the front of [æt ðə 'frʌnt‿əv] an der Spitze (von), im vorderen Bereich **II**
in front of [ɪn 'frʌnt‿əv] vor **I**
frozen ['frəʊzn] (tief)gefroren **III U3,** 43
fruit [fru:t] Obst, Frucht **II**
full [fʊl] voll **II**
fun [fʌn] Spaß **III U4,** 60
to be fun [bi 'fʌn] Spaß machen; witzig sein **I**
to have fun [hæv 'fʌn] Spaß haben, sich amüsieren **I**

to make fun of [ˌmeɪk ˈfʌn‿əv] sich lustig machen über **III U4,** 69
funny [ˈfʌni] lustig, witzig **I**
furniture [ˈfɜːnɪtʃə] Möbel **I**
future [ˈfjuːtʃə] Zukunft **II**

G

gallery [ˈgælri] (Kunst)Galerie **II**
game [geɪm] Spiel **I**
game show [ˈgeɪm ˌʃəʊ] Spielshow **II**
Mind the **gap.** [ˌmaɪnd ðə ˈgæp] Vorsicht beim Ein- und Aussteigen. **II**
garage [ˈgærɑːʒ] Garage; Werkstatt; Tankstelle **I**
garden [ˈgɑːdn] Garten **I**
gash [gæʃ] tiefe Schnittwunde **III U5,** 87
to **gasp** [gɑːsp] tief einatmen, tief Luft holen; keuchen **III U2,** 34
ticket **gate** [ˈtɪkɪt ˌgeɪt] Fahrkartenschranke **II**
genitive [ˈdʒenɪtɪv] Genitiv **II**
gentle [ˈdʒentl] sanft, liebenswürdig **II**
geography [dʒiˈɒgrəfi] Geografie; Erdkunde **II**
German [ˈdʒɜːmən] Deutsch; deutsch, aus Deutschland **I**
*to **get** [get] holen, bringen; bekommen **I**; werden **II**
Don't get your hopes up too high. [dəʊnt get jɔː ˌhəʊps ʌp tuː ˈhaɪ] Mach dir nicht zu viele Hoffnungen. **III U5,** 78
Get lost! [get ˈlɒst] Hau ab! **II**
to get attention [get əˈtentʃn] jmdn. auf sich aufmerksam machen **III U5,** 84
to get back [get ˈbæk] zurückkommen **II**
to get bored [get ˈbɔːd] sich langweilen **III U6,** 94
to get dressed [get ˈdrest] sich anziehen **III U3,** 44
to get in the way [ˌget‿ɪn ðə ˈweɪ] stören, im Weg stehen **III U3,** 52
to get into [get‿ˈɪntə] (ein)steigen **I**
to get into trouble [ˌget‿ɪntə ˈtrʌbl] in Schwierigkeiten geraten **II**
to get lost [get ˈlɒst] sich verirren **I**
to get off [get‿ˈɒf] aussteigen **II**
to get on [get‿ˈɒn] einsteigen **II**; auskommen **III U3,** 43
to get ready [get ˈredi] sich vorbereiten; sich fertig machen **III U2,** 32
to get rid of [get ˈrɪd‿əv] loswerden **III U3,** 47
to get sb to do sth [ˈget ˌsʌmbədi tə ˈduː ˌsʌmθɪŋ] jmdn. dazu bewegen, etwas zu tun **III U5,** 86
to get tired of [get ˈtaɪəd‿əv] etwas satt bekommen **III U4,** 67
to get to [ˈget tə] kommen zu, kommen nach, erreichen **I**
to get up [get ˈʌp] aufstehen **I**
to get used to (sth) [get‿ˈjuːzd tə] sich an (etwas) gewöhnen **II**
to get your own back [get jər‿ˈəʊn bæk] sich rächen **II**
You've got me there! [jʊv ˌgɒt mi ˈðeə] Da habt ihr mich kalt erwischt! **I**
ghost [gəʊst] Geist **III U2,** 34
giant [dʒaɪənt] Riesen-, riesig **III U6,** 93
girl [gɜːl] Mädchen **I**
girlfriend [ˈgɜːlfrend] Freundin *(in einer Paarbeziehung)* **III U2,** 33
gist [dʒɪst] das Wesentliche **III U2,** 32
*to **give** [gɪv] geben; schenken **I**
giving advice [ˌgɪvɪŋ ədˈvaɪs] einen Rat geben **III U6,** 96
to give a (group) presentation [gɪv‿ə ˌgruːp‿ˌprezn'teɪʃn] eine (Gruppen)präsentation machen **II**
to give one's opinion [ˌgɪv wʌnz əˈpɪnjən] seine Meinung äußern **III U5,** 85
to give reasons [gɪv ˈriːznz] Gründe nennen, Gründe angeben **II**
to give tours [gɪv ˈtʊəz] Stadtrundfahrten leiten **I**
to give up [gɪv‿ˈʌp] aufgeben **II**
glad [glæd] froh **II**
glass [glɑːs] Glas **II**
glasses *(pl.)* [ˈglɑːsɪz] Brille **III U1,** 16
*to **go** [gəʊ] gehen, fahren **I**; führen **I**
go on, please [gəʊ‿ˈɒn pliːz] Mach/Macht bitte weiter. **I**
Let's go! [lets ˈgəʊ] Lass(t) uns anfangen!/Lass(t) uns gehen! **I**
to be gone [biː ˈgɒn] verschwunden sein, weg sein **II**
to go back [gəʊ ˈbæk] zurückgehen **I**
to go crazy [gəʊ ˈkreɪzi] ausflippen, durchdrehen **III U3,** 49
to go curly [gəʊ ˈkɜːli] sich kräuseln **III U3,** 43
to go down [gəʊ ˈdaʊn] hinuntergehen; entlanggehen **I**; nach unten gehen **I**
to go home [gəʊ ˈhəʊm] nach Hause gehen **I**
to go on [gəʊ‿ˈɒn] (an)dauern **III U1,** 8
to go on holiday [gəʊ ɒn ˈhɒlədeɪ] in Urlaub gehen, in Urlaub fahren **I**
to go out with [gəʊ‿ˈaʊt wɪð] (aus)gehen mit **III U3,** 49
to go shopping [gəʊ ˈʃɒpɪŋ] einkaufen gehen **I**
to go surfing [gəʊ ˈsɜːfɪŋ] surfen gehen **I**
to go to bed [gəʊ tə ˈbed] ins Bett gehen **I**
to go up [gəʊ ˈʌp] nach oben gehen **I**
to go with [gəʊ ˈwɪð] passen zu, gehören zu **I**
What's going on? [wɒts ˌgəʊɪŋ‿ˈɒn] Was ist denn hier los? **III U3,** 53
goal [gəʊl] Tor **I**
goggles *(pl.)* [ˈgɒglz] Skibrille, Schwimmbrille **III U1,** 16
gold [gəʊld] Gold **III U2,** 24
gold medal [gəʊld ˈmedl] Goldmedaille **III U1,** 13
golden [ˈgəʊldn] golden ⟨**III U1,** 18⟩
golden boots [ˌgəʊldn ˈbuːts] goldene Stiefel, Zauberstiefel **II**
golf [gɒlf] Golf **II**
good [gʊd] gut **I**
a good way to … [ə‿ˌgʊd ˈweɪ tə] eine gute Möglichkeit … **II**
Good luck! [ˌgʊd ˈlʌk] Viel Glück! **II**
Good morning. [gʊd ˈmɔːnɪŋ] Guten Morgen. **I**
to be good at [bi ˈgʊd‿ət] gut sein in/bei **I**
to be good with [bi ˈgʊd wɪð] gut umgehen können mit **I**
goodbye [gʊdˈbaɪ] auf Wiedersehen **I**
good-looking [ˌgʊdˈlʊkɪŋ] gut aussehend **II**
*to have **(got)** [hæv ˈgɒt] besitzen, haben **I**
government [ˈgʌvnmənt] Regierung **III U2,** 30
grammar [ˈgræmə] Grammatik **I**
grammar school [ˈgræmə ˌskuːl] Gymnasium **II**
grandad [ˈgrændæd] Opa **I**
grandfather [ˈgrænˌfɑːðə] Großvater **I**
grandma [ˈgrænmɑː] Oma **I**
grandmother [ˈgrænmʌðə] Großmutter **I**
great-great-grandmother [ˌgreɪtgreɪtˈgrænmʌðə] Urgroßmutter **III U2,** 35
grass [grɑːs] Gras **I**
great [greɪt] toll, großartig **I**; groß, riesig **I**
great-great-grandmother [ˌgreɪtgreɪtˈgrænmʌðə] Urgroßmutter **III U2,** 35

Greek [gri:k] griechisch, aus Griechenland; Griechisch **I**
green [gri:n] grün **I**
grey [greɪ] grau **I**
grid [grɪd] Raster, Tabelle **I**
ground [graʊnd] Boden ⟨**III U3,** 54⟩
group [gru:p] Gruppe **I**
*to **grow** [grəʊ] wachsen **III U3,** 43
grumpy ['grʌmpi] mürrisch, schlecht gelaunt **III U3,** 52
to **guess** [ges] (er)raten; vermuten **I**
guide [gaɪd] Führer/-in **II**
guidebook ['gaɪdbʊk] Reiseführer **II**
guitar [gɪ'tɑ:] Gitarre **I**
gun [gʌn] Schusswaffe **III U6,** 102
guy [gaɪ] Typ, Kerl; *pl.:* Leute **III U3,** 53

H

habit ['hæbɪt] Gewohnheit ⟨**III U5,** 87⟩
hair [heə] Haar, Haare **II**
half pl. **halves** [hɑ:f; hɑ:vz] (die) Hälfte; Halbzeit **III U1,** 13
half [hɑ:f] halb **I**
half-sister ['hɑ:fˌsɪstə] Halbschwester **I**
half-time [ˌhɑ:f'taɪm] Halbzeit **III U1,** 19
*to meet **halfway** [mi:t hɑ:f'weɪ] (sich auf halbem Weg) entgegenkommen **III U3,** 46
hall [hɔ:l] Halle, Saal **II**; Flur, Korridor **II**
hand [hænd] Hand **I**
Hands on [hændz‿'ɒn] Pack's an! **I**
like the back of my hand [laɪk ðə ˌbæk‿əv maɪ 'hænd] wie meine Westentasche, in- und auswendig **II**
to hold hands [həʊld 'hændz] Händchen halten **II**
*to **hang** [hæŋ] hängen **II**
to hang out (with) [ˌhæŋ 'aʊt wɪð] sich treffen (mit); rumhängen (mit) **III U4,** 69
to **happen** ['hæpn] passieren, geschehen **I**
happy ['hæpi] glücklich, fröhlich **I**
Happy Birthday! [ˌhæpi 'bɜ:θdeɪ] Alles Gute zum Geburtstag! **I**
harbour ['hɑ:bə] Hafen **I**
hard [hɑ:d] schwierig, schwer; hart **II**; stark **II**
to try hard [traɪ 'hɑ:d] sich anstrengen **II**
hat [hæt] Hut **III U3,** 43
to **hate** [heɪt] hassen, nicht mögen **III U2,** 24
*to **have** [hæv] haben, besitzen **II**; essen; trinken **II**
to have (got) [hæv 'gɒt] besitzen, haben **I**
to have a party [hæv ə 'pɑ:ti] eine Party feiern **I**
to have breakfast [hæv 'brekfəst] frühstücken **I**
to have fun [hæv 'fʌn] Spaß haben, sich amüsieren **I**
to have no idea [hæv ˌnəʊ‿aɪ'dɪə] keine Ahnung haben **III U2,** 35
to have to ['hæv tə] müssen **III U2,** 28
he [hi:] er **I**
head [hed] Kopf **II**
headache ['hedeɪk] Kopfschmerzen, Kopfweh **II**
heading ['hedɪŋ] Überschrift, Titel **I**
headline ['hedlaɪn] Schlagzeile **III U5,** 84
health [helθ] Gesundheit **II**
healthy ['helθi] gesund **II**
*to **hear** [hɪə] hören **I**
heart [hɑ:t] Herz **I**
eight of hearts [ˌeɪt‿əv 'hɑ:ts] Herzacht *(beim Kartenspiel)* **I**
to learn by heart [ˌlɜ:n baɪ 'hɑ:t] auswendig lernen **I**
heavy ['hevi] schwer, stark **II**
heavy industry [ˌhevi 'ɪndəstri] Schwerindustrie **III U4,** 59
heir [eə] Erbe, Erbin **III U2,** 25
helicopter ['helɪkɒptə] Helikopter, Hubschrauber **II**
Hello. [hel'əʊ] Hallo. **I**
to say hello [seɪ hel'əʊ] jemanden begrüßen **I**
to say hello to [seɪ hel'əʊ tə] grüßen, Grüße ausrichten **I**
helmet ['helmət] Helm **III U1,** 9
help [help] Hilfe **I**
to **help** [help] helfen **I**
to help oneself (to) [help wʌn'self tə] sich bedienen **III U3,** 44
helpful ['helpfl] hilfsbereit; hilfreich, nützlich **II**
her [hɜ:] ihr/-e **I**
here [hɪə] hier **I**; hierher, hierhin **I**
Here it is. [ˌhɪər‿ɪt‿'ɪz] Hier ist es. **I**
Here you are. [ˌhɪə ju‿'ɑ:] Bitte schön. **I**
in here [ɪn 'hi:ə] hier drin **I**
hero pl. **heroes** ['hɪərəʊ, 'hɪərəʊz] Held **II**
herself [hɜ:'self] sie (selbst), sich (selbst); selber **III U3,** 45
Hey! [heɪ] Hey! **I**
Hi. [haɪ] Hi./Hallo. **I**
*to **hide** [haɪd] (sich) verstecken **II**
high [haɪ] hoch; groß **II**
high-tech ['haɪtek] hoch technisiert **II**
hike [haɪk] Wanderung **II**
hiker ['haɪkə] Wanderer **II**
hill [hɪl] Berg; Hügel **II**
himself [hɪm'self] er (selbst), sich (selbst); selber **III U3,** 44
his [hɪz] sein/-e **I**
history ['hɪstri] Geschichte **II**
*to **hit** [hɪt] schlagen; treffen **II**
hm [m] hm **I**
hobby pl. **hobbies** ['hɒbi; 'hɒbiz] Hobby **I**
ice **hockey** ['aɪs ˌhɒki] Eishockey **III U1,** 9
*to **hold** [həʊld] halten, festhalten **I**
to hold hands [həʊld 'hændz] Händchen halten **II**
to hold up [həʊld 'ʌp] hochhalten **I**
hole [həʊl] Loch **I**
holiday(s) ['hɒlədeɪ; 'hɒlədeɪz] Ferien, Urlaub **I**
beach holiday ['bi:tʃ ˌhɒlədeɪ] Strandurlaub **I**
holiday home ['hɒlədeɪ ˌhəʊm] *(hier:)* Tierpension **I**
planning your holidays [ˌplænɪŋ jə 'hɒlədeɪz] den Urlaub planen **I**
to go on holiday [gəʊ ɒn 'hɒlədeɪ] in Urlaub gehen, in Urlaub fahren **I**
holiday-maker ['hɒlədeɪˌmeɪkə] Urlauber/-in **I**
home [həʊm] Zuhause **I**
animal home ['ænɪml həʊm] Tierheim **II**
at home [æt 'həʊm] zu Hause **I**
holiday home ['hɒlədeɪ ˌhəʊm] *(hier:)* Tierpension **I**
Home alone. [həʊm ə'ləʊn] Allein zu Hause. **III U3,** 51
home crowd ['həʊm ˌkraʊd] heimisches Publikum **II**
home page ['həʊm ˌpeɪdʒ] Homepage **I**
home sweet home ['həʊm ˌswi:t 'həʊm] trautes Heim *(Sprichwort)* **I**
old people's home [əʊld 'pi:plz həʊm] Altersheim **III U3,** 44
on the way home [ˌɒn ðe weɪ 'həʊm] auf dem Weg nach Hause **I**
to go home [gəʊ 'həʊm] nach Hause gehen **I**
homework ['həʊmwɜ:k] Hausaufgabe, Hausaufgaben **I**
Hooray! [hʊ'reɪ] Hurra! **I**
to **hop** [hɒp] hüpfen **II**
hope [həʊp] Hoffnung **II**

Don't get your hopes up too high. [dəʊnt get jɔ: ˌhəʊps ʌp tu: 'haɪ] Mach dir nicht zu viele Hoffnungen. **III U5,** 78
to **hope** [həʊp] hoffen **II**
horrible ['hɒrəbl] schrecklich, furchtbar **II**
horror ['hɒrə] Horror, Schrecken, Entsetzen **II**
horse [hɔ:s] Pferd **I**
hospital ['hɒspɪtl] Krankenhaus, Hospital **II**
host [həʊst] Gastgeber/-in **II**
host family ['həʊst ˌfæmli] Gastfamilie **II**
youth **hostel** ['ju:θ ˌhɒstl] Jugendherberge **II**
hot [hɒt] heiß; gefragt **III U2,** 30
hot dog ['hɒt dɒg] Hot Dog *(Würstchen im Brötchen)* **II**
hotel [həʊ'tel] Hotel **II**
hot-headed [hɒt'hedɪd] hitzköpfig **II**
hotline ['hɔtlaɪn] Hotline **III U5,** 85
hour [aʊə] Stunde **I**
for (many) hours [fə ˌmeni 'aʊəz] stundenlang **I**
24-hour [twenti,fɔ:‿'aʊə] 24-Stunden- **I**
house [haʊs] Haus **I**
at my house [ət 'maɪ haʊs] bei mir zu Hause **I**
to move house [mu:v 'haʊs] umziehen **III U4,** 58
houseboat ['haʊsbəʊt] Hausboot **III U4,** 66
housewife pl. **housewives** ['haʊswaɪf; 'haʊswaɪvz] Hausfrau **III U5,** 77
how [haʊ] wie **I**
How about ...? [haʊ ə'baʊt] Wie wäre es mit ...? **I**
How are you? [ˌhaʊ‿ɑ: 'jə] Wie geht es dir/Ihnen? **I**
How many ... ? [haʊ 'meni] Wie viele ... ? **I**
How much ... ? [haʊ 'mʌtʃ] Wie viel ... ? **I**
How much is ... ? ['haʊ mʌtʃ‿ɪz] Wie viel kostet ... ? **I**
How old are you? [haʊ‿'əʊld‿ɑ: 'ju:] Wie alt bist du? **I**
How to ... ['haʊ tə] Wie man ... **I**
a/one **hundred** [ə 'hʌndrəd; wʌn 'hʌndrəd] einhundert **I**
hungry ['hʌŋgri] hungrig **II**
hurry ['hʌri] Eile, Hast **I**
to be in a hurry [bi ɪn ə 'hʌri] es eilig haben, in Eile sein **I**
to **hurry up** [ˌhʌri 'ʌp] sich beeilen **I**
*to **hurt** [hɜ:t] verletzen; weh tun **II**

I

I [aɪ] ich **I**
I don't care! [aɪ ˌdəʊnt 'keə] Das ist mir egal! **III U3,** 43
I'd rather [aɪd 'rɑ:ðə] ich würde lieber **III U4,** 60
I see. [aɪ 'si:] Ich verstehe./Aha! **III U6,** 100
ice [aɪs] Eis **III U1,** 8
ice hockey ['aɪs ˌhɒki] Eishockey **III U1,** 9
ice skating ['aɪs ˌskeɪtɪŋ] Schlittschuhlaufen **II**
ice-cream [ˌaɪs'kri:m] Eiscreme, Eis **I**
idea [aɪ'dɪə] Idee **I**
to have no idea [hæv ˌnəʊ‿aɪ'dɪə] keine Ahnung haben **III U2,** 35
identification [aɪdentɪfɪ'keɪʃn] Identifizierung, Identifikation **II**
idiot ['ɪdiət] Idiot/-in **II**
if [ɪf] wenn, falls; ob **II**
if-clause ['ɪfklɔ:z] if-Satz **II**
ill [ɪl] krank; schlecht **II**
to **imagine** [ɪ'mædʒɪn] sich (etwas) vorstellen **II**
important [ɪm'pɔ:tnt] wichtig **I**
to **improve** [ɪm'pru:v] (sich) verbessern **II**
in [ɪn] aktuell, in, trendy **II**
in [ɪn] in, im **I**; aus, von, jede/-r/-s (zweite/dritte ...) **III U3,** 42
in a draw [ɪn‿ə 'drɔ:] unentschieden **III U1,** 19
in a friendly way [ɪn‿ə ˌfrendli 'weɪ] freundlich *(Adverb)* **II**
in English [ɪn‿'ɪŋglɪʃ] auf Englisch **I**
in front of [ɪn 'frʌnt‿əv] vor **I**
in here [ɪn 'hi:ə] hier drin **I**
in the evening [ɪn ði‿'i:vnɪŋ] abends **I**
in the street [ɪn ðə 'stri:t] auf der Straße **I**
indefinite [ɪn'defɪnət] unbestimmt **III U4,** 60
independent [ˌɪndɪ'pendənt] unabhängig **III U2,** 25
indirect speech [ˌɪndɪrekt 'spi:tʃ] indirekte Rede **III U6,** 94
Industrial Revolution [ɪnˌdʌstriəl revˈlu:ʃn] Industrielle Revolution **III U2,** 24
industry ['ɪndəstri] Industrie, Industrieanlage **III U4,** 58
heavy industry [ˌhevi 'ɪndəstri] Schwerindustrie **III U4,** 59
oil industry ['ɔɪl‿ˌɪndəstri] Ölindustrie **II**
infinitive [ɪn'fɪnətɪv] Infinitiv **II**
to **inform** [ɪn'fɔ:m] informieren **II**
information *(no pl.)* [ˌɪnfə'meɪʃn] Information, Informationen **I**
information centre [ˌɪnfə'meɪʃn 'sentə] Touristeninformation **I**
in-line skating [ˌɪnlaɪn 'skeɪtɪŋ] Inlineskates fahren **II**
inside [ɪn'saɪd] innen, im Innern; hinein, nach drinnen; in **II**
musical **instrument** [ˌmju:zɪkl‿'ɪnstrəmənt] Musikinstrument **II**
interactive [ˌɪntər'æktɪv] interaktiv **III U4,** 67
interested in ['ɪntrəstɪd] interessiert an **I**
interesting ['ɪntrəstɪŋ] interessant **I**
Internet ['ɪntənet] Internet **I**
to surf on the Internet [ˌsɜ:f‿ɒn ði‿'ɪntənet] im Internet surfen **I**
interview ['ɪntəvju:] Interview; Befragung **II**
to **interview** ['ɪntəvju:] interviewen **III U1,** 20
into ['ɪntə] in (hinein) **I**
to **introduce** [ˌɪntrə'dju:s] einführen, einleiten **III U6,** 94
invention [ɪn'venʃn] Erfindung **III U2,** 24
invitation [ˌɪnvɪ'teɪʃn] Einladung **I**
to **invite** [ɪn'vaɪt] einladen **I**
to invite ... out [ɪnˌvaɪt 'aʊt] ... (zu etwas) einladen **I**
irregular [ɪ'regjələ] unregelmäßig **II**
island ['aɪlənd] Insel **I**
it [ɪt] es **I**
It's a pity. [ˌɪts‿ə 'pɪti] Das ist schade./Es ist schade ... **III U4,** 67
It's two pounds. [ɪts ˌtu: 'paʊndz] Es kostet zwei Pfund. **I**
Italian [ɪ'tæliən] italienisch, aus Italien; Italienisch **I**
its [ɪts] sein **I**
itself [ɪt'self] sich (selbst); selber **III U3,** 45

J

life-**jacket** ['laɪfˌdʒækɪt] Schwimmweste, Rettungsweste **II**
January ['dʒænjuri] Januar **I**
jealous (of) ['dʒeləs‿əv] neidisch; eifersüchtig **III U3,** 47
jeans *(pl.)* [dʒi:nz] Jeans **I**
jewellery ['dʒu:əlri] Schmuck **III U2,** 33
job [dʒɒb] Arbeit, Aufgabe, Tätigkeit **I**
to **jog** [dʒɒg] joggen **II**
to **join** [dʒɔɪn] beitreten **II**

joke [dʒəʊk] Witz **I**
to **joke** [dʒəʊk] scherzen **III U2,** 33
journey ['dʒɜ:ni] Reise **III U6,** 93
joy [dʒɔɪ] Freude, Vergnügen ⟨**III U2,** 36⟩
judge [dʒʌdʒ] Richter/-in **II**
judo ['dʒu:dəʊ] Judo **II**
July [dʒʊ'laɪ] Juli **I**
jumbled ['dʒʌmbld] durcheinander geraten, vermischt **I**
jump [dʒʌmp] Sprung **III U1,** 16
ski jump ['ski: dʒʌmp] Skispringen **III U1,** 16
to **jump** [dʒʌmp] springen **I**
to jump out of one's skin [ˌdʒʌmp‿aʊt‿əv wʌnz 'skɪn] sich zu Tode erschrecken **III U6,** 101
ski **jumper** ['ski: ˌdʒʌmpə] Skispringer **III U1,** 16
June [dʒu:n] Juni **I**
junk [dʒʌŋk] Gerümpel; Ramsch **III U3,** 47
junkie ['dʒʌŋki] Junkie **III U5,** 81
just [dʒʌst] nur **I**; einfach **I**; gerade (eben), soeben **I**
just now [ˌdʒʌst 'naʊ] gerade, im Augenblick **I**

K

karaoke machine [ˌkæri'əʊki mə'ʃi:n] Karaokegerät **I**
*to **keep** [ki:p] behalten, aufbewahren **I**
to keep + *adj.* [ki:p] ... bleiben **II**
to keep fit [ki:p 'fɪt] fit bleiben **II**
to keep out [ki:p‿'aʊt] draußen halten; draußen bleiben **III U2,** 24
keyword ['ki:wɜ:d] Stichwort; Schlüsselbegriff **III U4,** 66
kick [kɪk] Tritt, Stoß **III U1,** 20
to **kick** [kɪk] schießen; treten **I**
kid [kɪd] Kind, Jugendlicher, Jugendliche **I**
to **kill** [kɪl] töten, umbringen **II**
kind [kaɪnd] Art, Sorte **II**
kind [kaɪnd] freundlich, nett **II**
king [kɪŋ] König **II**
to **kiss** [kɪs] küssen **II**
kitchen ['kɪtʃɪn] Küche **I**
kite [kaɪt] Drachen **I**
kite festival ['kaɪt ˌfestɪvl] Drachenfest **I**
to fly a kite [flaɪ ə 'kaɪt] einen Drachen steigen lassen **I**
knee [ni:] Knie **II**
knife pl. **knives** [naɪf; naɪvz] Messer **II**
knight [naɪt] Ritter **III U2,** 25
*to **know** [nəʊ] kennen; wissen **I**
I don't know! [ˌaɪ dəʊnt 'nəʊ] Ich weiß (es) nicht! **I**

L

lady ['leɪdi] Dame; Frau **III U2,** 33
cleaning lady ['kli:nɪŋ ˌleɪdi] Putzfrau **III U3,** 43
lake [leɪk] See **II**
LAN *(Local Area Network)* [læn; ˌləʊkl ˌeəriə 'netwɜ:k] LAN **III U5,** 85
land [lænd] Land **I**
on land [ɒn 'lænd] an Land **III U4,** 66
to **land** [lænd] landen **II**
landscape ['lændskeɪp] Landschaft **III U4,** 59
language ['læŋgwɪdʒ] Sprache **I**
first language ['fɜ:st ˌlæŋgwɪdʒ] Muttersprache **III U6,** 93
second language ['seknd ˌlæŋgwɪdʒ] Zweitsprache **III U6,** 100
laptop ['læptɒp] Laptop **I**
large (L) [lɑ:dʒ] groß **I**
extra large (XL) ['ekstrə ˌlɑ:dʒ] besonders groß **I**
lark [lɑ:k] Lerche ⟨**III U1,** 18⟩
last [lɑ:st] letzte/-r/-s **I**
late [leɪt] (zu) spät **I**
2L8 (= too late) [tu: 'leɪt] zu spät *(Abkürzung in SMS oder E-Mail)* **III U3,** 43
Sorry I'm late. [ˌsɒri‿aɪm 'leɪt] Tut mir leid, dass ich zu spät komme. **I**
to be late [bi 'leɪt] zu spät kommen, spät dran sein **I**
to be late for school [bi ˌleɪt fə 'sku:l] zu spät zur Schule kommen **I**
later ['leɪtə] später **I**
See you later. [si: jə 'leɪtə] Bis später. **II**
Latin ['lætɪn] Latein **II**
for **laughs** [fə 'lɑ:fs] zum Spaß **III U4,** 68
to **laugh** [lɑ:f] lachen **I**
to laugh at ['lɑ:f‿ət] auslachen **II**
*to **lay the table** [ˌleɪ ðə 'teɪbl] den Tisch decken **II**
leap [li:p] Sprung, Satz **III U6,** 93
*to **learn** [lɜ:n] lernen **I**
to learn by heart [ˌlɜ:n baɪ 'hɑ:t] auswendig lernen **I**
learner ['lɜ:nə] Lernende/-r **II**
at **least** [ət 'li:st] wenigstens, mindestens **III U4,** 68
*to **leave** [li:v] (ver)lassen; abfahren **II**; hinterlassen **III U3,** 50
Leave him alone! [ˌli:v hɪm‿ə'ləʊn] Lass ihn in Ruhe! **II**
left [left] linke/-r/-s; links **I**
on the left [ɒn ðə 'left] auf der linken Seite, links **I**
on your left/right [ɒn jə 'left, 'raɪt] links/rechts, auf der linken/rechten Seite **I**
leg [leg] Bein **I**
leisure ['leʒə] Freizeit, Freizeit- **III U4,** 66
*to **lend (to)** [lend] leihen; verleihen **II**
less [les] weniger **III U4,** 58
lesson ['lesn] Unterrichtsstunde **I**
dancing lessons *(pl.)* ['dɑ:nsɪŋ ˌlesnz] Tanzunterricht, Tanzstunden **I**
*to **let** [let] lassen **I**
let's (= let us) [lets; let‿'ʌs] lass(t) uns **I**
Let's go! [lets 'gəʊ] Lass(t) uns anfangen!/Lass(t) uns gehen! **I**
let's listen [lets 'lɪsn] lass(t) uns zuhören **I**
letter ['letə] Buchstabe **I**
level ['levl] Niveau, Level; Höhe **II**
library ['laɪbri] Bibliothek **II**
to **lick** [lɪk] (ab)lecken **I**
lie [laɪ] Lüge **III U3,** 43
to tell a lie [ˌtel‿ə 'laɪ] lügen **III U3,** 43
life pl. **lives** [laɪf; laɪvz] Leben **I**
life-jacket ['laɪfˌdʒækɪt] Schwimmweste, Rettungsweste **II**
light [laɪt] Licht; Lampe **II**
lighthouse ['laɪthaʊs] Leuchtturm **I**
lights *(pl.)* [laɪts] Beleuchtung **III U3,** 53
to **like** [laɪk] mögen **I**
I don't like them. [aɪ dəʊnt 'laɪk ˌðəm] Sie gefallen mir nicht. **I**
like [laɪk] wie **I**
like the back of my hand [laɪk ðə ˌbæk‿əv maɪ 'hænd] wie meine Westentasche, in- und auswendig **II**
like this [laɪk 'ðɪs] so, auf diese Weise **I**
What is ... like? [ˌwɒt‿ɪz 'laɪk] Wie ist ... ? **II**
what it looks like [ˌwɒt‿ɪt 'lʊks laɪk] wie es aussieht **I**
line [laɪn] Linie; Zeile **I**; (Telefon)leitung **III U2,** 35
time line ['taɪm laɪn] Zeitstrahl **II**
to **link** [lɪŋk] verbinden **I**
list [lɪst] Liste **I**
shopping list ['ʃɒpɪŋ ˌlɪst] Einkaufszettel **II**
to **listen** ['lɪsn] zuhören **I**
let's listen [lets 'lɪsn] lass(t) uns zuhören **I**
to listen for ['lɪsn fə] heraushören **I**
to listen to ['lɪsn tə] jemandem zuhören **I**; hören auf **III U3,** 49
Listening ['lɪsnɪŋ] *(hier:)* Hörverstehensübung **I**
little ['lɪtl] klein **I**; wenig **I**
a little [ə 'lɪtl] ein wenig, etwas **I**

to **live** [lɪv] wohnen, leben **I**
living room ['lɪvɪŋ ru:m] Wohnzimmer **I**
loch [lɒx] See *(in Schottland)* **II**
locker ['lɒkə] Schließfach **II**
to **log on (to)** [lɒg‿'ɒntə] sich (in etw.) einloggen ⟨**III P1,** 23⟩
Londoner ['lʌndənə] Londoner/-in **II**
lonely ['ləʊnli] einsam **III U2,** 33
long [lɒŋ] lang **I**
(not) any longer [nɒt ˌeni 'lɒŋgə] (nicht) mehr, (nicht) länger **II**
look [lʊk] Aussehen **III U5,** 82
to **look** [lʊk] schauen, sehen, gucken **I**; nachschauen, suchen **I**; aussehen **I**
to look after [lʊk‿'ɑ:ftə] sich kümmern um; aufpassen auf **I**
to look at ['lʊk‿æt] anschauen, ansehen **I**
to look for ['lʊk fə] suchen (nach) **I**
to look up [lʊk‿'ʌp] nachschlagen, nachschauen **I**
what it looks like [ˌwɒt‿ɪt 'lʊks laɪk] wie es aussieht **I**
lord [lɔ:d] Lord, Herr **III U2,** 33
lorry ['lɒri] Lastwagen **II**
*to **lose** [lu:z] verlieren **II**
Get lost! [get 'lɒst] Hau ab! **II**
to be lost [bi 'lɒst] sich verirrt haben **II**
to get lost [get 'lɒst] sich verirren **I**
a **lot of** [ə 'lɒt‿əv] viel/-e, eine Menge **I**
lots of ['lɒts‿əv] viel/-e, jede Menge **I**
loud [laʊd] laut **I**
love [lʌv] Null *(Tennis)* **III U1,** 13; Liebe **III U4,** 60; Liebe Grüße, Herzliche Grüße *(am Briefende)* **II**
*to fall in **love** [ˌfɔ:l‿ɪn 'lʌv] sich verlieben **II**
to **love** [lʌv] lieben **I**
luck [lʌk] Glück **III U1,** 12
bad luck [bæd 'lʌk] Pech, Unglück **III U3,** 43
Good luck! [ˌgʊd 'lʌk] Viel Glück! **II**
to be out of luck [ˌbi: aʊt‿əv 'lʌk] kein Glück haben **III U1,** 19
What a stroke of luck! [wɒt‿ə ˌstrəʊk‿əv 'lʌk] Was für ein Glückstreffer! **III U1,** 19
lucky ... ['lʌki] ... Glücklicher, ... Glückliche **II**
That was lucky! [ˌðæt wəz 'lʌki] Glück gehabt! **III U1,** 19
to be lucky [bi 'lʌki] Glück haben **I**
You were lucky there! [jʊ wə ˌlʌki 'ðeə] Da hast du aber Glück gehabt! **III U1,** 19
lunch [lʌnʃ] Mittagessen **I**
lunchtime ['lʌnʃtaɪm] Mittagszeit, Mittagspause **I**
the **lungs** *(pl.)* [lʌŋz] die Lunge **III U1,** 13

M

machine [mə'ʃi:n] Maschine, Apparat, Gerät; Automat **I**
karaoke machine [ˌkæri'əʊki mə'ʃi:n] Karaokegerät **I**
magazine [ˌmægə'zi:n] Zeitschrift **I**
magic ['mædʒɪk] Magie, Zauberei **III U5,** 86
voice **mail** ['vɔɪs meɪl] Voicemail; Mailbox **III U3,** 50
main [meɪn] Haupt- **III U5,** 77
main clause ['meɪn klɔ:z] Hauptsatz **II**
*to **make** [meɪk] machen, bilden **I**
Make up your mind! [ˌmeɪk‿'ʌp jə 'maɪnd] Entscheide dich! **I**
to make a decision [ˌmeɪk‿ə dɪ'sɪʒn] eine Entscheidung treffen **III U3,** 52
to make a face [meɪk ə 'feɪs] ein Gesicht ziehen **II**
to make friends [ˌmeɪk 'frendz] Freundschaft schließen **II**
to make fun of [ˌmeɪk 'fʌn‿əv] sich lustig machen über **III U4,** 69
to make it ['meɪk‿ɪt] es schaffen **III U6,** 102
to make money [ˌmeɪk 'mʌni] Geld verdienen **II**
to make sure [ˌmeɪk 'ʃɔ:] sichergehen **III U3,** 52
make-up ['meɪkʌp] Make-up **III U3,** 43
male voice choir [ˌmeɪl vɔɪs 'kwaɪə] Männerchor **III U4,** 59
man pl. **men** [mæn; men] Mann **I**
to **manage (to do sth)** ['mænɪdʒ] es schaffen (etw. zu tun) **III U3,** 52
manager ['mænɪdʒə] Geschäftsführer/-in **I**
maniac ['meɪniæk] Verrückte/-r, Wahnsinnige/-r **III U5,** 81
mankind [mæn'kaɪnd] Menschheit **III U6,** 93
many ['meni] viele **I**
How many ... ? [haʊ 'meni] Wie viele ... ? **I**
map [mæp] Stadtplan, Landkarte **I**
treasure map ['treʒə ˌmæp] Schatzkarte **I**
marathon ['mærəθn] Marathon **III U1,** 13
March [mɑ:tʃ] März **I**
the third of March [ðə ˌθɜ:d‿əv 'mɑ:tʃ] der dritte März **I**
market ['mɑ:kɪt] Markt **I**
married to ['mærid tə] verheiratet mit **I**
to **marry** ['mæri] heiraten **III U3,** 43
mask [mɑ:sk] Maske **III U3,** 52
match [mætʃ] Wettkampf; Spiel; Match **II**
to **match** [mætʃ] zuordnen **I**

mate [meɪt] (Schiffs)offizier; Freund/-in **I**
raw **material** [ˌrɔ: mə'tɪəriəl] Rohstoff **III U2,** 30
Maths [mæθs] Mathematik **II**
may [meɪ] (vielleicht) können; dürfen **I**
May I? [meɪ‿aɪ] Darf ich? **II**
May [meɪ] Mai **I**
maybe ['meɪbi] vielleicht **I**
me [mi:] mich; mir **I**
Me? [mi:; mi] Ich? **I**
meal [mi:l] Mahlzeit, Essen **I**
*to **mean** [mi:n] bedeuten; meinen **I**
I didn't mean to ... [aɪ ˌdɪdnt 'mi:n tə] Ich wollte nicht ... **III U4,** 62
mean [mi:n] knauserig, geizig **II**
meaning ['mi:nɪŋ] Bedeutung **I**
meat [mi:t] Fleisch **II**
gold **medal** [gəʊld 'medl] Goldmedaille **III U1,** 13
medium pl. **media** ['mi:diəm, 'mi:diə] Medium, Medien **III U5,** 76
medium (M) ['mi:diəm] mittel(groß) **I**
*to **meet** [mi:t] (sich) treffen **I**; kennenlernen **III U3,** 43
meeting people ['mi:tɪŋ ˌpi:pl] Leute kennenlernen, Leute treffen **I**
Pleased to meet you. [ˌpli:zd tə 'mi:t‿ju] Sehr erfreut./Freut mich, Sie/dich kennenzulernen. **II**
to meet halfway [mi:t hɑ:f'weɪ] (sich auf halbem Weg) entgegenkommen **III U3,** 46
to **mend** [mend] heilen; reparieren **I**
to **mention** ['menʃn] erwähnen **III U6,** 94
menu ['menju:] Speisekarte **II**
mess [mes] Unordnung, Durcheinander **I**
What a mess! [wɒt‿ə 'mes] Was für eine Unordnung! **I**
message ['mesɪdʒ] Nachricht **II**
metal ['metl] Metall **III U2,** 35
metre ['mi:tə] Meter **II**
microwave ['maɪkrəʊweɪv] Mikrowelle **III U3,** 43
middle name ['mɪdl ˌneɪm] zweiter Vorname **III U2,** 33
might [maɪt] könnte(n) **III U1,** 17
mile [maɪl] Meile **I**
milk [mɪlk] Milch **I**
to **milk** [mɪlk] melken **I**
million ['mɪljən] Million **II**
millions of ['mɪljənz‿əv] Millionen von **II**
Make up your **mind**! [ˌmeɪk‿'ʌp jə 'maɪnd] Entscheide dich! **I**
to **mind** [maɪnd] etwas dagegen haben; einem etwas ausmachen **III U3,** 46

Mind the gap. [ˌmaɪnd ðə ˈgæp] Vorsicht beim Ein- und Aussteigen. **II**
Never mind! [ˌnevə ˈmaɪnd] Macht nichts.; Mach dir nichts draus!; Schon gut. **III U4,** 62
coal **mine** [ˈkəʊl maɪn] Kohlenbergwerk, Kohlengrube **III U4,** 59
minute [ˈmɪnɪt] Minute **I**
to **miss** [mɪs] vermissen **II**
missing [ˈmɪsɪŋ] fehlend, verschwunden **I**
missionary [ˈmɪʃnri] Missionar/-in **III U6,** 93
to **mist up** [mɪst‿ˈʌp] (sich) beschlagen **III U1,** 16
mistake [mɪˈsteɪk] Fehler **II**
mixed [mɪkst] gemischt **I**
mixed bag [ˌmɪkst ˈbæg] bunte Mischung **I**
mmm [m] mmm, lecker **I**
mobile [ˈməʊbaɪl] Handy, Mobiltelefon **I**
fashion **model** [ˈfæʃn ˌmɒdl] Model, Mannequin **II**
modern [ˈmɒdn] modern **III U2,** 26
moment [ˈməʊmənt] Moment, Augenblick **I**
Monday [ˈmʌndeɪ] Montag **I**
money [ˈmʌni] Geld **I**
pocket money [ˈpɒkɪt ˌmʌni] Taschengeld **II**
to make money [ˌmeɪk ˈmʌni] Geld verdienen **II**
to raise money [reɪz ˈmʌni] Geld sammeln, Geld aufbringen **III U5,** 85
monkey [ˈmʌŋki] Affe **I**
monster [ˈmɒnstə] Monster **II**
month [mʌnθ] Monat **I**
moon [mu:n] Mond **III U6,** 93
more [mɔ:] mehr; weitere **I**
(not) any more [nɒt ˌeni ˈmɔ:] (nicht) mehr **III U3,** 43
morning [ˈmɔ:nɪŋ] Morgen, Vormittag **I**
Good morning. [gʊd ˈmɔ:nɪŋ] Guten Morgen. **I**
this morning [ðɪs ˈmɔ:nɪŋ] heute Morgen **I**
most [məʊst] das meiste; die meisten **II**
mother [ˈmʌðə] Mutter **I**
mother tongue [ˈmʌðə tʌŋ] Muttersprache **II**
motorway [ˈməʊtəweɪ] Autobahn **III U4,** 66
mountain [ˈmaʊntɪn] Berg **I**
mountain bike [ˈmaʊntɪn baɪk] Mountainbike **II**
mouse pl. **mice** [maʊs; maɪs] Maus **I**
mouth [maʊθ] Mund **II**
*to be on the **move** [bi: ɒn‿ðə ˈmu:v] unterwegs sein **III U4,** 58
to **move** [mu:v] (sich) bewegen **II**
to move (house) [mu:v ˈhaʊs] umziehen **III U4,** 58
MP3 player [ˌempi:ˈθri: ˌpleɪə] MP3-Player **III U3,** 51
Mr [ˈmɪstə] Herr *(Anrede)* **I**
Mrs [ˈmɪsɪz] Frau *(Anrede)* **I**
much [mʌtʃ] viel **I**
How much … ? [haʊ ˈmʌtʃ] Wie viel … ? **I**
How much is … ? [ˈhaʊ mʌtʃ‿ɪz] Wie viel kostet … ? **I**
to **muck out** [mʌk‿ˈaʊt] ausmisten **I**
mug [mʌg] Becher **I**
mum [mʌm] Mama **I**
museum [mju:ˈzi:əm] Museum **I**
music [ˈmju:zɪk] Musik **I**
musical instrument [ˌmju:zɪkl‿ˈɪnstrəmənt] Musikinstrument **II**
must [mʌst] müssen **I**
mustn't [ˈmʌsnt] nicht dürfen **I**
a must-see [ə ˌmʌst ˈsi:] … muss man gesehen haben **III U4,** 66
my [maɪ] mein/-e **I**
My name is …. [maɪ ˈneɪm‿ɪz] Ich heiße … **I**
myself [maɪˈself] ich/mir/mich (selbst); selber **III U3,** 44

N

name [neɪm] Name **I**
middle name [ˈmɪdl ˌneɪm] zweiter Vorname **III U2,** 33
My name is …. [maɪ ˈneɪm‿ɪz] Ich heiße … **I**
What's your name? [wɒts jɔ: ˈneɪm] Wie heißt du? **I**
nationality [ˌnæʃnˈæləti] Nationalität **I**
near [nɪə] nahe, in der Nähe von **I**
neck [nek] Hals, Nacken, Genick **II**
to **need** [ni:d] brauchen **I**
negative [ˈnegətɪv] Verneinungsform **III U2,** 28
negative [ˈnegətɪv] negativ, verneint **II**
neighbour [ˈneɪbə] Nachbar/-in **I**
nervous [ˈnɜ:vəs] nervös, aufgeregt **I**
never [ˈnevə] nie, niemals **I**
Never mind! [ˌnevə ˈmaɪnd] Macht nichts.; Mach dir nichts draus!; Schon gut. **III U4,** 62
new [nju:] neu **I**
news *(sing.)* [nju:z] Nachricht(en), Neuigkeit(en) **II**
newsagent [ˈnju:zˌeɪdʒnt] Zeitschriftengeschäft **I**
newspaper [ˈnju:sˌpeɪpə] Zeitung **III U5,** 76
popular newspaper [ˌpɒpjələ ˈnju:sˌpeɪpə] Boulevardzeitung **III U5,** 76
next [nekst] nächste/-r/-s **I**
next door [nekst ˈdɔ:] nebenan **II**
next to [ˈnekst tə] neben **I**
nice [naɪs] nett, sympathisch **I**; schön, gut **I**
nickname [ˈnɪkneɪm] Spitzname **III U5,** 76
night [naɪt] Nacht; Abend **I**
nil [nɪl] null *(beim Sport)* **III U1,** 19
nine [naɪn] neun **I**
nineteen [ˌnaɪnˈti:n] neunzehn **I**
ninety [ˈnaɪnti] neunzig **I**
no [nəʊ] kein/-e **I**
No way! [ˌnəʊ ˈweɪ] Was?!/Echt?!/Nie im Leben! **III U2,** 26
no [nəʊ] nein **I**
nobody [ˈnəʊbədi] niemand **II**
to **nod** [nɒd] nicken **III U2,** 34
noise [nɔɪz] Lärm, Krach; Geräusch **III U5,** 85
It's **none of your business!** [ɪts ˌnʌn‿əv jə ˈbɪznɪs] Das geht dich nichts an! **II**
noodle [ˈnu:dl] Nudel **III U6,** 93
normal [ˈnɔ:ml] normal **II**
Norman [ˈnɔ:mən] Normanne, Normannin; normannisch **III U2,** 25
north [nɔ:θ] Norden **I**
North Sea [ˌnɔ:θ ˈsi:] Nordsee **I**
up North [ʌp ˈnɔ:θ] im Norden **III U4,** 63
nose [nəʊz] Nase **II**
to stick up one's nose [ˌstɪk‿ʌp wʌnz ˈnəʊz] die Nase rümpfen ⟨**III U5,** 87⟩
not [nɒt] nicht **I**
not even [nɒt ˈi:vn] (noch) nicht einmal **I**
not until [nɒt ʌnˈtɪl] erst (dann), wenn **III U1,** 10
note [nəʊt] Notiz, Nachricht **I**
to take notes [teɪk ˈnəʊts] sich Notizen machen **I**
nothing [ˈnʌθɪŋ] nichts **II**
noun [naʊn] Nomen, Hauptwort **I**
November [nəˈvembə] November **I**
now [naʊ] jetzt, nun, gerade **I**; heute ⟨**III U5,** 87⟩; ⟨**III U6,** 103⟩
right now [raɪt ˈnaʊ] jetzt, sofort, gerade **I**
nowhere [ˈnəʊweə] nirgendwo; nirgendwohin **II**
number [ˈnʌmbə] Nummer, Hausnummer; Zahl **I**

O

o'clock [ə'klɒk] Uhr (*Zeitangabe bei vollen Stunden*) **I**
object ['ɒbdʒɪkt] Objekt, Satzergänzung **I**
obvious ['ɒbviəs] offensichtlich ⟨**III U5,** 87⟩
ocean ['əʊʃn] Ozean **I**
October [ɒk'təʊbə] Oktober **I**
odd [ɒd] seltsam, komisch **III U2,** 34
oddity ['ɒdɪti] Eigenartigkeit, Kuriosität **III U1,** 14
of [ɒv; əv] von **I**
four of them ['fɔ:r‿əv ðəm] vier davon (*Personen, Tiere …*) **I**
of course [əv 'kɔ:s] natürlich, selbstverständlich **I**
to **offer** ['ɒfə] (an)bieten **III U3,** 53
office ['ɒfɪs] Büro **II**
post office ['pəʊst‿ɒfɪs] Postamt **II**
official [ə'fɪʃl] offiziell **III U3,** 54
offside [ˌɒf'saɪd] abseits **III U1,** 19
often ['ɒfn] oft, häufig **I**
oh [əʊ] null (*bei Telefonnummern*) **I**
Oh! [əʊ] Oh! **I**
Oh dear! [əʊ 'dɪə] Oje! **II**
oil [ɔɪl] Öl **II**
oil industry ['ɔɪl‿ɪndəstri] Ölindustrie **II**
oil platform ['ɔɪl ˌplætfɔ:m] Bohrinsel **II**
OK [əʊ'keɪ] okay **I**
old [əʊld] alt **I**
How old are you? [haʊ‿'əʊld‿ɑ: 'ju:] Wie alt bist du? **I**
old people's home [əʊld 'pi:plz həʊm] Altersheim **III U3,** 44
year-old [ˌjɪər‿'əʊld] -jährige/r; -jährig **II**
old-fashioned [əʊld'fæʃnd] altmodisch **III U2,** 33
Olympic [ə'lɪmpɪk] Olympia-, olympisch **II**
on [ɒn] an(geschaltet) **II**
on [ɒn] auf; an **I**
on a train [ɒn‿ə 'treɪn] im Zug **I**
on average [ɒn‿'ævrɪdʒ] durchschnittlich, im Durchschnitt **III U4,** 58
on foot [ɒn 'fʊt] zu Fuß **III U6,** 102
on one's own [ɒn wʌnz‿'əʊn] (ganz) allein(e) **III U3,** 52
on stage [ɒn 'steɪdʒ] auf der Bühne **II**
on the beach [ɒn ðə 'bi:tʃ] am Strand **I**
on the bottom [ɒn ðə 'bɒtəm] unten **I**
on the left [ɒn ðə 'left] auf der linken Seite, links **I**
on the right [ɒn ðə 'raɪt] auf der rechten Seite, rechts **I**
on the top [ɒn ðə 'tɒp] oben **I**
on time [ɒn 'taɪm] pünktlich **III U6,** 102
on top of [ɒn 'tɒp‿əv] auf … hinauf, oben (auf) **I**
on Tuesdays [ɒn 'tju:zdeɪz] dienstags **I**
on TV [ɒn ˌti:'vi:] im Fernsehen **I**
on your right/left [ɒn jə 'raɪt, 'left] rechts/links, auf der rechten/linken Seite **I**
once [wʌns] einmal **III U1,** 12
Once upon a time … ['wʌns‿əˌpɒn‿ə 'taɪm] Es war einmal … **III U2,** 24
at once [ət 'wʌns] auf einmal; sofort **I**
one [wʌn] eins **I**
one by one [ˌwʌn baɪ 'wʌn] eine/-r/-s nach dem/der anderen **III U3,** 53
one evening [wʌn‿'i:vnɪŋ] eines Abends **I**
one Saturday afternoon [wʌn 'sætədeɪ ˌɑ:ftə'nu:n] an einem Samstag Nachmittag **I**
online [ˌɒn'laɪn] online **I**
only ['əʊnli] einzige/-r/-s **II**
only child [ˌəʊnli 'tʃaɪld] Einzelkind **I**
only ['əʊnli] erst, bloß; nur **II**
onto ['ɒntə] auf … hinauf **II**
Oops! [u:ps] Hoppla! **I**
to **open** ['əʊpn] öffnen, aufmachen **I**; eröffnen **III U1,** 11
open ['əʊpn] geöffnet, offen; aufgeschlagen **I**
open-air [ˌəʊpn'eə] Openair-, Freilicht-, im Freien **III U2,** 26
open day [ˌəʊpn 'deɪ] Tag der offenen Tür **III U2,** 29
opinion [ə'pɪnjən] Meinung **III U5,** 85
to give one's opinion [ˌgɪv wʌnz ə'pɪnjən] seine Meinung äußern **III U5,** 85
opposite ['ɒpəzɪt] Gegenteil **II**
opposite ['ɒpəzɪt] gegenüber **I**
or [ɔ:] oder **I**; sonst **III U3,** 43
orange ['ɒrɪndʒ] orange **I**
orchestra ['ɔ:kɪstrə] Orchester **I**
order ['ɔ:də] Reihenfolge **I**
to **order** ['ɔ:də] bestellen **II**
to **organise** ['ɔ:gənaɪz] organisieren **III U5,** 85
orienteering [ˌɔ:riən'tɪərɪŋ] Orientierungslauf **II**
other ['ʌðə] andere/-r/-s, weitere/-r/-s **I**
each other [i:tʃ‿'ʌðə] einander, sich (gegenseitig) **III U3,** 43
the others [ði‿'ʌðəz] die anderen **I**
Ouch! [aʊtʃ] Aua! **III U3,** 44
ought to ['ɔ:t‿tə] sollte(n) **III U2,** 29
our [aʊə; ɑ:] unser/-e **I**
ourselves [aʊə'selvz] wir (selbst), uns (selbst); selber **III U3,** 44
out [aʊt] heraus, hinaus, nach draußen **I**
out of ['aʊt‿əv] aus … heraus **II**
outline ['aʊtlaɪn] Umriss, Silhouette **III U5,** 87
outside [ˌaʊt'saɪd] außen, draußen, im Freien; außerhalb **I**
oval ['əʊvl] oval, eiförmig **III U1,** 8
over ['əʊvə] über **I**
over there [ˌəʊvə 'ðeə] (nach) dort drüben **I**
overweight [ˌəʊvə'weɪt] übergewichtig **II**
to **own** [əʊn] besitzen **II**
own [əʊn] eigene/-r/-s **I**
her own room [hər‿əʊn 'ru:m] ihr eigenes Zimmer **I**
on one's own [ɒn wʌnz‿'əʊn] (ganz) allein(e) **III U3,** 52
to get your own back [get jər‿'əʊn bæk] sich rächen **II**
owner ['əʊnə] Besitzer, Besitzerin **I**

P

to **pack** [pæk] (ein)packen **I**
page [peɪdʒ] Seite **I**
home page ['həʊm ˌpeɪdʒ] Homepage **I**
pain [peɪn] Schmerz **II**
to be a pain [bi‿ə 'peɪn] einem auf die Nerven gehen **I**
paint [peɪnt] Farbe **II**
to **paint** [peɪnt] (an)malen, streichen **II**
pair [peə] Paar **I**
a pair of [ə 'peər‿əv] ein Paar **III U4,** 60
palace ['pælɪs] Palast **II**
paper ['peɪpə] Papier **II**
paragraph ['pærəgrɑ:f] Paragraph, Absatz **III U2,** 35
paramedic [ˌpærə'medɪk] Sanitäter/-in **III U6,** 97
parents (*pl.*) ['peərnts] Eltern **I**
park [pɑ:k] Park **I**
theme park ['θi:m pɑ:k] Themenpark **II**
to **park** [pɑ:k] parken **I**
part [pɑ:t] Teil **I**
partner ['pɑ:tnə] Partner/-in **I**
party ['pɑ:ti] Party, Feier **I**
birthday party ['bɜ:θdeɪ ˌpɑ:ti] Geburtstagsfeier **I**

to have a party [hæv ə 'pɑ:ti] eine Party feiern **I**
passenger ['pæsndʒə] Passagier/-in, Beifahrer/-in, Fahrgast **II**
passive ['pæsɪv] Passiv **III U5,** 79
passport ['pɑ:spɔ:t] (Reise-)Pass **II**
password ['pɑ:swɜ:d] Passwort ⟨**III P1,** 23⟩
past [pɑ:st] Vergangenheit **II**
past perfect [ˌpɑ:st 'pɜ:fɪkt] Plusquamperfekt **III U2,** 31
past [pɑ:st] nach *(bei Uhrzeitangaben)* **I**
path [pɑ:θ] Pfad, Weg **II**
patient ['peɪʃnt] Patient/-in **III U5,** 87
patient ['peɪʃnt] geduldig **II**
pause [pɔ:z] Pause **II**
*to **pay** [peɪ] bezahlen **II**
P.E. (Physical Education) [pi:'i:; ˌfɪzɪkl edʒʊ'keɪʃn] Sportunterricht **II**
pen [pen] Füller **I**
penalty ['penlti] Elfmeter; Strafe **III U1,** 19
pencil ['pensl] Bleistift **I**
pencil-case ['pensl keɪs] Federmäppchen **I**
penny pl. **pence** [peni; pens] Penny, Pence *(brit. Währungseinheit)* **I**
people *(pl.)* ['pi:pl] Leute *(pl.)*, Menschen *(pl.)* **I**
old people's home [əʊld 'pi:plz həʊm] Altersheim **III U3,** 44
per [pɜ:; pə] pro **I**
per cent [pə'sent] Prozent **III U6,** 93
past **perfect** [ˌpɑ:st 'pɜ:fɪkt] Plusquamperfekt **III U2,** 31
perfect ['pɜ:fɪkt] perfekt, vollkommen **II**
to **perform** [pə'fɔ:m] aufführen, auftreten **II**
perfume ['pɜ:fju:m] Parfüm **II**
peroxide [pə'rɒksaɪd] Peroxyd *(Bleichmittel für Haare)*; mit Peroxyd gebleicht ⟨**III U4,** 65⟩
person pl. **people** ['pɜ:sn; pi:pl] Person, Mensch **I**
personal ['pɜ:snəl] persönlich **II**
pet [pet] Haustier **I**
phone [fəʊn] Telefon **I**
phone call ['fəʊn ˌkɔ:l] (Telefon)anruf **I**
phone number ['fəʊn ˌnʌmbə] Telefonnummer **I**
to **phone** [fəʊn] anrufen **I**
photo ['fəʊtəʊ] Foto **I**
to **photograph** ['fəʊtəgrɑ:f] fotografieren **III U5,** 79
phrase [freɪz] Satz, Redewendung **I**
classroom phrases *(pl.)* ['klɑ:srʊm ˌfreɪzɪz] Redewendungen für den Unterricht **I**
physical ['fɪzɪkl] körperlich **II**
pick-up ['pɪkʌp] Pick-up, Kleintransporter **I**
to **pick up** [pɪk_'ʌp] abholen, mitnehmen **I**; aufheben **II**
picnic ['pɪknɪk] Picknick **I**
picture ['pɪktʃə] Bild **I**
piece [pi:s] Stück **II**
pier [pɪə] Pier, Hafendamm **I**
pig [pɪg] Schwein **I**
pigeon ['pɪdʒən] Taube **II**
pile [paɪl] Stapel, Haufen **III U5,** 86
pink [pɪŋk] rosa, pink **I**
pip [pɪp] Kern **III U3,** 43
pipe [paɪp] Rohr **III U5,** 87
pirate ['paɪrət] Pirat, Seeräuber **I**
pitch [pɪtʃ] Spielfeld, Platz **III U1,** 8
to **pitter-patter** ['pɪtəˌpætə] prasseln, klopfen, trappeln **I**
It's a **pity.** [ˌɪts_ə 'pɪti] Das ist schade./ Es ist schade … **III U4,** 67
pizza ['pi:tsə] Pizza **I**
pizza place ['pi:tsə ˌpleɪs] Pizzeria **I**
place [pleɪs] Ort **I**; Platz **III U1,** 17
changing places [ˌtʃeɪndʒɪŋ 'pleɪsɪz] Ortswechsel **III U4,** 67
plan [plæn] Plan **II**
to **plan** [plæn] planen **I**
planning your holidays [ˌplænɪŋ jə 'hɒlədeɪz] den Urlaub planen **I**
plane [pleɪn] Flugzeug **II**
planet ['plænɪt] Planet **II**
plank [plæŋk] Brett, Planke **I**
planner ['plænə] Kalender, Planer **II**
plant [plɑ:nt] Pflanze **III U6,** 93
plate [pleɪt] Teller **II**
platform ['plætfɔ:m] Bahnsteig; Plattform **II**
oil platform ['ɔɪl ˌplætfɔ:m] Bohrinsel **II**
play [pleɪ] Spiel, Theaterstück **II**
role play ['rəʊl pleɪ] Rollenspiel **I**
to **play** [pleɪ] spielen **I**; (ab)spielen *(CD, Radio etc.)* **I**
to play a trick on [ˌpleɪ_ə 'trɪk_ɒn] einen Streich spielen **II**
player ['pleɪə] Spieler/-in, Mitspieler/-in **II**
MP3 player [ˌempi:'θri: ˌpleɪə] MP3-Player **III U3,** 51
playground ['pleɪgraʊnd] Schulhof; Spielplatz **I**
please [pli:z] bitte **I**
Pleased to meet you. [ˌpli:zd tə 'mi:t_ju] Sehr erfreut./Freut mich, Sie/dich kennenzulernen. **II**
plural ['plʊərl] Plural, Mehrzahl **I**
pm [ˌpi:'em] nachmittags *(Uhrzeit)* **I**
pocket ['pɒkɪt] Tasche, Hosentasche **II**
pocket money ['pɒkɪt ˌmʌni] Taschengeld **II**
pod [pɒd] Gondel **II**
poet ['pəʊɪt] Dichter/-in **III U2,** 25
You've got a **point.** [ju:v gɒt_ə 'pɔɪnt] Da ist was dran. **III U3,** 46
to **point** [pɔɪnt] zeigen **I**
police [pə'li:s] Polizei **I**
police department [pə'li:s dɪˌpɑ:tmənt] Polizeidienststelle **III U5,** 85
police officer [pəˌli:s 'ɒfɪsə] Polizeibeamte/-r **III U6,** 97
police station [pə'li:s ˌsteɪʃn] Polizeirevier, Polizeiwache **I**
Polish ['pəʊlɪʃ] polnisch, aus Polen; Polnisch **I**
polite [pə'laɪt] höflich **I**
politeness [pə'laɪtnəs] Höflichkeit **II**
Pooh! [pu:] Igitt! **I**
pool [pu:l] Pool **III U4,** 69
the **poor** [ðə 'pɔ:] die Armen **III U4,** 60
poor [pɔ:; pʊə] arm **II**
pop star ['pɒp stɑ:] Popstar **I**
popular ['pɒpjələ] beliebt, populär **II**
popular newspaper [ˌpɒpjələ 'nju:sˌpeɪpə] Boulevardzeitung **III U5,** 76
positive ['pɒzətɪv] positiv **II**
postbox ['pəʊstbɒks] Briefkasten *(öffentlich)* **II**
postcard ['pəʊskɑ:d] Postkarte **I**
post office ['pəʊst_ɒfɪs] Postamt **II**
poster ['pəʊstə] Poster **I**
couch **potato** ['kaʊtʃ pəˌteɪtəʊ] Fernsehglotzer/-in, Couchpotato **III U5,** 81
pound [paʊnd] Pfund *(Währung)* **I**
It's two pounds. [ɪts ˌtu: 'paʊndz] Es kostet zwei Pfund. **I**
power ['paʊə] Strom, Elektrizität, Energie **III U2,** 24
to **practise** ['præktɪs] üben **II**
prairie ['preəri] Prärie **III U6,** 101
Premiership ['premiərʃɪp] *erste Division, vgl. Deutsche Bundesliga* **II**
to **prepare** [prɪ'peə] vorbereiten; zubereiten **III U2,** 29
preposition [ˌprepə'zɪʃn] Präposition **II**
pre-reading [pri:'ri:dɪŋ] vor dem Lesen **III U2,** 32
prescription [prɪ'skrɪpʃn] Rezept *(für Arzneimittel)* **II**
present ['preznt] Gegenwart; Präsens **I**; Geschenk **I**
present progressive [ˌpreznt prə'gresɪv] Verlaufsform des Präsens/ der Gegenwart **I**

simple present [ˌsɪmpl ˈpreznt] Gegenwart, Präsens **I**
presentation [ˌprezn'teɪʃn] Präsentation, Vortrag **II**
to give a (group) presentation [gɪv‿ə ˌgru:p‿ˌprezn'teɪʃn] eine (Gruppen)präsentation machen **II**
present perfect [ˌpreznt 'pɜ:fɪkt] das Perfekt **II**
press conference ['pres ˌkɒnfrns] Pressekonferenz **III U1,** 16
price [praɪs] Preis **II**
priest [pri:st] Priester **II**
primary school ['praɪmri ˌsku:l] Grundschule **I**
princess [prɪn'ses] Prinzessin **III U6,** 101
prison ['prɪzn] Gefängnis **III U2,** 31
prisoner ['prɪznə] Gefangene/-r **II**
prize [praɪz] Preis, Gewinn **I**
probably ['prɒbəbli] möglicherweise, wahrscheinlich **III U3,** 47
problem ['prɒbləm] Problem **I**
product ['prɒdʌkt] Produkt, Erzeugnis **III U5,** 82
cleaning product ['kli:nɪŋ ˌprɒdʌkt] Reinigungsmittel, Putzmittel **III U5,** 77
programme ['prəʊgræm] Programmheft **III U3,** 53; Programm; Sendung **III U5,** 77
project ['prɒdʒekt] Projekt **I**
to **promise** ['prɒmɪs] versprechen **II**
pronoun ['prəʊnaʊn] Pronomen, Fürwort **I**
relative pronoun [ˌrelətɪv 'prəʊnaʊn] Relativpronomen **III U1,** 13
self-pronoun ['self ˌprəʊnaʊn] Reflexivpronomen **III U3,** 44
props *(pl.)* [prɒps] Requisiten **III U3,** 53
pros and cons *(pl.)* [ˌprəʊz‿n 'kɒnz] Pro und Kontra **III U5,** 81
Protestant ['prɒtɪstnt] Protestant/-in; protestantisch **III U2,** 24
*to be **proud (of)** [bi: 'praʊd‿əv] stolz sein (auf) **III U4,** 59
P.S.E. (Personal and Social Education) [ˌpi:jes'i:; ˌpɜ:snəl‿ənd ˌsəʊʃl‿edʒʊ'keɪʃn] Sozialkunde **II**
the **public** [ðə 'pʌblɪk] die Öffentlichkeit **III U5,** 77
public ['pʌblɪk] öffentlich **I**
pullover ['pʊləʊvə] Pullover **II**
Punjabi [pʌn'dʒɑ:bi:] Pandschabi; pandschabisch **III U4,** 63
pupil ['pju:pl] Schüler/-in **I**
purple ['pɜ:pl] violett, lila **I**
purr [pɜ:] *(Schnurren einer Katze)* **I**
purse [pɜ:s] Portemonnaie, Geldbeutel **III U3,** 48

to **push** [pʊʃ] stoßen, schieben, drücken, schubsen **II**
*to **put** [pʊt] stellen, setzen, legen **I**
to put in [pʊt 'ɪn] einsetzen **I**
to put on (a play) [ˌpʊt‿ɒn‿ə 'pleɪ] (ein Theaterstück) aufführen **III U3,** 53

Q

quality ['kwɒləti] Qualität; Qualitäts- **III U5,** 76
quarter ['kwɔ:tə] Viertel **I**
queen [kwi:n] Königin **II**
question ['kwestʃən] Frage **I**
question tag ['kwestʃən ˌtæg] Frageanhängsel, Bestätigungsfrage **II**
question word ['kwestʃən ˌwɜ:d] Fragewort **I**
queue [kju:] Schlange **II**
to **queue** [kju:] anstehen, sich anstellen **III U1,** 20
quick [kwɪk] schnell **II**
quiet [kwaɪət] leise, ruhig, still **I**
quite [kwaɪt] ziemlich; ganz, völlig **III U4,** 69
quiz [kwɪz] Quiz, Ratespiel **I**

R

race [reɪs] Wettlauf, Rennen **III U1,** 9
racket ['rækɪt] Schläger *(Tennis-)* **III U1,** 9; Lärm, Krach ⟨**III U1,** 19⟩
radio ['reɪdiəʊ] Radio **I**
radio station ['reɪdiəʊ ˌsteɪʃn] Radiosender **I**
railway ['reɪlweɪ] Eisenbahn **III U6,** 101
rain [reɪn] Regen **I**
to **rain** [reɪn] regnen **I**
rainy ['reɪni] regnerisch **II**
to **raise money** [reɪz 'mʌni] Geld sammeln, Geld aufbringen **III U5,** 85
ramp [ræmp] Rampe **III U5,** 86
rap [ræp] Rap **I**
I'd **rather** [aɪd 'rɑ:ðə] ich würde lieber **III U4,** 60
raw material [ˌrɔ: mə'tɪəriəl] Rohstoff **III U2,** 30
R.E. (Religious Education) [ɑ:'r‿i:; rɪˌlɪdʒəs‿edʒʊ'keɪʃn] Religion *(Schulfach)* **II**
to **react** [ri'ækt] reagieren ⟨**III U3,** 53⟩
*to **read** [ri:d] lesen **I**
reading a story ['ri:dɪŋ ə 'stɔ:ri] eine Geschichte lesen **I**
to read to [ri:d 'tə] jmdm. vorlesen **I**

reader ['ri:də] Leser/-in **II**
ready ['redi] fertig, bereit **I**
to get ready [get 'redi] sich vorbereiten; sich fertig machen **III U2,** 32
real [rɪəl] echt, richtig, wirklich **II**
realistic [ˌrɪə'lɪstɪk] realistisch **III U5,** 77
really ['rɪəli] wirklich **II**
reason ['ri:zn] Grund **II**
to give reasons [gɪv 'ri:znz] Gründe nennen, Gründe angeben **II**
recently ['ri:sntli] kürzlich, vor kurzem, neulich; in letzter Zeit **III U4,** 59
recipe ['resɪpi] Rezept **I**
to **recommend** [ˌrekə'mend] empfehlen **III U6,** 96
record ['rekɔ:d] Schallplatte **II**; Rekord **III U1,** 13
red [red] rot **I**
referee [ˌrefr'i:] Schiedsrichter/-in **III U1,** 8
reflexive [rɪ'fleksɪv] reflexiv **III U3,** 45
region ['ri:dʒn] Region; Gegend **III U4,** 58
regional ['ri:dʒnl] regional **III U4,** 59
register ['redʒɪstə] Namensliste; Register **II**
to take the register [ˌteɪk ðə 'redʒɪstə] „Anwesenheitskontrolle" **II**
regular ['regjələ] regelmäßig; gleichmäßig **II**
rehearsal [rɪ'hɜ:sl] Probe **III U3,** 53
to **rehearse** [rɪ'hɜ:s] proben **III U3,** 53
reign [reɪn] Herrschaft **III U2,** 30
relative ['relətɪv] Verwandte/-r **III U4,** 60
relative clause [ˌrelətɪv 'klɔ:z] Relativsatz **III U1,** 13
relative pronoun [ˌrelətɪv 'prəʊnaʊn] Relativpronomen **III U1,** 13
to **relax** [rɪ'læks] (sich) entspannen, (sich) ausruhen; sich beruhigen **III U3,** 44
religious [rɪ'lɪdʒəs] religiös, gläubig **II**
to **remember** [rɪ'membə] sich erinnern (an); denken an **I**
to **remind (about)** [rɪ'maɪnd‿əˌbaʊt] erinnern (an) **II**
to **repeat** [rɪ'pi:t] wiederholen **I**
reply [rɪ'plaɪ] Antwort **III U4,** 65
to **reply** [rɪ'plaɪ] antworten, erwidern, entgegnen **III U2,** 33
report [rɪ'pɔ:t] Bericht **II**
to **report** [rɪ'pɔ:t] berichten, wiedergeben **III U6,** 94; ⟨**III U5,** 87⟩
reporting what someone said [rɪˌpɔ:tɪŋ wɒt sʌmwʌn 'sed] wiedergeben, was jemand gesagt hat **III U6,** 95

reporter [rɪ'pɔ:tə] Reporter/-in **II**
*to **reread** [ri:'ri:d] noch einmal lesen **III U5,** 78
to **rescue** ['reskju:] retten **III U5,** 87
research [ri:'sɜ:tʃ] Recherche; Forschung; Untersuchung **III U4,** 66
reservation [ˌrezə'veɪʃn] Reservierung **III U6,** 104
rest [rest] Rest **II**
restaurant ['restrɑ:ŋ] Restaurant, Gaststätte **I**
result [rɪ'zʌlt] Ergebnis, Resultat ⟨**III U5,** 87⟩
*to **retell** [ri:'tel] nacherzählen; nochmals erzählen **I**
return [rɪ'tɜ:n] Hin- und Rückfahrkarte **III U6,** 104
revision [rɪ'vɪʒn] Wiederholung **I**
Industrial **Revolution** [ɪnˌdʌstriəl revˈlu:ʃn] Industrielle Revolution **III U2,** 24
*to **rewrite** [ri:'raɪt] umschreiben; neu schreiben **III U5,** 85
rhyme [raɪm] Reim **I**
rhythm ['rɪðm] Rhythmus ⟨**III U6,** 103⟩
rich [rɪtʃ] reich **I**
*to get **rid of** [get 'rɪd‿əv] loswerden **III U3,** 47
*to **ride** [raɪd] reiten, fahren **I**
right [raɪt] rechte/-r/-s; rechts **I**; richtig **I**
Right? [raɪt] Stimmt's?/Nicht wahr? **III U6,** 100
on the right [ɒn ðə 'raɪt] auf der rechten Seite, rechts **I**
on your right/left [ɒn jə 'raɪt, 'left] rechts/links, auf der rechten/linken Seite **I**
to be right [bɪ 'raɪt] Recht haben **I**
to turn right [ˌtɜ:n 'raɪt] (nach) rechts abbiegen **I**
right away [raɪt‿ə'weɪ] sofort **II**
right now [raɪt 'naʊ] jetzt, sofort, gerade **I**
*to **ring** [rɪŋ] klingeln, läuten **I**
risk [rɪsk] Risiko **II**
to take a risk [ˌteɪk‿ə 'rɪsk] ein Risiko eingehen **II**
to **risk (sth)** [rɪsk] (etw.) riskieren **II**
river ['rɪvə] Fluss **I**
road [rəʊd] Straße **I**
rock [rɒk] Fels, Riff, Stein **I**
rock climbing ['rɒk ˌklaɪmɪŋ] Klettern **II**
to **rock** [rɒk] rocken ⟨**III U5,** 87⟩
rock and roll [ˌrɒk‿n‿'rəʊl] Rock 'n' Roll **II**
rocky ['rɒki] felsig, steinig **I**
role [rəʊl] Rolle **II**
role play ['rəʊl pleɪ] Rollenspiel **I**
Roman ['rəʊmən] Römer/-in; römisch **II**
roof [ru:f] Dach **III U5,** 87
room [ru:m] Zimmer, Raum **I**
changing room ['tʃeɪndʒɪŋ ru:m] Umkleidekabine **II**
living room ['lɪvɪŋ ru:m] Wohnzimmer **I**
from all **round the world** [frəm‿'ɔ:l ˌraʊnd ðə 'wɜ:ld] aus aller Welt **I**
round the garden [raʊnd ðə 'gɑ:dn] durch den ganzen Garten **I**
routine [ru:'ti:n] Routine **I**
to **row** [rəʊ] rudern **I**
rowing ['rəʊɪŋ] Rudern **III U1,** 13
royal ['rɔɪəl] königlich **II**
to **rub out** [rʌb‿'aʊt] wegreiben, ausradieren **II**
rubber ['rʌbə] Radiergummi **I**
rubber ball [ˌrʌbə 'bɔ:l] Gummiball **I**
rubbish ['rʌbɪʃ] Unsinn, Quatsch; Müll; Gerümpel **III U1,** 12
rude [ru:d] unhöflich; unverschämt **III U4,** 62
rugby ['rʌgbi] Rugby **III U1,** 9
to **ruin** ['ru:ɪn] zerstören, ruinieren **I**
rule [ru:l] Regel **I**
ruler ['ru:lə] Lineal **I**
*to **run** [rʌn] laufen, rennen **I**
to run after [rʌn‿'ɑ:ftə] hinterherrennen **I**
to run away [rʌn‿ə'weɪ] weglaufen **I**
Russian ['rʌʃn] russisch, aus Russland; Russisch **I**

S

sad [sæd] traurig **I**
safe [seɪf] sicher, ungefährlich **I**
safety ['seɪfti] Sicherheit **II**
to **sail** [seɪl] segeln **I**
salad ['sæləd] Salat **II**
the **same** [ðə 'seɪm] der-/die-/dasselbe, der/die/das Gleiche **I**
sand [sænd] Sand **I**
sand castle ['sænd ˌkɑ:sl] Sandburg **I**
sandwich ['sænwɪdʒ] Sandwich **I**
sandy ['sændi] sandig **I**
Saturday ['sætədeɪ] Samstag **I**
to **save** [seɪv] sparen **II**; retten **III U6,** 101
Saxon ['sæksn] Sachse, Sächsin; sächsisch **III U2,** 24
*to **say** [seɪ] sagen **I**
saying what you've got ['seɪɪŋ ˌwɒt jʊv 'gɒt] sagen, was jemand hat **I**
to say hello [seɪ hel'əʊ] jemanden begrüßen **I**
to say hello to [seɪ hel'əʊ tə] grüßen, Grüße ausrichten **I**
to **scan** [skæn] durchsuchen, abtasten **III U4,** 66
scanning ['skænɪŋ] Durchsuchen nach Details; Abtasten **III U4,** 66
scared [skeəd] verängstigt **I**
to be scared for [bi 'skeəd fə] Angst haben um **I**
scarf pl. **scarves** [skɑ:f; skɑ:vz] Schal, Tuch **I**
scary ['skeəri] beängstigend, unheimlich **I**
scene [si:n] Szene **III U3,** 42
scented ['sentɪd] duftend ⟨**III U4,** 65⟩
school [sku:l] Schule **I**
boarding school ['bɔ:dɪŋ ˌsku:l] Internat **II**
grammar school ['græmə ˌsku:l] Gymnasium **II**
primary school ['praɪmri ˌsku:l] Grundschule **I**
school day ['sku:l deɪ] Schultag **I**
schools officer ['sku:lz ˌɒfɪsə] *(hier:)* Beauftragte/-r für Schulklassen **I**
school things *(pl.)* ['sku:l ˌθɪŋz] Schulsachen *(pl.)* **I**
to be late for school [bi ˌleɪt fə 'sku:l] zu spät zur Schule kommen **I**
schoolbag ['sku:lbæg] Schultasche **I**
science ['saɪəns] (Natur-)Wissenschaft **II**
science fiction [ˌsaɪəns 'fɪkʃn] Sciencefiction **II**
scientist ['saɪəntɪst] Wissenschaftler/-in **III U1,** 13
to **score** [skɔ:] punkten; ein Tor schießen **II**
Scot [skɒt] Schotte, Schottin **II**
Scottish ['skɒtɪʃ] schottisch **II**
scream [skri:m] Schrei **III U6,** 102
to **scream** [skri:m] schreien, kreischen **III U6,** 102
script [skrɪpt] Drehbuch, Skript **III U5,** 78
sea [si:] Meer, die See **I**
North Sea [ˌnɔ:θ 'si:] Nordsee **I**
search engine ['sɜ:tʃ ˌendʒɪn] Suchmaschine **III U4,** 68; ⟨**III P1,** 23⟩
seaside ['si:saɪd] (Meeres)küste **I**
seaside town [ˌsi:saɪd 'taʊn] Küstenstadt **I**
season ['si:zn] Jahreszeit; Saison **I**
seat [si:t] Sitz, Sitzplatz **III U6,** 101
second ['seknd] Sekunde **I**
second language ['seknd ˌlæŋgwɪdʒ] Zweitsprache **III U6,** 100
secret ['si:krət] Geheimnis **II**
secret ['si:krət] geheim **III U3,** 49

*to **see** [si:] sehen **I**
a must-see [ə ˌmʌst 'si:] ... muss man gesehen haben **III U4,** 66
I see. [aɪ 'si:] Ich verstehe./Aha! **III U3,** 46
See you later. [si: jə 'leɪtə] Bis später. **II**
See you there. [si: jə 'ðeə] Wir sehen uns dort. **I**
to **seem** [si:m] scheinen **III U4,** 63
self-catering [ˌself'keɪtrɪŋ] Selbstversorger- **III U6,** 104
self-pronoun ['self ˌprəʊnaʊn] Reflexivpronomen **III U3,** 44
selfish ['selfɪʃ] selbstsüchtig **III U3,** 43
*to **sell** [sel] verkaufen **I**
*to **send** [send] schicken **II**
sixth **sense** [ˌsɪksθ 'sens] sechster Sinn **III U2,** 34
sentence ['sentəns] Satz **I**
September [sep'tembə] September **I**
servant ['sɜ:vnt] Bedienstete/-r; Diener/-in **III U2,** 33
service ['sɜ:vɪs] Service, Dienst; Verbindung *(Zug, Bus)* **III U6,** 97
seven ['sevn] sieben **I**
seventeen [ˌsevn'ti:n] siebzehn **I**
seventy ['sevnti] siebzig **I**
s-genitive [es'dʒenɪtɪv] s-Genitiv **I**
*to **shake** [ʃeɪk] zittern, beben **II**; schütteln **II**
Shall I . . . ? [ʃæl͜ aɪ] Soll ich ... ? **II**
to **share** [ʃeə] teilen **II**
shark [ʃɑ:k] Hai **II**
she [ʃi:] sie **I**
shed [ʃed] Stall **I**; Schuppen, Gartenhäuschen **I**
sheep pl. **sheep** [ʃi:p] Schaf **I**
shelf pl. **shelves** [ʃelf; ʃelvz] Regal, Regalbrett **I**
*to **shine** [ʃaɪn] scheinen; glänzen **III U2,** 33
shiny ['ʃaɪni] glänzend ⟨**III U3,** 54⟩
ship [ʃɪp] Schiff **I**
shock [ʃɒk] Schock, Schreck **I**
*to be **shocked** [bi: 'ʃɒkt] geschockt sein **II**
shoe [ʃu:] Schuh **I**
*to **shoot** [ʃu:t] schießen **III U6,** 102
shop [ʃɒp] Geschäft, Laden **I**
computer shop [kəm'pju:tə ˌʃɒp] Computergeschäft **I**
shop assistant ['ʃɒp͜ əˌsɪstnt] Verkäufer/-in **II**
sports shop ['spɔ:ts ˌʃɒp] Sportgeschäft **I**
shopping ['ʃɒpɪŋ] Einkaufen **I**
shopping list ['ʃɒpɪŋ ˌlɪst] Einkaufszettel **II**
to do the shopping [ˌdu: ðə 'ʃɒpɪŋ] Einkäufe machen, Besorgungen machen **II**
to go shopping [gəʊ 'ʃɒpɪŋ] einkaufen gehen **I**
short [ʃɔ:t] kurz **I**; klein **II**
shot [ʃɒt] Schuss, Schlag **II**
should [ʃʊd] sollte/-est/-en/-et **I**
shoulder ['ʃəʊldə] Schulter **II**
shout [ʃaʊt] Schrei, Ruf **III U1,** 20
to **shout** [ʃaʊt] rufen, schreien **I**
show [ʃəʊ] Show, Schau, Aufführung **III U5,** 80
game show ['geɪm ˌʃəʊ] Spielshow **II**
*to **show** [ʃəʊ] zeigen **I**
to **shuffle** ['ʃʌfl] mischen **I**
Shut up! [ʃʌt͜ 'ʌp] Halt die Klappe! **III U3,** 51
shuttle ['ʃʌtl] Pendelzug **II**
shy [ʃaɪ] schüchtern **II**
sick [sɪk] schlecht, übel; krank **II**
side [saɪd] Seite **III U6,** 102
sides [saɪdz] Skript beim Casting **III U5,** 78
sights *(pl.)* [saɪts] Sehenswürdigkeiten **I**
sightseeing ['saɪtsi:ɪŋ] Besichtigungstour **II**
sign [saɪn] Schild, Zeichen **II**
to **sign** [saɪn] unterschreiben **III U5,** 78
signal ['sɪgnl] Zeichen, Signal **I**
silly ['sɪli] Dummkopf **I**
silly ['sɪli] albern, dumm **I**
silver ['sɪlvə] Silber ⟨**III U3,** 54⟩
silver ['sɪlvə] silbern ⟨**III U1,** 18⟩
simple ['sɪmpl] einfach, simpel **II**
*to **sing** [sɪŋ] singen **I**
singer ['sɪŋə] Sänger/-in **II**
singing lessons ['sɪŋɪŋ ˌlesnz] Gesangsunterricht, Gesangsstunden **II**
single ['sɪŋgl] Single *(CD)* **II**; einfache Fahrkarte **III U6,** 104
third person **singular** [θɜ:d ˌpɜ:sn 'sɪŋgjələ] dritte Person Singular (Einzahl) **I**
*to **sink** [sɪŋk] untergehen, sinken **I**
Sioux pl. **Sioux** [su:, su:z] Sioux-Indianer **III U6,** 102
Sir [sɜ:] Sir *(Anrede für einen Ritter)* **II**
sister ['sɪstə] Schwester **I**
*to **sit** [sɪt] sitzen **I**
to sit down [sɪt 'daʊn] sich hinsetzen **I**
situation [ˌsɪtju'eɪʃn] Situation **III U1,** 11
six [sɪks] sechs **I**
sixteen [ˌsɪk'sti:n] sechzehn **I**
sixty ['sɪksti] sechzig **I**
size [saɪz] Größe **I**
skateboard ['skeɪtbɔ:d] Skateboard **I**
skateboarding ['skeɪtbɔ:dɪŋ] Skateboardfahren **III U1,** 9
skater ['skeɪtə] Skater/-in **III U5,** 88
in-line **skating** [ˌɪnlaɪn 'skeɪtɪŋ] Inlineskates fahren **II**
ski [ski:] Ski **III U1,** 16
ski jump ['ski: dʒʌmp] Skispringen **III U1,** 16
ski jumper ['ski: ˌdʒʌmpə] Skispringer **III U1,** 16
skill [skɪl] Fertigkeit **I**
communication skills [kəˌmju:nɪ'keɪʃn ˌskɪlz] Sprechfertigkeiten, Kommunikationsfertigkeiten **I**
to **skim** [skɪm] überfliegen **III U4,** 66
skimming ['skɪmɪŋ] Überfliegen **III U4,** 66
skin [skɪn] Haut; Fell **III U6,** 101
to jump out of one's skin [ˌdʒʌmp͜ aʊt͜ əv wʌnz 'skɪn] sich zu Tode erschrecken **III U6,** 101
skirt [skɜ:t] Rock **II**
sky [skaɪ] Himmel **II**
sleep [sli:p] Schlaf **III U1,** 20
*to **sleep** [sli:p] schlafen **I**
*to **slide** [slaɪd] gleiten; rutschen **III U1,** 17
to **slow down** [sləʊ 'daʊn] langsamer werden **III U6,** 101
slow [sləʊ] langsam **I**
slum [slʌm] Slum, Elendsviertel **III U2,** 30
small [smɔ:l] klein **I**
small talk ['smɔ:l ˌtɔ:k] Smalltalk **III U6,** 100
smell [smel] Geruch, Duft, Gestank **I**
*to **smell** [smel] riechen; duften **III U4,** 63
to **smile** [smaɪl] lächeln **I**
to smile at ['smaɪl͜ ət] anlächeln **II**
smoke [sməʊk] Rauch **I**
to **smoke** [sməʊk] rauchen **II**
smooth [smu:θ] glatt **III U5,** 82
snack bar ['snæk bɑ:] Café **II**
snow [snəʊ] Schnee **III U1,** 13
to **snow** [snəʊ] schneien **III U1,** 20
so [səʊ] so **I**
so far ['səʊ fɑ:] bis jetzt **II**
so [səʊ] also, folglich, deshalb **I**
soap *(no pl.)* [səʊp] Seife **III U5,** 77
soap (opera) ['səʊp ˌɒprə] Seifenoper, Soap **III U5,** 77
soccer ['sɒkə] Fußball **III U5,** 82
social ['səʊʃl] sozial, Gesellschaft- **II**
sofa ['səʊfə] Sofa, Couch **I**
soldier ['səʊldʒə] Soldat/-in **II**
some [sʌm] einige, ein paar; etwas **I**
somebody ['sʌmbədi] jemand **II**
someone ['sʌmwʌn] jemand **II**

something ['sʌmθɪŋ] etwas **II**
sometimes ['sʌmtaɪmz] manchmal **I**
somewhere ['sʌmweə] irgendwo **II**
son [sʌn] Sohn **II**
song [sɒŋ] Lied, Song **I**
soon [su:n] bald **I**
as soon as [əz 'su:n‿əz] sobald **II**
I'm **sorry.** [aɪm 'sɒrɪ] Es tut mir leid. **I**
Sorry I'm late. [ˌsɒri‿aɪm 'leɪt] Tut mir leid, dass ich zu spät komme. **I**
to feel sorry for [fi:l 'sɒri] Mitleid haben mit; bedauern **III U3,** 46
to **sort** [sɔ:t] sortieren **I**
to sort out [sɔ:t 'aʊt] klären, regeln **I**
sound [saʊnd] Geräusch **I**; Laut **I**
to **sound** [saʊnd] klingen **III U4,** 63; ⟨**III U3,** 54⟩
south [saʊθ] Süden **I**
southbound ['saʊθbaʊnd] in Richtung Süden **II**
souvenir [ˌsu:vn'ɪə] Andenken, Souvenir **I**
space [speɪs] Weltraum ⟨**III U5,** 87⟩
spaghetti [spə'geti] Spaghetti **I**
Spanish ['spænɪʃ] spanisch, aus Spanien; Spanisch **I**
*to **speak (to)** [spi:k tə] sprechen (mit) **I**
speaker ['spi:kə] Sprecher/-in **II**
special ['speʃl] besondere/-r/-s **I**
direct **speech** [ˌdɪrekt 'spi:tʃ] direkte Rede **III U6,** 94
indirect speech [ˌɪndɪrekt 'spi:tʃ] indirekte Rede **III U6,** 94
to **spell** [spel] buchstabieren **I**
speller ['spelə] jemand, der gut/schlecht in Rechtschreibung ist **II**
spelling ['spelɪŋ] Rechtschreibung **II**
*to **spend** [spend] verbringen *(Urlaub, Zeit etc.)* **I**
to spend (on) [spend] ausgeben (für) **II**
spider ['spaɪdə] Spinne **II**
spinach *(no pl.)* ['spɪnɪtʃ] Spinat **III U5,** 86
*to **split up** [splɪt‿'ʌp] sich trennen **III U3,** 43
spoon [spu:n] Löffel **II**
sport [spɔ:t] Sport, Sportart **I**
sports shop ['spɔ:ts ˌʃɒp] Sportgeschäft **I**
spring [sprɪŋ] Frühling **I**
Brussels **sprout** [ˌbrʌslz 'spraʊt] Rosenkohl **III U3,** 43
Sssh! [ʃ] Psst! **I**
stage [steɪdʒ] Bühne **III U2,** 26
on stage [ɒn 'steɪdʒ] auf der Bühne **II**
stamp [stæmp] Briefmarke **II**
*to **stand** [stænd] stehen **I**; ertragen, ausstehen **III U3,** 44
Stand clear of the doors. [ˌstænd klɪə‿əv ðə 'dɔ:z] Zurückbleiben, bitte. **II**
star [stɑ:] Star **I**
pop star ['pɒp stɑ:] Popstar **I**
to **start** [stɑ:t] anfangen, beginnen **I**
station ['steɪʃn] Station, Bahnhof **I**
radio station ['reɪdiəʊ ˌsteɪʃn] Radiosender **I**
to **stay** [steɪ] bleiben **II**
*to **steal** [sti:l] stehlen **II**
steam engine ['sti:m ˌendʒɪn] Dampfmaschine **III U2,** 24
steel [sti:l] Stahl **III U2,** 25
step [step] Schritt, Stufe **III U6,** 93
step-father ['stepˌfɑ:ðə] Stiefvater **I**
stewardess ['stju:ədɪs] Stewardess **III U6,** 101
stick [stɪk] Stock, Schläger **III U1,** 8
*to **stick up one's nose** [ˌstɪk‿ʌp wʌnz 'nəʊz] die Nase rümpfen ⟨**III U5,** 87⟩
still [stɪl] noch, immer noch **I**
*to **stink** [stɪŋk] stinken **I**
stomach ['stʌmək] Magen, Bauch **II**
stop [stɒp] Haltestelle **II**
to **stop** [stɒp] aufhören, beenden **I**
department **store** [dɪ'pɑ:tmənt ˌstɔ:] Kaufhaus **I**
storm [stɔ:m] Sturm, Unwetter, Gewitter **I**
stormy ['stɔ:mi] stürmisch **I**
story ['stɔ:ri] Geschichte, Erzählung **I**
straight [streɪt] gerade(aus); direkt **I**
straight on [streɪt‿'ɒn] geradeaus **I**
strange [streɪndʒ] merkwürdig, seltsam; fremd **III U2,** 34
street [stri:t] Straße **I**
in the street [ɪn ðə 'stri:t] auf der Straße **I**
stress [stres] Betonung **III U2,** 36
to **stress** [stres] betonen, hervorheben **III U2,** 36
strict [strɪkt] streng **II**
strong [strɒŋ] stark, kräftig **I**
student ['stju:dnt] Schüler/-in, Student/-in **II**
studio ['stju:diəʊ] Studio **III U5,** 77
style [staɪl] Stil **II**
subject ['sʌbdʒɪkt] Subjekt, Satzgegenstand **I**; Schulfach; Thema **II**
success [sək'ses] Erfolg **II**
such [sʌtʃ] solche/-r/-s **III U2,** 34
suddenly ['sʌdnli] plötzlich, auf einmal **I**
sugar ['ʃʊgə] Zucker **I**
to **suggest** [sə'dʒest] vorschlagen **III U2,** 29
suggestion [sə'dʒestʃn] Vorschlag **III U2,** 29
suit [su:t] Anzug; Kostüm **II**
summer ['sʌmə] Sommer **I**
sun [sʌn] Sonne **I**
Sunday ['sʌndeɪ] Sonntag **I**
sunglasses *(pl.)* ['sʌnˌglɑ:sɪz] Sonnenbrille **I**
sunny ['sʌni] sonnig **II**
super ['su:pə] super **III U5,** 78
superlative [su:'pɜ:lətɪv] Superlativ **II**
supermarket ['su:pəˌmɑ:kɪt] Supermarkt **II**
sure [ʃɔ:; ʃʊə] sicher **I**
to **surf** [sɜ:f] (wind)surfen **I**
to go surfing [gəʊ 'sɜ:fɪŋ] surfen gehen **I**
to surf on the Internet [ˌsɜ:f‿ɒn ði‿'ɪntənet] im Internet surfen **I**
surprise [sə'praɪz] Überraschung **I**
to **surprise** [sə'praɪz] überraschen **III U1,** 20
survey ['sɜ:veɪ] Umfrage; Studie ⟨**III U5,** 87⟩
to **survive** [sə'vaɪv] überleben **I**
sweat [swet] Schweiß **III U1,** 14
sweatshirt ['swetʃɜ:t] Sweatshirt **I**
sweet [swi:t] süß **I**
sweets *(pl.)* [swi:ts] Süßigkeiten **I**
sweet shop ['swi:t ˌʃɒp] Süßwarenladen **I**
*to **swim** [swɪm] schwimmen **I**
to go swimming [gəʊ 'swɪmɪŋ] schwimmen gehen **I**
swimmer ['swɪmə] Schwimmer/-in **II**
swimming ['swɪmɪŋ] Schwimmen **III U1,** 13
swimming pool ['swɪmɪŋ ˌpu:l] Schwimmbad, Schwimmbecken **I**
swimsuit ['swɪmsu:t] Badeanzug **I**

T

table ['teɪbl] Tisch **I**
to clear the table [ˌklɪə ðə 'teɪbl] den Tisch abräumen **II**
to lay the table [ˌleɪ ðə 'teɪbl] den Tisch decken **II**
tablet ['tæblət] Tablette **II**
question **tag** ['kwestʃən ˌtæg] Frageanhängsel, Bestätigungsfrage **II**
to **tag along** ['tæg ə'lɒŋ] hinterherlaufen, hinterhertrotten ⟨**III U5,** 87⟩
*to **take** [teɪk] (weg)nehmen **I**; (mit)nehmen; bringen **I**; dauern, (Zeit) brauchen **III U6,** 93
Take your time. [ˌteɪk jɔ: 'taɪm] Lass dir Zeit. **III U4,** 62

to take a call [ˌteɪk͜ə ˈkɔːl] (Telefon) abheben, einen Anruf entgegennehmen **III U3,** 50
to take a photo [ˌteɪk͜ə ˈfəʊtəʊ] ein Foto machen **I**
to take a risk [ˌteɪk͜ə ˈrɪsk] ein Risiko eingehen **II**
to take notes [teɪk ˈnəʊts] sich Notizen machen **I**
to take off [teɪk͜ˈɒf] abnehmen, ausziehen, herunternehmen **I**; abheben **II**
to take out [teɪk͜ˈaʊt] ausführen **I**
to take the chance [ˌteɪk ðə ˈtʃɑːns] die Gelegenheit nutzen **III U6,** 102
to take the register [ˌteɪk ðə ˈredʒɪstə] „Anwesenheitskontrolle" **II**
to take turns [teɪk ˈtɜːnz] sich abwechseln **I**
talk [tɔːk] Gespräch, Unterhaltung; Unterredung **III U3,** 52
small talk [ˈsmɔːl ˌtɔːk] Smalltalk **III U6,** 100
to **talk** [tɔːk] sprechen, reden **I**
to talk about [tɔːk əˈbaʊt] sprechen über **I**
to talk to [tɔːk tə] sprechen mit, reden mit **I**
talkwise [ˈtɔːkwaɪz] „redegewandt" **III U1,** 12
tall [tɔːl] groß; hoch **II**
taste [teɪst] Geschmack **III U4,** 60
to **taste** [teɪst] schmecken **III U4,** 63
tasty [ˈteɪsti] lecker **I**
taxi [ˈtæksi] Taxi **I**
tea [tiː] Tee **I**; (frühes) Abendessen **III U4,** 60
*to **teach** [tiːtʃ] unterrichten, lehren, beibringen **I**
teacher [ˈtiːtʃə] Lehrer, Lehrerin **I**
German teacher [ˈdʒɜːmən ˌtiːtʃə] Deutschlehrer/-in **I**
team [tiːm] Team, Gruppe **I**
technology [tekˈnɒlədʒi] Technologie; Computerunterricht **II**
high-tech [ˈhaɪtek] hoch technisiert **II**
teenager [ˈtiːneɪdʒə] Teenager; Jugendliche/-r **II**
telegram [ˈtelɪɡræm] Telegramm **III U2,** 34
telephone [ˈtelɪfəʊn] Telefon **III U3,** 43
*to **tell** [tel] erzählen, sagen **I**
to tell a lie [ˌtel͜ə ˈlaɪ] lügen **III U3,** 43
to tell the time [ˌtel ðə ˈtaɪm] die Uhr lesen **I**
temperature [ˈtemprətʃə] Fieber; Temperatur **II**
ten [ten] zehn **I**
tennis [ˈtenɪs] Tennis **III U1,** 9
tense [tens] Zeit, Zeitform (*grammatisch*) **II**
terminal [ˈtɜːmɪnl] Terminal **II**
terrible [ˈterəbl] schrecklich, schlimm, furchtbar **I**
territory [ˈterɪtri] Gebiet, Revier, Territorium **I**
test [test] Test, Prüfung **I**
to **test** [test] testen, prüfen **II**
text [tekst] Text **I**; SMS **II**
factual text [ˌfæktʃʊəl ˈtekst] Sachtext **III U4,** 66
to **text** [tekst] eine SMS schicken **I**
than [ðæn; ðən] als **II**
thank you [ˈθæŋk ju] danke **I**
thanks [θæŋks] danke **I**
thanks a lot [ˌθæŋks͜ə ˈlɒt] vielen Dank **I**
thanks to [ˈθæŋks tə] dank (dir/Ihnen), wegen **I**
that *(Betonung)* [ðæt] so **II**
that [ðæt; ðət] dass **I**
that [ðæt] das; jenes **I**
that day [ðæt ˈdeɪ] an jenem Tag **I**
That was lucky! [ˌðæt wəz ˈlʌki] Glück gehabt! **III U1,** 19
that [ðæt; ðət] die *(Relativpronomen)* **I**; der, dem, den, die, das *(Relativpronomen)* **III U1,** 13
the [ðə; ði] der, die (*auch pl.*), das **I**
the ... the ... [ðə ... ðə] je ... desto ... **II**
the six/... of us [ðə ˈsɪks͜əv͜əs] uns sechs/... **II**
theatre [ˈθɪətə] Theater **II**
their [ðeə] ihr, ihre *(Plural)* **I**
them [ðem; ðəm] sie **I**
theme [θiːm] Thema; Motto **II**
theme park [ˈθiːm pɑːk] Themenpark **II**
themselves [ðəmˈselvz] sie/sich (selbst); selber **III U3,** 44
then [ðen] dann, danach **I**; damals ⟨**III U6,** 103⟩
there [ðeə] da, dort **I**; dorthin, dahin **I**
over there [ˌəʊvə ˈðeə] (nach) dort drüben **I**
There she is. [ˈðeə ʃi͜ɪz] Da ist sie ja. **I**
You've got me there! [jʊv ˌɡɒt mi ˈðeə] Da habt ihr mich kalt erwischt! **I**
these [ðiːz] diese (hier) **I**
they [ðeɪ] sie **I**
thief pl. **thieves** [θiːf; θiːvz] Dieb, Diebin **I**
thin [θɪn] dünn **II**
to end in thin air [end͜ɪn θɪn͜ˈeə] im Nichts enden **II**
thing [θɪŋ] Ding, Sache **I**
school things *(pl.)* [ˈskuːl ˌθɪŋz] Schulsachen *(pl.)* **I**
*to **think** [θɪŋk] finden, glauben, (nach)denken **I**
to think about [θɪŋk͜əˈbaʊt] halten von, denken über **I**
to think of [ˈθɪŋk͜əv] (sich) ausdenken, sich etwas einfallen lassen **I**; halten von, denken über **I**
third [θɜːd] dritte/-r/-s **I**
the third of March [ðə ˌθɜːd͜əv ˈmɑːtʃ] der dritte März **I**
thirteen [θɜːˈtiːn] dreizehn **I**
thirty [ˈθɜːti] dreißig **I**
this [ðɪs] diese/-r/-s **I**
like this [laɪk ˈðɪs] so, auf diese Weise **I**
this is ... [ˈðɪs͜ɪz] hier ist ... *(am Telefon)* **I**
this morning [ðɪs ˈmɔːnɪŋ] heute Morgen **I**
those [ðəʊz] diese (dort), jene **I**
a/one **thousand** [ə ˈθaʊznd; wʌnˈθaʊznd] eintausend **I**
three [θriː] drei **I**
thriller [ˈθrɪlə] Thriller; spannender Krimi; Schauergeschichte **III U6,** 96
throne [θrəʊn] Thron **III U2,** 30
through [θruː] durch **II**
*to **throw** [θrəʊ] werfen **I**
thunderstorm [ˈθʌndəstɔːm] Gewitter **II**
Thursday [ˈθɜːzdeɪ] Donnerstag **I**
ticket [ˈtɪkɪt] Ticket, Fahrschein; Eintrittskarte **II**
ticket gate [ˈtɪkɪt ˌɡeɪt] Fahrkartenschranke **II**
to **tidy (up)** [taɪdi ˈʌp] aufräumen, in Ordnung bringen **III U3,** 43
to **tie** [taɪ] binden, zubinden **III U5,** 87
tiger [ˈtaɪɡə] Tiger **I**
tight [taɪt] fest, eng **III U5,** 87
time [taɪm] Zeit **I**; Mal **II**
all the time [ˌɔːl ðə taɪm] die ganze Zeit **II**
at the same time [ət ðə ˌseɪm ˈtaɪm] zur selben Zeit, gleichzeitig **I**
from time to time [frəm ˌtaɪm tə ˈtaɪm] von Zeit zu Zeit **I**
It's time to go home. [ɪts ˌtaɪm tə ɡəʊ ˈhəʊm] Es ist Zeit, nach Hause zu gehen. **I**
on time [ɒn ˈtaɪm] pünktlich **III U6,** 102
Once upon a time ... [ˈwʌns͜əˌpɒn͜ə ˈtaɪm] Es war einmal ... **III U2,** 24
Take your time. [ˌteɪk jɔː ˈtaɪm] Lass dir Zeit. **III U4,** 62
time line [ˈtaɪm laɪn] Zeitstrahl **II**

to tell the time [ˌtel ðə 'taɪm] die Uhr lesen **I**
What time is it, please? [wɒt 'taɪm‿ɪz‿ɪt ˌpli:z] Wie spät ist es, bitte? **I**
timebox ['taɪmbɒks] Zeitmaschine **II**
timetable ['taɪmteɪbl] Stundenplan; Fahrplan **II**
tin [tɪn] Dose, Büchse **I**
tiny ['taɪni] klein, winzig **I**
tip [tɪp] Tipp, Ratschlag **I**
tired ['taɪəd] müde **I**
dog-tired [dɒg'taɪəd] hundemüde **I**
to get tired of [get 'taɪəd‿əv] etwas satt bekommen **III U4,** 67
title ['taɪtl] Titel **I**
to [tu:; tʊ; tə] nach, zu, in **I**; an **I**; vor *(bei Uhrzeitangaben)* **I**
toast [təʊst] Toast **II**
today [tə'deɪ] heute **I**
toe [təʊ] Zeh **II**
together [tə'geðə] zusammen; gemeinsam **I**
toilet ['tɔɪlət] Toilette **I**
tomorrow [tə'mɒrəʊ] morgen **II**
tone [təʊn] (Signal)ton **III U3,** 50
tongue [tʌŋ] Zunge **II**
mother tongue ['mʌðə tʌŋ] Muttersprache **II**
too [tu:] auch **I**; zu **I**
too much [tu: 'mʌtʃ] zu viel **I**
tooth pl. **teeth** [tu:θ; ti:θ] Zahn **I**
to brush one's teeth [brʌʃ wʌnz 'ti:θ] (seine) Zähne putzen **III U3,** 43
top [tɒp] oberes Ende, Spitze **I**; Top **II**
on the top [ɒn ðə 'tɒp] oben **I**
on top of [ɒn 'tɒp‿əv] auf ... hinauf, oben (auf) **I**
top 10 [ˌtɒp 'ten] Top 10, die besten Zehn **I**
topic ['tɒpɪk] Thema **III U4,** 66
top-up card ['tɒp‿ʌp kɑ:d] Aufladekarte *(fürs Handy)* **II**
tour [tʊə] Reise, Tour, Rundgang **I**
to give tours [gɪv 'tʊəz] Stadtrundfahrten leiten **I**
tourist ['tʊərɪst] Tourist, Touristin **I**
tower ['taʊə] Turm **III U2,** 31
town [taʊn] Stadt **I**
seaside town [ˌsi:saɪd 'taʊn] Küstenstadt **I**
toy [tɔɪ] Spielzeug **II**
track [træk] Bahn, Laufbahn; Weg **III U1,** 9; Gleis; Spur **III U6,** 101
tradition [trə'dɪʃn] Tradition **III U1,** 16
traffic ['træfɪk] Verkehr **II**
train [treɪn] Zug **I**
on a train [ɒn‿ə 'treɪn] im Zug **I**
to **train** [treɪn] trainieren **II**
trainer ['treɪnə] Trainer/-in **II**
trainers ['treɪnəz] Turnschuhe **II**
training ['treɪnɪŋ] Training, Ausbildung **II**
translate [trænz'leit] übersetzen **III U3,** 47
transport *(no pl.)* ['trænspɔ:t] Verkehrsmittel, Beförderung **I**
*to be **trapped** [bi: 'træpt] in der Falle sitzen **III U6,** 99
travel agency ['trævl ˌeɪdʒnsi] Reisebüro **III U6,** 104
Tube travel ['tju:b ˌtrævl] U-Bahn-Fahren **II**
to **travel** ['trævl] reisen, fahren **II**
travelcard ['trævlkɑ:d] Netzkarte **II**
traveller ['trævlə] Reisende/-r **III U6,** 93
travelling ['trævlɪŋ] (das) Reisen **II**
treasure ['treʒə] Schatz **I**
treasure map ['treʒə ˌmæp] Schatzkarte **I**
tree [tri:] Baum **I**
trendy ['trendi] trendy **III U4,** 60
trick [trɪk] Trick, Kunststück **I**
card trick ['kɑ:d ˌtrɪk] Kartenkunststück **I**
to play a trick on [ˌpleɪ‿ə 'trɪk‿ɒn] einen Streich spielen **II**
trip [trɪp] Reise, Fahrt, Ausflug **I**
class trip [ˌklɑ:s 'trɪp] Klassenfahrt, Klassenausflug **I**
trouble ['trʌbl] Ärger **I**
to get into trouble [ˌget‿ɪntə 'trʌbl] in Schwierigkeiten geraten **II**
trousers *(pl.)* ['traʊzəz] Hose **II**
true [tru:] wahr **II**
to **try** [traɪ] versuchen, probieren **II**
to try hard [traɪ 'hɑ:d] sich anstrengen **II**
to try on [traɪ‿'ɒn] anprobieren **I**
to try out [traɪ‿'aʊt] ausprobieren **III U4,** 69
T-shirt ['ti:ʃɜ:t] T-Shirt **I**
tube [tju:b] Tube **III U5,** 82
Tube [tju:b] U-Bahn **II**
Tube travel ['tju:b ˌtrævl] U-Bahn-Fahren **II**
Tuesday ['tju:zdeɪ] Dienstag **I**
tunnel ['tʌnl] Tunnel **I**
Turkish ['tɜ:kɪʃ] türkisch, aus der Türkei; Türkisch **I**
*to take **turns** [teɪk 'tɜ:nz] sich abwechseln **I**
Your turn. ['jɔ: tɜ:n] Du bist dran. **I**
to **turn** [tɜ:n] einbiegen, abbiegen **I**
to turn down [tɜ:n 'daʊn] abweisen ⟨**III U5,** 87⟩
to turn into [tɜ:n‿'ɪntə] (sich) verwandeln in; werden **III U3,** 47
to turn off [tɜ:n‿'ɒf] abschalten, ausschalten **III U3,** 45
to turn right [ˌtɜ:n 'raɪt] (nach) rechts abbiegen **I**
tutor ['tju:tə] Klassenlehrer, Klassenlehrerin **I**
tutor group ['tju:tə gru:p] Klasse *(in einer englischen Schule)* **I**
tutorial [tju:'tɔ:riəl] Tutorium **II**
TV [ˌti:'vi:] Fernseher **I**
on TV [ɒn ˌti:'vi:] im Fernsehen **I**
twelve [twelv] zwölf **I**
twenty ['twenti] zwanzig **I**
twenty-one [ˌtwenti'wʌn] einundzwanzig **I**
twin [twɪn] Zwilling, Zwillings- **III U3,** 43
two [tu:] zwei **I**
type [taɪp] Typ, Art, Sorte **III U3,** 47

U

ugh [ʊh] i, igitt **I**
uh [ə] äh **I**
um [əm] ähm **III U6,** 100
umpire ['ʌmpaɪə] Schiedsrichter/-in **III U1,** 9
uncle ['ʌŋkl] Onkel **I**
under ['ʌndə] unter **I**
Underground ['ʌndəgraʊnd] U-Bahn **I**
to **underline** [ˌʌndə'laɪn] unterstreichen **I**
*to **understand** [ˌʌndə'stænd] verstehen **II**
uniform ['ju:nɪfɔ:m] Uniform **II**
European **Union** [jʊərəˌpi:ən 'ju:njən] Europäische Union **III U2,** 25
unit ['ju:nɪt] Lektion, Kapitel, Einheit **I**
universal [ju:nɪ'vɜ:sl] allgemein, universell **II**
universe ['ju:nɪvɜ:s] Universum **II**
*to be **unlucky** [ˌbi: ʌn'lʌki] Pech haben **III U1,** 19
until [ʌn'tɪl] bis **II**
not until [nɒt ʌn'tɪl] erst (dann), wenn **III U1,** 10
unusual [ʌn'ju:ʒl] ungewöhnlich **III U1,** 13
What's up? [wɒts‿'ʌp] Was ist los? **I**
*to come **up to** [kʌm‿'ʌp tə] zukommen auf **II**
up North [ʌp 'nɔ:θ] im Norden **III U4,** 63
upstairs [ʌp'steəz] oben, im Obergeschoss **I**
UR (= you are) [ju: 'ɑ:] du bist *(Abkürzung in SMS oder E-Mail)* **III U3,** 43

us [ʌs; əs] uns **I**
to **use** [ju:z] benutzen, verwenden, gebrauchen **I**
to get used to (sth) [get‿'ju:zd tə] sich an (etwas) gewöhnen **II**
using the present progressive ['ju:zɪŋ ðə ˌpreznt prə'gresɪv] das *present progressive* benutzen **I**
useful ['ju:sfl] nützlich, hilfreich **I**
user name ['ju:zəˌneɪm] Benutzername ⟨**III P1,** 23⟩
usually ['ju:ʒli] gewöhnlich, normalerweise **I**

V

van [væn] Lieferwagen, Transporter **III U1,** 16
vegetable ['vedʒtəbl] Gemüse **II**
vegetarian [ˌvedʒɪ'teəriən] Vegetarier/-in **III U3,** 43
verb [vɜ:b] Verb, Zeitwort **I**
very ['veri] sehr **I**
vet [vet] Tierarzt, Tierärztin **I**
Victorian [vɪk'tɔ:riən] viktorianisch; Viktorianer/-in **III U2,** 30
video ['vɪdiəʊ] Video **I**
view [vju:] Aussicht, (Aus)blick, Sicht **II**
village ['vɪlɪdʒ] Dorf **I**
vineyard ['vɪnjəd] Weinberg ⟨**III U6,** 103⟩
violence *(no pl.)* ['vaɪəlns] Gewalt **III U5,** 77
violent ['vaɪəlnt] gewalttätig **III U5,** 85
vision ['vɪʒn] Vision **III U2,** 34
to **visit** ['vɪzɪt] besuchen **I**
visitor ['vɪzɪtə] Besucher/-in **I**
vocabulary [və'kæbjəlri] Vokabular, Wortschatz **I**
voice [vɔɪs] Stimme **II**
male voice choir [ˌmeɪl vɔɪs 'kwaɪə] Männerchor **III U4,** 59
voice mail ['vɔɪs meɪl] Voicemail; Mailbox **III U3,** 50
volleyball ['vɒlibɔ:l] Volleyball **I**
to **vote for** ['vəʊt fɔ:] wählen; stimmen für **II**

W

to **wait** [weɪt] warten **I**
to wait for ['weɪt fə] warten auf **I**
waiter ['weɪtə] Kellner, Bedienung **II**
waitress ['weɪtrɪs] Kellnerin, Bedienung **II**
*to **wake up** [weɪk‿'ʌp] aufwecken; aufwachen **I**
to **walk** [wɔ:k] gehen *(zu Fuß)* **I**
to walk on [wɔ:k‿'ɒn] weitergehen, weiterlaufen ⟨**III U1,** 18⟩
to walk past [wɔ:k 'pɑ:st] vorbeigehen, vorbeilaufen **III U5,** 87
to walk the dog [wɔ:k ðə 'dɒg] den Hund ausführen **I**
wall [wɔ:l] Wand, Mauer **I**
to **want** [wɒnt] wollen, mögen **I**
I want to . . . [aɪ 'wɒnt tə] ich möchte . . ./ich will . . . **I**
to want to know [ˌwɒnt tə 'nəʊ] wissen wollen **I**
World **War II** [ˌwɜ:ld ˌwɔ: 'tu:] der Zweite Weltkrieg **III U2,** 25
wardrobe ['wɔ:drəʊb] Kleiderschrank **I**
warm [wɔ:m] warm **I**
to **warn sb** [wɔ:n] jmdn. warnen; jmdn. ermahnen **III U6,** 97
warning ['wɔ:nɪŋ] Warnung **II**
to **wash** [wɒʃ] waschen **I**
to wash up [wɒʃ‿'ʌp] abwaschen, abspülen **II**
watch [wɒtʃ] Armbanduhr **II**
to **watch** [wɒtʃ] ansehen; beobachten **I**
to watch out [wɒtʃ 'aʊt] aufpassen **I**
water ['wɔ:tə] Wasser **I**
waterfront ['wɔ:təfrʌnt] Hafenviertel; Ufer **III U4,** 68
wave [weɪv] Welle, Woge **I**; Wink **III U1,** 20
to **wave** [weɪv] winken **III U1,** 17
waving [weɪvɪŋ] wogend ⟨**III U4,** 65⟩
wax [wæks] Wachs **III U2,** 26
waxed [wækst] gewachst **II**
way [weɪ] Weg **I**; Art und Weise **II**
a good way to . . . [əˌgʊd 'weɪ tə] eine gute Möglichkeit . . . **II**
finding the way [ˌfaɪndɪŋ ðə 'weɪ] den Weg finden **I**
No way! [ˌnəʊ 'weɪ] Was?!/Echt?!/Nie im Leben! **III U2,** 26
on his way [ˌɒn hɪz 'weɪ] auf dem Weg, unterwegs **I**
to get in the way [ˌget‿ɪn ðə 'weɪ] stören, im Weg stehen **III U3,** 52
we [wi:; wi] wir **I**
weak [wi:k] schwach **II**
*to **wear** [weə] anhaben, tragen **II**
weather ['weðə] Wetter **II**
web [web] Netz **II**
web browser ['web ˌbraʊzə] Webbrowser **III U5,** 77
webpage ['web peɪdʒ] Webseite ⟨**III P1,** 23⟩
website ['websaɪt] Website **II**
Wednesday ['wenzdeɪ] Mittwoch **I**
week [wi:k] Woche **I**
days of the week *(pl.)* [ˌdeɪz‿ɒv ðə 'wi:k] Wochentage *(pl.)* **I**
weekend [ˌwi:k'end] Wochenende **I**
at the weekend [æt ðə ˌwi:k'end] am Wochenende **I**
to **weigh** [weɪ] wiegen **II**
weird [wɪəd] merkwürdig, seltsam **III U4,** 68
welcome ['welkəm] Empfang **III U6,** 95
You're **welcome.** [jɔ: 'welkəm] Bitte schön./Nichts zu danken./Gern geschehen. **I**
welcome ['welkəm] Willkommen **II**
well [wel] gut **II**
well [wel] tja, nun **I**
welly pl. **wellies** ['weli; weliz] Gummistiefel **I**
Welsh [welʃ] walisisch; Walisisch **III U4,** 59
west [west] Westen **I**
wet [wet] nass **II**
what [wɒt] was **I**
What about . . . ? [wɒt‿ə'baʊt] Was ist mit . . . ? **I**
What a stroke of luck! [wɒt‿ə ˌstrəʊk‿əv 'lʌk] Was für ein Glückstreffer! **III U1,** 19
what else [ˌwɒt‿'els] was (sonst) noch **II**
What is . . . like? [ˌwɒt‿ɪz 'laɪk] Wie ist . . . ? **II**
what it looks like [ˌwɒt‿ɪt 'lʊks laɪk] wie es aussieht **I**
what's (= what is) [wɒts; ˌwɒt 'ɪz] was ist **I**
What's for homework, please? [wɒts fə 'həʊmwɜ:k ˌpli:z] Was haben wir als Hausaufgabe auf, bitte? **I**
What's that song? [wɒts ðæt 'sɒŋ] Was ist das für ein Lied? **I**
What's up? [wɒts‿'ʌp] Was ist los? **I**
What's your name? [wɒts jɔ: 'neɪm] Wie heißt du? **I**
What time is it, please? [wɒt 'taɪm‿ɪz‿ɪt ˌpli:z] Wie spät ist es, bitte? **I**
wheel [wi:l] Steuerrad, Steuer, Rad **I**
wheelchair ['wi:ltʃeə] Rollstuhl **III U1,** 12
when [wen] wenn, als **I**; wann **I**
where [weə] wo, wohin, woher **I**
Where are you from? [ˌweər‿ə jə 'frɒm] Woher kommst du? **I**
wherever [weə'revə] wo(hin) auch immer, egal wo(hin) **III U2,** 35
whether ['weðə] ob **III U6,** 97
which [wɪtʃ] welche/-r/-s **I**
which [wɪtʃ] der, dem, den, die, das *(Relativpronomen)* **III U1,** 13

while [waɪl] während **II**
whistle ['wɪsl] Pfiff, Pfeifen **III U6,** 102
white [waɪt] weiß **I**
who [hu:] wer **I**
Who's in it? [hu:z 'ɪn‿ɪt] Wer spielt mit? **III U6,** 96
who [hu:] der, dem, den, die *(Relativpronomen)* **III U1,** 13
whoever [hu:'evə] wer auch immer **III U2,** 35
whole [həʊl] ganz **I**
whose [hu:z] dessen, deren *(Relativpronomen)* **III U1,** 13
why [waɪ] warum **I**
wicked ['wɪkɪd] super, cool *(Umgangssprache)* **II**
wife pl. **wives** [waɪf, waɪvz] Ehefrau **II**
wild [waɪld] wild **I**
will [wɪl] Wille **I**
*to **win** [wɪn] gewinnen **I**
wind [wɪnd] Wind **I**
window ['wɪndəʊ] Fenster **I**
windy ['wɪndi] windig **I**
wing [wɪŋ] Flügel **III U4,** 59
winner ['wɪnə] Gewinner/-in **I**
winter ['wɪntə] Winter **I**
wise [waɪz] weise **III U3,** 43
wish [wɪʃ] Wunsch ⟨**III U3,** 48⟩
to **wish** [wɪʃ] (sich) wünschen **III U3,** 47
witch [wɪtʃ] Hexe **III U3,** 51
with [wɪð] mit **I**
to be with ... [bi 'wɪð] bei ... sein **I**
without [wɪ'ðaʊt] ohne **II**
woman pl. **women** ['wʊmən; 'wɪmɪn] Frau **I**
wonder ['wʌndə] Wunder **I**
to **wonder** ['wʌndə] sich fragen **III U2,** 34
wood [wʊd] Holz **III U2,** 24
Woof! [wʊf] Wau! **I**
Woosh! [wʊʃ] Zisch! **I**
word [wɜ:d] Wort **I**
question word ['kwestʃən ˌwɜ:d] Fragewort **I**
signal word ['sɪgnl ˌwɜ:d] Signalwort **I**
word bank ['wɜ:d ˌbæŋk] Wortsammlung **I**
word order ['wɜ:d‿ɔ:də] Wortstellung, Satzstellung **I**
word web ['wɜ:d web] Wortnetz **I**
wordwise ['wɜ:dwaɪz] „wortschlau", „wortgewandt" **I**
work [wɜ:k] Arbeit **II**
to **work** [wɜ:k] funktionieren **I**; arbeiten **I**
worker ['wɜ:kə] Arbeiter/-in **II**
workshop ['wɜ:kʃɒp] Werkstatt; Workshop **III U2,** 24
world [wɜ:ld] Welt **I**
in the world [ɪn ðə 'wɜ:ld] auf der Welt **I**
World War II [ˌwɜ:ld ˌwɔ: 'tu:] der Zweite Weltkrieg **III U2,** 25
worried ['wʌrɪd] beunruhigt, besorgt **I**
to **worry** ['wʌri] sich Sorgen machen **I**
Don't worry. [dəʊnt 'wʌri] Mach dir keine Sorgen. **I**
to be **worth** [bi 'wɜ:θ] wert sein **III U5,** 82
I'd like to ... *(= I would like to)* [aɪd 'laɪk tə] ich möchte .../ich würde gerne ... **I**
Wow! [waʊ] Wow!/Toll! **I**
*to **write** [raɪt] schreiben **I**
to write down [raɪt 'daʊn] aufschreiben **I**
wrong [rɒŋ] falsch **I**
to be wrong [bi 'rɒŋ] Unrecht haben, sich irren **I**
to do wrong [du: 'rɒŋ] Unrecht tun ⟨**III U2,** 36⟩

Y

year [jɪə] Jahr; Jahrgangsstufe, Klasse, Schuljahr **I**
for (many) years [fə ˌmeni 'jɪəz] jahrelang **I**
year-old [ˌjɪər‿'əʊld] -jährige/r; -jährig **II**
yellow ['jeləʊ] gelb **I**
yes [jes] ja **I**
yesterday ['jestədeɪ] gestern **II**
yet [jet] schon; noch **II**
you [ju:] du **I**
And you. [ənd 'ju:] Gleichfalls. **III U6,** 100
young [jʌŋ] jung **I**
your [jɔ:] dein, deine **I**; Ihr(e) **I**
yourself [jɔ:'self] dich selbst **I**; du/dir/dich/Sie/sich (selbst); selber **III U3,** 44
yourselves [jɔ:'selvz] ihr/euch/Sie/sich (selbst); selber **III U3,** 44
youth [ju:θ] Jugend **III U5,** 85
youth hostel ['ju:θ ˌhɒstl] Jugendherberge **II**
yuk [jʌk] i, igitt **I**

Z

zero ['zɪərəʊ, əʊ] null **I**
zoo [zu:] Zoo **I**
zoom-in [zu:m'ɪn] Heranzoomen, Heranfahren **I**
Zzz ... [z] Schnarch! **I**

Boys' names

Adam ['ædəm] **II**
Alex ['ælɪks] **III U2,** 32
Angus ['æŋgəs] **II**
Ben [ben] **I**
Bill [bɪl] **II**
Bob [bɒb] **II**
Bruce [bru:s] **II**
Charlie ['tʃɑ:li] **II**
Clarence ['klærns] **III U2,** 33
Danny ['dæni] **III U5,** 77
David ['deɪvɪd] **I**
Don [dɒn] **II**
Eddie ['edi] Eddie **III U1,** 16
Edward ['edwəd] **II**
Fabien [fɑ:bjɛ̃] **II**
Frank [fræŋk] **II**
Gavin ['gævɪn] **III U4,** 62
Harold ['hærəld] **III U2,** 25
Jake [dʒeɪk] **III U3,** 43
James [dʒeɪmz] **I**
Joey ['dʒəʊi] **II**
Jon [dʒɒn] **II**
Jonathan ['dʒɒnəθn] **I**
Joseph ['dʒəʊzɪf] **II**
Justin ['dʒʌstɪn] **II**
Kevin ['kevɪn] **II**
Luke [lu:k] **III U3,** 49
Marcus ['mɑ:kəs] **II**
Mark [mɑ:k] **III U2,** 26
Martin ['mɑ:tɪn] **I**
Matt [mæt] **III U5,** 78
Max [mæks] **III U4,** 62
Michael ['maɪkl] **III U4,** 68
Micky ['mɪki] **II**
Nelson ['nelsn] **I**
Nick [nɪk] **III U6,** 94
Pete [pi:t] **II**
Phil [fɪl] **I**
Philip ['fɪlɪp] **III U2,** 25
Reginald ['redʒɪnld] **III U2,** 33
Rhodri ['rɒdri] **III U4,** 67
Richard ['rɪtʃəd] **I**
Rob [rɒb] **I**
Robert ['rɒbət] **II**
Romeo ['rəʊmiəʊ] **III U2,** 25
Ryan [raɪən] **III U6,** 92
Sam [sæm] **I**
Samuel ['sæmjʊəl] **I**
Scott [skɒt] **I**
Tariq ['tærɪk] **III U4,** 61
Ted [ted] **I**
Terry ['teri] **I**
Tim [tɪm] **I**
Timothy ['tɪməθi] **III U2,** 32
Tom [tɒm] **I**
Walter ['wɒltə] **II**

Wayne [weɪn] **II**
William ['wɪljəm] **III U2,** 25

Girls' names

Amanda [ə'mændə] **I**
Amy ['eɪmi] **III U3,** 43
Anne [æn] **II**
Aouda [ə'u:də] **III U6,** 101
Chloe ['kləʊi] **III U2,** 32
Colleen ['kɒli:n] **II**
Debbie ['debi] **I**
Denise [də'ni:z] **I**
Diana [daɪ'ænə] **II**
Elena ['elənə] **I**
Elsie ['elsi] **I**
Emma ['emə] **I**
Farah ['fɑ:rə] **I**
Fiona [fi'əʊnə] **I**
Gayathriy ['gaɪətri] **II**
Grace [greɪs] **I**
Gwendolyn ['gwendəlɪn] **III U2,** 32
Henrietta [ˌhenri'etə] **III U2,** 33
Jade [dʒeɪd] **I**
Jane [dʒeɪn] **II**
Janice ['dʒænɪs] **II**
Jill [dʒɪl] **II**
Julie ['dʒu:li] **II**
Juliet ['dʒu:liət] **III U2,** 25
Katie ['keɪti] **II**
Kelly ['keli] **III U6,** 94
Kelsey ['kelsi] **III**
Kim [kɪm] **I**
Leanne [li'æn] **III U5,** 77
Linda ['lɪndə] **III U3,** 49
Lisa ['li:sə] **I**
Maria [mə'ri:ə] **II**
Mariah [mə'raɪə] **III U5,** 86
Marsha ['mɑ:ʃə] **III U4,** 71
Mary ['meəri] **II**
Megan ['megən] **III U4,** 64
Mel [mel] **III U3,** 43
Miriam ['mɪriəm] **III U3,** 43
Molly ['mɒli] **II**
Nasreen [nəs'ri:n] **I**
Nicola ['nɪklə] **I**
Nicole [nɪ'kəʊl] **II**
Nisha ['nɪʃə] **II**
Polly ['pɒli] **II**
Rachel ['reɪtʃl] **I**
Rhona ['rəʊnə] **III U4,** 60
Rukhshana [ruk'ʃɑnə] **II**
Sarah ['seərə] **I**
Serena [sə'ri:nə] **III U1,** 9
Shirin ['ʃɪrɪn] **III U4,** 60
Sue [su:] **I**
Susan ['su:zn] **I**
Tess [tes] **I**
Tina ['ti:nə] **II**
Tracy ['treɪsi] **I**
Venus ['vi:nəs] **III U1,** 9
Vicky ['vɪki] **III U2,** 25
Yoko ['jəʊkəʊ] **I**
Zeba ['zi:bə] **III U4,** 63

Surnames

Barker ['bɑ:kə] **I**
Berners-Lee [ˌbɜ:nəz'li:] **III U5,** 77
Brook [brʊk] **I**
Brown [braʊn] **I**
Carlton ['kɑ:ltn] **II**
Carter ['kɑ:tə] **I**
Chapuis [ʃapɥi] **II**
Church [tʃɜ:tʃ] **II**
Clooney ['klu:ni] **II**
Collins ['kɒlɪnz] **III U1,** 17
Cumberland ['kʌmbələnd] **III U2,** 33
Darling ['dɑ:lɪŋ] **I**
Devine [dɪ'vaɪn] **II**
Douglas ['dʌgləs] **II**
Green [gri:n] **I**
Jackson ['dʒæksn] **I**
Khan [kɑ:n] **III U4,** 60
Kumar [ku:'mɑ:] **II**
Lacy ['leɪsi] **III U2,** 34
Lotric ['lɒtrɪtʃ] **III U1,** 17
MacGregor [mə'gregə] **II**
MacMouse [mək'maʊs] **II**
McGeoch [mə'gɪəx] **II**
Nelson ['nelsn] **I**
Newman ['nju:mən] **I**
Patterson ['pætəsn] **III U3,** 43
Peterson ['pi:təsn] **I**
Pilch [pɪltʃ] **I**
Pinner ['pɪnə] **II**
Redfern ['redfɜ:n] **II**
Robinson ['rɒbɪnsn] **III U2,** 34
Simpson ['sɪmsən] **II**
Smith [smɪθ] **I**
Spencer ['spensə] **I**
Stavros ['stævrəs] **I**
Steward ['stju:əd] **II**
Stirling ['stɜ:lɪŋ] **III U5,** 78
Taylor ['teɪlə] **I**
Tiny ['taɪni] **I**
Tohomas [tə'həʊməs] **II**
Wendover ['wendəʊvə] **I**
Williams ['wɪljəmz] **II**

Place names

Aberdeen [ˌæbə'di:n] **II**
Abertawe ['æbətɔ:] **III U4,** 67
Albert Dock [ˌælbət 'dɒk] **III U4,** 63
Bamburgh ['bæmbrə] **I**
Bannockburn ['bænəkbɜ:n] **II**
Berlin [bɜ:'lɪn] **I**
Birmingham ['bɜ:mɪŋəm] **III U1,** 10; **III U2,** 25
Blackheath Park [ˌblækhi:θ 'pɑ:k] **I**
Bond Street ['bɒnd ˌstri:t] **II**
Boulogne [bʊ'lɔɪn] **II**
Brighton ['braɪtn] **I**
Bristol ['brɪstl] **I**
Calais ['kæleɪ] **II**
Calgary ['kælgri] **III U1,** 16
Canary Wharf [kə'neəri ˌwɔ:f] **I**
Cardiff ['kɑ:dɪf] **I**
Charlton ['tʃɑ:ltn] **I**
Church Street ['tʃɜ:tʃ ˌstri:t] **I**
Covent Garden [ˌkɒvnt 'gɑ:dn] **II**
Dover ['dəʊvə] **II**
Edinburgh ['edɪnbrə] **II**
Fort William [ˌfɔ:t 'wɪljəm] **II**
Gatwick ['gætwɪk] **II**
Golden Mile [ˌgəʊldn 'maɪl] **I**
Goodge Street ['gu:dʒ ˌstri:t] **II**
Greenwich ['grenɪdʒ] **I**
Greenwich Park [ˌgrenɪdʒ 'pɑ:k] **I**
Hamburg ['hæmbɜ:g] **II**
Harlech ['hɑ:lek] **I**
Heathrow [hi:θ'rəʊ] **II**
High Road ['haɪ ˌrəʊd] **I**
Hither Farm Road ['hɪðə fɑ:m ˌrəʊd] **I**
Holburne Road ['hɒlbɜ:n ˌrəʊd] **I**
Hollywood ['hɒliwʊd] **III U5,** 84
Hyde Park [ˌhaɪd 'pɑ:k] **II**
Inverness [ˌɪnvə'nes] **II**
Istanbul [ˌɪstæn'bʊl] **I**
Kidbrooke Park Road [ˌkɪdbrʊk 'pɑ:k ˌrəʊd] **I**
Kirkton ['kɜ:ktn] **II**
Knightsbridge ['naɪtsbrɪdʒ] **II**
Leicester ['lestə] **I**
Leicester Square ['lestə ˌskweə] **II**
Leytonstone ['leɪtnstəʊn] **II**
Liverpool ['lɪvəpu:l] ⟨**III U1,** 18⟩; **III U4,** 59
London ['lʌndən] **I**
Madrid [mə'drɪd] **I**
Malaga ['mæləgə] **III U2,** 33
Manchester ['mæntʃɪstə] **II**
Medicine Bow ['medsn ˌbəʊ] **III U6,** 102
Milan [mɪ'læn] ⟨**III U6,** 103⟩
Nairobi [naɪ'rəʊbi] **I**
New Town ['nju: taʊn] **II**
New York [ˌnju: 'jɔ:k] **III U6,** 100
Observatory Station [əbˌzɜ:vətri 'steɪʃn] **I**
Old Town ['əʊld taʊn] **II**
Oxford Circus Station ['ɒksfəd ˌsɜ:kəs ˌsteɪʃn] **II**

Oxford Street ['ɒksfəd ˌstri:t] II
Paris ['pærɪs] I
Penzance [pen'zæns] I
Piccadilly Circus [ˌpɪkədɪli 'sɜ:kəs] II
Pond Road ['pɒnd ˌrəʊd] I
Queens [kwi:nz] II
Queensway ['kwi:nzweɪ] II
Reading ['redɪŋ] III U4, 66
Rhossili ['rɒsli] III U4, 67
Richmond ['rɪtʃmənd] II
Royal Mile [ˌrɔɪəl 'maɪl] II
San Francisco [ˌsæn frən'sɪskəʊ] III U6, 101
Shanghai [ʃæŋ'haɪ] I
Southampton [saʊ'θæmtən] III U5, 86
Southend-on-Sea [ˌsaʊθ'end_ɒn 'si:] I
St. Anne's Square [snt'ænz skweə] III U4, 58
Stirling ['stɜ:lɪŋ] II
Stockwell Street ['stɒkwel ˌstri:t] I
Swansea ['swɒnzi] III U1, 11
Sydney ['sɪdni] III U6, 95
Tennessee [ˌtenə'si:] II
Tokyo ['təʊkiəʊ] I
Toulouse [tu:'lu:z] II
Trafalgar Square [trə'fælgə skweə] II
Victoria Station [vɪk'tɔ:riə ˌsteɪʃn] II
Waterloo Station [ˌwɔ:tə'lu: ˌsteɪʃn] II
Wendover Road ['wendəʊvə ˌrəʊd] I
Williamson Tunnels ['wɪljəmsn ˌtʌnlz] III U4, 68
Wimbledon ['wɪmbldn] II
Windsor ['wɪndzə] III U4, 58
Yucatan [ju:kə'tɑ:n] ⟨III U6, 103⟩

Geographical names

Asia ['eɪʒə] Asien III U6, 93
Atlantic [ət'læntɪk] III U2, 27
Australia ['ɒstreɪliə] Australien III U2, 30
Ben Nevis [ˌben 'nevɪs] II
Big Harcar Rock [bɪg ˌhɑ:kə 'rɒk] I
Bondi Beach [ˌbɒndaɪ 'bi:tʃ] III U6, 95
Bordeaux [bɔ:'dəʊ] ⟨III U6, 103⟩
Borneo ['bɔ:niəʊ] ⟨III U6, 103⟩
Britain ['brɪtn] Großbritannien I
Canada ['kænədə] Kanada II
Channel ['tʃænl] Ärmelkanal *(Teil der Nordsee zwischen Großbritannien und Frankreich)* II
China ['tʃaɪnə] III U6, 93
Cornwall ['kɔ:nwɔ:l] I
Dorchester ['dɔ:tʃɪstə] III U5, 85
Egypt ['i:dʒɪpt] Ägypten III U2, 30
England ['ɪŋglənd] I
Essex ['esɪks] II
Europe ['jʊərəp] Europa II
Farne Islands [fɑ:n 'aɪləndz] I
Finland ['fɪnlənd] Finland III U1, 17
France [frɑ:nts] Frankreich II
Germany ['dʒɜ:məni] Deutschland I
Gower Coast ['gaʊə kəʊst] III U4, 67
Great Britain [ˌgreɪt 'brɪtn] Großbritannien III U1, 17
Great Wall of China [ˌgreɪt ˌwɔ:l_əv 'tʃaɪnə] III U1, 13
Greece [gri:s] Griechenland I
Highlands ['haɪləndz] II
India ['ɪndiə] Indien III U2, 25
Isle of Dogs [ˌaɪl əv 'dɒgz] I
Italy ['ɪtli] Italien I
Jamaica [dʒə'meɪkə] III U1, 13
Japan [dʒə'pæn] III U6, 93
Lancashire ['læŋkəʃə] II
Loch Fyne [ˌlɒx 'faɪn] II
Loch Lochy [ˌlɒx 'lɒxi] II
Loch Lomond [ˌlɒx 'ləʊmənd] II
Loch Ness [ˌlɒx 'nes] II
Loch Rannoch [ˌlɒx 'rænəx] II
Loch Tay [ˌlɒx 'teɪ] II
Louisiana [luˌi:zi'ænə] ⟨III U5, 83⟩
Majorca [mə'jɔ:kə] III U2, 33
Mersey ['mɜ:zi] III U4, 65
Mexico ['meksɪkəʊ] III U2, 24
Mount Snowdon [ˌmaʊnt 'snəʊdn] I
Nevada [nə'vɑ:də] III U6, 101
Normandy ['nɔ:məndi] die Normandie III U2, 25
North America [ˌnɔ:θ ə'merɪkə] Nordamerika III U2, 30
Pakistan [ˌpɑ:kɪ'stɑ:n] III U4, 60
Panama [ˌpænə'mɑ:] III U2, 27
Poland ['pəʊlənd] Polen I
River Mersey [ˌrɪvə 'mɜ:zi] III U4, 59
River Thames [ˌrɪvə 'temz] I
Rocky Mountains [ˌrɒki 'maʊntɪnz] III U6, 101
Russia ['rʌʃə] Russland I
Scotland ['skɒtlənd] Schottland II
Sennen Beach [ˌsenən 'bi:tʃ] I
Silicon Valley [ˌsɪlɪkən 'væli] III U4, 66
South Africa [ˌsaʊθ_'æfrɪkə] Südafrika III U6, 100
Spain [speɪn] I
St Michael's Mount [snˌmaɪklz 'maʊnt] I
Sudan [su:'dɑ:n] ⟨III U6, 103⟩
The Shetlands [ðə 'ʃetləndz] die Shetlandinseln II
Turkey ['tɜ:ki] Türkei I
UK [ju:'keɪ] Vereinigtes Königreich von Großbritannien und Nordirland II
Utah ['ju:tɑ:] III U6, 101
Wales [weɪlz] I
Wyoming [waɪ'əʊmɪŋ] III U6, 101
Yugoslavia [ju:gəʊ'slɑ:viə] Jugoslawien III U1, 17

Other names

Aberdeen Hiking Club [ˌæbədi:n 'haɪkɪŋ klʌb] II
Airbus ['eəbʌs] III U4, 59
Anfield Road [ˌænfi:ld 'rəʊd] III U4, 68
Angelo's ['ændʒləʊz] I
Arapaho [ə'ræpəhəʊ] Arapaho-Indianer ⟨III U6, 103⟩
Armada [ɑ:'mɑ:də] III U2, 25
Barker ['bɑ:kə] I
Battle of Hastings [ˌbætl_əv 'heɪstɪŋz] III U2, 25
BBC (British Broadcasting Corporation) [ˌbi:bi:'si: (ˌbrɪtɪʃ 'brɔ:dkɑ:stɪŋ kɔ:prˌeɪʃn)] II
Beagle ['bi:gl] III U6, 93
Beatlemania [ˌbi:tl'meɪniə] III U4, 65
the Beeb [ðə 'bi:b] III U5, 76
Beryl Alpha [ˌberl 'ælfə] II
Black and Tan [ˌblæk_n_'tæn] *(Biermischgetränk)* ⟨III U4, 65⟩
Bonza ['bɒnzə] I
Brent Charlie [ˌbrent 'tʃɑ:li] II
Britannia [brɪ'tæniə] Britannien III U2, 24
British Airways [ˌbrɪtɪʃ 'eəweɪz] II
British Empire [ˌbrɪtɪʃ 'empaɪə] III U2, 25
Bu [bu:] II
Buckingham Palace [ˌbʌkɪŋəm 'pælɪs] II
Busted ['bʌstɪd] II
buzz [bʌz] *(hier:) Name eines Spiels* I
Caddris [kædrɪs] II
CCTV [ˌsi:si:ti:'vi:] Videoüberwachung II
Cèilidh Mòr [ˌkeɪli 'mɔ:] II
Central Line ['sentrl ˌlaɪn] II
Chihuahua [tʃɪ'wɑ:wə] II
Chocolate Islands ['tʃɒklət ˌaɪləndz] I
Coaster's Café [ˌkəʊstəz 'kæfeɪ] II
Commonwealth ['kɒmənwelθ] III U2, 30
Cool Cat [ˌku:l 'kæt] I
Cool Runnings [ˌku:l 'rʌnɪŋz] III U1, 13
Coronation Street [kɒrəˌneɪʃn 'stri:t] III U5, 77
Covent Garden Market [ˌkɒvnt 'gɑ:dn ˌmɑ:kɪt] II
CSI: Miami [si:es'aɪ maɪˌæmi] III U5, 87
Cumberland Hall [ˌkʌmbələnd 'hɔ:l] III U2, 34
Cutty Sark [ˌkʌti 'sɑ:k] I
Danny Way [ˌdæni 'weɪ] III U1, 11
DAZZ [dæz] III U4, 71
Decathlon [dɪ'kæθlɒn] II
Docklands Light Railway [ˌdɒklændz laɪt 'reɪlweɪ] I

Dr Jones [ˌdɒktə ˈdʒəʊnz] **II**
EastEnders [i:stˈendəz] **III U5,** 77
Eisteddfod [aɪˈsteðvɒd] **III U4,** 61
Emmerdale [ˈeməndeɪl] **III U5,** 77
Epic Skatepark [ˌepɪk ˈskeɪtpɑ:k] **III U1,** 10
ER (Emergency Room) [i:ˈɑ:r; ɪˈmɜ:dʒnsi ru:m] **III U5,** 87
Eskimo [ˈeskɪməʊ] 〈**III U6,** 103〉
Fightstar [ˈfaɪtstɑ:] **II**
Foyles [fɔɪlz] **II**
Gizzette Hair Gel [ˌgɪzet heə ˈgel] **III U5,** 82
the Globe Theatre [ˈgləʊb ˌθɪətə] das Globe-Theater **III U2,** 25
Google [ˈgu:gl] **II**
Graceland [ˈgreɪslənd] **II**
Greensleeves [ˈgri:nsli:vz] **III U2,** 36
Greenwich Foot Tunnel [ˌgrenɪdʒ ˈfʊt tʌnl] **I**
Greenwich Market [ˌgrenɪdʒ ˈmɑ:kɪt] **I**
Guinness World of Records [ˌgɪnɪs wɜ:ld‿əv ˈrekɔ:dz] **II**
Hadrian's Wall [ˌheɪdriənz ˈwɔ:l] **III U2,** 24
Hamleys [ˈhæmliz] **II**
Harrods [ˈhærədz] **II**
Historia [hɪˈstɔ:riə] **III U2,** 25
Hobbyland [ˈhɒbilænd] Hobbyland **I**
Hogwarts [ˈhɒgwɔ:ts] **II**
HTML [eɪtʃti:emˈel] **III U5,** 77
Jubilee Line [ˈdʒu:bɪli: laɪn] **II**
Koolkats [ˈku:lkæts] **II**
Kyoto Hotel [ˈkjəʊtəʊ həʊˌtel] **III U5,** 84
Liverpool FC [ˌlɪvəpu:l efˈsi:] **III U4,** 59
Liverpool Football Club [ˌlɪvəpu:l ˈfʊtbɔ:l klʌb] **III U4,** 68
Londinium [lʌnˈdɪniəm] **II**
London Dungeon [ˌlʌndən ˈdʌndʒn] **II**
London Eye [ˌlʌndən‿ˈaɪ] **II**
London Marathon [ˌlʌndən ˈmærəθn] **III U1,** 13
London Zoo [ˌlʌndən ˈzu:] **III U2,** 31
Lycos [ˈlaɪkəz] **III U5,** 76
M4 [emˈfɔ:] **III U4,** 66
Madame Tussaud's [ˌmædəm tʊˈsɔ:dz] **III U2,** 26
Manchester United [ˌmæntʃɪstə ju:ˈnaɪtɪd] **II**
ManU *(Abkürzung für* Manchester United*)* [ˌmænˈju:] **III U5,** 87
Maritime Museum [ˈmærɪtaɪm mju:ˈzi:əm] **II**
Millennium Dome [mɪˈleniəm ˌdəʊm] **I**
Moonlight [ˈmu:nlaɪt] **III U4,** 71
Mousehole Harbour [ˌmaʊzl ˈhɑ:bə] **I**
Mudchute Farm [ˌmʌdʃu:t ˈfɑ:m] **I**
Murray's [ˈmʌriz] **II**

National Waterfront Museum [ˌnæʃnl ˌwɔ:təfrʌnt mju:ˈzi:əm] **III U4,** 60
Natural History Museum [ˌnætʃrl ˈhɪstri mju:ˌzi:əm] **II**
Neighbours [ˈneɪbəz] **III U5,** 77
New World [ˌnju: ˈwɜ:ld] **III U2,** 24
Olympic Games [əʊˌlɪmpɪk ˈgeɪmz] Olympiade, Olympische Spiele **III U1,** 9
Passepartout [ˌpæspəˈtu:] **III U6,** 101
Phileas Fogg [fɪˌliə ˈfɒg] **III U6,** 101
Piazza [piˈætsə] **II**
Playstation [ˈpleɪˌsteɪʃn] **III U1,** 11
RCA [ɑ:rsi:ˈeɪ] **III U5,** 76
Real Madrid [rɪˌɑ:l məˈdrɪd] **II**
Regent's Park [ˌri:dʒnts ˈpɑ:k] **III U2,** 31
Rivermead Leisure Complex [ˌrɪvəmi:d ˌleʒə ˈkɒmpleks] **III U4,** 66
Royal Observatory [ˌrɔɪəl əbˈzɜ:vətri] **I**
Rusty [ˈrʌsti] **I**
Sayonara [saiˈəʊnɑ:lɑ:] **III U5,** 84
Shout [ʃaʊt] **III U5,** 76
Sidewalk [ˈsaɪdwɔ:k] **III U1,** 11
Smash hits [ˈsmæʃ hɪt] **III U5,** 76
Spin [spɪn] **III U5,** 82
Squeak [skwi:k] **II**
Starry [ˈstɑ:ri] **III U4,** 71
Starstruck [ˈstɑ:strʌk] **II**
Superbowl [ˈsu:pəbəʊl] **III U1,** 13
Superteen [ˈsu:pəti:n] **II**
Sweet Home Alabama [ˈswi:t həʊm æləˌbæma] 〈**III U5,** 83〉
Tallis Newsletter [ˌtælɪs ˈnju:zletə] **II**
Tate Modern [ˌteɪt ˈmɒdn] **II**
Teen Buzz [ˈti:n bʌz] **II**
Thames Barrier [ˌtemz ˈbæriə] **I**
The Lord of the Rings [ðə ˌlɔ:d‿əv ðə ˈrɪŋz] **III U6,** 96
The Quarrymen [ðə ˈkwɒrimən] **III U4,** 65
Thomas Tallis [ˌtɒməs ˈtælɪs] **I**
Thomas Tallis School [ˌtɒməs ˈtælɪs ˌsku:l] **I**
Tiger [ˈtaɪgə] **I**
Tokyo Tigers [ˌtəʊkiəʊ ˈtaɪgəz] **I**
Tom-Toms [ˈtɒm tɒmz] **II**
Top Fit [ˌtɒp ˈfɪt] **II**
the Tower of London [ðə ˌtaʊər‿əv ˈlʌndən] **III U2,** 31
4U [fə ˈju] **I**
Walk the line [wɔ:k ðə ˈlaɪn] 〈**III U5,** 83〉
Water Park [ˈwɔ:tə ˌpɑ:k] **I**
World Cup [wɜ:ld ˈkʌp] Fußballweltmeisterschaft **II**
World Stage [ˌwɜ:ld ˈsteɪdʒ] **III U2,** 26
World Wide Web [ˌwɜ:ld waɪd ˈweb] **III U5,** 77
Zerfee [ˈzɜ:rfi:] **II**
Zest [zest] **II**

Famous names

Captain Cook [ˌkæptɪn ˈkʊk] **III U6,** 93
50 Cent [ˌfɪfti ˈsent] **III U5,** 77
Charles Darwin [ˌtʃɑ:lz ˈdɑ:wɪn] **III U6,** 93
David Beckham [ˌdeɪvɪd ˈbekəm] **II**
Elizabeth I [ɪˌlɪzəbəθ ðə ˈfɜ:st] **III U2,** 24
Ellen MacArthur [ˌelən məˈkɑ:θə] **III U6,** 93
Elvis Presley [ˌelvɪs ˈpresli] **II**
Francis Drake [ˌfrɑ:nsɪs ˈdreɪk] **III U2,** 24
Gladys Aylward [ˌglædɪs ˈeɪlwəd] **III U6,** 93
Harry Potter [ˌhæri ˈpɒtə] **II**
James Watt [ˌdʒeɪmz ˈwɒt] **III U2,** 24
Kelly Holmes [ˌkeli ˈhəʊmz] **II**
Lance Armstrong [ˌlænts ˈɑ:mstrɒŋ] **III U1,** 14
Marco Polo [ˌmɑ:kəʊ ˈpəʊləʊ] **III U6,** 93
Matthew Pinsent [ˌmæθju: ˈpɪnsnt] **III U1,** 13
Matti Nykanen [ˌmati ˈnɪkanən] **III U1,** 17
Michael Phelps [ˌmaɪkl ˈfelps] **III U1,** 13
Mickey Mouse [ˈmɪki maʊs] **I**
Neil Armstrong [ni:l ˈɑ:mstrɒŋ] **III U6,** 93
Oliver Twist [ˌɒlɪvə ˈtwɪst] 〈**III U5,** 81〉
Orlando Bloom [ɔ:ˌlændəʊ ˈblu:m] **II**
Queen Victoria [ˌkwi:n vɪkˈtɔ:riə] **III U2,** 25
Reese Witherspoon [ˈri:s ˌwɪðəspu:n] 〈**III U5,** 83〉
Robbie Williams [ˌrɒbi ˈwɪljəmz] **III U2,** 26
Roger Federer [ˌrɒdʒə ˈfedərə] **III U1,** 14
Runrig [ˈrʌnrɪg] **II**
Stephen Hoskins [ˌsti:vn ˈhɒskɪnz] **III U2,** 30
Tanny Grey-Thompson [ˈtæni ˌgreɪˈtɒmpsn] **III U1,** 13
The Arctic Monkeys [ˌɑ:ktɪk ˈmʌŋkiz] **III U5,** 77
The Beatles [ðə bi:tlz] **III U4,** 59
The Spice Girls [ˈspaɪs ˌgɜ:lz] **II**
Tiger Woods [ˌtaɪgə ˈwʊdz] **III U1,** 14
Victoria Adams [vɪkˌtɔ:rɪə ˈædəmz] **II**
William Shakespeare [ˌwɪljəm ˈʃeɪkspɪə] **III U2,** 25
William the Conqueror [ˌwɪljəm ðə ˈkɒŋkrə] **III U2,** 31

List of irregular verbs

infinitive	simple past	past participle	German
to **be** [biː]	**was / were** [wɒz, wɜː]	**been** [biːn]	sein
to **become** [bɪˈkʌm]	**became** [bɪˈkeɪm]	**become** [bɪˈkʌm]	werden
to **bleed** [bliːd]	**bled** [bled]	**bled** [bled]	bluten
to **break** [breɪk]	**broke** [brəʊk]	**broken** [ˈbrəʊkn]	(zer)brechen; kaputtmachen
to **bring** [brɪŋ]	**brought** [brɔːt]	**brought** [brɔːt]	(mit)bringen
to **build** [bɪld]	**built** [bɪlt]	**built** [bɪlt]	bauen
to **burn** [bɜːn]	**burnt / burned** [bɜːnt, bɜːnd]	**burnt / burned** [bɜːnt, bɜːnd]	(ver)brennen
to **buy** [baɪ]	**bought** [bɔːt]	**bought** [bɔːt]	kaufen
to **catch** [kætʃ]	**caught** [kɔːt]	**caught** [kɔːt]	fangen
to **choose** [tʃuːz]	**chose** [tʃəʊz]	**chosen** [ˈtʃəʊzn]	(aus)wählen
to **come** [kʌm]	**came** [keɪm]	**come** [kʌm]	kommen
to **cost** [kɒst]	**cost** [kɒst]	**cost** [kɒst]	kosten
to **deal (with)** [diːl]	**dealt** [delt]	**dealt** [delt]	(be)handeln
to **do** [duː]	**did** [dɪd]	**done** [dʌn]	machen, tun
to **draw** [drɔː]	**drew** [druː]	**drawn** [drɔːn]	zeichnen
to **drink** [drɪŋk]	**drank** [dræŋk]	**drunk** [drʌŋk]	trinken
to **drive** [draɪv]	**drove** [drəʊv]	**driven** [ˈdrɪvn]	fahren
to **eat** [iːt]	**ate** [et, eɪt]	**eaten** [ˈiːtn]	essen
to **fall** [fɔːl]	**fell** [fel]	**fallen** [ˈfɔːlən]	(herunter)fallen, hinfallen
to **feed** [fiːd]	**fed** [fed]	**fed** [fed]	füttern
to **feel** [fiːl]	**felt** [felt]	**felt** [felt]	(sich) fühlen
to **fight** [faɪt]	**fought** [fɔːt]	**fought** [fɔːt]	kämpfen, (sich) streiten
to **find** [faɪnd]	**found** [faʊnd]	**found** [faʊnd]	finden
to **fly** [flaɪ]	**flew** [fluː]	**flown** [fləʊn]	fliegen
to **forget** [fəˈget]	**forgot** [fəˈgɒt]	**forgotten** [fəˈgɒtn]	vergessen
to **get** [get]	**got** [gɒt]	**got** [gɒt]	holen, bringen; (be)kommen; werden
to **give** [gɪv]	**gave** [geɪv]	**given** [ˈgɪvn]	geben
to **go** [gəʊ]	**went** [went]	**gone** [gɒn]	gehen
to **grow** [grəʊ]	**grew** [gruː]	**grown** [grəʊn]	wachsen
to **hang** [hæŋ]	**hung** [hʌŋ]	**hung** [hʌŋ]	hängen
to **have** [hæv]	**had** [hæd]	**had** [hæd]	haben
to **hear** [hɪə]	**heard** [hɜːd]	**heard** [hɜːd]	hören
to **hide** [haɪd]	**hid** [hɪd]	**hidden** [ˈhɪdn]	(sich) verstecken
to **hit** [hɪt]	**hit** [hɪt]	**hit** [hɪt]	schlagen; treffen
to **hold** [həʊld]	**held** [held]	**held** [held]	halten
to **hurt** [hɜːt]	**hurt** [hɜːt]	**hurt** [hɜːt]	verletzen, weh tun
to **keep** [kiːp]	**kept** [kept]	**kept** [kept]	behalten
to **know** [nəʊ]	**knew** [njuː]	**known** [nəʊn]	wissen; kennen
to **lay** [leɪ]	**laid** [leɪd]	**laid** [leɪd]	legen
to **learn** [lɜːn]	**learnt/learned** [lɜːnt, lɜːnd]	**learnt/learned** [lɜːnt, lɜːnd]	lernen

infinitive	simple past	past participle	German
to **leave** [li:v]	**left** [left]	**left** [left]	(ver)lassen, abfahren
to **lend** [lend]	**lent** [lent]	**lent** [lent]	leihen
to **let** [let]	**let** [let]	**let** [let]	lassen
to **lose** [lu:z]	**lost** [lɒst]	**lost** [lɒst]	verlieren
to **make** [meɪk]	**made** [meɪd]	**made** [meɪd]	machen, tun
to **mean** [mi:n]	**meant** [ment]	**meant** [ment]	bedeuten; meinen
to **meet** [mi:t]	**met** [met]	**met** [met]	(sich) treffen
to **pay** [peɪ]	**paid** [peɪd]	**paid** [peɪd]	(be)zahlen
to **put** [pʊt]	**put** [pʊt]	**put** [pʊt]	setzen, stellen, legen
to **read** [ri:d]	**read** [red]	**read** [red]	lesen
to **ride** [raɪd]	**rode** [rəʊd]	**ridden** ['rɪdn]	fahren, reiten
to **ring** [rɪŋ]	**rang** [ræŋ]	**rung** [rʌŋ]	klingeln, läuten
to **run** [rʌn]	**ran** [ræn]	**run** [rʌn]	rennen, laufen
to **say** [seɪ]	**said** [sed]	**said** [sed]	sagen
to **see** [si:]	**saw** [sɔ:]	**seen** [si:n]	sehen
to **sell** [sel]	**sold** [səʊld]	**sold** [səʊld]	verkaufen
to **send** [send]	**sent** [sent]	**sent** [sent]	schicken
to **shake** [ʃeɪk]	**shook** [ʃʊk]	**shaken** ['ʃeɪkn]	schütteln
to **shine** [ʃaɪn]	**shone** [ʃɒn]	**shone** [ʃɒn]	scheinen; glänzen
to **shoot** [ʃu:t]	**shot** [ʃɒt]	**shot** [ʃɒt]	schießen
to **show** [ʃəʊ]	**showed** [ʃəʊd]	**shown** [ʃəʊn]	zeigen
to **sing** [sɪŋ]	**sang** [sæŋ]	**sung** [sʌŋ]	singen
to **sink** [sɪŋk]	**sank** [sæŋk]	**sunk** [sʌŋk]	sinken
to **sit** [sɪt]	**sat** [sæt]	**sat** [sæt]	sitzen
to **sleep** [sli:p]	**slept** [slept]	**slept** [slept]	schlafen
to **slide** [slaɪd]	**slid** [slɪd]	**slid** [slɪd]	rutschen; gleiten
to **smell** [smel]	**smelt / smelled** [smelt, smeld]	**smelt / smelled** [smelt, smeld]	riechen
to **speak** [spi:k]	**spoke** [spəʊk]	**spoken** ['spəʊkn]	sprechen
to **spend** [spend]	**spent** [spent]	**spent** [spent]	ausgeben; verbringen
to **stand** [stænd]	**stood** [stʊd]	**stood** [stʊd]	stehen
to **steal** [sti:l]	**stole** [stəʊl]	**stolen** ['stəʊlən]	stehlen
to **swim** [swɪm]	**swam** [swæm]	**swum** [swʌm]	schwimmen
to **take** [teɪk]	**took** [tʊk]	**taken** ['teɪkn]	(mit)nehmen, bringen
to **teach** [ti:tʃ]	**taught** [tɔ:t]	**taught** [tɔ:t]	lehren
to **tell** [tel]	**told** [təʊld]	**told** [təʊld]	erzählen, sagen
to **think** [θɪŋk]	**thought** [θɔ:t]	**thought** [θɔ:t]	denken, glauben
to **throw** [θrəʊ]	**threw** [θru:]	**thrown** [θrəʊn]	werfen
to **understand** [ˌʌndə'stænd]	**understood** [ˌʌndə'stʊd]	**understood** [ˌʌndə'stʊd]	verstehen
to **wake** [weɪk]	**woke** [wəʊk]	**woken** ['wəʊkn]	(auf)wecken; (auf)wachen
to **wear** [weə]	**wore** [wɔ:]	**worn** [wɔ:n]	anhaben, tragen
to **win** [wɪn]	**won** [wʌn]	**won** [wʌn]	gewinnen, siegen
to **write** [raɪt]	**wrote** [rəʊt]	**written** ['rɪtn]	schreiben

⟨In the classroom⟩

What you can say to your teacher

Can you help me, please?	Können Sie mir bitte helfen?
I don't understand this.	Ich verstehe das nicht.
Can you explain that again, please?	Können Sie das bitte noch einmal erklären?
What do we have to do?	Was müssen wir denn machen?
What's that in English / German?	Was heißt das auf Englisch / Deutsch?
Can I say: ... ? / What does ... mean?	Kann ich sagen: ... ? / Was bedeutet ... ?
How do you do this exercise?	Wie macht man diese Übung?
Is this right? I'm not sure.	Ist das richtig? Ich bin nicht sicher.
Sorry, I don't know.	Tut mir Leid, das weiß ich nicht.
Can you write it on the board, please?	Können Sie das bitte an die Tafel schreiben?
Can I ask a question, please?	Kann ich bitte eine Frage stellen?
Sorry, can you repeat the question / sentence, please?	Entschuldigung, können Sie die Frage / den Satz bitte wiederholen?
Can you play the CD again, please?	Können Sie die CD bitte nochmal abspielen?
Can we do another example, please?	Können wir noch ein Beispiel machen?
Whose turn is it?	Wer ist dran?
What's for homework, please?	Was haben wir als Hausaufgabe auf?
I'm not feeling well.	Ich fühle mich nicht gut.
I've got a headache.	Ich habe Kopfweh.
Can I open the window, please?	Darf ich bitte das Fenster öffnen?
Can I go to the toilet, please?	Darf ich bitte auf die Toilette gehen?

What your teacher can say to you

Open your books at page	Schlagt Seite ... auf.
Turn to page	Blättert auf Seite ... um.
Read the text on page	Lest den Text auf Seite ...
Who would like to write on the transparency?	Wer möchte auf die Folie schreiben?
Come to the board, please.	Komm bitte an die Tafel.
Who would like to play the CD?	Wer möchte die CD abspielen?
You're going to hear the CD twice.	Ihr werdet die CD zweimal hören.
Please play track 5 again.	Spiel bitte den Track Nr. 5 noch einmal.
Who would like to play the part of ... ?	Wer möchte die Rolle von ... spielen?
Write the answers in your exercise books.	Schreibt die Antworten in eure Übungshefte.
Would you collect the exercise books / worksheets, please?	Würdest du bitte die Übungshefte / Arbeitsblätter einsammeln?
Do this exercise for homework.	Macht diese Übung als Hausaufgabe.
Be quiet, please. Sit down, please.	Seid bitte ruhig. Setz dich / Setzt euch, bitte.
Please speak up.	Sprich / Sprecht bitte lauter.
No prompting, please.	Nicht vorsagen, bitte.
Excellent!	Prima!
You can do better. Try again.	Das kannst du besser. Versuch es noch einmal.
That's it. Well done.	So ist es richtig. Gut gemacht.

Talking about stories, poems, songs, ...

I like / don't like this story.	Diese Geschichte gefällt mir / gefällt mir nicht.
I think it's good, interesting, brilliant, funny, really exciting.	Ich finde sie gut, interessant, toll, witzig, wirklich spannend.
I think it's sad, terrible, boring.	Ich finde sie traurig, schrecklich, langweilig.
I think Alex / Janice / ... is an interesting, strange, annoying character.	Ich finde den Charakter von Alex / Janice / ... interessant, seltsam, lästig.

Talking about charts and numbers

As you can see in this chart ...	Wie man in diesem Diagramm sehen kann, ...
The results show that ...	Die Ergebnisse zeigen, dass ...
More than half / a third / 20 percent ...	Mehr als die Hälfte / ein Drittel / 20 Prozent ...
Less than half / a third / 20 percent ...	Weniger als die Hälfte / ein Drittel / 20 Prozent ...
We were surprised that ...	Uns überraschte, dass ...

Discussion phrases

What do you think? / What's your opinion?	Was meinst du?
Do you have any comments on ... ?	Möchtest du etwas zu ... sagen?
In my opinion ...	Meiner Meinung nach ...
As far as I know ...	Soweit ich weiß ...
It's a fact that ...	Tatsache ist, dass ...
Actually, ...	Tatsächlich / Eigentlich ...
Basically, ...	Im Grunde ...
I think you are right / wrong.	Ich denke, du hast Recht / Unrecht.
I agree. / I disagree.	Ich stimme zu. / Ich bin anderer Meinung.
Well, you've got a point, but ...	Das mag etwas daran sein, aber ...
Well, I must admit that ..., but ...	Ich muss zwar zugeben, dass ..., aber ...
However, ...	Jedoch ...
On the one hand ..., on the other hand ...	Einerseits ..., anderseits ...

Presentation phrases

The theme of my presentation is ...	Das Thema meines Vortrags ist ...
I'm going to talk about ...	Ich werde über ... sprechen.
I wanted to find out whether ...	Ich wollte herausfinden, ob ...
To begin with, ...	Als Erstes, ...
First of all, ...	Zuallererst ...
Secondly, ...	Zweitens ...
Now let's turn to / have a look at ...	Nun lasst uns zu ... kommen / lasst uns betrachten.
Another important point is ...	Ein weiterer wichtiger Punkt ist ...
Here you can see ...	Hier könnt ihr ... sehen.
This is the reason why ...	Dies ist der Grund, warum ...
And now I'd like to summarize the main points.	Und nun möchte ich die zentralen Punkte zusammenfassen.

Lösungen zu den Check-out-Seiten

Unit 1 page 21

Exercise 1
Hier sollst du über deine Lieblingssportart sprechen – so lange ohne Pause wie möglich.
Musterlösung: I really like soccer very much. I started to play for our club team, FC Renningen, three years ago. I'm a forward, so if I'm lucky, I put in a goal or two every game. A game is really exciting for all of us, and we have great fun in our team. After some games I'm very tired – and sometimes I'm not tired at all. I feel better after a game when we've won, of course! We all try hard. We're playing FC Unterhausen next Sunday. They're a good team, but we are, too.

Exercise 2
1. Anne is playing tennis with Fiona on Sunday. 2. Phil and Ben are meeting at the sports centre on Saturday. 3. Rob is teaching Jill to row on Sunday morning. 4. Tina and Justin are training together at the weekend. 5. Laura's father is driving her to the skatepark tomorrow.

Exercise 3
a) 1. An umpire must be someone who knows the rules of the game. 2. Fans often wear the colours of the team (that / which) they follow. 3. Everyone wants to work with a trainer whose athletes win a lot of races. 4. Rowing champions are often people whose lungs are very big. 5. Wheelchair athletes use wheels that / which don't weigh much. 6. Basketball is easier for players who are very tall. 7. Rugby is a sport (that / which) you play with an oval ball. 8. You should always be polite to the person (who / that) you are playing against.

b) *You do not need the relative pronoun in sentences 2, 7 and 8.*

Exercise 4
Musterlösung: 1. Don't be silly! I don't agree. Girls can do skateboarding as well as boys. 2. That's what I think, too. I like sport, but at weekends there is too much sport on TV. It's better to do sport, not to watch it! 3. Sorry, but you're wrong. Golf can be very exciting, and it's not easy to get the ball in the hole. 4. I don't agree. The Olympics are for everyone, and people with no chance can be a surprise, too. Think of Eddie the Eagle!

Exercise 1
1. had to 2. was not able 3. had to / were allowed to 4. was not able to 5. have already had to / was already allowed to 6. will be allowed to 7. will be able to 8. will not be able to

Unit 2 page 37

Exercise 2
Musterlösung: 1. I suggest we collect ideas in class first and then look on the Internet at home. Perhaps our parents have some ideas. 2. Maybe we could visit the London Zoo or the Tower of London. There's lots of jewellery there! 3. We can look for some good London tips on the Internet, too. Or we could look in a library. 4. Won't it be expensive if we go by train? Or could we fly? 5. But let's check the train times and the prices first. I'd like to know how many hours it is to London. 6. I think we ought to phone the information centre here at home; or we could phone the London tourist office. 7. What do you think: Where can we eat lunch in London? Should we take sandwiches with us or buy them there? 8. When we've found out everything, why don't we write a short report and then give a presentation in the class? Everyone in our team must help with the presentation.

Exercise 3
1. After Chloe had found the diary in an old box in her mum's wardrobe, she went to her room. 2. After she had gone to her room, she read the first few pages of the diary. 3. After Chloe's mum had talked to her, Chloe was shocked. / After she had read the diary, Chloe talked to her mum. 4. After Chloe had told her mum Alex's first name, Chloe and her family suddenly left the house. 5. After they had gone, Alex went to their house, but he couldn't find them.

Exercise 4
Musterlösung: a) Let's visit the new DaimlerChrysler Museum in Stuttgart! – Oh, great! I'd really like to see it. Let's go there on Saturday morning.
b) 1. I'd like to find out how old the oldest car is. 2. How fast was the oldest car? 3. Where does the name 'Mercedes' come from? 4. My favourite Mercedes is the beautiful old 300 SL, but I don't know when they built it. 5. What is the fastest Mercedes called? Is it the famous "Silberpfeil"?

Unit 3 page 55

Exercise 1
1. Miriam and Jake have (just) kissed each other. 2. Mr Patterson has (just) hurt himself. 3. Mrs Patterson has (just) bought herself some new shoes. 4. Mel and Amy have just thrown spaghetti at each other. 5. The computer has (just) turned itself off.

Exercise 2
a) 1. weren't, would have 2. wouldn't buy, had
3. was, would cook 4. had, would drive

b) 1. hadn't left, wouldn't have visited 2. wouldn't have had, hadn't gone 3. had stayed, wouldn't have had, wouldn't have worn, hadn't worn, wouldn't have got, wouldn't have been

Exercise 3

Musterlösung: Hello, …, this is … Can I speak to …, please? – Oh – could I leave a message with you? – Thanks. Here's the message: There's a great film at the Delphi on Saturday afternoon. Let's see it together. Please call me back. Thanks!

Exercise 4

Musterlösung:

Friend: My brother always takes my CDs and DVDs, and then I can't find them. Can you give me any advice?

You: Hm, you've got a problem. It's not nice of him, but maybe he forgets to bring them back to you.

Friend: Well, maybe! But he does it all the time.

You: If I were you, I'd talk to him first. Be friendly, but tell him that he must stop this. What about this: He can use your CDs and DVDs, but he must put them back soon.

Friend: OK, thanks a lot. That's a good idea.

You: And if he still takes your CDs and DVDs and doesn't put them back, you can always talk to your mum or dad about it.

Unit 4 page 71

Exercise 1

1. the 2. *no definite article* 3. *no definite article* 4. the 5. *no definite article* 6. the 7. *no definite article* 8. *no definite article* 9. *no definite article* 10. the 11. the 12. the

Exercise 2

1. a 2. the 3. *no article* 4. *no article* 5. a 6. *no article* 7. *no article* 8. *no article* 9. *no article* 10. an 11. *no article*

Exercise 3

1. excited 2. interesting 3. beautifully 4. easily 5. perfectly 6. nice 7. quietly 8. beautiful

Exercise 4

Musterlösung: a) 1. Hello. Can I help you to carry it? 2. Thank you. That's very kind of you. 3. I do apologize, I'm really sorry! 4. Thanks, you've been a great help. 5. No problem. 6. Yes, I did. I'm terribly sorry.

b) 1. Satz: A: I like this supermarket, they've got everything. But how can I get this all home? Oh, this bag is so heavy! B: Hello. Can I help you to carry it? A: Well, that's terribly nice of you. Thanks. It's not far. B: Ugh! This really is heavy. What's in this bag? A: Uh, well – twenty tins of tasty dog food!

3. Satz: A. I heard what you said! I'm the 'idiot' you were talking about. B: I do apologize, I'm really sorry! Can I explain it to you? A: Yes, OK. B: Well, sometimes you wear funny hats, and … I don't like hats … A: … but *I* do! You know, everyone in my family wears hats – we love them. That's the way our family is – a little crazy, but we're nice! B: And I wasn't very nice. I didn't mean to be rude. A: That's OK now. No problem!

Unit 5 page 89

Exercise 1

1. is seen 2. was discovered 3. had not been offered, had been given 4. was asked 5. is filmed 6. is sent 7. will be included

Exercise 2

1. After Bill's accident, he was taken to hospital by an ambulance. 2. He was given Brussels sprouts and spinach by the people in hospital every day. 3. But soon he was brought spaghetti. 4. He was visited by his mates every day. / "I was visited by my mates every day." 5. Ricky was rescued by Janice. 6. After Ricky had been rescued by Janice, she was invited by TV, newspapers and a magazine to tell her exciting story. 7. She was sent new T-shirts by people and firms from all over England. 8. Soon she will be asked to tell her story by the BBC, too.

Exercise 3

Musterlösung: a) 1. A bike accident 2. Yesterday – boy on bike from class 7b – go home – didn't see little dog – bark – surprise – fall over – hurt leg – ambulance – leg broken – not go to school – three weeks – better now 3. Yesterday a boy from class 7b got on his bike after school. He wanted to go home. There was a little dog outside the school that he didn't see. The dog barked, and that surprised the boy. He fell over and his leg was hurt. He was taken to hospital by an ambulance. His leg is broken. The boy won't be able to go to school for three weeks. He must stay at home, but he is feeling better now.

Exercise 4

Musterlösung: Read *Teen BUZZ*! The greatest teen magazine in the world! *Teen BUZZ* tells you all about fave celebs, about this year's hottest clothes, about the newest hits, about the greatest parties. This is the trendiest pop world magazine you can buy. Buy it – for only three tiny little pounds every Friday, and get the BIG information! Don't be a couch potato. Buy it NOW!

Unit 6 page 105

Exercise 1

He said that he had arrived in Toulouse OK. He told me that Robert and his family were very nice. He said he hadn't had time to see much yet. But he was sure that he was going to love his time in France. – He asked if

Manchester United had won yesterday / the day before. – He hoped he would get tickets for the game there tomorrow / the next day. – He asked whether I / we had heard from Dad, and whether he was enjoying his trip. – He said that he had to go because Robert wanted him. He told me that he would call again soon. He said maybe he could speak to Mum then, and he said bye.

Exercise 2

1. ... pack it. 2. ... warned you not to lose it. 3. ... asked you to get cheese. 4. ... told you to bring yours. 5. ... was told not to wear them. 6. ... advised us to get here early.

Exercise 3

Musterlösung:

A: I'm from Japan. This is my first time in London. B: Your first time? Well, hey! I'm Italian, and it's my first time here, too. I'm told there's a lot to see here. A: You're right, my London guidebook has got 500 pages. It's difficult to decide which place you should visit first! B: Exactly, it's not easy! I'd like to go on the London Eye – would you? A: Oh, yes, I really would. My guidebook says that it's next to the Thames. B: Yes, I know. Maybe that's why it's very expensive. A: Everything is expensive here – it's like Japan! Let's go there together tomorrow. I'm sure there's a great view from the top. What do you think?

Exercise 4

Musterlösung: Positiv: I like *Green Line* 3 because I've learnt a lot and I can say lots of things in English now. Unit 1, because I do lots of sport (I'm no couch potato!). Unit 2, because the comic and the texts are fun, although I'm not really interested in history. Unit 5, because the things which are said about the media are realistic.

Negativ: Unit 4: The text 'Changing places' isn't so good because I still can't imagine what the places are really like! Unit 3: The text 'Chatroom messages' isn't realistic: It's too short, and don't you usually chat with more than two people?

Bildquellen:

UM1/UM4: Corbis/Skelley; S. 8: (1) Getty Images/Forster; (2) Getty Images/Petersen; (3) Picture-Alliance/Naden; S. 9: (1) Getty Images/MN Chan; (2) Picture-Alliance/DPPI; (3) MEV; (4) Picture-Alliance/epa; S. 10: Alamy Images RF/Photospin; S. 11: Fotosearch RF/Stockbyte; S. 12: Das Fotoarchiv/RF; S. 13: Corbis/McNamee; S. 14: © 1995 by Macmillan Children's Books, London, ISBN 0-330-34281-9; S. 15: Corbis/Reuters/Atkinson; S. 16: (1–2) Getty Images/Schneider; S. 17: (1) Fotosearch RF/Digital Vision; (2) Getty Images/Cannon; (3) Corbis/Bettmann; (5) Getty Images/Powell; S. 18: (1–2) Picture-Alliance/Dal Zennaro; S. 20: (1, 4, 6) Fotosearch RF/PhotoDisc; (2, 3) Getty Images RF/PhotoDisc; (5) Corbis/KARAHALIS/Re; S. 22: Avenue Images GmbH/Ingram Publishing; S. 23: (1) Getty Images RF/PhotoDisc; (2) Fotolia LLC/RF/eblue; S. 26–27: Alamy Images RM/IML Image Group; S. 28: Alamy Images RM/Koca; S. 29: Education Photos/Walmsley; S. 30: (1) Corbis/Bettmann; (2) Wikimedia Foundation Inc.; S. 31: (1) Avenue Images GmbH/Image Source; (2) Historic Royal Palaces; (3) Alamy Images RM/AA World Travel; (4) Topham Picturepoint/Woodmansterne; S. 32: Joker/Gerard; S. 41: Fotofinder; S. 42: (1) defd; (2) Cinetext; (3) BBC Broadcasting Corporation South; (4) The Moviestore Collection; S. 43: (1) Klett-Archiv/Hill; (2) Avenue Images GmbH/StockDisc; S. 44: Klett-Archiv/Hill; S. 46: iStockphoto/RF/Levstek; S. 47: Klett-Archiv/Hill; S. 49: Fotosearch RF; S. 50: Fotosearch RF/Stockbyte; S. 51: Klett-Archiv/Hill; S. 53: Corbis/Cardinale; S. 54: Corbis/Kaufmann; S. 56: (1, 4) Stockfood Photo Stock Agency; (2–3) Getty Images RF/PhotoDisc; S. 57: (1) obs; (2) Thomas Tallis Scholl: www.school-portal.co.uk; S. 58: (1) Alamy Images RM/Lyons; (2) iStockphoto/RF/Mansi; (3) Getty Images RF/Photodisc; S. 59: (1) Alamy Images RM/eye35.com; (2) iStockphoto/RF/Bendy; (3) Alamy Images RM/Howes/Wild Places Photo; S. 60: Corbis/Fisher; S. 61: Alamy Images RM/Morgan; S. 63: (1) Avenue Images GmbH/Image Source; (2) Wikimedia Foundation Inc./Public Domain; S. 64: iStockphoto/RF/Waiheng; S. 65: (1) Marco Polo Agence Photographique/Bouillot; (2) Superbild/Bouillot; (3) Picture-Alliance/KPA; S. 66: DigitalVision; S. 67: Alamy Images RM: (1) Wiedel; (2) Photolibary; (3) Lyons; S. 68: (1) Alamy Images RM/Titmuss; (2) JupiterImages/RF/photos.com; (3) www.williamsontunnels.co.uk/Bridson; S. 69: Corbis: (1) Fisher; (2) /Edifice/Darley; (3) Corbis/Ward; S. 70: Getty Images/Taxi/Murray; S. 71: Alamy Images RM/Photolibary; S. 75: Corbis/Nowitz; S. 76: (1) www.shoutmag.co.uk; (2) www.timesonline.co.uk; S. 77: (1) Bananastock RF; (2) Picture-Alliance/dpa; (3) iStockphoto/RF/Duplass; S. 78: (1) Corbis/zefa/Holz; (2) Visum/C&M Fragasso; S. 79: Avenue Images GmbH/Ingram Publishing; S. 81: (1) iStockphoto/RF/Prikhodko; (2) Avenue Images GmbH/image100; (3, 4) Fotosearch RF/Design Pics; (5) iStockphoto/RF/Alvarez; (6) Young and Rubicon/Noel Ford; S. 82: (1) Alamy Images RM/Digital Vision; (2) iStockphoto/RF/Russ; S. 83: Alamy Images RM/Allstar; S. 84: Corbis/Hellestad; S. 86: (1) Fotolia LLC/RF/Stitt; (2) Avenue Images GmbH/Image Source; S. 87: Fotolia LLC/RF/Stitt; S. 88: Corbis/Sands/NY New; S. 90: (1) Reprinted with Special Permission of King Features Syndicate; (2–3) Ingram Publishing; S. 91: Getty Images/Vincent; S. 92: (1, 2) Avenue Images GmbH/Stockbyte; S. 93: (1) Corbis/Bettman; (2) Wikimedia Foundation Inc.; (3) ullstein bild/Reuters; S. 94: (1) Marco Polo Agence Photographique; (2) Mauritius/age; S. 95: (1) MEV; (2) Avenue Images GmbH/Image Source; S. 97: (1) Corbis/Trotter/Eye Ubiquitous; (2) Getty Images/Image Bank/Yellow Dog; (3) Getty Images/Image Bank/Yellow Do; (4) JupiterImages/RF/photos.com; S. 98: Avenue Images GmbH/Image Source/RF; S. 100: Corbis/Creasource; S. 101: Corbis/Creasource; S. 104: (1) Getty Images/Image Bank; (2) Avenue Images GmbH/Banana Stock; (3) Getty Images/taxi/Bray; S. 105: Avenue Images GmbH/Stock Disc; S. 109: Alamy Images RM/Pitt; S. 110: (1) Alamy Images RM/Greenberg; (2) Fotosearch RF/Stockbyte; S. 112: Avenue Images GmbH/Image Source; S. 113: (1) Victoria & Albert Museum/V&A Images; (2) Imageshop RF; S. 115: Das Fotoarchiv/RF; S. 116: Picture-Alliance/akg; S. 117: Wikimedia Foundation Inc./Public Domain; S. 118: (1) iStockphoto/RF/Deshaies; (2) D. C. Thomson; S. 119: (1) D. C. Thomson; (2) iStockphoto/RF/Deshaies; S. 120: (1) MEV; (2) Niehoff; S. 122: (2) Lade; (3) Fotosearch RF/PhotoDisc; (4, 5, 8) Corel Corporation; (6) Corbis/zefa/Ruckszi; (7) Getty Images RF/Photo Disc; S. 123: (1) defd; (2) Sipa Press/Nana Productions; (3–4) Klett-Archiv/Hill; S. 155: (1) Fotosearch RF/PhotoDisc; (2) Fotosearch RF/Digital Vision; S. 158: (1) Corbis/Westmorland; (2) Image 100/RF; S. 160: Fotosearch RF/PhotoDisc; S. 161: Avenue Images GmbH/Stock Disc; S. 162: Getty Images RF/Photodisc; S. 164: (1) iStockphoto/RF/Lee; (2) Avenue Images GmbH/Digital Vision; S. 167: Fotosearch RF/Image 100; S. 169: Corbis/Woolfitt; S. 170: Mauritius/Pöhlmann; S. 176: (1) iStockphoto/RF; (2) Getty Images RF/Photodisc; S. 180: Corel Corporation; S. 217: (1) Getty Images RF/Photodisc; (2) Interfoto; (3–4) AKG; (5) Wikimedia Foundation Inc.; (6) Corbis/Bettmann

Song- und Textquellen:

S. 16–17: © Scholastic Publ. London, Tim Lardner; S. 18: © Williamson Music Int. Für D/A/CH/osteuropäische Länder: EMI Music Publishing (Germany GmbH), Hamburg, Williamson Music Int.; S. 36: © Traditional; S. 39–39: © Scholastic Children's Book, Philip Pulman; S. 54: © by NIGHT GARDEN MUSIC/WARNER TAMERLINE PUBL., NEUE WELT MUSIKVERLAG GMBH, Hamburt, WARNER/CHAPPELL MUSIC GERMANY GMBH & CO.; S. 65: © Heatside Music Ltd., Rudolf Slezak Musikverlag GmbH, D-22089 Hamburg; S. 72–73: © The O'Brian Press Ltd. Eoin Colfer; S. 88: © Almo-Music Copr./Ferry Hills Songs/Mr. Spock Music/Rainbow Fish Publ./Warner-Tamerlane Publ. Co., NEUE WELT MUSICKVERLAG GMBH, Hamburg, Rondor Musikverlag GmbH, Berlin; S. 103: © WARNER/CHAPPELL MUSIC LTD, NEUE WELT MUSIKVERLAG GMBH &CO.KG; S. 106–107: © Cambridge University Press, Robert Louis Stevenson; S. 118–119: © Shout, D.C. Thomson & Co. Ltd

Dictionary (German–English)

A

abbiegen to turn **I**
(nach) rechts abbiegen to turn right **I**
Abend evening **I**; night **I**
eines Abends one evening **I**
Abendessen dinner **III U4,** 66
(frühes) Abendessen tea **III U4,** 60
abends in the evening **I**
Abenteuer adventure **I**
aber but **I**
abfahren to leave **II**
Abflug departure **II**
(Telefon) abheben to take a call **III U3,** 50
abheben to take off **II**
abholen to pick up **I**
ablecken to lick **I**
ablenken to distract **III U5,** 87
Abmachung arrangement **III U1,** 10
abmalen to copy **I**
den Tisch **abräumen** to clear the table **II**
Abreise departure **II**
Absatz paragraph **III U2,** 35
abschalten to turn off **III U3,** 45
abschreiben to copy **I**
Abseilen abseiling **II**
abseits offside **III U1,** 19
absichtlich deliberate **II**
abspielen to play **I**
abspülen to wash up **II**
abstrakt abstract **III U4,** 60
abtasten to scan **III U4,** 66
abwaschen to wash up **II**
sich **abwechseln** to take turns **I**
acht eight **I**
achtzehn eighteen **I**
achtzig eighty **I**
Acker field **I**
Action action **III U2,** 26
Adjektiv adjective **I**
Adler eagle **III U1,** 16
Adressbuch address book **I**
Adresse address **I**
Aerobic aerobics **II**
Affe monkey **I**
Agent/-in agent **III U5,** 78
aggressiv aggressive **II**
Aha! I see. **III U3,** 46
ähm um **III U6,** 100
Akte file **III U5,** 78
Aktiv active **III U5,** 80
Aktivität activity **I**
aktuell in **II**
Akzent accent **III U4,** 67
albern silly **I**
alle everybody **II**
alle/-s (davon) all of it **II**
alle/-s all **I**
alle zehn Minuten every ten minutes **I**
aus aller Welt from all round the world **I**
allein alone **I**
allergisch auf allergic to **I**
alles everything **I**
allgemein universal **II**
Alphabet alphabet **I**
alphabetisch alphabetical **I**
als than **II**; as **II**
als when **I**
also so **I**
alt old **I**
Alter age **III U2,** 25
Altersheim old people's home **III U3,** 44
altmodisch old-fashioned **III U2,** 33
aus **Amerika** American **III U1,** 9
amerikanisch American **III U1,** 9
Amerikanisch American **III U1,** 9
sich **amüsieren** to have fun **I**; to enjoy oneself **III U3,** 44
an to **I**; on **I**; at **I**
an der Spitze (von) at the front of **II**
anbellen to bark at **I**
anbieten to offer **III U3,** 53
andauern to go on **III U1,** 8
Andenken souvenir **I**
andere/-r/-s other **I**
die anderen the others **I**
ein/-e andere/-r/-s another **I**
anders different **I**
Anfang beginning **III U5,** 85
anfangen to begin **II**; to start **I**
anfeuern to cheer **III U4,** 68
Angeln fishing **II**
an(geschaltet) on **II**
angreifen to attack **III U2,** 25
Angst haben um to be scared for **I**
anhaben to wear **II**
Anhänger/-in fan **II**
anklicken to click on **I**
ankommen to arrive **II**
Ankündigung announcement **II**
Ankunft arrival **II**
anlächeln to smile at **II**
anmalen to paint **II**
Anorak anorak **II**
anpreisen to advertise **III U5,** 77
anprobieren to try on **I**
Anruf phone call **I**; call **II**
einen Anruf entgegennehmen to take a call **III U3,** 50
Anrufbeantworter answerphone **III U3,** 43
anrufen to call **III U3,** 45; to phone **I**
Anrufer/-in caller **III U3,** 50
anschauen to look at **I**
ansehen to watch **I**; to look at **I**
anstehen to queue **III U1,** 20
sich **anstellen** to queue **III U1,** 20
sich **anstrengen** to try hard **II**
Antiquität antique **II**
Antwort answer **I**; reply **III U4,** 65
antworten to answer **I**; to reply **III U2,** 33
Anzeige ad(vertisement) **III U5,** 82
sich **anziehen** to get dressed **III U3,** 44
Anzug suit **II**
Apfel apple **I**
Apparat machine **I**
applaudieren to applaud **III U3,** 53
April April **I**
Arbeit job **I**; work **II**
arbeiten to work **I**
Arbeiter/-in worker **II**
Areal area **III U6,** 97
Ärger trouble **I**
ärgerlich annoying **III U6,** 100
arm poor **II**
die Armen the poor **III U4,** 60
Arm arm **II**
Armbanduhr watch **II**
Armee army **II**
Aroma flavour **I**
Art kind **II**; form **II**; type **III U3,** 47
Art und Weise way **II**
Artikel article **II**
Arzt doctor **II**
Ärztin doctor **II**
Asiate, Asiatin Asian **III U4,** 63
asiatisch Asian **III U4,** 63
Assistent/-in assistant **III U5,** 78
Athlet/-in athlete **III U1,** 13
Aua! Ouch! **III U3,** 44
auch too **I**; also **III U1,** 13
Audio- audio **III U4,** 65
auf on **I**; at **I**
auf der linken Seite on the left **I**
auf Englisch in English **I**
auf ... hinauf on top of **I**; onto **II**
aufbewahren to keep **I**
aufessen to eat up **III U3,** 43
aufführen to perform **II**
(ein Theaterstück) aufführen to put on (a play) **III U3,** 53
Aufführung show **III U5,** 80
Aufgabe job **I**
aufgeben to give up **II**
aufgeregt nervous **I**; excited **I**
aufheben to pick up **II**
aufhören to stop **I**
Aufladekarte *(fürs Handy)* top-up card **II**
aufmachen to open **I**
jmdn. auf sich **aufmerksam machen** to get attention **III U5,** 84
aufpassen to watch out **I**
aufpassen auf to look after **I**
aufprallen to crash **I**
aufräumen to tidy (up) **III U3,** 43
aufregend exciting **II**
aufschreiben to write down **I**
aufstehen to get up **I**
auftreten to perform **II**
aufwachen to wake up **I**
aufwecken to wake up **I**

Auge eye **I**
Augenblick moment **I**
im Augenblick just now **I**
August August **I**
aus from **I**
aus ... heraus out of **II**
Ausbildung training **II**
Ausblick view **II**
Auschecken check-out **I**
(sich) **ausdenken** to think of **I**
Auseinandersetzung argument **III U5,** 85
ausflippen to go crazy **III U3,** 49
Ausflug trip **I**
ausführen to take out **I**
den Hund ausführen to walk the dog **I**
ausfüllen to fill in **I**
ausgeben (für) to spend (on) **II**
ausgehen mit to go out with **III U3,** 49
Ausguck crow's nest **I**
auskommen to get on **III U3,** 43
auslachen to laugh at **II**
(sich) **ausleihen** to borrow **II**
ausmisten to muck out **I**
ausprobieren to try out **III U4,** 69
ausradieren to rub out **II**
Grüße **ausrichten** to say hello to **I**
(sich) **ausruhen** to relax **III U3,** 44
Ausrüstung equipment **II**
ausschalten to turn off **III U3,** 45
aussehen to look **I**
Aussehen look **III U5,** 82
außen outside **I**
außerhalb outside **I**
außerirdisches Wesen alien **II**
Außerirdische/-r alien **II**
Aussicht view **II**
Ausstattung equipment **II**
aussteigen to get off **II**
Ausstellung exhibition **III U4,** 63
Austausch exchange **III U4,** 58
austauschen to exchange **III U5,** 85
auswählen to choose **I**
ausziehen to take off **I**
Auto car **I**
Autobahn motorway **III U4,** 66
Automat machine **I**

B

babyleicht easy-peasy **I**
Bäcker/-in baker **II**
Bad(ezimmer) bathroom **I**
ein Bad nehmen to have a bath **III U2,** 31
Badeanzug swimsuit **I**
Bahn track **III U1,** 9
Bahnhof station **I**
Bahnsteig platform **II**
bald soon **I**
Ball ball **I**
Band band **I**
Base *(beim Baseball)* base **III U1,** 8
Baseball baseball **III U1,** 8
Basketball basketball **I**
Bauch stomach **II**
bauen to build **I**
Bauernhof farm **I**
Baum tree **I**
beamen to beam **II**
beängstigend scary **I**
beantworten to answer **I**
beben to shake **II**
Becher mug **I**
bedauern to feel sorry for **III U3,** 46
bedeuten to mean **I**
Bedeutung meaning **I**
sich **bedienen** to help oneself (to) **III U3,** 44
Bedienstete/-r servant **III U2,** 33
Bedienung waitress **II**; waiter **II**
sich **beeilen** to hurry up **I**
beeindruckend awesome **III U5,** 77
beenden to finish **I**; to stop **I**
sich **befassen mit** to deal with **III U4,** 62
Befehl command **III U6,** 98
befolgen to follow **II**
befördern to carry **II**
Beförderung transport *(no pl.)* **I**
Befragung interview **II**
begeistert excited **I**
Beginn beginning **III U5,** 85
beginnen to start **I**; to begin **II**
jemanden **begrüßen** to say hello **I**
behalten to keep **I**
behindert disabled **III U1,** 13
bei at **I**
beibringen to teach **I**
beide both **II**
Beifahrer/-in passenger **II**
Bein leg **I**
beinahe almost **II**
Beispiel example **I**
beitreten to join **II**
bekommen to get **I**
Beleuchtung lights *(pl.)* **III U3,** 53
beliebt popular **II**
bellen to bark **I**
sich **benehmen** to behave **III U3,** 43
benutzen to use **I**
beobachten to watch **I**
Bereich field **II**
bereit ready **I**
bereits already **I**
Berg mountain **I**; hill **II**
Bericht report **II**; article **II**
berichten to report **III U6,** 94
berichtigen to correct **I**
sich **beruhigen** to relax **III U3,** 44
berühmt famous **I**
berühmte Persönlichkeit celeb(rity) **III U5,** 76
beschäftigt (mit) busy (with) **I**
(sich) **beschlagen** to mist up **III U1,** 16
beschreiben to describe **I**
Besetzung cast **III U3,** 51
Besichtigungstour sightseeing **II**
besiegen to defeat **III U2,** 25
besitzen to have got **I**; to have **II**; to own **II**
Besitzer/-in owner **I**
besondere/-r/-s special **I**
besonders especially **III U3,** 47
besorgt worried **I**
Besorgungen machen to do the shopping **II**
besser better **II**
bestehen to exist **III U4,** 59
bestellen to order **II**
beste/-r/-s best **I**
bestimmt definite **III U4,** 60
besuchen to visit **I**; to attend **III U5,** 85
Besucher/-in visitor **I**
betonen to stress **III U2,** 36
Betonung stress **III U2,** 36
betreten to enter **II**
Bett bed **I**
beunruhigt worried **I**
bevor before **I**
(sich) **bewegen** to move **II**
bewusst deliberate **II**
bezahlen to pay **II**
Bibliothek library **II**
bieten to offer **III U3,** 53
Bild picture **I**
bilden to make **I**
Bildung education **II**
billig cheap **I**
binden to tie **III U5,** 87
Biografie biography **III U6,** 96
(spätestens) **bis** by **III U4,** 65
bis until **II**
bis before **I**
bis jetzt so far **II**
bitte please **I**
Bitte schön. Here you are. **I**; You're welcome. **I**
blau blue **I**
bleiben to stay **II**
draußen bleiben to keep out **III U2,** 24
fit bleiben to keep fit **II**
Bleistift pencil **I**
Blick view **II**
bloß only **II**
Blume flower **I**
Blut blood **III U5,** 87
bluten to bleed **II**
Bob bobsleigh **III U1,** 13
Boden bottom **I**; earth **II**
Bohrinsel oil platform **II**
Boot boat **I**
böse bad **I**
Boss boss **II**
Boulevardzeitung popular newspaper **III U5,** 76
Box box **I**
Boygroup boy band **I**
brauchen to need **I**
braun brown **I**
brechen to break **I**; to crack **III U5,** 86

Bremse brake III U1, 9
brennen to burn II
Brett plank I; board I
Briefkasten postbox II
Briefmarke stamp II
Brille glasses *(pl.)* III U1, 16
bringen to take I; to bring I; to get I
Brite, Britin Briton III U2, 26
britisch British I
Broschüre brochure I
Brot bread II
Brücke bridge I
Bruder brother I
Buch book I
buchen to book III U6, 104
Bücherwurm bookworm III U5, 81
Büchse tin I
Buchstabe letter I
buchstabieren to spell I
Büffel buffalo pl. buffalo III U6, 101
Bühne stage III U2, 26
  auf der Bühne on stage II
Burg castle I
Büro office II
Bus bus pl. buses I
Bushaltestelle bus stop I

C

Café café I; snack bar II
Cafeteria cafeteria I
Campingplatz campsite II
Cartoon cartoon III U1, 12
Casting casting III U5, 78
CD CD I
Center centre I
Champion champion II
Chance chance III U1, 10
Charakter character II
Chatroom chatroom III U3, 47
chatten to chat III U3, 47
Chef/-in boss II
Chemiekasten chemistry set I
Chemikalie chemical III U6, 97
Chip card I
nach Christus AD *(= Anno Domini)* III U2, 24
Comic(heft) comic III U2, 25
Computer computer I
Computergeschäft computer shop I
Computerklub computer club I
Computerunterricht Technology II
cool cool I; wicked II
Couch sofa I
Couchpotato couch potato III U5, 81
Cousin/-e cousin I
Curry *(Gewürz oder Gericht)* curry III U4, 63

D

da because I
da there I
Dach roof III U5, 87
etwas dagegen haben to mind III U3, 46
dahin there I
Dame lady III U2, 33
Dampf steam III U2, 24
Dampfmaschine steam engine III U2, 24
danach then I; after that I
dank thanks to I
vielen Dank thanks a lot I
danke thank you I; thanks I
Nichts zu danken. You're welcome. I
dann then I
das the I; that I
dass that I
Datum date I
dauern to go on III U1, 8; to take III U6, 93
Definition definition III U1, 14
dein(e) your I
denken to think I
  denken an to remember I
  denken über to think of I; to think about I
der the I
der *(Relativpronomen)* who III U1, 13; which III U1, 13; that III U1, 13
deren whose III U1, 13
der-/die-/dasselbe the same I
deshalb so I
dessen whose III U1, 13
je … desto … the … the … II
Detail detail III U2, 32
deutsch German I
Deutsch German I
aus Deutschland German I
Deutschlehrer/-in German teacher I
Dezember December I
Diabetes diabetes II
Dialog dialogue I
dich selbst yourself I
Dichter/-in poet III U2, 25
die the I
die *(Relativpronomen)* that I; who III U1, 13; which III U1, 13
Dieb/-in thief pl. **thieves** I
Diener/-in servant III U2, 33
Dienst service III U6, 97
Dienstag Tuesday I
dienstags on Tuesdays I
diese (dort) those I
  diese (hier) these I
diese/-r/-s this I
Ding thing I
Dinosaurier dinosaur II
direkt straight I
  direkte Rede direct speech III U6, 94
Discjockey DJ I
Discman Discman I
Disco disco III U2, 28
Diskothek disco III U2, 28
diskutieren to discuss III U5, 79
Diskutieren discussing III U5, 81
Distanz distance III U6, 104
DJ DJ I
Dock dock III U4, 68
Donnerstag Thursday I
Dorf village I
dort there I
  (nach) dort drüben over there I
dorthin there I
Dose tin I
Drachen kite I
  einen Drachen steigen lassen to fly a kite I
Drachenfest kite festival I
Drama drama II
draußen outside I
  draußen bleiben to keep out III U2, 24
  draußen halten to keep out III U2, 24
  nach draußen out I
dreckig dirty I
Drehbuch script III U5, 78
drehen to film III U5, 79
drei three I
dreißig thirty I
dreizehn thirteen I
dritte/-r/-s third I
drücken to push II
du you I
  du (selbst) yourself III U3, 44
Dudelsack bagpipes *(pl.)* II
Duft smell I
duften to smell III U4, 63
dumm silly I
Dummkopf silly I
dunkel dark I
dünn thin II
durch through II
durchdrehen to go crazy III U3, 49
durcheinander geraten jumbled I
Durcheinander mess I
Durchsage announcement II
im Durchschnitt on average III U4, 58
durchschnittlich on average III U4, 58
durchsuchen to scan III U4, 66
dürfen may I; can I; to be allowed to (do sth) III U2, 26
  nicht dürfen mustn't I
DVD DVD II

E

E-Card e-card III U5, 77
echt real II
Ecke corner II
Das ist mir egal! I don't care! III U3, 43
Ehefrau wife pl. wives II
Ei egg I
eifersüchtig jealous (of) III U3, 47
eiförmig oval III U1, 8
Eigenartigkeit oddity III U1, 14
eigene/-r/-s own I

Eigenschaftswort adjective **I**
eigentlich actually **III U2,** 35
Eile hurry **I**
in Eile sein to be in a hurry **I**
ein/-e a, an **I**
ein/-e andere/-r/-s another **I**
noch ein/-e another **I**
einander each other **III U3,** 43
tief **einatmen** to gasp **III U2,** 34
einbiegen to turn **I**
Einbrecher/-in burglar **III U6,** 99
Einchecken check-in **I**
einfach easy **I**; simple **II**; basic **III U5,** 85
einfach just **I**
sich etwas **einfallen lassen** to think of **I**
einfangen to catch **I**
einführen to introduce **III U6,** 94
Eingang entrance **II**
Einheit unit **I**
einhundert a/one hundred **I**
einige a few **I**; some **I**
Einkäufe machen to do the shopping **II**
einkaufen gehen to go shopping **I**
Einkaufen shopping **I**
Einkaufszettel shopping list **II**
einladen to invite **I**
... (zu etwas) einladen to invite ... out **I**
Einladung invitation **I**
einleiten to introduce **III U6,** 94
einmal once **III U1,** 12
(noch) nicht einmal not even **I**
auf einmal suddenly **I**; at once **I**
Es war einmal ... Once upon a time ... **III U2,** 24
einpacken to pack **I**
einreisen to enter **II**
eins one **I**
einsam lonely **III U2,** 33
einsammeln to collect **I**
einschlafen to fall asleep **I**
einsetzen to put in **I**
einsteigen to get into **I**; to get on **II**
eintausend a/one thousand **I**
Eintrittskarte ticket **II**
Einzelheit detail **III U2,** 32
Einzelkind only child **I**
einzige-r/-s only **II**
Eis ice-cream **I**; ice **III U1,** 8
Eiscreme ice-cream **I**
Eisenbahn railway **III U6,** 101
Eishockey ice hockey **III U1,** 9
Elefant elephant **III U2,** 25
Elektrizität power **III U2,** 24
Elendsviertel slum **III U2,** 30
elf eleven **I**
Elfmeter penalty **III U1,** 19
elisabethanisch Elizabethan **III U2,** 25
Eltern parents *(pl.)* **I**
E-Mail e-mail **I**
Empfang welcome **III U6,** 95
empfehlen to recommend **III U6,** 96
Ende end **II**; ending **III U2,** 35
enden to finish **I**; to end **I**
endlich finally **I**
Energie power **III U2,** 24
eng tight **III U5,** 87
aus **England** English **I**
englisch English **I**
Englisch English **I**
englischsprachig English-speaking **II**
Ensemble cast **III U3,** 51
entdecken to discover **III U5,** 78
Entfernung distance **III U6,** 104
(sich auf halbem Weg) **entgegenkommen** to meet halfway **III U3,** 46
entgegnen to reply **III U2,** 33
entlanggehen to go down **I**
(sich) **entscheiden** to decide **III U3,** 44
Entscheidung decision **III U3,** 52
eine Entscheidung treffen to make a decision **III U3,** 52
sich **entschuldigen** to apologize **III U4,** 62
Entschuldigung. Excuse me. **I**
Entsetzen horror **II**
(sich) **entspannen** to relax **III U3,** 44
enttäuschend disappointing **III U6,** 94
Entwicklung evolution **III U6,** 93
er he **I**
er (selbst) himself **III U3,** 44
Erbe/Erbin heir **III U2,** 25
Erdbeben earthquake **II**
Erdboden earth **II**
Erde earth **II**
Erdkunde Geography **II**
Ereignis event **III U1,** 10
erfinden to invent **III U2,** 25
Erfindung invention **III U2,** 24
Erfolg success **II**
jmdn. **erinnern (an)** to remind (about) **II**
sich erinnern (an) to remember **I**
Erkältung cold **III U5,** 86
erklären to explain **I**
erklimmen to climb **I**
erlauben to allow **III U5,** 85
jmdn. **ermahnen** to warn sb **III U6,** 97
ernähren to feed **III U2,** 33
eröffnen to open **III U1,** 11
erraten to guess **I**
(telefonisch) **erreichen** to contact **III U3,** 50
erreichen to get to **I**
erschaffen to create **III U5,** 77
sich zu Tode **erschrecken** to jump out of one's skin **III U6,** 101
erst only **II**
als **Erstes** first **I**
erste/-r/-s first **I**
ertragen to stand **III U3,** 44
ertränken to drown **III U2,** 34
ertrinken to drown **III U2,** 34
Erwachsene/-r adult **III U6,** 104
erwähnen to mention **III U6,** 94
erwarten to expect **II**
erwidern to reply **III U2,** 33
erzählen to tell **I**
Erzählung story **I**
Erzeugnis product **III U5,** 82
Erziehung education **II**
es it **I**
Es war einmal ... Once upon a time ... **III U2,** 24
essen to eat **I**
Essen meal **I**; food **I**
etwas a little **I**; some **I**; something **II**
euer, eure your **I**
Euro *(Währung)* euro **II**
aus **Europa** European **I**
Europäer/-in European **I**
europäisch European **I**
Europäische Union European Union **III U2,** 25
Evolution evolution **III U6,** 93
exakt exact **III U1,** 15
Exemplar copy **III U5,** 76
existieren to exist **III U4,** 59
Extra extra **III U4,** 69

F

Fabrik factory **III U2,** 24
fähig sein (zu) to be able to (do sth) **III U2,** 26
Fähre ferry **II**
fahren to drive **I**; to go **I**; to ride **I**; to travel **II**
in Urlaub fahren to go on holiday **I**
Fahrer/-in driver **I**
Fahrgast passenger **II**
einfache **Fahrkarte** single **III U6,** 104
Hin- und Rückfahrkarte return **III U6,** 104
Fahrkartenschranke ticket gate **II**
Fahrplan timetable **II**
Fahrpreis fare **II**
Fahrrad bike **I**
Fahrschein ticket **II**
Fahrt trip **I**
fair fair **I**
Fakt fact **II**
in der **Falle sitzen** to be trapped **III U6,** 99
fallen to fall **I**; to fall off **III U5,** 86
falls if **II**
falsch wrong **I**; false **II**
Familie family **I**
Familienstammbaum family tree **I**
Fan fan **II**
fangen to catch **I**
fantastisch fantastic **III U6,** 100
Farbe colour **I**; paint **II**
färben to dye **II**
Farmer/-in farmer **III U2,** 30
fast almost **II**
Februar February **I**
Federmäppchen pencil-case **I**
fehlend missing **I**
Fehler mistake **II**
Feier party **I**
feiern to celebrate **II**
eine Party feiern to have a party **I**

Feind/-in enemy **II**
Feld field **III U1,** 8
Fell skin **III U6,** 101
Fels rock **I**
felsig rocky **I**
Fenster window **I**
Ferien holiday(s) **I**
Fernseher TV **I**
im Fernsehen on TV **I**
Fernsehglotzer/-in couch potato **III U5,** 81
fertig ready **I**
fertig stellen to finish **I**; to complete **III U6,** 101
Fertigkeit skill **I**
fest tight **III U5,** 87
Fest festival **I**
festhalten to hold **I**
Festival festival **I**
Festung fortress **III U2,** 31
Feuer fire **II**
Feuerwehrfrau firefighter **III U6,** 97
Feuerwehrmann firefighter **III U6,** 97
Fieber temperature **II**
Figur character **II**
Film film **I**
filmen to film **III U5,** 79
finden to think **I**
finden to find **I**
Finger finger **II**
Firma firm **III U4,** 60
Fisch fish pl. fish **I**
Fisch und Pommes frites fish and chips **II**
Fischen fishing **II**
Fischerei fishing **II**
fit fit **II**
fit bleiben to keep fit **II**
Fitness fitness **II**
Fläche area **III U6,** 97
Flasche bottle **I**
flattern to flap **III U1,** 17
Fleisch meat **II**
fliegen to fly **I**
fliegend flying **III U2,** 35
Flug flight **II**
Flügel wing **III U4,** 59
Flughafen airport **II**
Flugzeug plane **II**
Flur hall **II**; corridor **II**
Fluss river **I**
Flussdiagramm flow chart **II**
folgen to follow **II**
folgende/-r/-s the following **III U2,** 28
folglich so **I**
Form form **I**
in Form fit **II**
Forschung research **III U4,** 66
Foto photo **I**
ein Foto machen to take a photo **I**
Fotoapparat camera **I**
fotografieren to photograph **III U5,** 79
Frage question **I**
fragen to ask **I**
nach ... fragen to ask for ... **I**
sich fragen to wonder **III U2,** 34
Fragewort question word **I**
französisch French **II**
Französisch French **II**
Frau woman pl. women **I**; lady **III U2,** 33
Frau *(Anrede)* Mrs **I**
frei free **II**
im Freien outside **I**; open-air **III U2,** 26
Freilicht- open-air **III U2,** 26
Freitag Friday **I**
Freizeit free time **I**; leisure **III U4,** 66
Freizeit- leisure **III U4,** 66
fremd strange **III U2,** 34
Freund/-in friend **I**; mate **I**
Freund *(in einer Paarbeziehung)* boyfriend **III U3,** 49
Freundin *(in einer Paarbeziehung)* girlfriend **III U2,** 33
freundlich kind **II**; friendly **II**
Freundschaft friendship **III U4,** 60
Freundschaft schließen to make friends **II**
friedlich calm **I**
Frisbeescheibe Frisbee **II**
frisch fresh **I**
froh glad **II**
fröhlich happy **I**
Frucht fruit **II**
früh early **I**
Frühling spring **I**
Frühstück breakfast **I**
frühstücken to have breakfast **I**
Frühstückszerealie cereal *(no pl.)* **III U5,** 86
Fuchs fox **I**
(sich) **fühlen** to feel **II**
führen to go **I**
Führer/-in guide **II**
Füller pen **I**
Füllwort filler **III U6,** 100
fünf five **I**
fünfzehn fifteen **I**
fünfzig fifty **I**
funktionieren to work **I**
für for **I**
furchtbar terrible **I**; horrible **II**; awful **III U4,** 60
furchterregend frightening **III U6,** 102
Fuß foot pl. feet **I**
zu Fuß on foot **III U6,** 102
Fußball football **I**; soccer **III U5,** 82
Fußboden floor **III U2,** 30
füttern to feed **I**

G

Gabel fork **II**
Galerie gallery **II**
Gang corridor **II**
ganz all **I**; whole **I**
Garage garage **I**
Garten garden **I**
Gartenhäuschen shed **I**
Gastfamilie host family **II**
Gastgeber/-in host **II**
Gaststätte restaurant **I**
Gebäude building **II**
geben to give **I**
es gibt there's (= there is) **I**; there are **I**
Gebiet territory **I**; field **II**; area **III U6,** 97
geboren werden to be born **II**
gebrauchen to use **I**
gebrochen broken **II**
Gebrüll bellow **III U6,** 101
Geburtsort birthplace **III U4,** 59
Geburtstag birthday **I**
Alles Gute zum Geburtstag! Happy Birthday! **I**
Geburtstagsfeier birthday party **I**
geduldig patient **II**
Gefahr danger **III U6,** 102
gefährlich dangerous **III U6,** 97
Gefangene/-r prisoner **II**
Gefängnis prison **III U2,** 31
gefroren frozen **III U3,** 43
Gefühl feeling **III U1,** 10
gegen against **I**
Gegend region **III U4,** 58
sich **(gegenseitig)** each other **III U3,** 43
Gegenteil opposite **II**
gegenüber opposite **I**
Gegenwart present **I**
geheim secret **III U3,** 49
Geheimnis secret **II**
gehen to go **I**
gehen *(zu Fuß)* to walk **I**
gehen mit to go out with **III U3,** 49
gehen um to be about **III U2,** 32
in Urlaub gehen to go on holiday **I**
ins Bett gehen to go to bed **I**
nach oben gehen to go up **I**
nach unten gehen to go down **I**
surfen gehen to go surfing **I**
über ... gehen to cross **I**
gehören zu to go with **I**
Geist ghost **III U2,** 34
geizig mean **II**
schlecht **gelaunt** grumpy **III U3,** 52
gelb yellow **I**
Geld money **I**
Geld verdienen to make money **II**
Geld sammeln to raise money **III U5,** 85
Geldbeutel *(BE)* purse **III U3,** 48
Gelegenheit chance **III U1,** 10
gemeinsam together **I**
gemischt mixed **I**
Gemüse vegetable **II**
genau exact **III U1,** 15
Genick neck **II**
genießen to enjoy **I**
genug enough **II**
genügend enough **II**
geöffnet open **I**
Geografie Geography **II**
Gepäck baggage *(sing.)* **II**
gerade just now **I**; right now **I**; now **I**; straight **I**

geradeaus straight **I**; straight on **I**
Gerät machine **I**
Geräusch sound **I**; noise **III U5,** 85
gerecht fair **I**
Gern geschehen. You're welcome. **I**
Geruch smell **I**
Gerümpel rubbish **III U1,** 12; junk **III U3,** 47
Gesangsunterricht singing lessons **II**
Geschäft shop **I**
Geschäftsführer/-in manager **I**
geschehen to happen **I**
Geschenk present **I**
Geschichte story **I**; History **II**
geschieden von divorced from **I**
Geschmack flavour **I**; taste **III U4,** 60
Geschmacksrichtung flavour **I**
geschockt sein to be shocked **II**
Gesellschaft- social **II**
Gesicht face **I**
  ein Gesicht ziehen to make a face **II**
Gespräch conversation **II**; talk **III U3,** 52
Gestank smell **I**
gestatten to allow **III U5,** 85
gestern yesterday **II**
gesund healthy **II**
Gesundheit health **II**
Getränk drink **I**
gewachst waxed **II**
Gewalt violence *(no pl.)* **III U5,** 77
gewalttätig violent **III U5,** 85
Gewinn prize **I**
gewinnen to win **I**
Gewinner/-in winner **I**; champion **II**
Gewitter storm **I**; thunderstorm **II**
sich an (etwas) **gewöhnen** to get used to (sth) **II**
gewöhnlich usually **I**
Gitarre guitar **I**
glänzen to shine **III U2,** 33
glänzend brilliant **II**
Glas glass **II**
glatt smooth **III U5,** 82
glauben to think **I**; to believe **I**
gläubig religious **II**
der/die/das **Gleiche** the same **I**
Gleichfalls. And you. **III U6,** 100
gleichmäßig regular **II**
gleichzeitig at the same time **I**
Gleis track **III U6,** 101
gleiten to slide **III U1,** 17
Glück luck **III U1,** 12
  Glück haben to be lucky **I**
  kein Glück haben to be out of luck **III U1,** 19
  Viel Glück! Good luck! **II**
glücklich happy **I**
Gold gold **III U2,** 24
Goldmedaille gold medal **III U1,** 13
Golf golf **II**
Gondel pod **II**
Grammatik grammar **I**
Gras grass **I**
grau grey **I**
aus **Griechenland** Greek **I**
griechisch Greek **I**
Griechisch Greek **I**
Grippe flu **II**
groß big **I**; great **I**; large (L) **I**; tall **II**; high **II**
  besonders groß extra large (XL) **I**
großartig great **I**; fantastic **III U6,** 100
Größe size **I**
Großmutter grandmother **I**
Großstadt city **I**
Großvater grandfather **I**
grün green **I**
Grund reason **II**
  Gründe angeben to give reasons **II**
  Gründe nennen to give reasons **II**
Grund- basic **III U5,** 85
grundlegend basic **III U5,** 85
Grundschule primary school **I**
Gruppe group **I**; team **I**
Grüße ausrichten to say hello to **I**
  Herzliche Grüße love **II**
  Liebe Grüße love **II**
grüßen to say hello to **I**
gucken to look **I**
Gummiball rubber ball **I**
Gummistiefel welly pl. wellies **I**
gut well **II**
gut good **I**; fine **I**; nice **I**
  gut aussehend good-looking **II**
  gut sein in/bei to be good at **I**
  Schon gut. Never mind! **III U4,** 62
Guthaben credit **II**
Gymnasium grammar school **II**

H

Haar hair **II**
Haare hair **II**
haben to have got **I**; to have **II**
Hafen harbour **I**
Hafendamm pier **I**
Hafenviertel waterfront **III U4,** 68
Hähnchen chicken **I**
Hai shark **II**
halb half **I**
Halbschwester half-sister **I**
Halbzeit half pl. halves **III U1,** 13; half-time **III U1,** 19
(die) **Hälfte** half pl. halves **III U1,** 13
Halle hall **II**
Hallo. Hi. **I**; Hello. **I**
Hals neck **II**
halten to hold **I**
  Halt die Klappe! Shut up! **III U3,** 51
  halten von to think of **I**; to think about **I**
  Händchen halten to hold hands **II**
Haltestelle stop **II**
Hamburger burger **II**
Hand hand **I**
  Händchen halten to hold hands **II**
handeln von to be about **III U2,** 32
Handlung action **III U2,** 26
Handwerker *(Pl.)* craftspeople *(pl.)* **II**
Handy mobile **I**
hängen to hang **II**
hart hard **II**
hassen to hate **III U2,** 24
Hast hurry **I**
Haufen pile **III U5,** 86
häufig often **I**
Haupt- main **III U5,** 77
Hauptstadt capital **II**
Hauptwort noun **I**
Haus house **I**
  auf dem Weg nach Hause on the way home **I**
  bei mir zu Hause at my house **I**
  nach Hause gehen to go home **I**
  zu Hause at home **I**
Hausaufgabe, Hausaufgaben homework **I**
Hausboot houseboat **III U4,** 66
Hausfrau housewife pl. housewives **III U5,** 77
Hausmeister/-in caretaker **I**
Hausnummer number **I**
Haustier pet **I**
  virtuelles Haustier cyberpet **I**
Haut skin **III U6,** 101
Heft exercise book **I**
heilen to mend **I**
Heimwerken DIY (= Do-it-yourself) **III U3,** 43
heiraten to marry **III U3,** 43
heiß hot **III U2,** 30
Held hero pl. heroes **II**
helfen to help **I**
Helikopter helicopter **II**
Helm helmet **III U1,** 9
Heranzoomen zoom-in **I**
heraus out **I**
herausfinden to find out **II**
Herausforderung challenge **III U6,** 93
heraushören to listen for **I**
Herbst autumn **I**
hereinkommen to come in **I**; to enter **II**
Herr *(Anrede)* Mr **I**
Herrschaft reign **III U2,** 30
herüberkommen to come over **I**
herum around **II**
herunter down **I**
herunterfallen to fall off **III U5,** 86
herunterladen to download **II**
herunternehmen to take off **I**
hervorheben to stress **III U2,** 36
Herz heart **I**
heute today **I**
Hexe witch **III U3,** 51
Hi. Hi. **I**
hier here **I**
  hier drin in here **I**
hierher here **I**
hierhin here **I**
Hilfe help **I**
hilfreich useful **I**; helpful **II**
hilfsbereit helpful **II**

Himmel sky **II**
hinab down **I**
hinaufklettern to climb **I**
hinaufsteigen to climb **I**
hinaus out **I**
hinein inside **II**
hineingehen to enter **II**
hinfallen to fall **I**; to fall over **I**
sich hinsetzen to sit down **I**
hinter behind **I**
Hintergrund background **III U5,** 85
hinterhergehen to follow **II**
hinterherrennen to run after **I**
hinterlassen to leave **III U3,** 50
hinunter down **I**
hinunterfallen to fall off **III U5,** 86
hinuntergehen to go down **I**
etw. (zu etw.) hinzufügen to add **II**
Hitparade charts **II**
hitzköpfig hot-headed **II**
Hobby hobby pl. hobbies **I**
hoch high **II**; tall **II**
hochhalten to hold up **I**
hoffen to hope **II**
Hoffnung hope **II**
höflich polite **I**
Höflichkeit politeness **II**
Höhe level **II**
Höhle cave **II**
holen to get **I**
Holz wood **III U2,** 24
Homepage home page **I**
Hör- audio **III U4,** 65
hören to hear **I**
hören auf to listen to **III U3,** 49
Horror horror **II**
Hose trousers *(pl.)* **II**
Hosentasche pocket **II**
Hospital hospital **II**
Hotel hotel **II**
Hotline hotline **III U5,** 85
Hubschrauber helicopter **II**
Hügel hill **II**
Huhn chicken **I**
Hühnchen chicken **I**
Hund dog **I**
Hundehütte doghouse **I**
hundemüde dog-tired **I**
hungrig hungry **II**
hüpfen to hop **II**
Hurra! Hooray! **I**
Hut hat **III U3,** 43

I

ich I **I**
ich (selbst) myself **III U3,** 44
Idee idea **I**
Identifikation identification **II**
Identifizierung identification **II**
Idiot/-in idiot **II**
igitt yuk **I**
ihr (selbst) yourselves **III U3,** 44
ihr/-e her **I**; their **I**
Ihr/-e your **I**
im Innern inside **II**
im vorderen Bereich at the front of **II**
immer always **I**
immer noch still **I**
immer wieder again and again **II**
in in **I**; at **I**; to **I**; inside **II**
in (hinein) into **I**
in Ordnung fine **I**
indirekte Rede indirect speech **III U6,** 94
Industrie industry **III U4,** 58
Industrieanlage industry **III U4,** 58
Industrielle Revolution Industrial Revolution **III U2,** 24
Information, Informationen information *(no pl.)* **I**
informieren to inform **II**
Ingenieur/-in engineer **III U4,** 60
Inlineskates fahren in-line skating **II**
innen inside **II**
Insel island **I**
inserieren to advertise **III U5,** 77
intelligent clever **II**
interaktiv interactive **III U4,** 67
interessant interesting **I**
an etwas interessiert sein to be into sth **III U4,** 60
interessiert an interested in **I**
Internat boarding school **II**
Internet Internet **I**
im Internet surfen to surf on the Internet **I**
Interview interview **II**
interviewen to interview **III U1,** 20
irgendein/-e/-er any **I**
irgendetwas anything **II**
irgendjemand anyone **II**; anybody **II**
irgendwelche any **I**
irgendwo somewhere **II**; anywhere **II**
sich irren to be wrong **I**
aus Italien Italian **I**
italienisch Italian **I**
Italienisch Italian **I**

J

ja yes **I**
Jahr year **I**
jahrelang for (many) years **I**
Jahreszeit season **I**
Jahrgangsstufe year **I**
Jahrhundert century **III U2,** 24
-jährig year-old **II**
-jährige/r year-old **II**
Januar January **I**
Jazzcafé jazz café **I**
je ... desto ... the ... the ... **II**
Jeans jeans *(pl.)* **I**
jedenfalls anyway **II**
jeder everyone **I**; everybody **II**
jeder (beliebige) anyone **II**; anybody **II**
jede/-r/-s every **I**; each **II**
jemals ever **II**
jemand someone **II**; somebody **II**
jene those **I**
an jenem Tag that day **I**
jenes that **I**
jetzt now **I**; right now **I**
joggen to jog **II**
jubeln to cheer **III U4,** 68
Judo judo **II**
Jugend youth **III U5,** 85
Jugendherberge youth hostel **II**
Jugendliche/-r kid **I**; teenager **II**
Juli July **I**
jung young **I**
Junge boy **I**
Juni June **I**
Junkie junkie **III U5,** 81

K

Kaiserin empress **III U2,** 30
Kaiserreich empire **III U2,** 25
Kalender planner **II**
kalt cold **I**
Kamera camera **I**
Kampf fight **II**; battle **II**
kämpfen to fight **I**
Kanal channel **III U1,** 13
Kantine eatery **I**
Kanu canoe **II**
Kapitän captain **I**
Kapitel unit **I**
kaputt broken **II**
kaputtgehen to break **I**
Karaokegerät karaoke machine **I**
Karte card **I**
Kartoffelchip crisp **I**
ein Karton ... a box of ... **I**
Käse cheese **I**
Kästchen box **I**
Kasten box **I**
Katholik/-in Catholic **III U2,** 24
katholisch Catholic **III U2,** 24
Katze cat **I**
Katzenfutter cat food **I**
kaufen to buy **I**
Kaufhaus department store **I**
kein/-e no **I**
Kellner waiter **II**
Kellnerin waitress **II**
kennen to know **I**
kennenlernen to meet **III U3,** 43
Kerl guy **III U3,** 53
Kern pip **III U3,** 43
Kerze candle **I**
keuchen to gasp **III U2,** 34
Kind child pl. children **I**; kid **I**
Kino cinema **I**
Kirche church **I**
klar clear **I**

klären to sort out **I**
Klasse class **I**; year **I**
Klasse *(in einer englischen Schule)* tutor group **I**
Klassenausflug class trip **I**
Klassenfahrt class trip **I**
Klassenkamerad/-in classmate **II**
Klassenlehrer/-in tutor **I**
Klassenzimmer classroom **I**
klatschen to clap **I**
Kleid dress **III U2,** 26
Kleider clothes *(pl.)* **I**
Kleiderschrank wardrobe **I**
Kleidung clothes *(pl.)* **I**
klein small **I**; little **I**; tiny **I**; short **II**
Kleintransporter pick-up **I**
Klettern rock climbing **II**
Klick click **III U2,** 35
Klicken click **III U2,** 35
klingeln to ring **I**
klingen to sound **III U4,** 63
Klischee cliché **II**
Klub club **I**
klug clever **II**
Knall bang **I**
knallen to bang **I**
knauserig mean **II**
Knie knee **II**
Koch, Köchin cook **I**
kochen to cook **II**
Kochklub cooking club **I**
Kohlenbergwerk coal mine **III U4,** 59
Kohlengrube coal mine **III U4,** 59
Kolonie colony **III U2,** 25
komisch odd **III U2,** 34
Komma comma **III U3,** 48
kommen to come **I**
Komm jetzt! Come on! **I**
Komm schon! Come on! **I**
kommen nach to get to **I**
kommen zu to get to **I**
zu spät kommen to be late **I**
Kommentar comment **II**
Kommunikationsfertigkeiten communication skills **I**
Komödie comedy **III U6,** 96
Komparativ comparative **II**
Kompass compass **II**
Konferenz conference **III U4,** 66
Konflikt conflict **III U5,** 77
König king **II**
Königin queen **II**
königlich royal **II**
können can **I**; to be able to (do sth) **III U2,** 26
konnte(n) could **II**
(vielleicht) können may **I**
könnte(n) might **III U1,** 17
Kontext context **III U1,** 19
Pro und Kontra pros and cons *(pl.)* **III U5,** 81
Kontrast contrast **III U4,** 58
kontrollieren to check **II**; to examine **II**; to control **III U1,** 8
Konversation conversation **II**
(sich) konzentrieren to concentrate **III U4,** 66
Konzert concert **III U5,** 77
Kopf head **II**
Kopfschmerzen headache **II**
Kopfweh headache **II**
Körper body **II**
körperlich physical **II**
Korridor hall **II**; corridor **II**
korrigieren to correct **I**
kosten to cost **II**
Wie viel kostet ... ? How much is ...? **I**
kostenlos free **III U2,** 30
Kostüm costume **III U3,** 51
Krach noise **III U5,** 85
kräftig strong **I**
Krähennest crow's nest **I**
krank sick **II**; ill **II**
Krankenhaus hospital **II**
Krankenwagen ambulance **III U5,** 87
sich kräuseln to go curly **III U3,** 43
kreischen to scream **III U6,** 102
Kricket cricket **III U1,** 8
Kristall crystal **I**
Kruste crust **III U3,** 43
Küche kitchen **I**
Kuchen cake **I**
Kuh cow **I**
Kult cult **III U4,** 58
Kultur culture **III U4,** 59
Kummerkastentante agony aunt **III U3,** 49
sich kümmern um to look after **I**
Kunde, Kundin customer **I**
Kunst Art **II**
Kunstgalerie gallery **II**
Kunsthandwerk arts and crafts *(pl.)* **II**
Kunststück trick **I**
Kuriosität oddity **III U1,** 14
Kurs course **II**
kurz short **I**
vor kurzem recently **III U4,** 59
kürzlich recently **III U4,** 59
küssen to kiss **II**
Küste seaside **I**; coast **I**
Küstenstadt seaside town **I**

L

lächeln to smile **I**
lachen to laugh **I**
Laden shop **I**
Lampe light **II**
LAN LAN *(Local Area Network)* **III U5,** 85
Land land **I**; country **II**
an Land on land **III U4,** 66
Landarbeiter/-in farmhand **I**
landen to land **II**
Landkarte map **I**
Landschaft landscape **III U4,** 59
Landwirt/-in farmer **III U2,** 30
lang long **I**
(nicht) länger (not) any longer **II**
langsam slow **I**
langsamer werden to slow down **III U6,** 101
sich langweilen to get bored **III U6,** 94
langweilig boring **I**
Laptop laptop **I**
Lärm noise **III U5,** 85
lassen to let **I**; to leave **II**
Lass dir Zeit. Take your time. **III U4,** 62
Lass ihn in Ruhe! Leave him alone! **II**
lästig annoying **III U6,** 100
Lastwagen lorry **II**
Latein Latin **II**
Laufbahn track **III U1,** 9
laufen to run **I**
laut loud **I**
Laut sound **I**
läuten to ring **I**
leben to live **I**
Leben life pl. lives **I**
lecken to lick **I**
lecker tasty **I**
leer empty **I**
legen to put **I**
lehren to teach **I**
Lehrer/-in teacher **I**
leicht easy **I**
Leichtathlet/-in athlete **III U1,** 13
Leichtathletik athletics **III U1,** 8
leider I'm afraid **III U3,** 50
leihen to lend (to) **II**
leise quiet **I**
Leitung line **III U2,** 35
Lektion unit **I**
lernen to learn **I**
auswendig lernen to learn by heart **I**
Lernende/-r learner **II**
lesen to read **I**
noch einmal lesen to reread **III U5,** 78
vor dem Lesen pre-reading **III U2,** 32
Leser/-in reader **II**
letzte/-r/-s last **I**
Leuchtturm lighthouse **I**
Leute people *(pl.)* **I**
Level level **II**
Licht light **II**
Liebe love **III U4,** 60
lieben to love **I**
liebenswürdig gentle **II**
Liebe/-r *(Anrede in Briefen)* dear **II**
Lieblings- favourite **I**
Lied song **I**
Lieferwagen van **III U1,** 16
Lifting facelift **III U4,** 59
lila purple **I**
Lineal ruler **I**
Linie line **I**
linke/-r/-s left **I**
links left **I**; on the left **I**
auf der linken Seite on the left **I**
Liste list **I**
Loch hole **I**

Löffel spoon **II**
Londoner/-in Londoner **II**
Lord lord **III U2,** 33
loswerden to get rid of **III U3,** 47
Luft air **I**
  tief Luft holen to gasp **III U2,** 34
Lüge lie **III U3,** 43
lügen to tell a lie **III U3,** 43
Lunge the lungs *(pl.)* **III U1,** 13
lustig funny **I**
  sich lustig machen über to make fun of **III U4,** 69

M

machen to do **I**; to make **I**
  ein Foto machen to take a photo **I**
  Mach dir nichts draus! Never mind! **III U4,** 62
  Macht nichts. Never mind! **III U4,** 62
  sich Notizen machen to take notes **I**
Mädchen girl **I**
Magen stomach **II**
Magie magic **III U5,** 86
Mahlzeit meal **I**
Mai May **I**
Mailbox voice mail **III U3,** 50
Make-up make-up **III U3,** 43
Mal time **II**
malen to paint **II**
Mama mum **I**
manchmal sometimes **I**
Mann man pl. men **I**
Mannequin fashion model **II**
Männerchor male voice choir **III U4,** 59
Mappe folder **I**
Marathon marathon **III U1,** 13
Markt market **I**
März March **I**
Maschine machine **I**
Maske mask **III U3,** 52
Match match **II**
Mathematik Maths **II**
Mauer wall **I**
Maus mouse pl. mice **I**
Medaille medal **III U1,** 13
Medien medium pl. media **III U5,** 76
Medium medium pl. media **III U5,** 76
Meer sea **I**
Meeresküste seaside **I**
Mehl flour **I**
mehr more **I**; extra **III U3,** 44
  (nicht) mehr (not) any longer **II**; (not) any more **III U3,** 43
Mehrzahl plural **I**
Meile mile **I**
mein/-e my **I**
meinen to mean **I**
Meinung opinion **III U5,** 85
  seine Meinung äußern to give one's opinion **III U5,** 85
das **meiste** most **II**
  die meisten most **II**
melken to milk **I**
eine **Menge** a lot of **I**
  jede Menge lots of **I**
Mensch person pl. people **I**
Menschenmenge crowd **III U4,** 68
Menschheit mankind **III U6,** 93
merkwürdig strange **III U2,** 34; weird **III U4,** 68
Messer knife pl. knives **II**
Metall metal **III U2,** 35
Meter metre **II**
mich me **I**
Mikrowelle microwave **III U3,** 43
Milch milk **I**
Milliarde billion **II**
Million million **II**
  Millionen von millions of **II**
mindestens at least **III U4,** 68
Minute minute **I**
mir me **I**
mischen to shuffle **I**
bunte **Mischung** mixed bag **I**
Missionar/-in missionary **III U6,** 93
mit with **I**
  mit (der U-Bahn) by (Underground) **I**
mitbringen to bring **I**
Mitleid haben mit to feel sorry for **III U3,** 46
mitnehmen to take **I**; to pick up **I**
Mitspieler/-in player **II**
Mittagessen lunch **I**
Mittagspause lunchtime **I**
Mittagszeit lunchtime **I**
mittel(groß) medium (M) **I**
Mittwoch Wednesday **I**
Möbel furniture **I**
Mobiltelefon mobile **I**
Mode fashion **II**
Model fashion model **II**
modern modern **III U2,** 26
mögen to want **I**; to like **I**
  ich möchte ... I'd like to ... *(= I would like to)* **I**
  nicht mögen to hate **III U2,** 24
möglicherweise probably **III U3,** 47
Möglichkeit chance **III U1,** 10
Moment moment **I**
Monat month **I**
Mond moon **III U6,** 93
Monster monster **II**
Montag Monday **I**
morgen tomorrow **II**
Morgen morning **I**
  Guten Morgen. Good morning. **I**
  heute Morgen this morning **I**
Motor engine **III U2,** 24
Motto theme **II**
Mountainbike mountain bike **II**
MP3-Player MP3 player **III U3,** 51
müde tired **I**
Müll rubbish **III U1,** 12
Mund mouth **II**
Münzgeld change **II**
mürrisch grumpy **III U3,** 52
Museum museum **I**
Musik music **I**
Musikgruppe band **I**
Musikinstrument musical instrument **II**
müssen must **I**; to have to **III U2,** 28
Mutter mother **I**
Muttersprache mother tongue **II**; first language **III U6,** 93

N

nach to **I**; after **I**
  nach *(bei Uhrzeitangaben)* past **I**
  nach Christus AD *(= Anno Domini)* **III U2,** 24
  nach drinnen inside **II**
Nachbar/-in neighbour **I**
nachdem after **I**
nachdenken to think **I**
nacherzählen to retell **I**
nachmachen to copy **III U5,** 76
Nachmittag afternoon **I**
nachmittags *(Uhrzeit)* pm **I**
Nachricht note **I**; message **II**
Nachricht(en) news *(sing.)* **II**
nachschauen to look **I**; to look up **I**
nachschlagen to look up **I**
nächste/-r/-s next **I**
Nacht night **I**
Nacken neck **II**
nahe near **I**; close **III U2,** 32
in der **Nähe von** near **I**
Nahrung food **I**
Nahrungsmittel food **I**
Name name **I**
Nase nose **II**
  die Nase voll haben von to be fed up (with) **I**
nass wet **II**
Nationalität nationality **I**
natürlich of course **I**
Naturwissenschaft Science **II**
Nebel fog **II**
neben next to **I**
nebenan next door **II**
neblig foggy **II**
negativ negative **II**
nehmen to take **I**
  nehmen *(Bus, Zug)* to catch **I**
neidisch jealous (of) **III U3,** 47
nein no **I**
nennen to call **I**
nervös nervous **I**
nett nice **I**; kind **II**; friendly **II**
Netz web **II**
Netzkarte travelcard **II**
neu new **I**
  neu schreiben to rewrite **III U5,** 85
neugierig curious **III U2,** 33
Neuigkeit(en) news *(sing.)* **II**

neulich recently **III U4,** 59
neun nine **I**
neunzehn nineteen **I**
neunzig ninety **I**
nicht not **I**
  auch nicht not … either **III U4,** 69
nichts nothing **II**
nicken to nod **III U2,** 34
nie never **I**
niemals never **I**
niemand nobody **II**
nirgendwo nowhere **II**
nirgendwohin nowhere **II**
Niveau level **II**
noch still **I**; yet **II**
  noch ein/-e another **I**
  noch einmal again **I**
nochmal again **I**
nochmals erzählen to retell **I**
Nomen noun **I**
Norden north **I**
  im Norden up North **III U4,** 63
Nordsee North Sea **I**
normal normal **II**
normalerweise usually **I**
Normanne, Normannin Norman **III U2,** 25
normannisch Norman **III U2,** 25
Notfall emergency **III U5,** 87
Notiz note **I**
  sich Notizen machen to take notes **I**
Notlage emergency **III U5,** 87
November November **I**
Nudel noodle **III U6,** 93
null zero **I**
  null *(Tennis)* love **III U1,** 13
  null *(beim Sport)* nil **III U1,** 19
  null *(bei Telefonnummern)* oh **I**
Nummer number **I**
nun well **I**
nun now **I**
nur just **I**; only **II**
nützlich useful **I**; helpful **II**

O

ob if **II**; whether **III U6,** 97
oben upstairs **I**; on the top **I**; above **III U5,** 87
  oben (auf) on top of **I**
oberes Ende top **I**
im **Obergeschoss** upstairs **I**
oberhalb above **III U5,** 87
Obst fruit **II**
obwohl although **II**
oder or **I**
offen open **I**
  Tag der offenen Tür open day **III U2,** 29
öffentlich public **I**
die **Öffentlichkeit** the public **III U5,** 77
offiziell official **III U3,** 54
öffnen to open **I**
oft often **I**
ohne without **II**
Ohr ear **I**
Oje! Oh dear! **II**
okay OK **I**
Oktober October **I**
Öl oil **II**
Ölindustrie oil industry **II**
Olympia- Olympic **II**
Olympiade Olympic Games **III U1,** 9
olympisch Olympic **II**
Oma grandma **I**
Onkel uncle **I**
online online **I**
Opa grandad **I**
Openair- open-air **III U2,** 26
orange orange **I**
Orchester orchestra **I**
Ordner folder **I**
in **Ordnung bringen** to tidy (up) **III U3,** 43
organisieren to organise **III U5,** 85
Orientierungslauf orienteering **II**
Ort place **I**
Ortswechsel changing places **III U4,** 67
Osten east **I**
östlich von east of **I**
oval oval **III U1,** 8
Ozean ocean **I**

P

ein **paar** a few **I**; some **I**
Paar pair **I**
  ein Paar a pair of **III U4,** 60
packen to pack **I**
Palast palace **II**
Pandschabi Punjabi **III U4,** 63
pandschabisch Punjabi **III U4,** 63
Papa dad **I**
Papier paper **II**
Paragraph paragraph **III U2,** 35
Parfüm perfume **II**
Park park **I**
parken to park **I**
Partner/-in partner **I**
Party party **I**
  eine Party feiern to have a party **I**
Pass passport **II**
Passagier/-in passenger **II**
passen zu to go with **I**
passieren to happen **I**
Patient/-in patient **III U5,** 87
Pause pause **II**; break **II**
Pech bad luck **III U3,** 43
  Pech haben to be unlucky **III U1,** 19
peinlich embarrassing **II**
Pendelzug shuttle **II**
Penny, Pence *(brit. Währungseinheit)* penny pl. pence **I**
per by (Underground) **I**
perfekt perfect **II**
Person person pl. people **I**
persönlich personal **II**
berühmte **Persönlichkeit** celeb(rity) **III U5,** 76
Pfad path **II**
Pfeifen whistle **III U6,** 102
Pferd horse **I**
Pfiff whistle **III U6,** 102
Pflanze plant **III U6,** 93
Pflicht duty **I**
Pfund *(Währung)* pound **I**
Picknick picnic **I**
Pick-up pick-up **I**
Pier pier **I**
pink pink **I**
Pirat pirate **I**
Pizza pizza **I**
Pizzeria pizza place **I**
Plan plan **II**; arrangement **III U1,** 10
planen to plan **I**
Planer planner **II**
Planet planet **II**
Planke plank **I**
Plattform platform **II**
Platz place **III U1,** 17; pitch **III U1,** 8
plaudern to chat **III U3,** 47
plötzlich suddenly **I**
Plural plural **I**
Polen Poland **I**
  aus Polen Polish **I**
Polizei police **I**
Polizeibeamte/-r police officer **III U6,** 97
Polizeidienststelle police department **III U5,** 85
Polizeirevier police station **I**
Polizeiwache police station **I**
polnisch Polish **I**
Polnisch Polish **I**
Pommes frites chips *(pl.)* **II**
  Fisch und Pommes frites fish and chips **II**
Pool pool **III U4,** 69
Popstar pop star **I**
populär popular **II**
positiv positive **II**
Postamt post office **II**
Poster poster **I**
Postkarte postcard **I**
Prärie prairie **III U6,** 101
Präsentation presentation **II**
prasseln to pitter-patter **I**
Preis prize **I**; price **II**
preiswert cheap **I**
Pressekonferenz press conference **III U1,** 16
Priester priest **II**
prima brilliant **II**
Prinzessin princess **III U6,** 101
pro per **I**
  pro Tag a day **II**
Pro und Kontra pros and cons *(pl.)* **III U5,** 81
Probe rehearsal **III U3,** 53
proben to rehearse **III U3,** 53
probieren to try **II**
Problem problem **I**

Produkt product **III U5,** 82
Programm programme **III U5,** 77; channel **III U1,** 13
Programmheft programme **III U3,** 53
Projekt project **I**
Protestant/-in Protestant **III U2,** 24
protestantisch Protestant **III U2,** 24
Prozent per cent **III U6,** 93
prüfen to test **II**; to check **II**
Prüfung test **I**
Publikum audience **III U3,** 53
Pullover pullover **II**
punkten to score **II**
pünktlich on time **III U6,** 102
Putzfrau cleaning lady **III U3,** 43
Putzmittel cleaning product **III U5,** 77

Q

Qualität quality **III U5,** 76
Qualitäts- quality **III U5,** 76
Quatsch rubbish **III U1,** 12
Quiz quiz **I**

R

Rabauke bully **II**
sich **rächen** to get your own back **II**
Rad wheel **I**
Radiergummi rubber **I**
Radio radio **I**
Radiosender radio station **I**
Rampe ramp **III U5,** 86
Ramsch junk **III U3,** 47
Rap rap **I**
Raster grid **I**
Rat advice **III U3,** 48
  einen Rat geben giving advice **III U6,** 96
raten to guess **I**
  (jmdm.) raten (etw. zu tun) to advise (sb to do sth) **III U6,** 97
Ratespiel quiz **I**
Ratschlag tip **I**; advice **III U3,** 48
Rauch smoke **I**
rauchen to smoke **II**
Raum room **I**
realistisch realistic **III U5,** 77
Recherche research **III U4,** 66
Rechnung bill **II**
Recht haben to be right **I**
rechte/-r/-s right **I**
rechts right **I**; on the right **I**
  auf der rechten Seite on the right **I**
Rechtschreibung spelling **II**
direkte **Rede** direct speech **III U6,** 94
  indirekte Rede indirect speech **III U6,** 94
reden to talk **I**
  reden mit to talk to **I**
Redewendung phrase **I**
Regal shelf pl. shelves **I**
Regalbrett shelf pl. shelves **I**
Regel rule **I**
regelmäßig regular **II**
regeln to sort out **I**
Regen rain **I**
Regierung government **III U2,** 30
Region region **III U4,** 58
regional regional **III U4,** 59
Regisseur-/in director **III U3,** 53
regnen to rain **I**
regnerisch rainy **II**
reich rich **I**
Reich empire **III U2,** 25
Reihenfolge order **I**
Reim rhyme **I**
reinigen to clean **III U2,** 34
Reinigungsmittel cleaning product **III U5,** 77
Reise tour **I**; trip **I**; journey **III U6,** 93
Reisebüro travel agency **III U6,** 104
Reisebus coach **III U6,** 97
Reiseführer guidebook **II**
Reisegepäck baggage *(sing.)* **II**
reisen to travel **II**
(das) **Reisen** travelling **II**
Reisende/-r traveller **III U6,** 93
Reisepass passport **II**
reiten to ride **I**
Reklame advertising *(no pl.)* **III U5,** 82
Rekord record **III U1,** 13
Religion *(Schulfach)* R.E. (Religious Education) **II**
religiös religious **II**
rennen to run **I**
Rennen race **III U1,** 9
Renovierung facelift **III U4,** 59
reparieren to mend **I**
Reporter/-in reporter **II**
Requisiten props *(pl.)* **III U3,** 53
reservieren to book **III U6,** 104
Reservierung reservation **III U6,** 104
Rest rest **II**
Restaurant restaurant **I**
retten to rescue **III U5,** 87; to save **III U6,** 101
Rettungsweste life-jacket **II**
Revier territory **I**
Industrielle **Revolution** Industrial Revolution **III U2,** 24
Rezept *(für Arzneimittel)* prescription **II**
  Rezept recipe **I**
Richter/-in judge **II**
richtig right **I**; correct **I**; real **II**
riechen to smell **III U4,** 63
Riesen- giant **III U6,** 93
Riesenrad ferris wheel **I**
riesig great **I**; giant **III U6,** 93
Riff rock **I**
Rinde crust **III U3,** 43
Risiko risk **II**
  ein Risiko eingehen to take a risk **II**
(etw.) **riskieren** to risk (sth) **II**
Ritter knight **III U2,** 25
Rock skirt **II**
Rock 'n' Roll rock and roll **II**
roh raw **III U2,** 30
Rohr pipe **III U5,** 87
Rohstoff raw material **III U2,** 30
Rolle role **II**
  jmdm. eine Rolle (in einem Film) geben to cast **III U5,** 78
Rollenbesetzung casting **III U5,** 78
Rollenspiel role play **I**
Rollstuhl wheelchair **III U1,** 12
Rolltreppe escalator **II**
Römer/-in Roman **II**
römisch Roman **II**
rosa pink **I**
Rosenkohl Brussels sprout **III U3,** 43
rot red **I**
Routine routine **I**
Rücken back **II**
Rückseite back **II**
rudern to row **I**
Rudern rowing **III U1,** 13
Ruf shout **III U1,** 20
rufen to shout **I**; to call **I**; to cry **II**
Rugby rugby **III U1,** 9
ruhig calm **I**; quiet **I**
ruinieren to ruin **I**
rumhängen (mit) to hang out (with) **III U4,** 69
Rundgang tour **I**
Rüpel bully **II**
russisch Russian **I**
Russisch Russian **I**
aus **Russland** Russian **I**
rutschen to slide **III U1,** 17

S

Saal hall **II**
Sache thing **I**
Sachse Saxon **III U2,** 24
Sächsin Saxon **III U2,** 24
sächsisch Saxon **III U2,** 24
Sachtext factual text **III U4,** 66
sagen to say **I**; to tell **I**
Saison season **I**
Salat salad **II**
sammeln to collect **I**
  Geld sammeln to raise money **III U5,** 85
Samstag Saturday **I**
Sand sand **I**
Sandburg sand castle **I**
sandig sandy **I**
Sandwich sandwich **I**
sanft gentle **II**
Sänger/-in singer **II**
Sanitäter/-in paramedic **III U6,** 97
etwas **satt bekommen** to get tired of **III U4,** 67
Satz phrase **I**; sentence **I**; leap **III U6,** 93
Satzstellung word order **I**
sauber clean **III U2,** 30
säubern to clean **III U2,** 34

sauer sein to be fed up (with) **I**
Schachtel box **I**
eine Schachtel ... a box of ... **I**
Das ist schade. It's a pity. **III U4,** 67
Es ist schade ... It's a pity. **III U4,** 67
Schaf sheep pl. sheep **I**
schaffen to create **III U5,** 77
(es) schaffen (etw. zu tun) to manage (to do sth) **III U3,** 52
es schaffen to make it **III U6,** 102
Schal scarf pl. scarves **I**
Schallplatte record **II**
Schalter desk **II**
Schatz treasure **I**
Schatzkarte treasure map **I**
Schau show **III U5,** 80
schauen to look **I**
Schauergeschichte thriller **III U6,** 96
Schauspieler actor **II**
Schauspielerin actress **III U3,** 53
scheinen to shine **III U2,** 33; to seem **III U4,** 63
schenken to give **I**
scherzen to joke **III U2,** 33
schicken to send **II**
schieben to push **II**
Schiedsrichter/-in referee **III U1,** 8; umpire **III U1,** 9
schießen to kick **I**; to shoot **III U6,** 102
Schiff ship **I**; boat **I**
Schild sign **II**
Schinkenpeck bacon **I**
Schlacht battle **II**
Schlaf sleep **III U1,** 20
schlafen to sleep **I**
schlafend asleep **I**
Schlafzimmer bedroom **I**
Schlag bang **I**; shot **II**
schlagen to bang **I**; to hit **II**
(mit den Flügeln) **schlagen** to flap **III U1,** 17
schlagen *(einen Ball)* to bat **III U1,** 20
Schläger racket **III U1,** 9; stick **III U1,** 8
Schläger *(beim Tischtennis, Baseball)* bat **III U1,** 8
Schlagzeile headline **III U5,** 84
Schlagzeug drums *(pl.)* **I**
Schlagzeuger/-in drummer **II**
Schlange queue **II**
schlau clever **II**
schlecht bad **I**; ill **II**
schlechter worse **II**
schlechteste/-r/-s worst **II**
schließen to close **I**
Schließfach locker **II**
schließlich finally **I**
schlimm terrible **I**
schlimmer worse **II**
schlimmste/-r/-s worst **II**
Schlittschuhlaufen ice skating **II**
Schloss castle **I**
Schluss end **II**; ending **III U2,** 35
Schlüsselbegriff keyword **III U4,** 66

schmecken to taste **III U4,** 63
Schmerz pain **II**
Schmuck jewellery **III U2,** 33
schmutzig dirty **I**
Schnee snow **III U1,** 13
(sich) schneiden to cut **III U5,** 87
schneien to snow **III U1,** 20
schnell fast **I**; quick **II**
tiefe Schnittwunde gash **III U5,** 87
Schock shock **I**
Schokolade chocolate **I**
Schokoplätzchen chocolate crispies *(pl.)* **I**
schon already **I**; yet **II**
schön beautiful **I**; nice **I**
Schotte, Schottin Scot **II**
schottisch Scottish **II**
Schrank cupboard **I**
Schreck shock **I**
Schrecken horror **II**
schrecklich terrible **I**; horrible **II**; awful **III U4,** 60
Schrei shout **III U1,** 20; scream **III U6,** 102
schreiben to write **I**
Schreibtisch desk **I**
schreien to shout **I**; to call **I**; to cry **II**; to scream **III U6,** 102
Schritt step **III U6,** 93
schubsen to push **II**
schüchtern shy **II**
Schuh shoe **I**
Schule school **I**
zu spät zur Schule kommen to be late for school **I**
Schüler/-in student **II**; pupil **I**
Schulfach subject **II**
Schulhof playground **I**
Schuljahr year **I**
Schulklasse class **I**
Schulsachen *(pl.)* school things *(pl.)* **I**
Schultag school day **I**
Schultasche schoolbag **I**
Schulter shoulder **II**
Schuppen shed **I**
Schuss shot **II**
Schüssel bowl **I**
Schusswaffe gun **III U6,** 102
schütteln to shake **II**
schwach weak **II**
schwarz black **I**
Schwein pig **I**
Schweiß sweat **III U1,** 14
schwer heavy **II**; hard **II**
Schwerindustrie heavy industry **III U4,** 59
Schwester sister **I**
schwierig hard **II**; difficult **III U3,** 50
Schwierigkeiten trouble **I**
in Schwierigkeiten geraten to get into trouble **II**
Schwierigkeiten bewältigen dealing with problems **III U4,** 62
Schwimmbad swimming pool **I**
Schwimmbecken swimming pool **I**
Schwimmbrille goggles *(pl.)* **III U1,** 16

schwimmen to swim **I**
schwimmen gehen to go swimming **I**
Schwimmen swimming **III U1,** 13
Schwimmer/-in swimmer **II**
Schwimmweste life-jacket **II**
Sciencefiction science fiction **II**
sechs six **I**
sechzehn sixteen **I**
sechzig sixty **I**
See lake **II**; sea **I**
See *(in Schottland)* loch **II**
Seeräuber pirate **I**
segeln to sail **I**
sehen to see **I**; to look **I**
Sehenswürdigkeiten sights *(pl.)* **I**
sehr very **I**
Seife soap *(no pl.)* **III U5,** 77
Seifenoper soap (opera) **III U5,** 77
sein to be **I**
da sein to be in **III U3,** 50
sauer sein to be fed up (with) **I**
spät dran sein to be late **I**
sein its **I**
sein/-e his **I**
Seite page **I**; side **III U6,** 102
Sekunde second **I**
selber myself **III U3,** 44; yourself **III U3,** 44; himself **III U3,** 44; herself **III U3,** 45; itself **III U3,** 45;ourselves **III U3,** 44; yourselves **III U3,** 44;themselves **III U3,** 44
selbst myself **III U3,** 44; yourself **III U3,** 44; himself **III U3,** 44; herself **III U3,** 45; itself **III U3,** 45; ourselves **III U3,** 44; yourselves **III U3,** 44; themselves **III U3,** 44
selbst even **I**
selbstsüchtig selfish **III U3,** 43
Selbstversorger- self-catering **III U6,** 104
selbstverständlich of course **I**
seltsam strange **III U2,** 34; odd **III U2,** 34; weird **III U4,** 68
Sendung programme **III U5,** 77
September September **I**
Service service **III U6,** 97
setzen to put **I**
Show show **III U5,** 80
sich (gegenseitig) each other **III U3,** 43
sich (selbst) myself **III U3,** 44; yourself **III U3,** 44; himself **III U3,** 44; herself **III U3,** 45; itself **III U3,** 45; ourselves **III U3,** 44; yourselves **III U3,** 44; themselves **III U3,** 44
sicher sure **I**; safe **I**
sicher gehen to make sure **III U3,** 52
Sicherheit safety **II**
Sicht view **II**
sie she **I**; them **I**; they **I**
sie selbst herself **III U3,** 45; themselves **III U3,** 44
sieben seven **I**
siebzehn seventeen **I**
siebzig seventy **I**
Sieger/-in champion **II**
Signal signal **I**

Signalton tone III U3, 50
Signalwort signal word I
Silhouette outline III U5, 87
simpel simple II
singen to sing I
Single *(CD)* single II
sinken to sink I
sechster Sinn sixth sense III U2, 34
Sioux-Indianer Sioux pl. Sioux III U6, 102
Situation situation III U1, 11
Sitz seat III U6, 101
sitzen to sit I
Sitzplatz seat III U6, 101
Skateboard skateboard I
Skateboardfahren skateboarding III U1, 9
Skater/-in skater III U5, 88
Ski ski III U1, 16
Skibrille goggles *(pl.)* III U1, 16
Skispringen ski jump III U1, 16
Skispringer ski jumper III U1, 16
Skript script III U5, 78
Slum slum III U2, 30
Smalltalk small talk III U6, 100
SMS text II
eine SMS schicken to text I
so like this I; so I
so ... wie as ... as II
Soap soap (opera) III U5, 77
sobald as soon as II
soeben just I
Sofa sofa I
sofort at once I; right now I; right away II
sogar even I
Sohn son II
solche/-r/-s such III U2, 34
Soldat/-in soldier II
sollte/-est/-en/-et should I
sollte(n) ought to III U2, 29
Sommer summer I
Sonne sun I
Sonnenbrille sunglasses *(pl.)* I
sonnig sunny II
Sonntag Sunday I
sonst or III U3, 43
sonst else II
sich Sorgen machen to worry I
sorgfältig careful II
Sorte flavour I; kind II; type III U3, 47
sortieren to sort I
Souvenir souvenir I
sowieso anyway II
sozial social II
Sozialkunde P.S.E. (Personal and Social Education) II
Spaghetti spaghetti I
aus Spanien Spanish I
spanisch Spanish I
Spanisch Spanish I
spannend exciting II
spannender Krimi thriller III U6, 96
sparen to save II
Spaß fun III U4, 60
Spaß haben to have fun I; to enjoy oneself III U3, 44
Spaß machen to be fun I
zum Spaß for laughs III U4, 68
(zu) spät late I
spät dran sein to be late I
zu spät kommen to be late I
später later I
Speck bacon I
Speicherkarte *(für Digitalkameras)* card I
Speisekarte menu II
Spiel game I; match II; play II
Spielautomaten arcade games *(pl.)* I
spielen to play I; to act I
spielen *(CD, Radio etc.)* to play I
Spieler/-in player II
Spielfeld field III U1, 8; court III U1, 9; pitch III U1, 8
Spielkarte card I
Spielplatz playground I
Spielzeug toy II
Spinat spinach *(no pl.)* III U5, 86
Spinne spider II
spitze awesome III U5, 77
Spitze top I
Spitzname nickname III U5, 76
Sport sport I
Sportart sport I
Sportgeschäft sports shop I
Sportunterricht P.E. (Physical Education) II
Sprache language I
sprechen to speak (to) I; to talk I
sprechen mit to talk to I
sprechen über to talk about I
Sprecher/-in speaker II
Sprechfertigkeiten communication skills I
Springbrunnen fountain III U2, 34
springen to jump I; to crack III U5, 86
Sprung jump III U1, 16; leap III U6, 93
Spülmaschine dishwasher II
Spur track III U6, 101
Stadt town I
Großstadt city I
Stadtplan map I
Stahl steel III U2, 25
Stall shed I
Stapel pile III U5, 86
Star star I
stark strong I; hard II; heavy II
Station station I
stehen to stand I
im Weg stehen to get in the way III U3, 52
stehlen to steal II
steigen to climb I
einen Drachen steigen lassen to fly a kite I
Stein rock I
steinig rocky I
stellen to put I
sterben to die I
Steuer wheel I
steuern to control III U1, 8
Steuerrad wheel I
Stewardess stewardess III U6, 101
Stichwort keyword III U4, 66
Stiefel boot II
Stiefvater step-father I
Stil style II
still quiet I
Stimme voice II
stimmen für to vote for II
stinken to stink I
Stock stick III U1, 8
stolz sein (auf) to be proud (of) III U4, 59
stören to get in the way III U3, 52
Stoß kick III U1, 20
stoßen to push II
Strafe penalty III U1, 19
Strand beach I
am Strand on the beach I
Strandurlaub beach holiday I
Straße street I; road I
auf der Straße in the street I
Straßenmusikant/-in busker II
einen Streich spielen to play a trick on II
streichen to paint II
Streit fight II; argument III U5, 85
sich streiten to fight I
sich streiten um to fight over I
streng strict II
Strom power III U2, 24
Stück piece II
Student/-in student II
Studio studio III U5, 77
Stufe step III U6, 93
Stuhl chair I
Stunde hour I
stundenlang for (many) hours I
Stundenplan timetable II
Sturm storm I
stürmisch stormy I
suchen to look I
suchen (nach) to look for I
Suchmaschine search engine III U4, 68
süchtig addicted (to) II
Süden south I
in Richtung Süden southbound II
super cool I; wicked II; super III U5, 78; awesome III U5, 77
Supermarkt supermarket II
Superstar superstar II
surfen to surf I
im Internet surfen to surf on the Internet I
süß sweet I
Süßigkeiten sweets *(pl.)* I
Süßwarenladen sweet shop I
Sweatshirt sweatshirt I
sympathisch nice I
Szene scene III U3, 42

T

Tabelle grid I
Tablette tablet II

Tafel board I
Tag day I
am Tag zuvor the day before III U6, 95
den ganzen Tag all day II
pro Tag a day II
Tag der offenen Tür open day III U2, 29
vor zwei Tagen two days earlier III U6, 95
Tagebuch diary I
täglich daily I
Tagung conference III U4, 66
Tankstelle garage I
Tante aunt I
tanzen to dance I
Tänzer/-in dancer II
Tanzunterricht dancing lessons *(pl.)* I
Tasche bag I; pocket II
Taschengeld pocket money II
Tasse cup II
eine Tasse ... a cup of I
Tätigkeit job I
Tatsache fact II
tatsächlich actually III U2, 35
Taube pigeon II
Taxi taxi I
Team team I
hoch technisiert high-tech II
Technologie Technology II
Tee tea I
Teenager teenager II
Teil part I
teilen to share II
teilnehmen to attend III U5, 85
Telefon phone I; telephone III U3, 43
Telefonleitung line III U2, 35
Telefonnummer phone number I
Telegramm telegram III U2, 34
Teller plate II
Temperatur temperature II
Tennis tennis III U1, 9
Terminal terminal II
Territorium territory I
Test test I
testen to test II
teuer expensive I
Text text I
Theater theatre II
Theaterstück play II
Thema theme II; subject II; topic III U4, 66
Themenpark theme park II
Thriller thriller III U6, 96
Thron throne III U2, 30
Ticket ticket II
tiefgefroren frozen III U3, 43
Tier animal I
Tierarzt, Tierärztin vet I
Tierheim animal home II
Tiger tiger I
Tipp tip I
Tisch table I
den Tisch abräumen to clear the table II
den Tisch decken to lay the table II

Titel title I; heading I
tja well I
Toast toast II
Tochter daughter II
Toilette toilet I
toll great I; brilliant II
Ton tone III U3, 50
Top top II
Tor goal I
ein Tor schießen to score II
Torte cake I
tot dead I
töten to kill II
Tour tour I
Tourist/-in tourist I
Touristeninformation information centre I
Tradition tradition III U1, 16
tragen to carry II
Trainer/-in trainer II
trainieren to train II
Training training II
Transporter van III U1, 16
trappeln to pitter-patter I
Traum dream I
träumen to dream III U1, 20
traurig sad I
treffen to meet I; to hit II
sich treffen to meet I
sich treffen (mit) to hang out (with) III U4, 69
trendy in II; trendy III U4, 60
sich trennen to split up III U3, 43
treten to kick I
Trick trick I
trinken to drink I
Tritt kick III U1, 20
trotzdem anyway II
tschüss bye I
T-Shirt T-shirt I
Tube tube III U5, 82
Tuch scarf pl. scarves I
tun to do I
Tunnel tunnel I
Tür door I
aus der Türkei Turkish I
türkisch Turkish I
Türkisch Turkish I
Türklingel doorbell III U3, 52
Turm tower III U2, 31
Turnschuhe trainers II
eine Tüte ... a bag of ... I
Tutorium tutorial II
Typ type III U3, 47; guy III U3, 53
Tyrann bully II

U

U-Bahn Underground I; Tube II
üben to practise II
über over I; about I; above III U5, 87
überall everywhere I; anywhere II
überfliegen to skim III U4, 66
Überfliegen skimming III U4, 66
übergewichtig overweight II
überleben to survive I
überprüfen to check II
überqueren to cross I
überraschen to surprise III U1, 20
Überraschung surprise I
Überschrift heading I
übersetzen to translate III U3, 47
überzeugen to convince III U5, 86
Übung exercise I
Ufer waterfront III U4, 68
Uhr (*Zeitangabe bei vollen Stunden*) o'clock I
Uhr clock I
die Uhr lesen to tell the time I
umbringen to kill II
umfallen to fall over I
gut umgehen können mit to be good with I
umgehen mit to deal with III U4, 62
umher around II
Umkleidekabine changing room II
Umriss outline III U5, 87
umschreiben to rewrite III U5, 85
umsteigen to change II
umziehen to move (house) III U4, 58
unabhängig independent III U2, 25
unbestimmt indefinite III U4, 60
und and I
unentschieden in a draw III U1, 19
Unfall accident II
ungefährlich safe I
ungewöhnlich unusual III U1, 13
Unglück bad luck III U3, 43
unheimlich scary I
unhöflich rude III U4, 62
Uniform uniform II
Europäische Union European Union III U2, 25
universell universal II
Universum universe II
Unordnung mess I
Unrecht haben to be wrong I
unregelmäßig irregular II
uns us I
unser/-e our I
Unsinn rubbish III U1, 12
unten on the bottom I; downstairs I
nach unten down I
unter under I
unteres Ende bottom I
untergehen to sink I
im Untergeschoss downstairs I
Unterhaltung conversation II; talk III U3, 52; entertainment *(no pl.)* III U5, 77 ;
Unterredung talk III U3, 52
unterrichten to teach I
Unterrichtsstunde lesson I
Unterschied difference III U3, 46; contrast III U4, 58
unterschiedlich different I

unterschreiben to sign **III U5,** 78
unterstreichen to underline **I**
untersuchen to examine **II**
Untersuchung research **III U4,** 66
unterwegs on his way **I**
  unterwegs sein to be on the move **III U4,** 58
unverschämt rude **III U4,** 62
Unwetter storm **I**
Urlaub holiday(s) **I**
Urlauber/-in holiday-maker **I**
Urgroßmutter great-great-grandmother **III U2,** 35
usw. (= und so weiter) etc. (= et cetera) **I**

V

Vater father **I**
Vati dad **I**
Vegetarier/-in vegetarian **III U3,** 43
(sich) **verändern** to change **III U5,** 76
verängstigt scared **I**
Veranstaltung event **III U1,** 10
verärgert angry **II**
Verband bandage **III U5,** 87
(sich) **verbessern** to improve **II**
verbinden to link **I**
verbindend connecting **II**
Verbindung *(Zug, Bus)* service **III U6,** 97
  sich in Verbindung setzen to contact **III U3,** 50
Verbindungslinie connecting line **III U2,** 32
verbrennen to burn **II**
verbringen *(Urlaub, Zeit etc.)* to spend **I**
verdienen to earn **III U3,** 46
  Geld verdienen to make money **II**
Verein club **I**
Vereinbarung arrangement **III U1,** 10
verfolgen to chase **I**
Vergangenheit past **II**
vergessen to forget **I**
Vergleich comparison **II**
vergleichen (mit) to compare (with/to) **II**
sich **verhalten** to behave **III U3,** 43
verheiratet mit married to **I**
sich **verirren** to get lost **I**
  sich verirrt haben to be lost **II**
verkaufen to sell **I**
Verkäufer/-in assistant **I**; shop assistant **II**
Verkehr traffic **II**
Verkehrsmittel transport *(no pl.)* **I**
verlassen to leave **II**
verleihen to lend (to) **II**
verletzen to hurt **II**
sich **verlieben** to fall in love **II**
verlieren to lose **II**
Verlies dungeon **II**
vermischt jumbled **I**
vermissen to miss **II**
vermuten to guess **I**
verneint negative **II**
Verneinungsform negative **III U2,** 28
verrückt crazy **II**
  jmdn. verrückt machen to drive someone crazy **III U3,** 43
Verrückter maniac **III U5,** 81
Versammlung assembly **II**
Verschönerung facelift **III U4,** 59
verschwinden to disappear **III U5,** 86
verschwunden missing **I**
  verschwunden sein to be gone **II**
Verspätung delay **III U6,** 101
versprechen to promise **II**
verständlich clear **I**
(sich) **verstecken** to hide **II**
verstehen to understand **II**
  Ich verstehe. I see. **III U3,** 46
versuchen to try **II**
Vertrag contract **III U5,** 78
vervollständigen to complete **I**
(sich) **verwandeln in** to turn into **III U3,** 47
Verwandte/-r relative **III U4,** 60
verwenden to use **I**
Verzögerung delay **III U6,** 101
Video video **I**
viel much **I**
  viel/-e a lot of **I**; lots of **I**
  viele many **I**
  Wie viel ... ? How much ... ? **I**
vielleicht maybe **I**
vier four **I**
Viertel quarter **I**
vierzehn fourteen **I**
vierzig forty **I**
Viktorianer/-in Victorian **III U2,** 30
viktorianisch Victorian **III U2,** 30
violett purple **I**
Vision vision **III U2,** 34
Vogel bird **I**
Voicemail voice mail **III U3,** 50
Vokabular vocabulary **I**
voll full **II**
Volleyball volleyball **I**
vollkommen perfect **II**
von from **I**; of **I**; by **III U5,** 80
  von ... bis from ... to **I**
  von ... entfernt from **I**
vor *(zeitlich)* ago **II**
  vor before **I**
  vor *(bei Uhrzeitangaben)* to **I**
  vor in front of **I**
vor allem especially **III U3,** 47
vorbeigehen to walk past **III U5,** 87
vorbeischauen to come over **I**
vorbereiten to prepare **III U2,** 29
  sich vorbereiten to get ready **III U2,** 32
Vorhang curtain **III U3,** 53
jmdm. **vorlesen** to read to **I**
Vormittag morning **I**
vormittags *(Uhrzeit)* am **I**
vorn(e) at the front **II**
zweiter **Vorname** middle name **III U2,** 33
Vorschlag suggestion **III U2,** 29
vorschlagen to suggest **III U2,** 29
vorsichtig careful **II**
vorsingen to audition **II**
vorspielen to audition **II**
vorsprechen to audition **II**
sich (etwas) **vorstellen** to imagine **II**
vortanzen to audition **II**
Vortrag presentation **II**

W

Wachs wax **III U2,** 26
wachsen to grow **III U3,** 43
Wagen carriage **II**
Wagon carriage **II**
wählen to choose **I**; to vote for **II**
Wahnsinnige/-r maniac **III U5,** 81
wahr true **II**
  Nicht wahr? Right? **III U6,** 100
während while **II**; during *(+ noun)* **III U4,** 66
wahrscheinlich probably **III U3,** 47
walisisch Welsh **III U4,** 59
Walisisch Welsh **III U4,** 59
Wand wall **I**
Wanderer hiker **II**
Wanderung hike **II**
wann when **I**
warm warm **I**
jmdn. **warnen** to warn sb **III U6,** 97
Warnung warning **II**
warten to wait **I**
  warten auf to wait for **I**
warum why **I**
was what **I**
  was (sonst) noch what else **II**
  Was ist los? What's up? **I**
  Was ist mit ... ? What about ... ? **I**
waschen to wash **I**
Wasser water **I**
Webbrowser web browser **III U5,** 77
Website website **II**
Wechselgeld change **II**
wechseln to change **II**
Wecker alarm clock **I**
weg away **I**
  weg sein to be gone **II**
Weg way **I**; path **II**; track **III U1,** 9
  auf dem Weg on his way **I**
wegen thanks to **I**
weglaufen to run away **I**
wegnehmen to take **I**
wegreiben to rub out **II**
weh tun to hurt **II**
Weide field **I**
Weihnachten Christmas **II**
weil because **I**
weinen to cry **II**
weise wise **III U3,** 43
auf diese **Weise** like this **I**
weiß white **I**
weit far **III U1,** 17
weitere more **I**
weitere/-r/-s other **I**

weiterfahren to continue **III U6,** 101
weitergehen to continue **III U6,** 101
weitermachen to continue **III U2,** 34
weiterreden to continue **III U2,** 34
weiterreisen to continue **III U6,** 101
welche/-r/-s which **I**
Welle wave **I**
Welt world **I**
auf der Welt in the world **I**
der Zweite **Weltkrieg** World War II **III U2,** 25
wenig little **I**
ein wenig a little **I**
wenige a few **I**
weniger less **III U4,** 58
wenigstens at least **III U4,** 68
wenn when **I**; if **II**
wer who **I**
wer auch immer whoever **III U2,** 35
Wer spielt mit? Who's in it? **III U6,** 96
werben to advertise **III U5,** 77
Werbepause commercial break **III U1,** 13
Werbespot commercial **III U1,** 13; ad(vertisement) **III U5,** 82
Werbung advertising *(no pl.)* **III U5,** 82
Werbung machen (für) to advertise **III U5,** 77
werden to get **II**; to become **II**; to turn into **III U3,** 47
werfen to throw **I**
Werk factory **III U2,** 24
Werkstatt garage **I**; workshop **III U2,** 24
wert sein to be worth **III U5,** 82
das **Wesentliche** gist **III U2,** 32
Westen west **I**
Wettbewerb competition **I**
Wette bet **III U6,** 101
Wetter weather **II**
Wettkampf match **II**
Wettlauf race **III U1,** 9
wichtig important **I**
wie how **I**
Wie viele ... ? How many ...? **I**
Wie wäre es mit ... ? How about ...? **I**
Wie man ... How to ... **I**
wie like **I**
Wie ist ... ? What is ... like? **II**
wieder again **I**
immer wieder again and again **II**
wiedergeben to report **III U6,** 94
wiederholen to repeat **I**
Wiederholung revision **I**
auf **Wiedersehen** goodbye **I**
wiegen to weigh **II**
Wiese field **I**
wild wild **I**
Wille will **I**
Willkommen welcome **II**
Wind wind **I**
windig windy **I**
windsurfen to surf **I**
Wink wave **III U1,** 20
winken to wave **III U1,** 17
Winter winter **I**
winzig tiny **I**
wir we **I**
wir selbst ourselves **III U3,** 44
wirklich really **II**; actually **III U2,** 35
wirklich real **II**
wissen to know **I**
Wissenschaft Science **II**
Wissenschaftler/-in scientist **III U1,** 13
Witz joke **I**
witzig funny **I**
witzig sein to be fun **I**
wo where **I**
egal **wo(hin)** wherever **III U2,** 35
wo(hin) auch immer wherever **III U2,** 35
Woche week **I**
Wochenende weekend **I**
am Wochenende at the weekend **I**
Wochentage *(pl.)* days of the week *(pl.)* **I**
Woge wave **I**
woher where **I**
wohin where **I**
Wohltätigkeitsverein charity **II**
wohnen to live **I**
Wohnung flat **I**
Wohnzimmer living room **I**
Wolke cloud **II**
wolkig cloudy **II**
wollen to want **I**
wissen wollen to want to know **I**
Workshop workshop **III U2,** 24
Wort word **I**
Wörterbuch dictionary **I**
Wortnetz word web **I**
Wortsammlung word bank **I**
Wortschatz vocabulary **I**
Wortstellung word order **I**
Wunder wonder **I**
wunderbar beautiful **I**
(sich) **wünschen** to wish **III U3,** 47
ich **würde gerne ...** I'd like to ... *(= I would like to)* **I**
wütend angry **II**

Z

Zahl number **I**
zählen to count **I**
Zahn tooth pl. teeth **I**
(seine) Zähne putzen to brush one's teeth **III U3,** 43
Zauberei magic **III U5,** 86
Zeh toe **II**
zehn ten **I**
Zeichen signal **I**; sign **II**
zeichnen to draw **I**
zeigen to show **I**
Zeile line **I**
Zeit time **I**
die ganze Zeit all the time **II**
in letzter Zeit recently **III U4,** 59
Lass dir Zeit. Take your time. **III U4,** 62
von Zeit zu Zeit from time to time **I**
(Zeit) brauchen to take **III U6,** 93
zur selben Zeit at the same time **I**
Zeitalter age **III U2,** 25
Zeitmaschine timebox **II**
Zeitschrift magazine **I**
Zeitschriftengeschäft newsagent **I**
Zeitstrahl time line **II**
Zeitung newspaper **III U5,** 76
Zeltplatz campsite **II**
Zentrum centre **I**
zerbrechen to break **I**; to crack **III U5,** 86
zerspringen to crack **III U5,** 86
zerstören to ruin **I**
ziemlich quite **III U4,** 69
Zimmer room **I**
zittern to shake **II**
Zoll customs *(sing.)* **II**
Zoo zoo **I**
zornig angry **II**
zu too **I**; to **I**
zu viel too much **I**
zubereiten to prepare **III U2,** 29
zubinden to tie **III U5,** 87
Zucker sugar **I**
Zuckerkrankheit diabetes **II**
zuerst first **I**; at first **II**
Zug train **I**
im Zug on a train **I**
zugeben to admit **III U5,** 86
Zuhause home **I**
zuhören to listen **I**
jemandem zuhören to listen to **I**
zujubeln to cheer **III U4,** 68
zukommen auf to come up to **II**
Zukunft future **II**
zumachen to close **I**
zum Schluss finally **I**
zunächst at first **II**
Zunge tongue **II**
zuordnen to match **I**
zurück back **I**
zurückgehen to go back **I**
zurückkommen to get back **II**
zusammen together **I**
Zusammenhang context **III U1,** 19
in Zusammenhang stehen to be connected **III U2,** 32
zusammenhängen to be connected **III U2,** 32
Zusammenstoß crash **III U1,** 20
zusammenstoßen (mit) to bump into **II**
zusammenstoßen to crash **I**
Zusatz extra **III U4,** 69
zusätzlich extra **III U6,** 100
zustimmen to agree **III U1,** 12
zwanzig twenty **I**
zwei two **I**
zweisprachig bilingual **III U4,** 60
Zweitsprache second language **III U6,** 100
Zwilling twin **III U3,** 43
Zwillings- twin **III U3,** 43
zwischen between **II**
zwölf twelve **I**

We know little of the earliest people in the British Isles. But they built famous stone rings which you can still visit today, such as Stonehenge.

Stonehenge, built 2500 – 2000 BC

43 BC – 410 AD

In 43 BC the Romans took most of Britain from the Celts who lived there. Scotland and its people were too wild, so the Romans built a big wall to protect themselves.

5th and 6th century

After the Romans had left, Germanic tribes conquered England. The Saxons were the most successful of them, but the Angles gave "England" its name: It means "Land of the Angles".

1066

William, Duke of Normandy, defeated the Saxon King Harold and conquered England.

The battle of Hastings (1066)

1215

King John had to sign the Magna Carta. This made the law stronger and the king weaker. Perhaps you already know King John from the Robin Hood stories!

1558 – 1603

When Elizabeth I was queen, England became rich and powerful and started to colonise North America. This was also the age of great British art – for example the poet William Shakespeare.

Elizabeth I, with the English victory over the Spanish Armada in the background (1588)

1776 – 1783

In 1776 the English colonists in North America wanted to become independent. They had to fight for it, but finally they succeeded in 1783.

18th and 19th century

Industrialisation started in England in the 18th century. Factories with machines and steam engines were built all over Britain. Steam engines were also used in the first locomotives in the early 19th century.

The Middleton Railway of 1812 was used to transport coal

1837 – 1901

During the time of Queen Victoria I, England had so many colonies all round the world that the sun always shone somewhere in the British Empire.

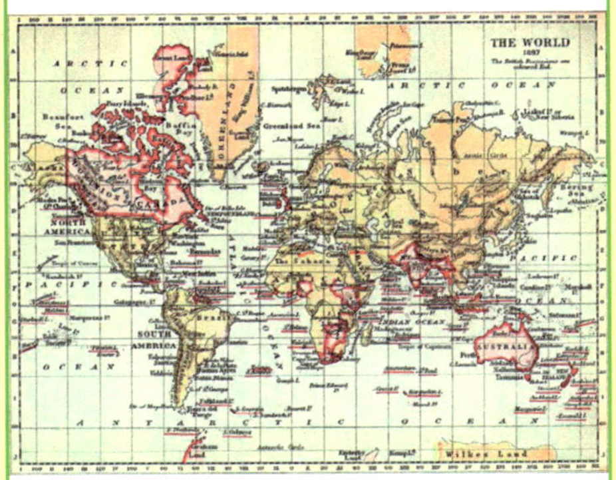

A world map of 1897: Everything in red belongs to the British Empire!

1914 – 1918 and 1939 – 1945

In the two world wars all of Europe suffered terrible losses.

1947

India became independent after long but peaceful protests. The leader of the independence movement was Mahatma Gandhi.

Mahatma Gandhi

1973

The UK joined the European Community, which in 1992 became the European Union.

Countries in which English is the / an official language

NAME Independent Commonwealth

Name Dependent territories of Commonwealth states (in brackets) SCALE 1 : 88,000,000